THE WORLD ACCORDING TO LUCY

PSYCHIATRIC
HELP 5¢
THE DOCTOR
IS IN

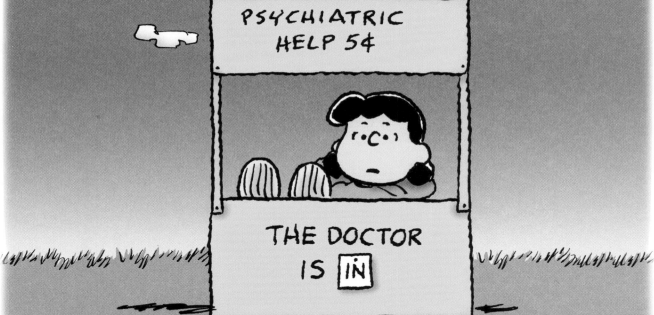

BY CHARLES M. SCHULZ

Ballantine Books * New York

A Ballantine Book
Published by The Ballantine Publishing Group
Copyright © 2002 by United Feature Syndicate, Inc.

www.ballantinebooks.com
www.snoopy.com

Library of Congress Catalog Card Number: 2001118649

ISBN 0-345-44271-7

Cover design by Paige Braddock, Charles M. Schulz Creative Associates

Manufactured in the United States of America

First Edition: April 2002

10 9 8 7 6 5 4 3 2 1

The World
According to
Lucy

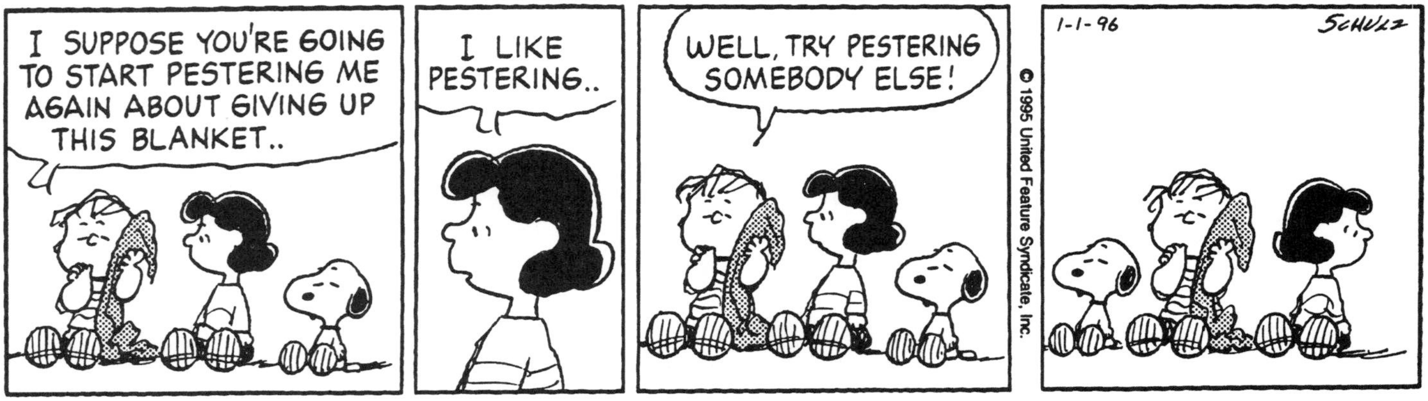
I SUPPOSE YOU'RE GOING TO START PESTERING ME AGAIN ABOUT GIVING UP THIS BLANKET..
I LIKE PESTERING..
WELL, TRY PESTERING SOMEBODY ELSE!
© 1995 United Feature Syndicate, Inc.
1-1-96
SCHULZ

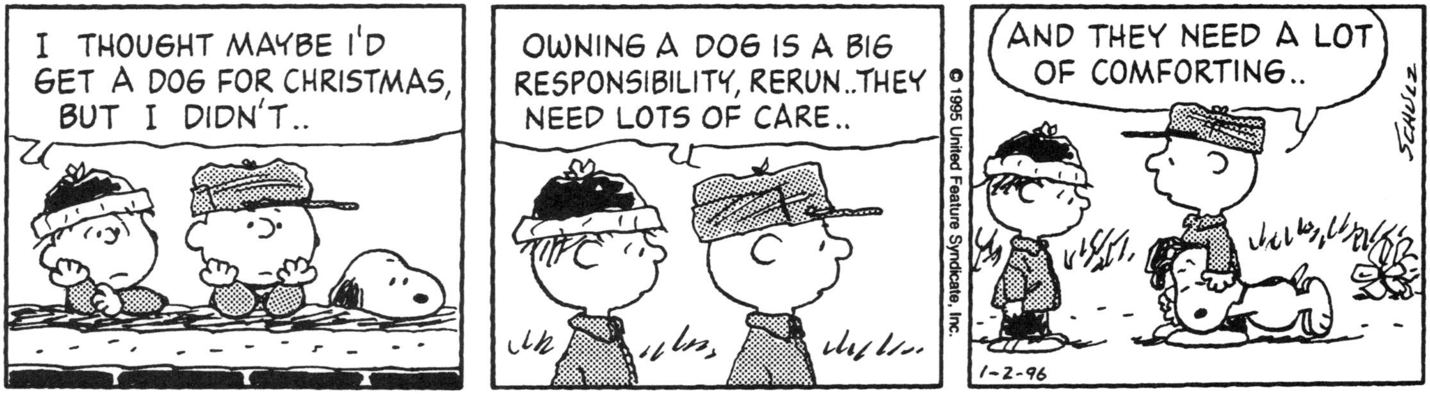
I THOUGHT MAYBE I'D GET A DOG FOR CHRISTMAS, BUT I DIDN'T..
OWNING A DOG IS A BIG RESPONSIBILITY, RERUN..THEY NEED LOTS OF CARE..
© 1995 United Feature Syndicate, Inc.
AND THEY NEED A LOT OF COMFORTING..
SCHULZ
1-2-96

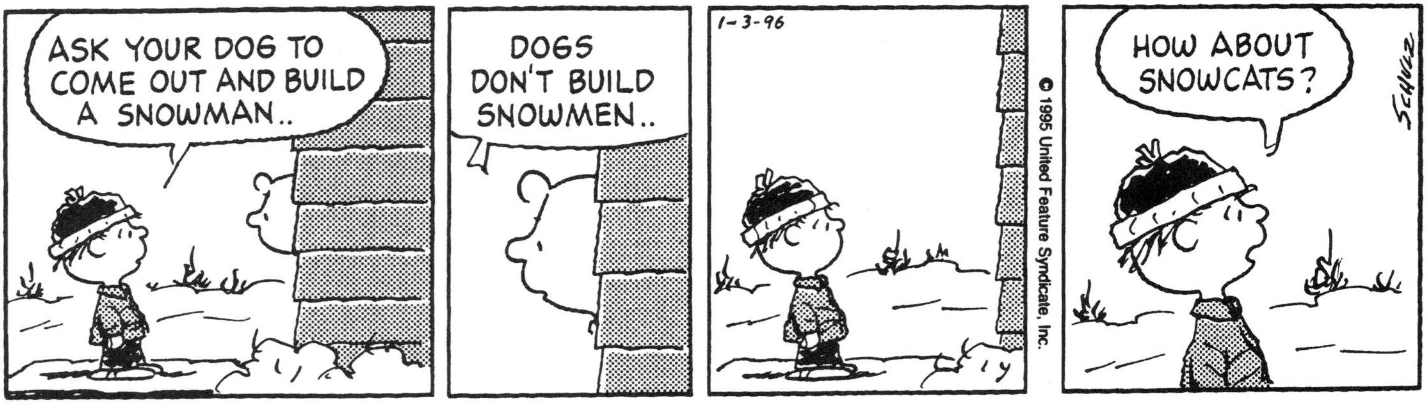
ASK YOUR DOG TO COME OUT AND BUILD A SNOWMAN..
DOGS DON'T BUILD SNOWMEN..
1-3-96
© 1995 United Feature Syndicate, Inc.
HOW ABOUT SNOWCATS?
SCHULZ

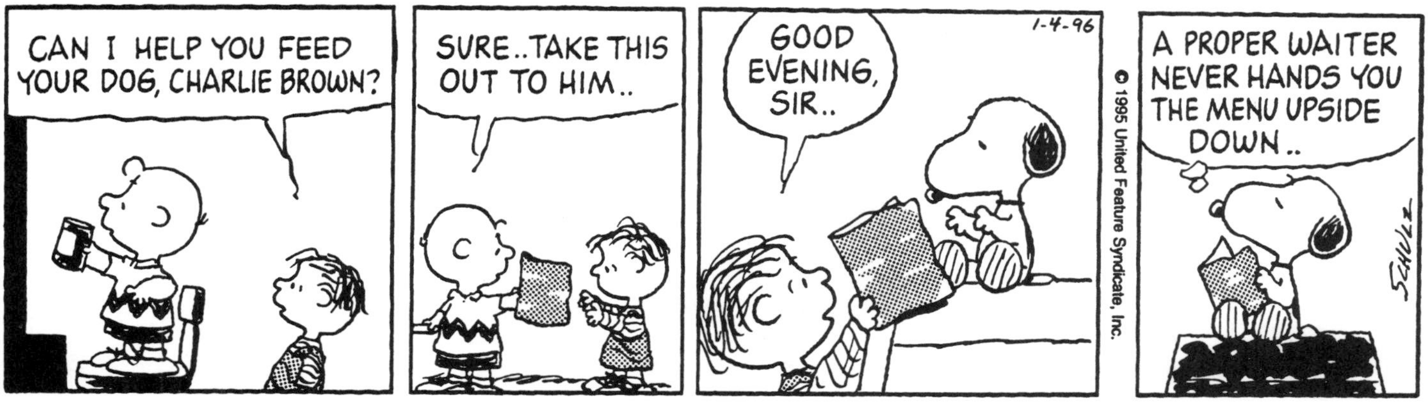
CAN I HELP YOU FEED YOUR DOG, CHARLIE BROWN?
SURE..TAKE THIS OUT TO HIM..
1-4-96
GOOD EVENING, SIR..
© 1995 United Feature Syndicate, Inc.
A PROPER WAITER NEVER HANDS YOU THE MENU UPSIDE DOWN..
SCHULZ

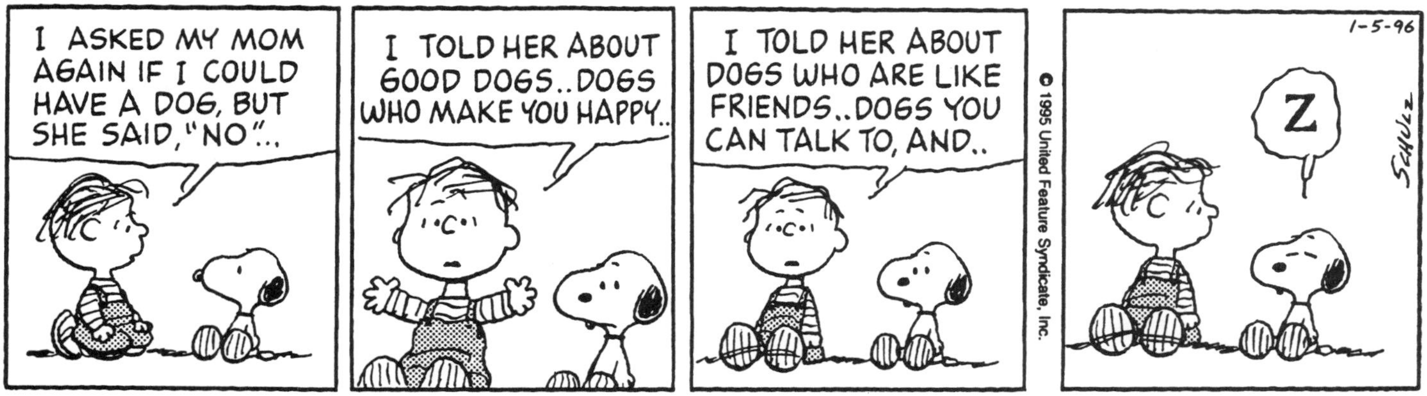
I ASKED MY MOM AGAIN IF I COULD HAVE A DOG, BUT SHE SAID, "NO"..
I TOLD HER ABOUT GOOD DOGS..DOGS WHO MAKE YOU HAPPY..
I TOLD HER ABOUT DOGS WHO ARE LIKE FRIENDS..DOGS YOU CAN TALK TO, AND..
© 1995 United Feature Syndicate, Inc.
1-5-96
Z
SCHULZ

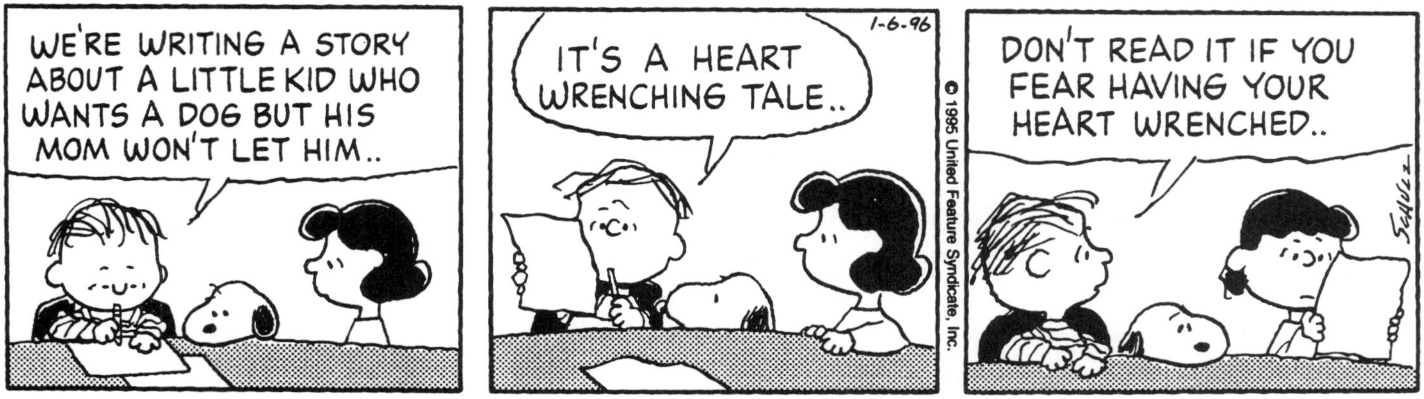
WE'RE WRITING A STORY ABOUT A LITTLE KID WHO WANTS A DOG BUT HIS MOM WON'T LET HIM..
1-6-96
IT'S A HEART WRENCHING TALE..
© 1995 United Feature Syndicate, Inc.
DON'T READ IT IF YOU FEAR HAVING YOUR HEART WRENCHED..
SCHULZ

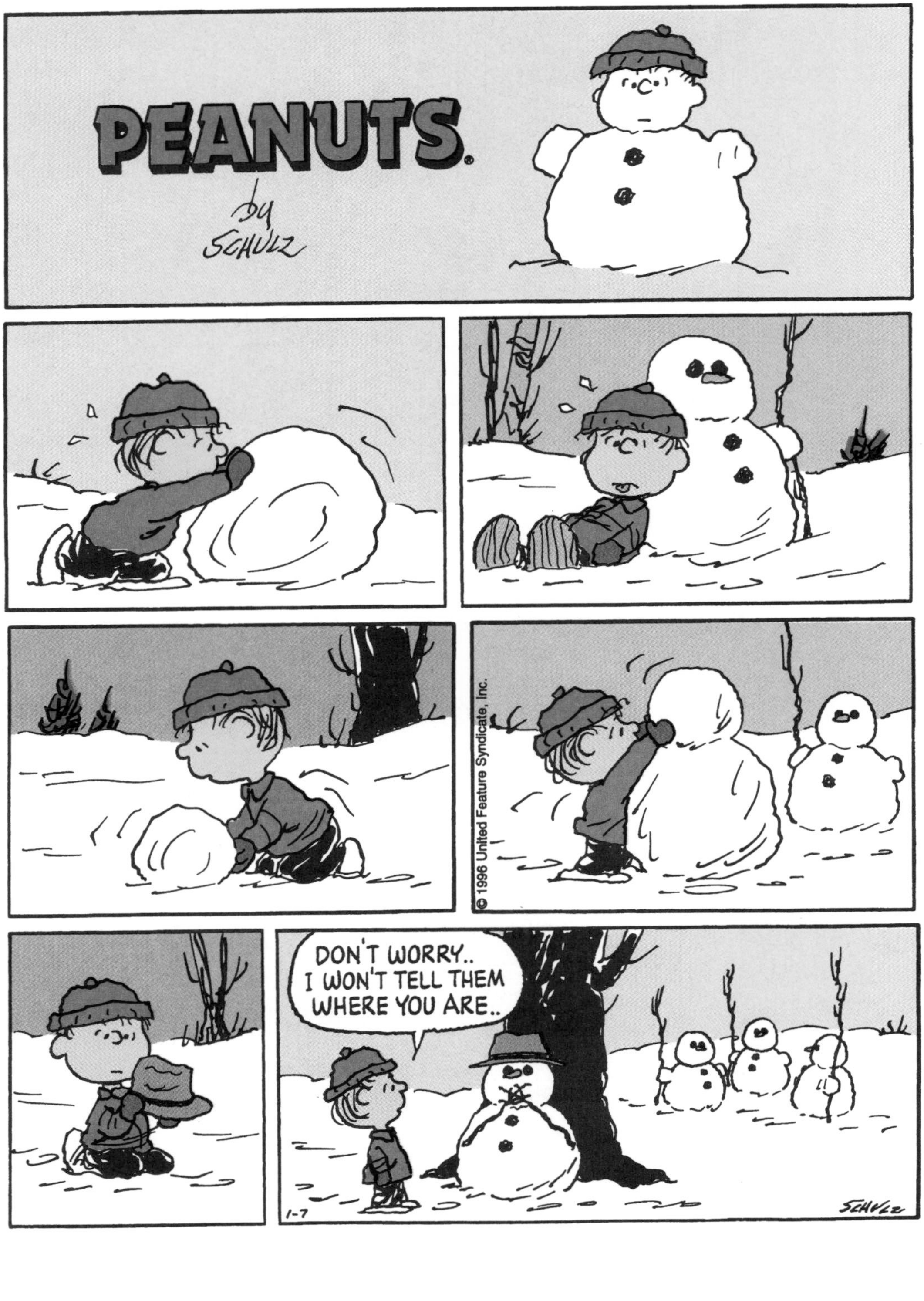
PEANUTS.
by SCHULZ
© 1996 United Feature Syndicate, Inc.
DON'T WORRY..
I WON'T TELL THEM
WHERE YOU ARE..
1-7
SCHULZ

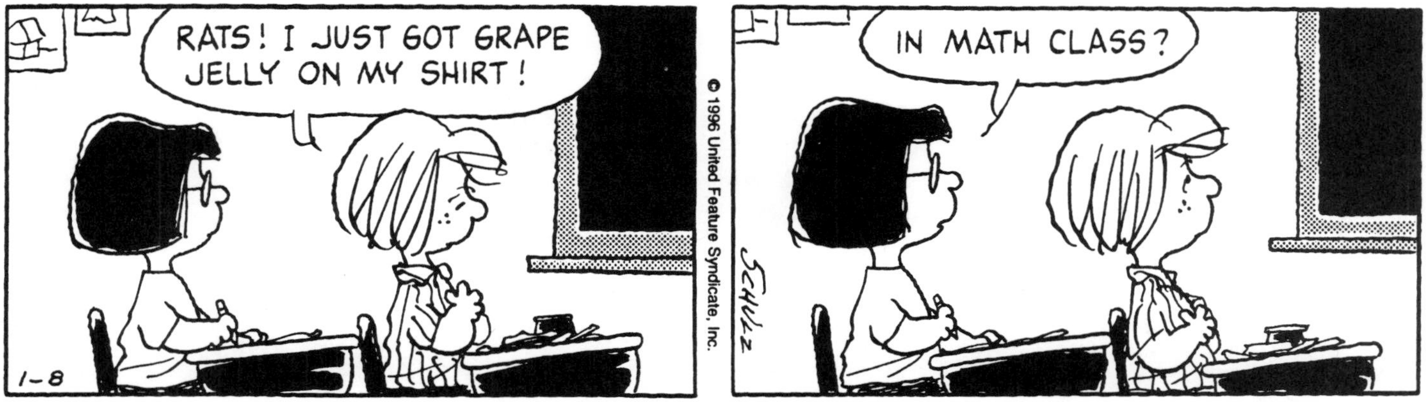
RATS! I JUST GOT GRAPE JELLY ON MY SHIRT!
1-8
© 1996 United Feature Syndicate, Inc.
SCHULZ
IN MATH CLASS?

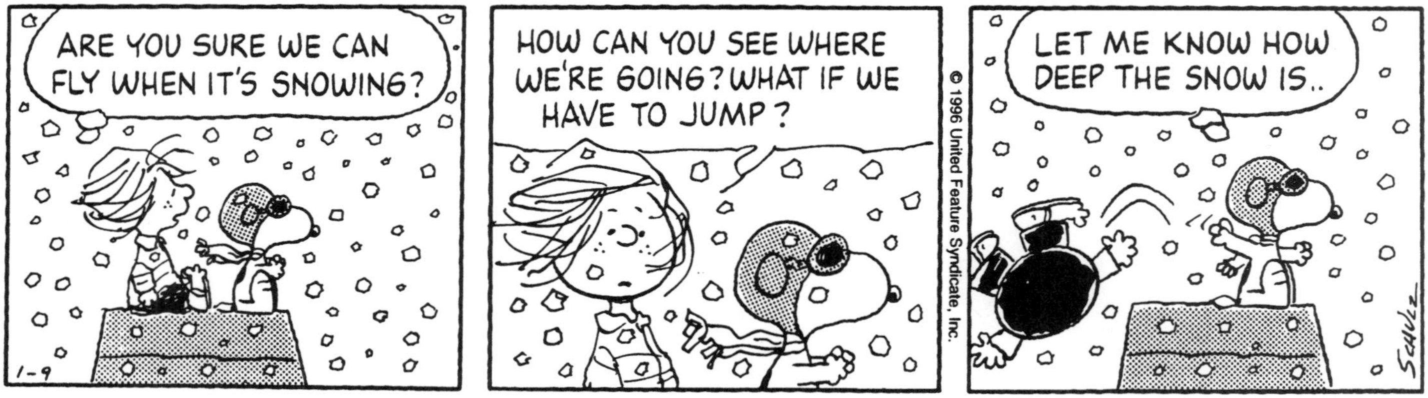
ARE YOU SURE WE CAN FLY WHEN IT'S SNOWING?
1-9
HOW CAN YOU SEE WHERE WE'RE GOING? WHAT IF WE HAVE TO JUMP?
© 1996 United Feature Syndicate, Inc.
LET ME KNOW HOW DEEP THE SNOW IS..
SCHULZ

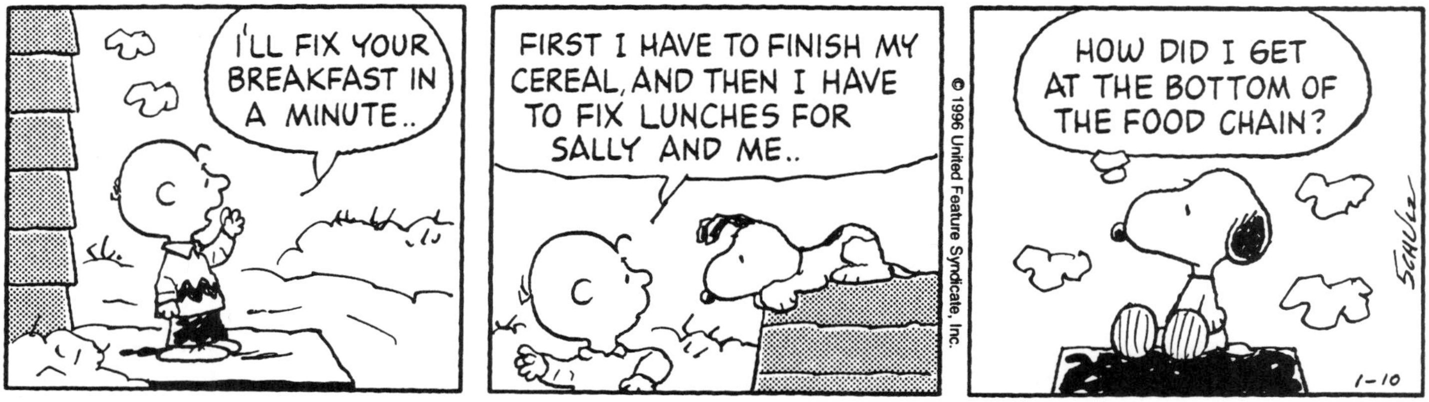
I'LL FIX YOUR BREAKFAST IN A MINUTE..
FIRST I HAVE TO FINISH MY CEREAL, AND THEN I HAVE TO FIX LUNCHES FOR SALLY AND ME..
© 1996 United Feature Syndicate, Inc.
HOW DID I GET AT THE BOTTOM OF THE FOOD CHAIN?
SCHULZ
1-10

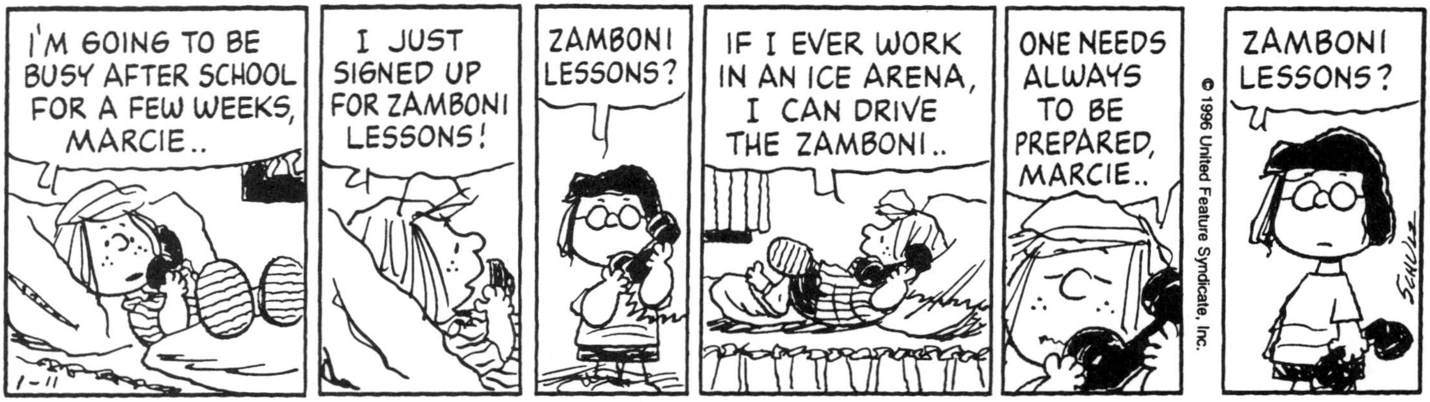
1-11
I'M GOING TO BE BUSY AFTER SCHOOL FOR A FEW WEEKS, MARCIE..
I JUST SIGNED UP FOR ZAMBONI LESSONS!
ZAMBONI LESSONS?
IF I EVER WORK IN AN ICE ARENA, I CAN DRIVE THE ZAMBONI..
ONE NEEDS ALWAYS TO BE PREPARED, MARCIE..
© 1996 United Feature Syndicate, Inc.
ZAMBONI LESSONS?

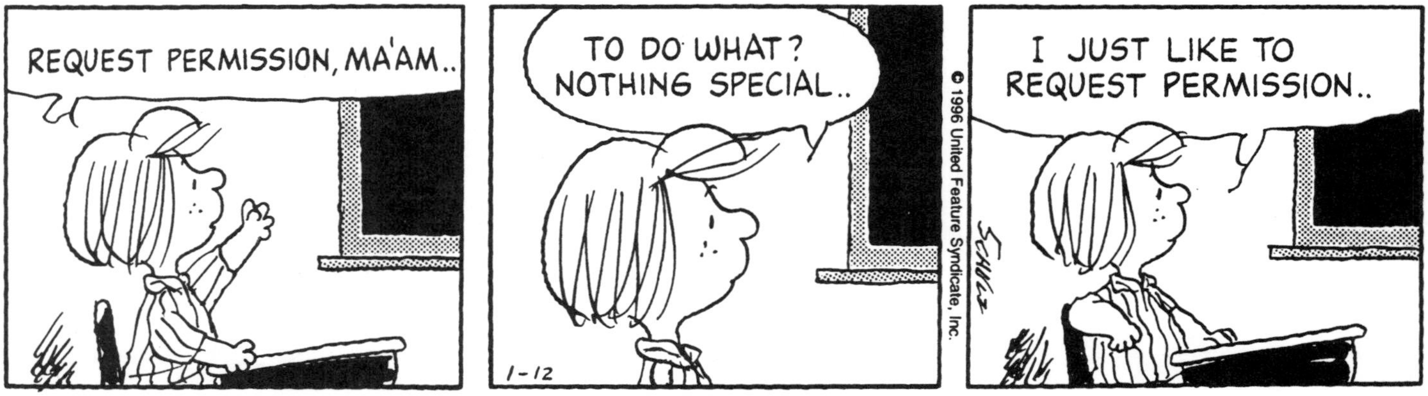
REQUEST PERMISSION, MA'AM..
TO DO WHAT? NOTHING SPECIAL..
1-12
© 1996 United Feature Syndicate, Inc.
I JUST LIKE TO REQUEST PERMISSION..

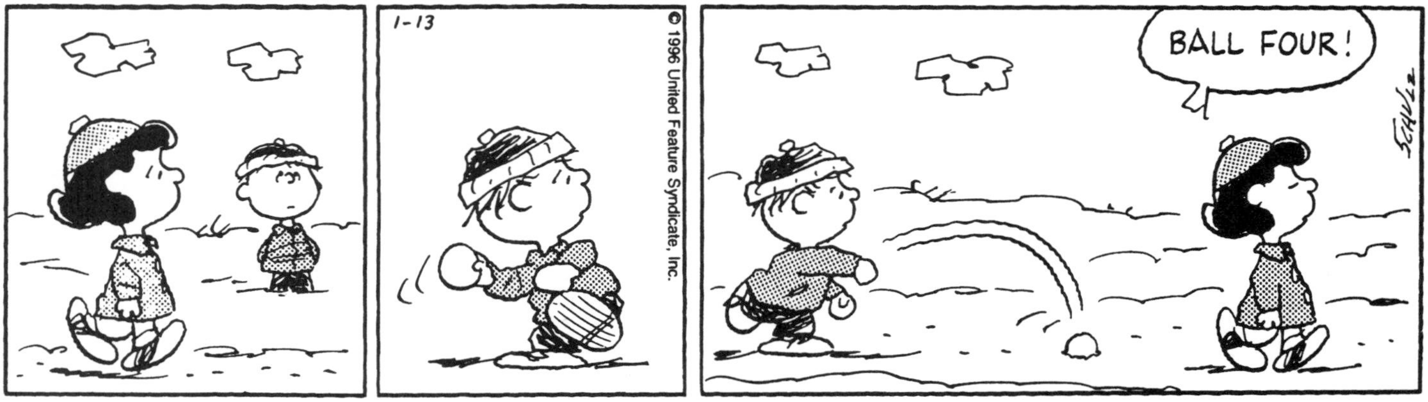
1-13
© 1996 United Feature Syndicate, Inc.
BALL FOUR!

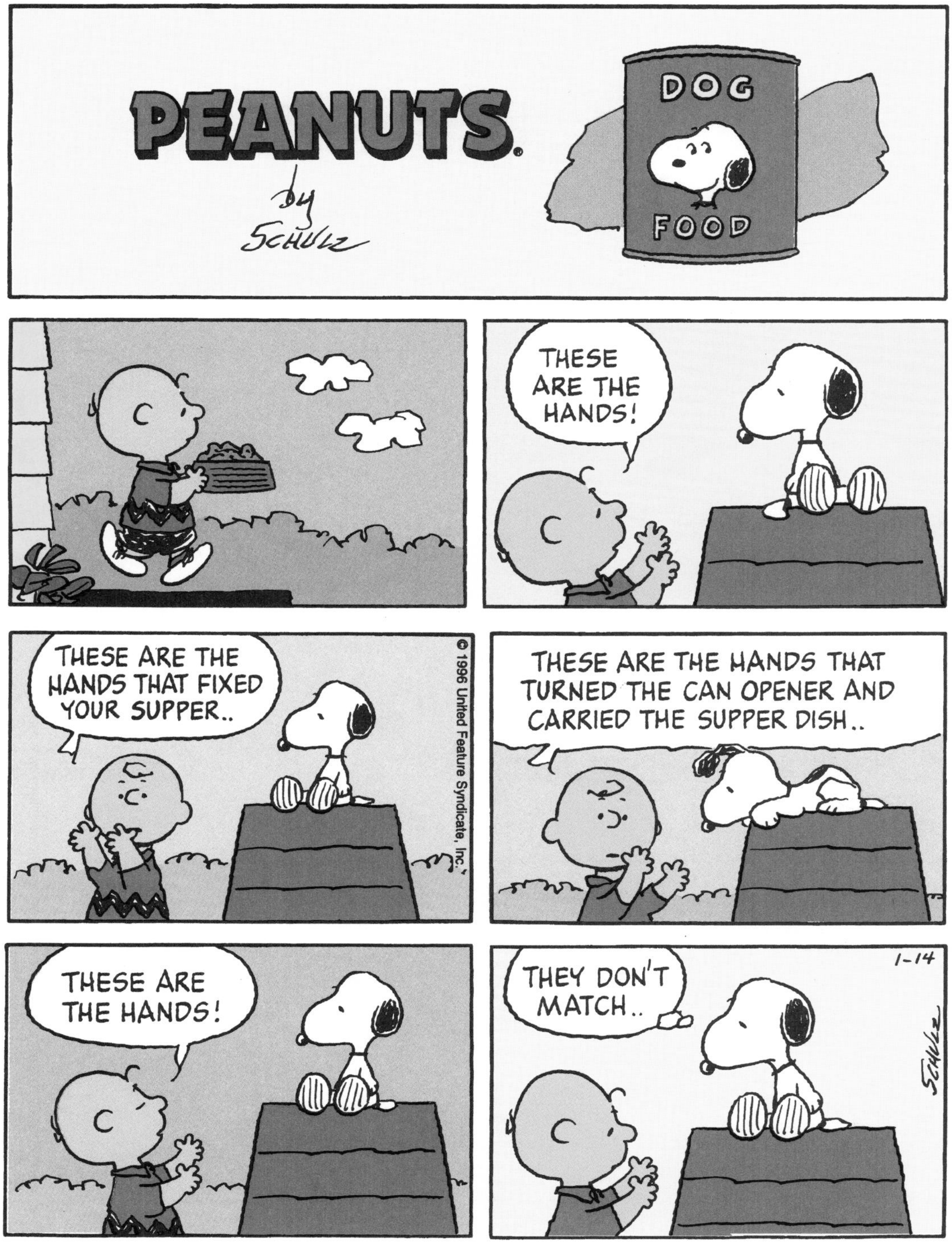
PEANUTS
by SCHULZ
DOG
FOOD
THESE ARE THE HANDS!
THESE ARE THE HANDS THAT FIXED YOUR SUPPER..
© 1996 United Feature Syndicate, Inc.
THESE ARE THE HANDS THAT TURNED THE CAN OPENER AND CARRIED THE SUPPER DISH..
THESE ARE THE HANDS!
1-14
THEY DON'T MATCH..
SCHULZ

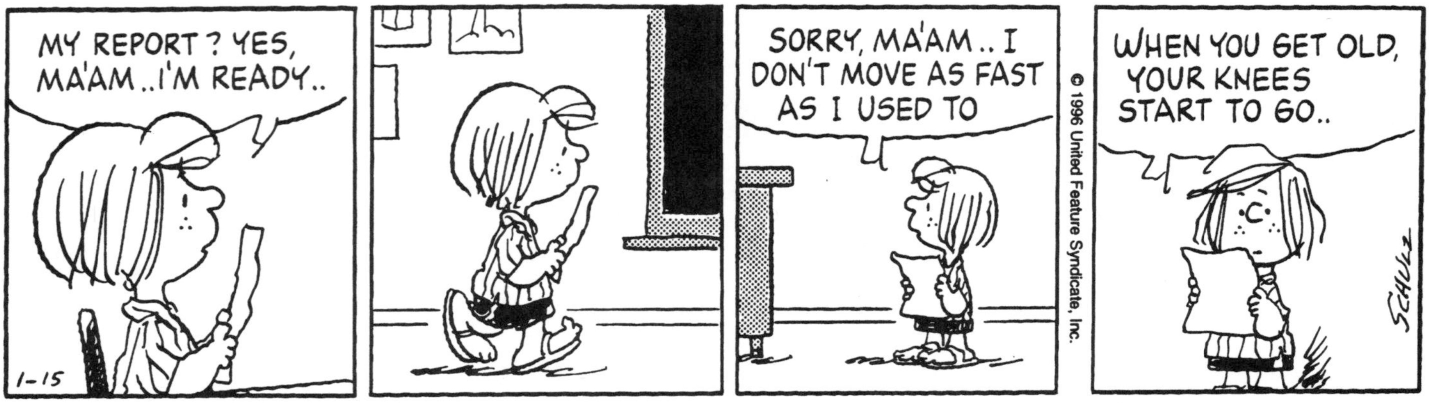
MY REPORT ? YES, MA'AM .. I'M READY..
1-15
SORRY, MA'AM .. I DON'T MOVE AS FAST AS I USED TO
© 1996 United Feature Syndicate, Inc.
WHEN YOU GET OLD, YOUR KNEES START TO GO..
SCHULZ

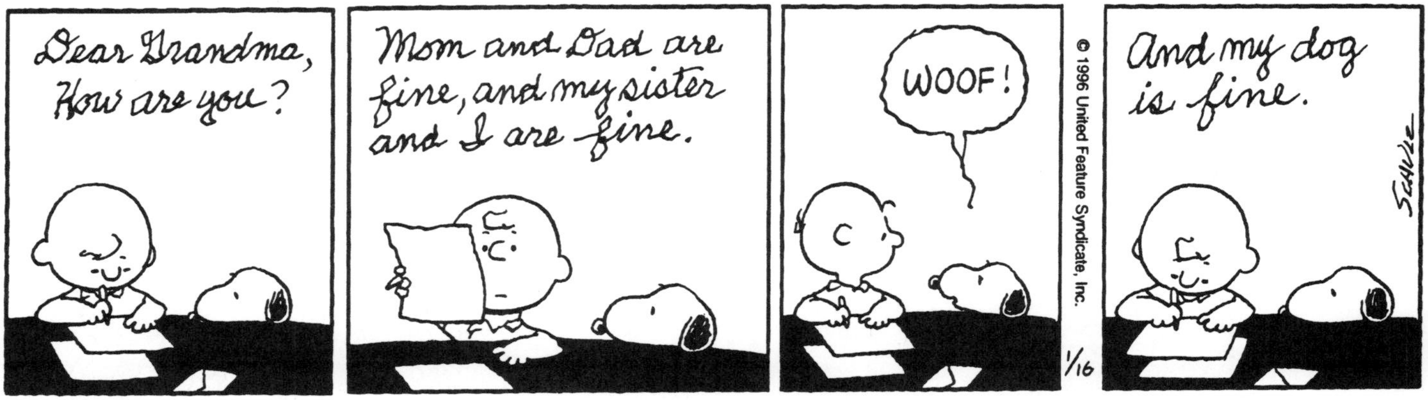
Dear Grandma, How are you?
Mom and Dad are fine, and my sister and I are fine.
WOOF!
© 1996 United Feature Syndicate, Inc.
1/16
And my dog is fine.
SCHULZ

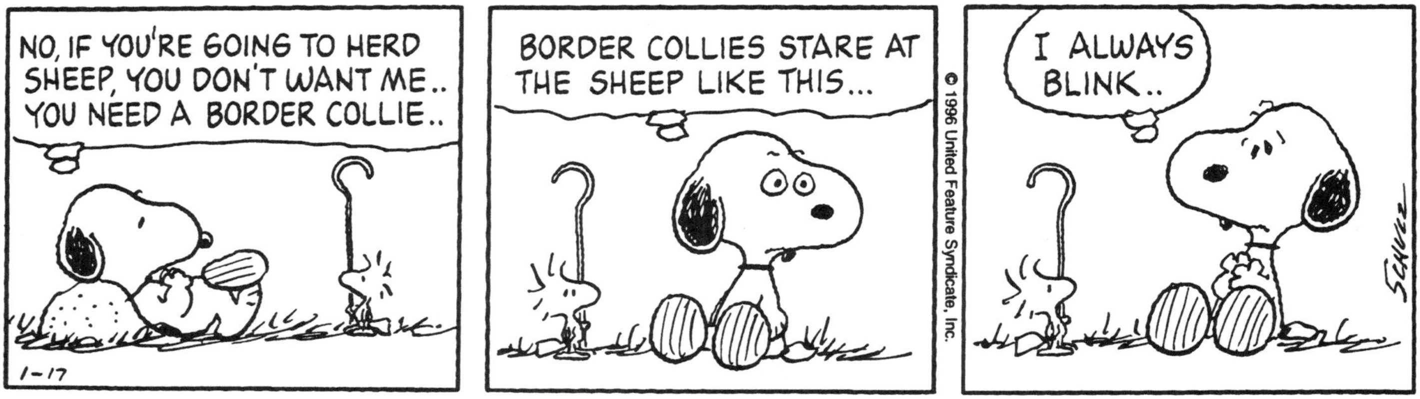
NO, IF YOU'RE GOING TO HERD SHEEP, YOU DON'T WANT ME.. YOU NEED A BORDER COLLIE..
1-17
BORDER COLLIES STARE AT THE SHEEP LIKE THIS...
© 1996 United Feature Syndicate, Inc.
I ALWAYS BLINK..
SCHULZ

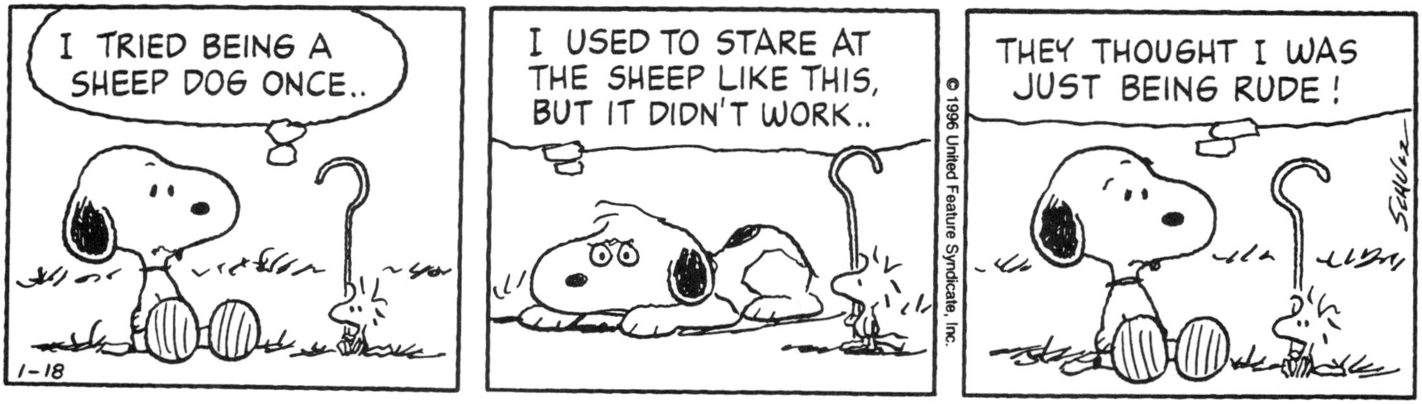
I TRIED BEING A SHEEP DOG ONCE..
1-18
I USED TO STARE AT THE SHEEP LIKE THIS, BUT IT DIDN'T WORK..
© 1996 United Feature Syndicate, Inc.
THEY THOUGHT I WAS JUST BEING RUDE!
SCHULZ

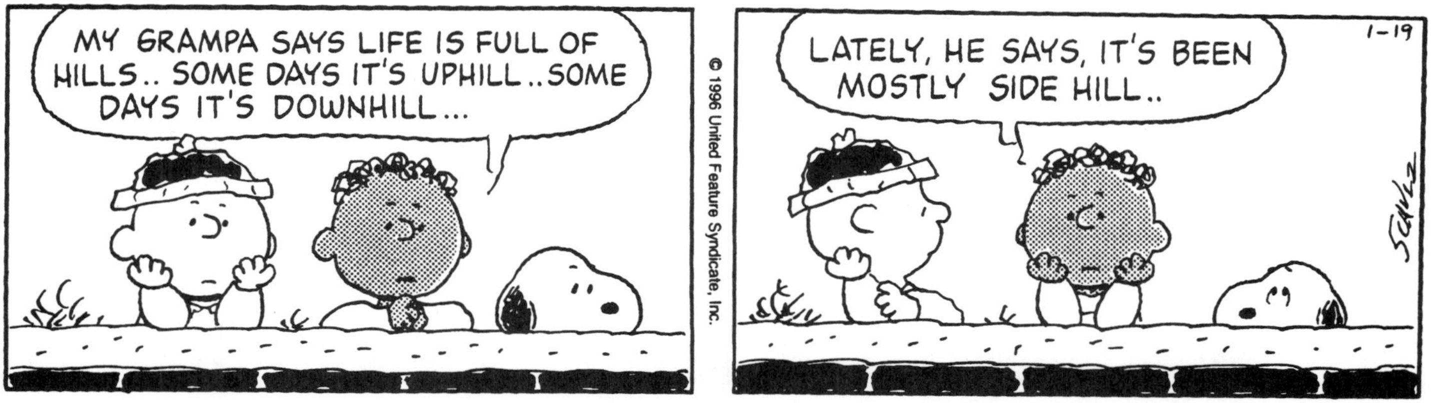
MY GRAMPA SAYS LIFE IS FULL OF HILLS.. SOME DAYS IT'S UPHILL..SOME DAYS IT'S DOWNHILL...
© 1996 United Feature Syndicate, Inc.
1-19
LATELY, HE SAYS, IT'S BEEN MOSTLY SIDE HILL..
SCHULZ

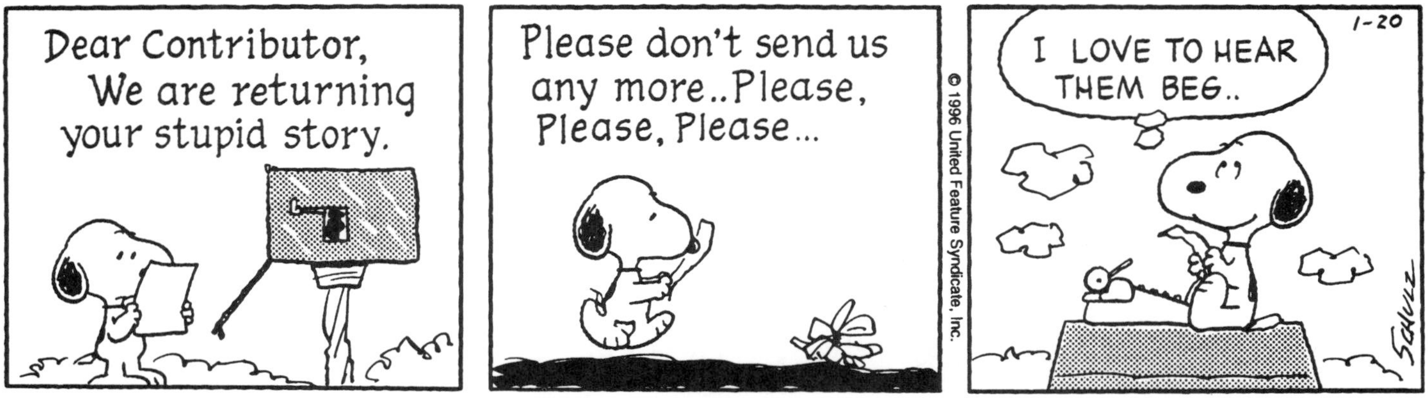
Dear Contributor,
We are returning your stupid story.
Please don't send us any more..Please, Please, Please...
© 1996 United Feature Syndicate, Inc.
1-20
I LOVE TO HEAR THEM BEG..
SCHULZ

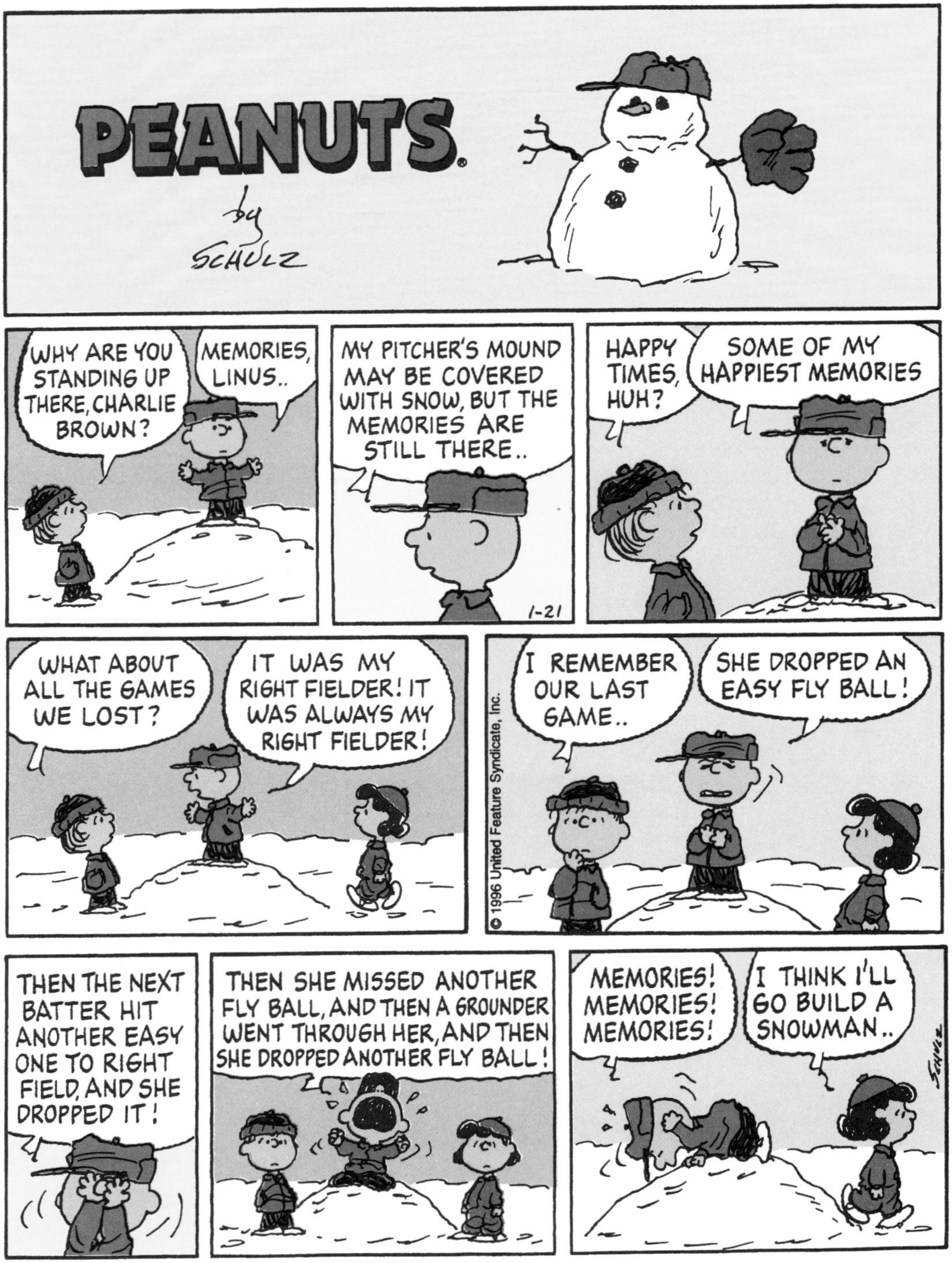
PEANUTS
by SCHULZ
WHY ARE YOU STANDING UP THERE, CHARLIE BROWN?
MEMORIES, LINUS..
MY PITCHER'S MOUND MAY BE COVERED WITH SNOW, BUT THE MEMORIES ARE STILL THERE..
1-21
HAPPY TIMES, HUH?
SOME OF MY HAPPIEST MEMORIES
WHAT ABOUT ALL THE GAMES WE LOST?
IT WAS MY RIGHT FIELDER! IT WAS ALWAYS MY RIGHT FIELDER!
© 1996 United Feature Syndicate, Inc.
I REMEMBER OUR LAST GAME..
SHE DROPPED AN EASY FLY BALL!
THEN THE NEXT BATTER HIT ANOTHER EASY ONE TO RIGHT FIELD, AND SHE DROPPED IT!
THEN SHE MISSED ANOTHER FLY BALL, AND THEN A GROUNDER WENT THROUGH HER, AND THEN SHE DROPPED ANOTHER FLY BALL!
MEMORIES! MEMORIES! MEMORIES!
I THINK I'LL GO BUILD A SNOWMAN..
SCHULZ

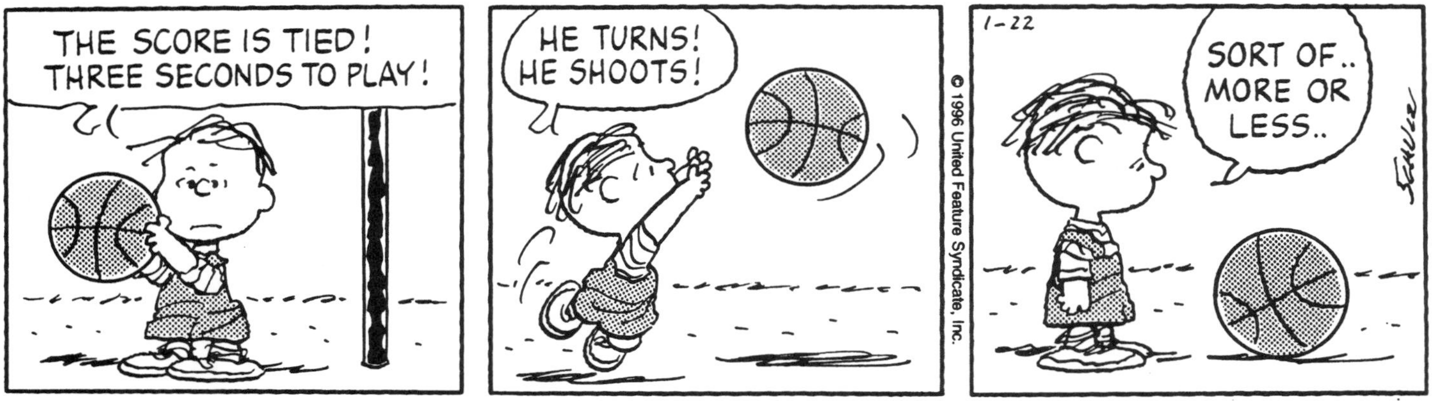
THE SCORE IS TIED! THREE SECONDS TO PLAY!
HE TURNS! HE SHOOTS!
© 1996 United Feature Syndicate, Inc.
1-22
SORT OF.. MORE OR LESS..
SCHULZ

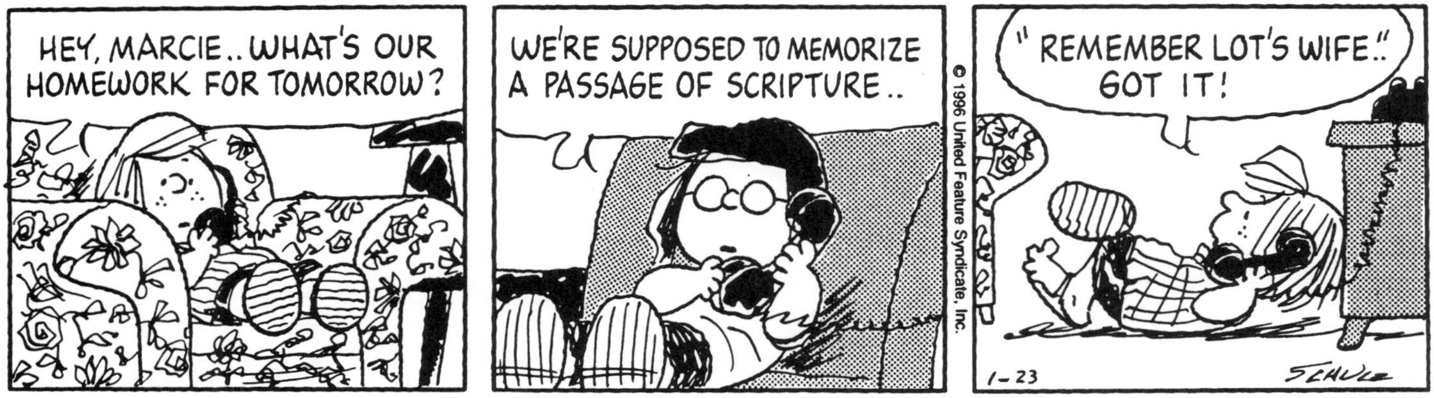
HEY, MARCIE.. WHAT'S OUR HOMEWORK FOR TOMORROW?
WE'RE SUPPOSED TO MEMORIZE A PASSAGE OF SCRIPTURE..
© 1996 United Feature Syndicate, Inc.
"REMEMBER LOT'S WIFE." GOT IT!
1-23
SCHULZ

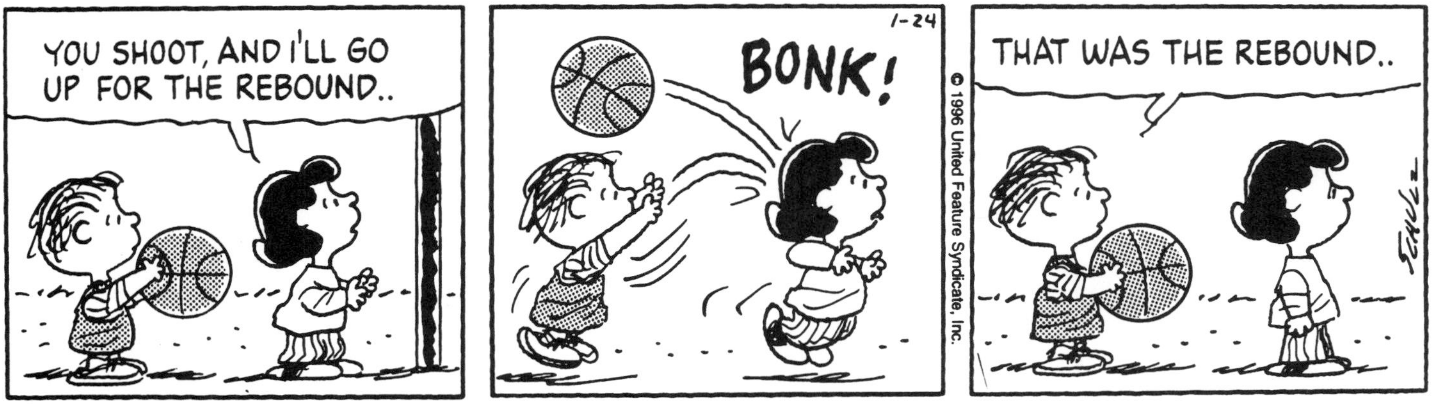
YOU SHOOT, AND I'LL GO UP FOR THE REBOUND..
1-24
BONK!
© 1996 United Feature Syndicate, Inc.
THAT WAS THE REBOUND..
SCHULZ

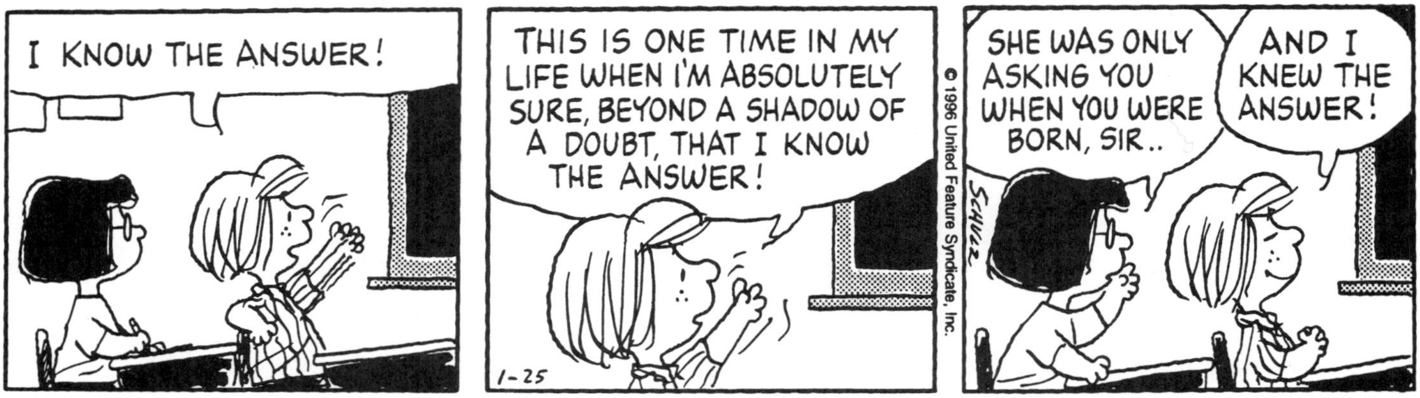
I KNOW THE ANSWER!
THIS IS ONE TIME IN MY LIFE WHEN I'M ABSOLUTELY SURE, BEYOND A SHADOW OF A DOUBT, THAT I KNOW THE ANSWER!
1-25
© 1996 United Feature Syndicate, Inc.
SCHULZ
SHE WAS ONLY ASKING YOU WHEN YOU WERE BORN, SIR..
AND I KNEW THE ANSWER!

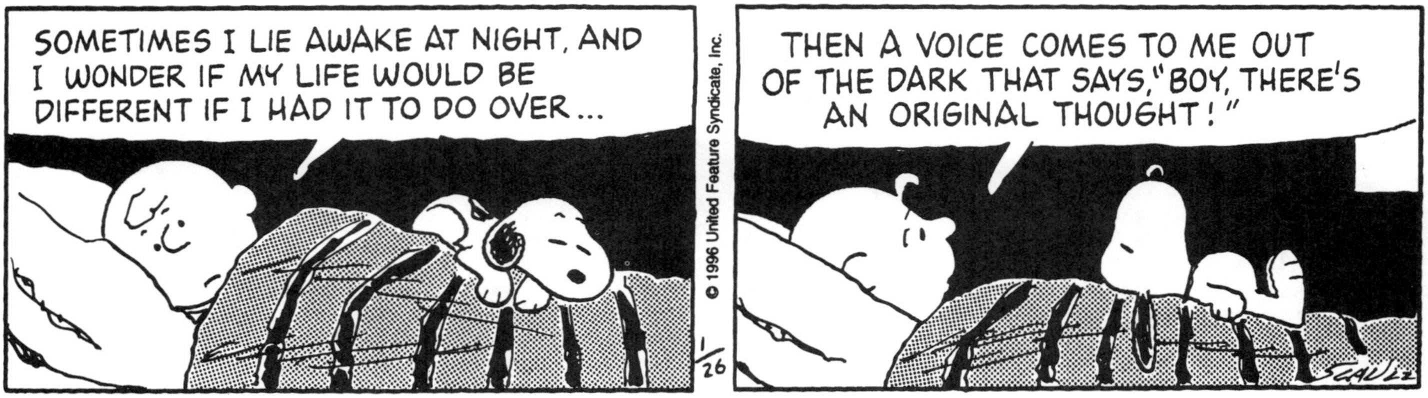
SOMETIMES I LIE AWAKE AT NIGHT, AND I WONDER IF MY LIFE WOULD BE DIFFERENT IF I HAD IT TO DO OVER...
© 1996 United Feature Syndicate, Inc.
1/26
THEN A VOICE COMES TO ME OUT OF THE DARK THAT SAYS, "BOY, THERE'S AN ORIGINAL THOUGHT!"
SCHULZ

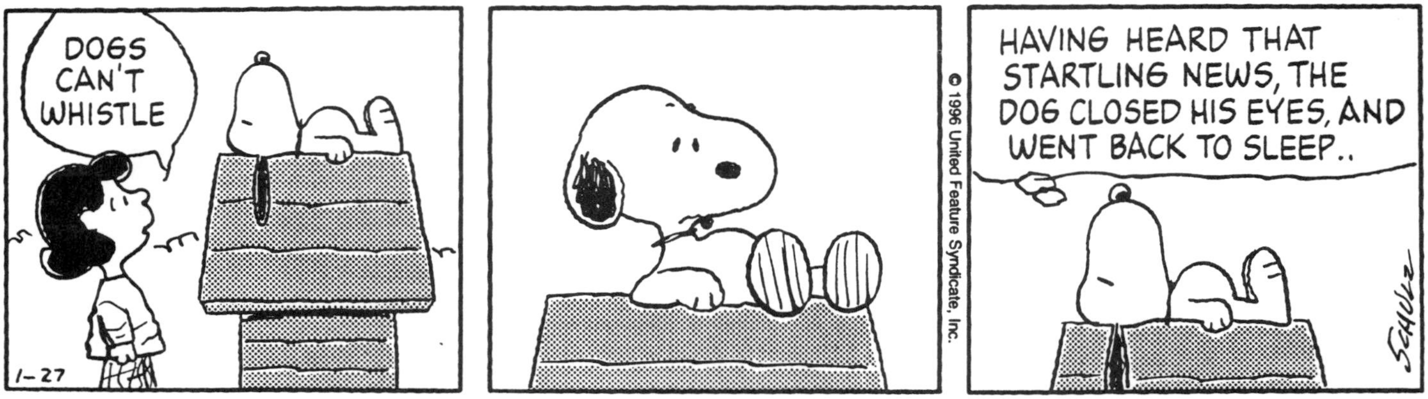
DOGS CAN'T WHISTLE
1-27
© 1996 United Feature Syndicate, Inc.
HAVING HEARD THAT STARTLING NEWS, THE DOG CLOSED HIS EYES, AND WENT BACK TO SLEEP..
SCHULZ

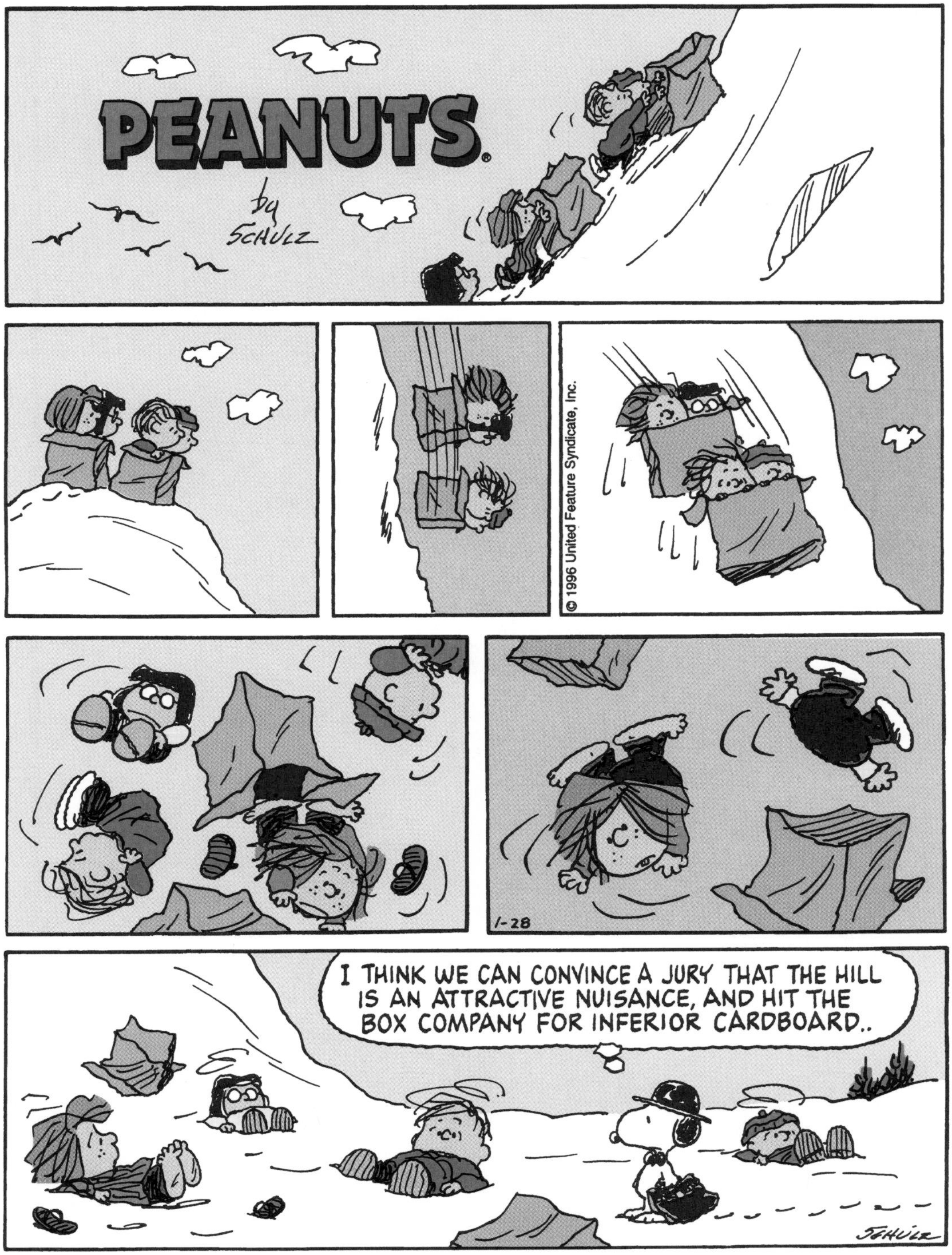

PEANUTS®
by SCHULZ
© 1996 United Feature Syndicate, Inc.
1-28
I THINK WE CAN CONVINCE A JURY THAT THE HILL IS AN ATTRACTIVE NUISANCE, AND HIT THE BOX COMPANY FOR INFERIOR CARDBOARD..
SCHULZ

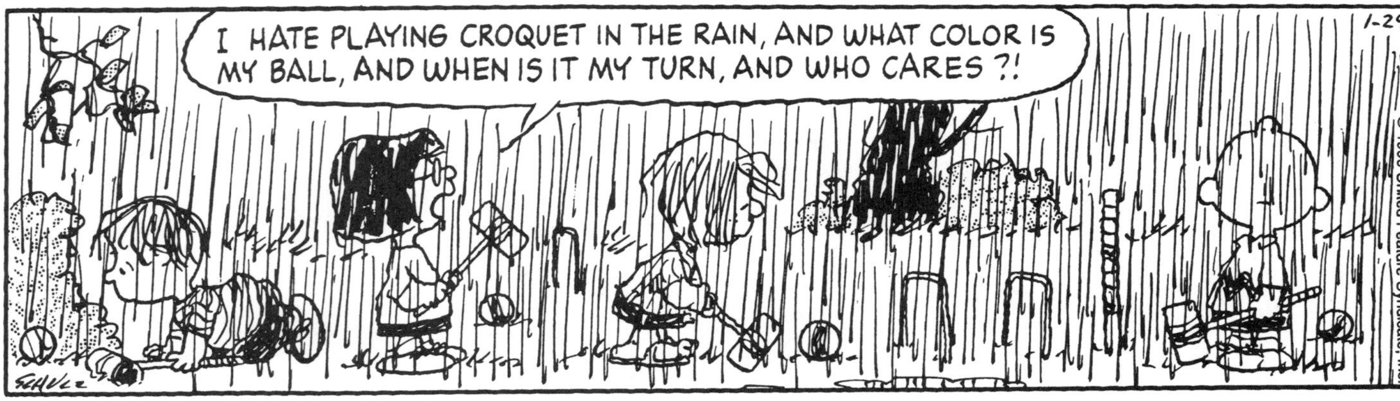
1-29
I HATE PLAYING CROQUET IN THE RAIN, AND WHAT COLOR IS MY BALL, AND WHEN IS IT MY TURN, AND WHO CARES ?!
© 1996 United Feature Syndicate, Inc.
SCHULZ

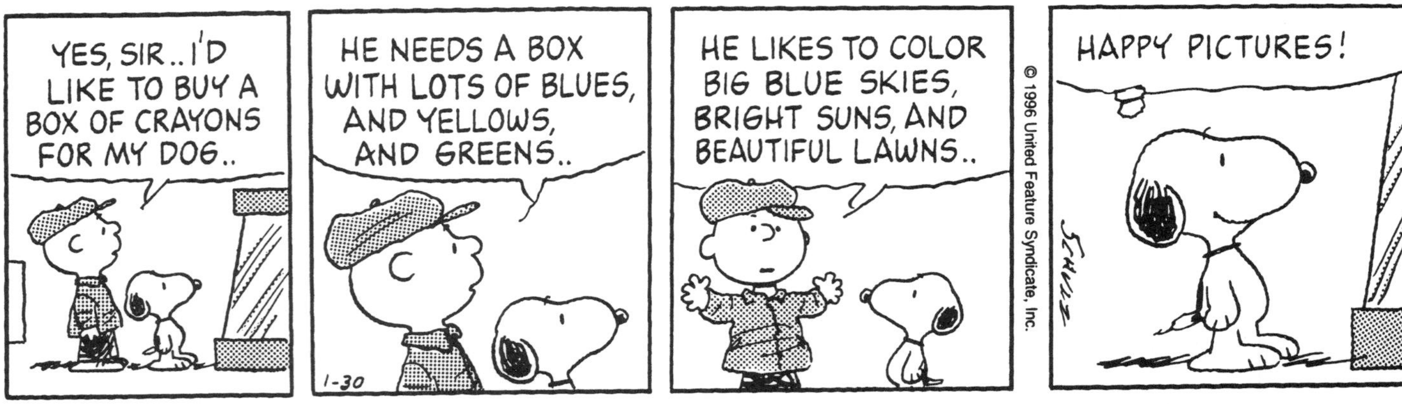
YES, SIR.. I'D LIKE TO BUY A BOX OF CRAYONS FOR MY DOG..
HE NEEDS A BOX WITH LOTS OF BLUES, AND YELLOWS, AND GREENS..
1-30
HE LIKES TO COLOR BIG BLUE SKIES, BRIGHT SUNS, AND BEAUTIFUL LAWNS..
© 1996 United Feature Syndicate, Inc.
HAPPY PICTURES!
SCHULZ

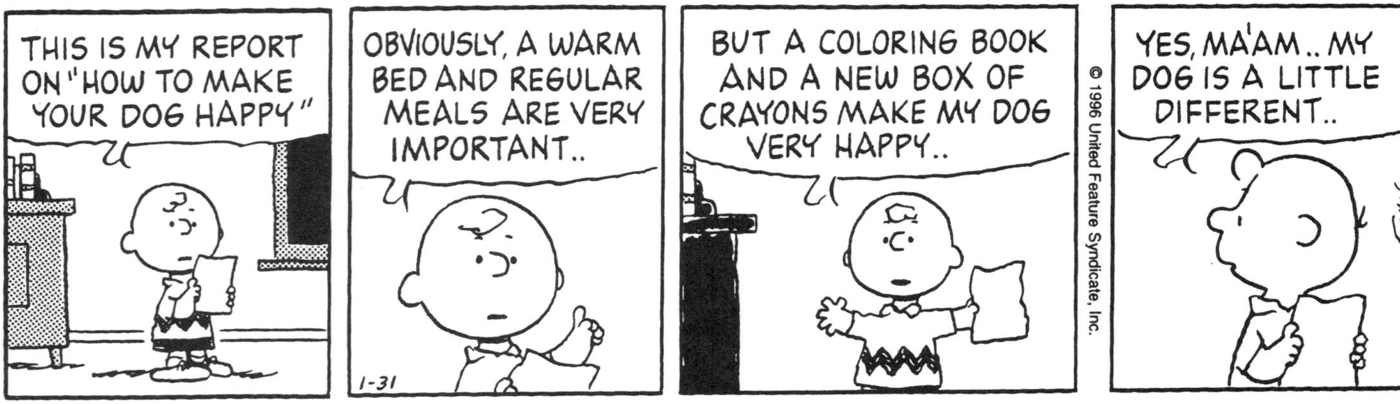
THIS IS MY REPORT ON "HOW TO MAKE YOUR DOG HAPPY"
OBVIOUSLY, A WARM BED AND REGULAR MEALS ARE VERY IMPORTANT..
1-31
BUT A COLORING BOOK AND A NEW BOX OF CRAYONS MAKE MY DOG VERY HAPPY..
© 1996 United Feature Syndicate, Inc.
YES, MA'AM.. MY DOG IS A LITTLE DIFFERENT..
SCHULZ

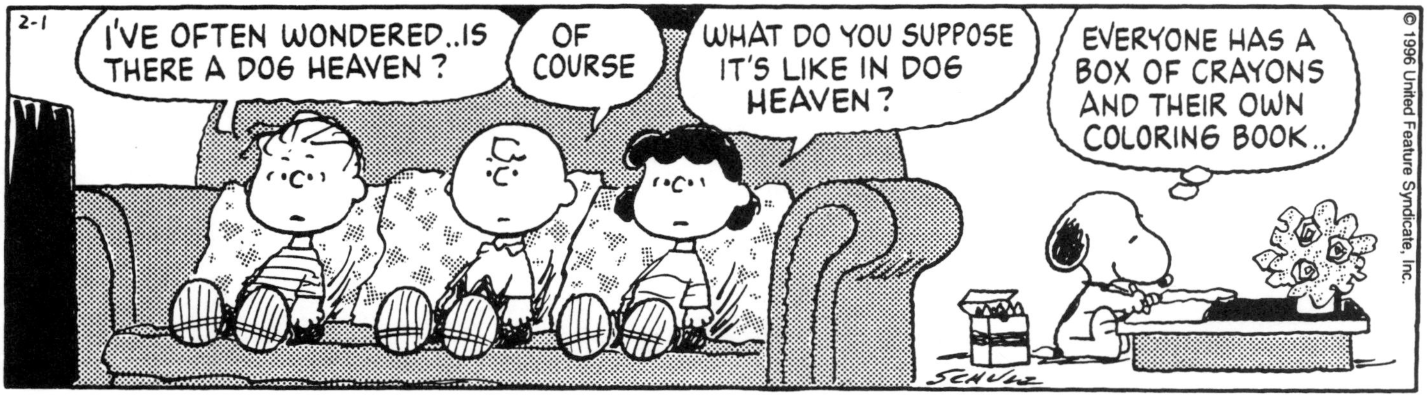
2-1
I'VE OFTEN WONDERED..IS THERE A DOG HEAVEN ?
OF COURSE
WHAT DO YOU SUPPOSE IT'S LIKE IN DOG HEAVEN ?
EVERYONE HAS A BOX OF CRAYONS AND THEIR OWN COLORING BOOK..
SCHULZ
© 1996 United Feature Syndicate, Inc.

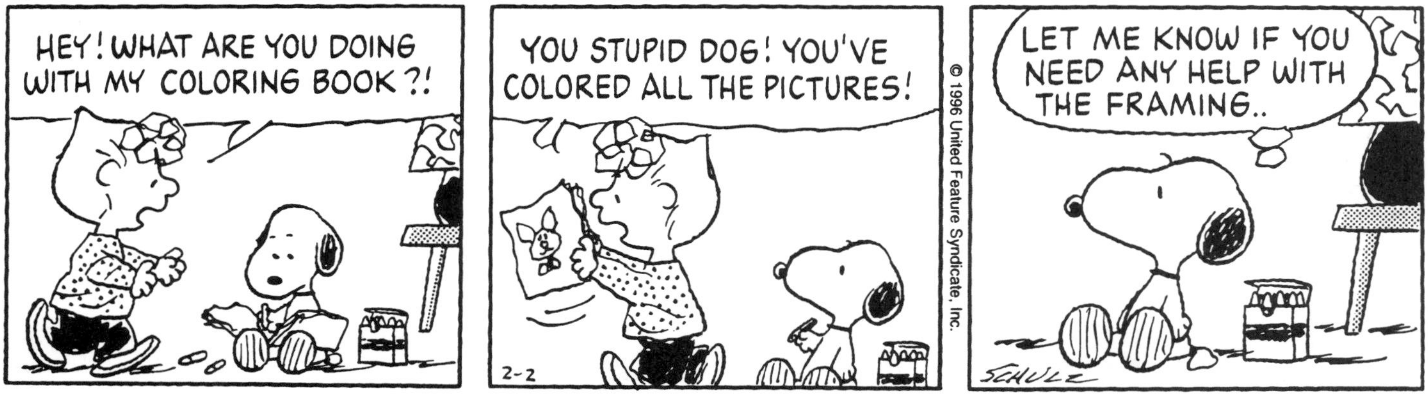
HEY! WHAT ARE YOU DOING WITH MY COLORING BOOK ?!
YOU STUPID DOG! YOU'VE COLORED ALL THE PICTURES!
2-2
© 1996 United Feature Syndicate, Inc.
LET ME KNOW IF YOU NEED ANY HELP WITH THE FRAMING..
SCHULZ

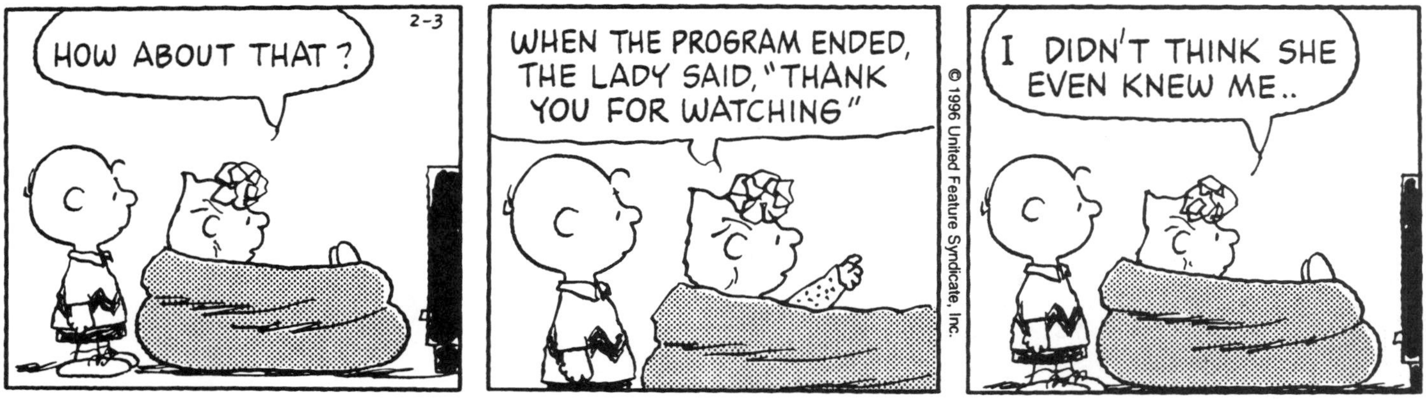
2-3
HOW ABOUT THAT ?
WHEN THE PROGRAM ENDED, THE LADY SAID, "THANK YOU FOR WATCHING"
© 1996 United Feature Syndicate, Inc.
I DIDN'T THINK SHE EVEN KNEW ME..

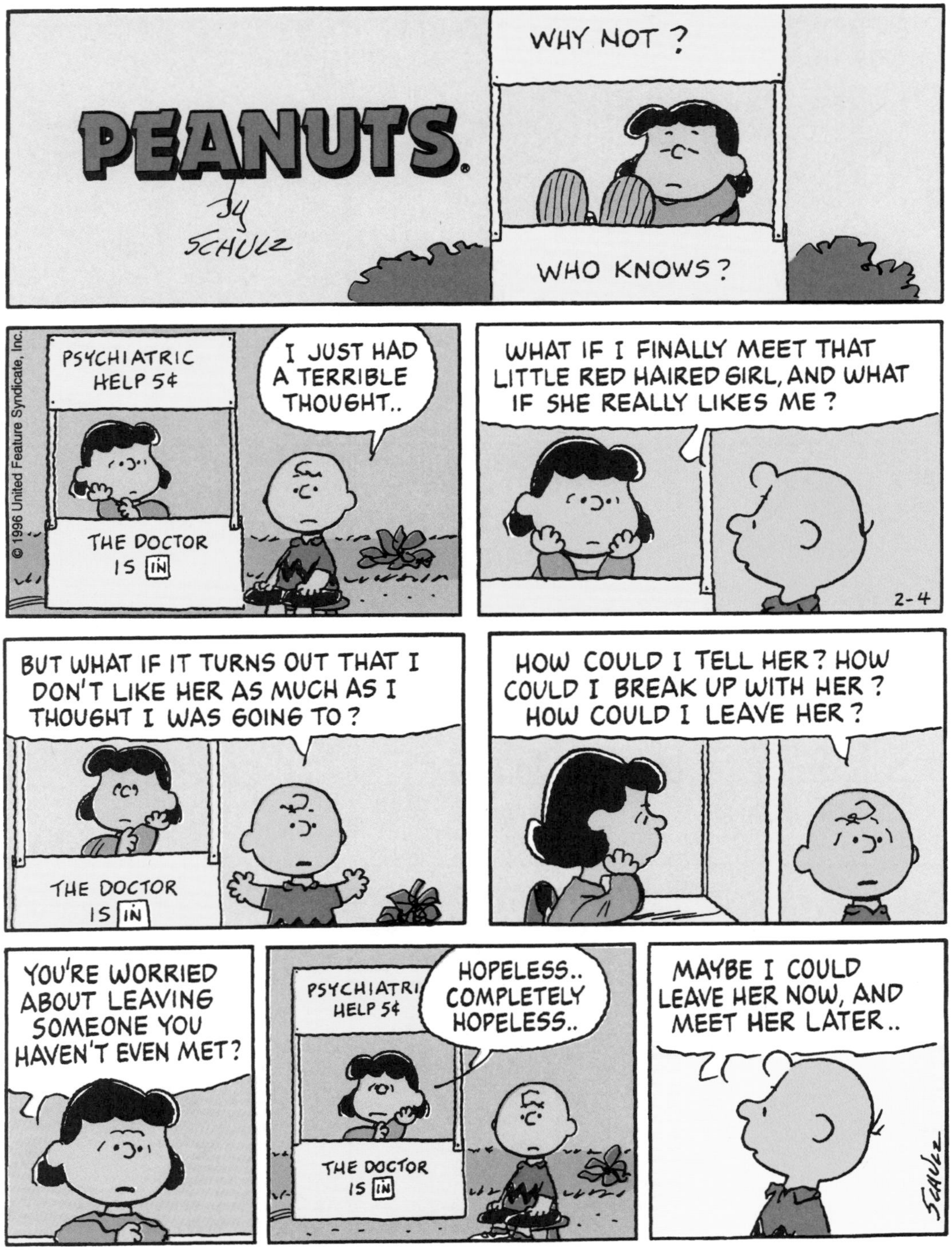
PEANUTS
by SCHULZ
WHY NOT ?
WHO KNOWS ?
© 1996 United Feature Syndicate, Inc.
PSYCHIATRIC HELP 5¢
THE DOCTOR IS IN
I JUST HAD A TERRIBLE THOUGHT..
WHAT IF I FINALLY MEET THAT LITTLE RED HAIRED GIRL, AND WHAT IF SHE REALLY LIKES ME ?
2-4
BUT WHAT IF IT TURNS OUT THAT I DON'T LIKE HER AS MUCH AS I THOUGHT I WAS GOING TO ?
THE DOCTOR IS IN
HOW COULD I TELL HER ? HOW COULD I BREAK UP WITH HER ? HOW COULD I LEAVE HER ?
YOU'RE WORRIED ABOUT LEAVING SOMEONE YOU HAVEN'T EVEN MET ?
PSYCHIATRI HELP 5¢
THE DOCTOR IS IN
HOPELESS.. COMPLETELY HOPELESS..
MAYBE I COULD LEAVE HER NOW, AND MEET HER LATER..
SCHULZ

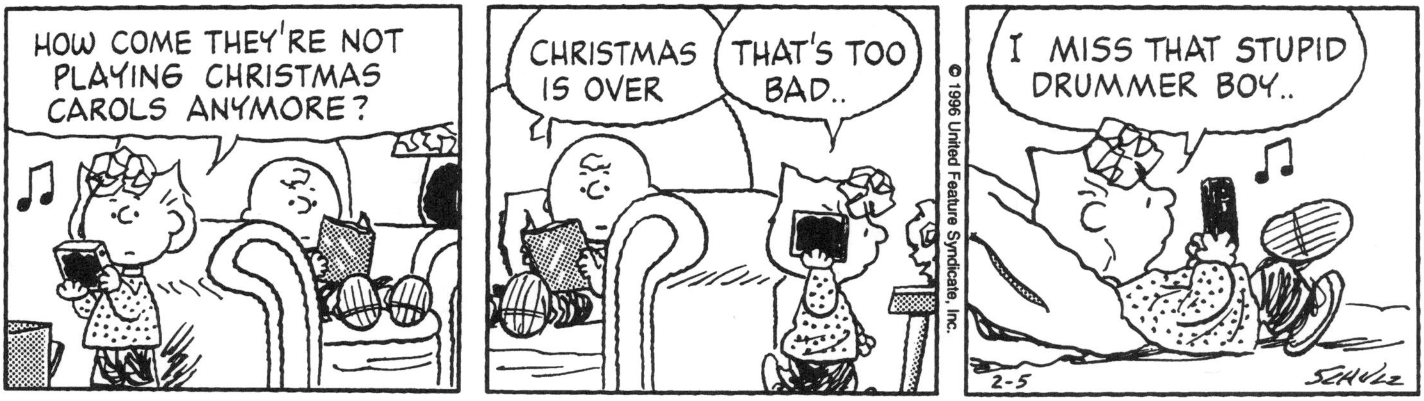
HOW COME THEY'RE NOT PLAYING CHRISTMAS CAROLS ANYMORE?
CHRISTMAS IS OVER
THAT'S TOO BAD..
I MISS THAT STUPID DRUMMER BOY..
© 1996 United Feature Syndicate, Inc.
2-5
SCHULZ

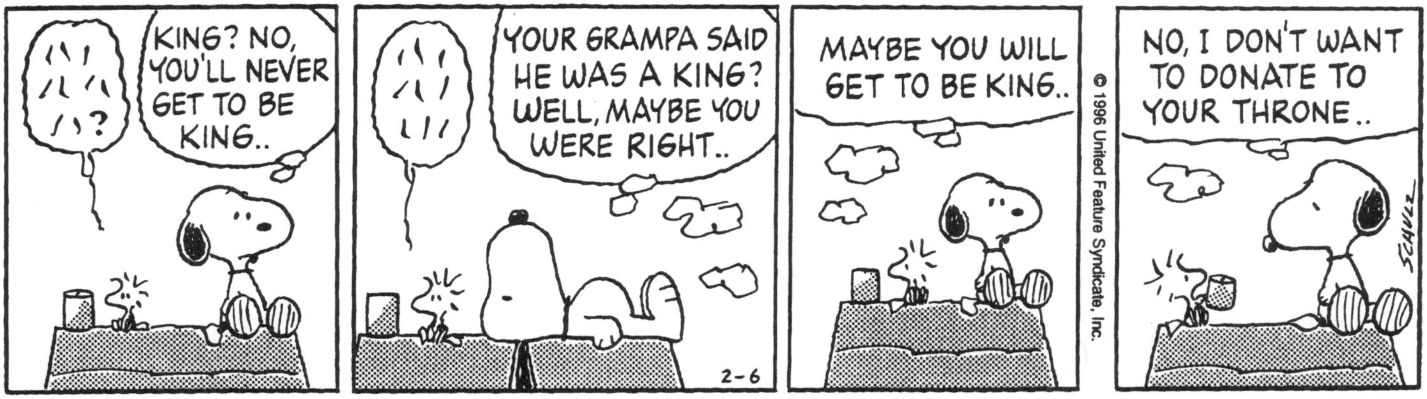
?
KING? NO, YOU'LL NEVER GET TO BE KING..
YOUR GRAMPA SAID HE WAS A KING? WELL, MAYBE YOU WERE RIGHT..
MAYBE YOU WILL GET TO BE KING..
NO, I DON'T WANT TO DONATE TO YOUR THRONE..
© 1996 United Feature Syndicate, Inc.
2-6
SCHULZ

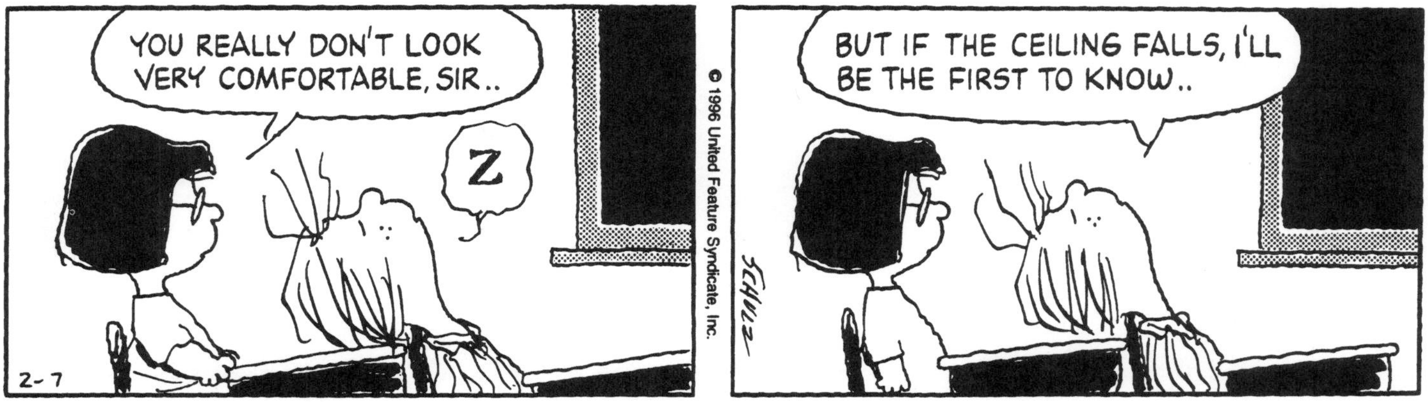
YOU REALLY DON'T LOOK VERY COMFORTABLE, SIR..
Z
BUT IF THE CEILING FALLS, I'LL BE THE FIRST TO KNOW..
© 1996 United Feature Syndicate, Inc.
2-7
SCHULZ

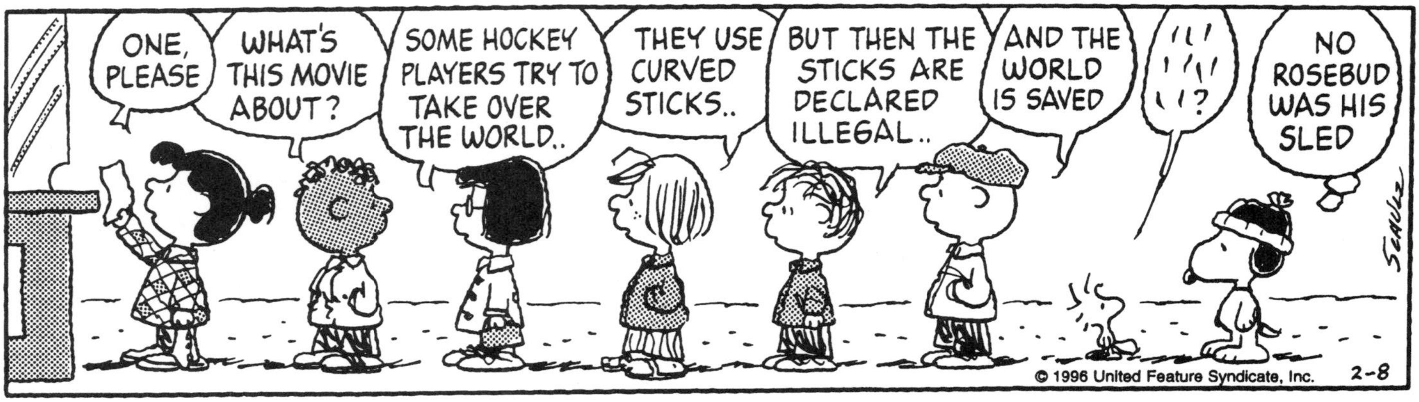
ONE, PLEASE
WHAT'S THIS MOVIE ABOUT?
SOME HOCKEY PLAYERS TRY TO TAKE OVER THE WORLD..
THEY USE CURVED STICKS..
BUT THEN THE STICKS ARE DECLARED ILLEGAL..
AND THE WORLD IS SAVED
NO ROSEBUD WAS HIS SLED
SCHULZ
© 1996 United Feature Syndicate, Inc.
2-8

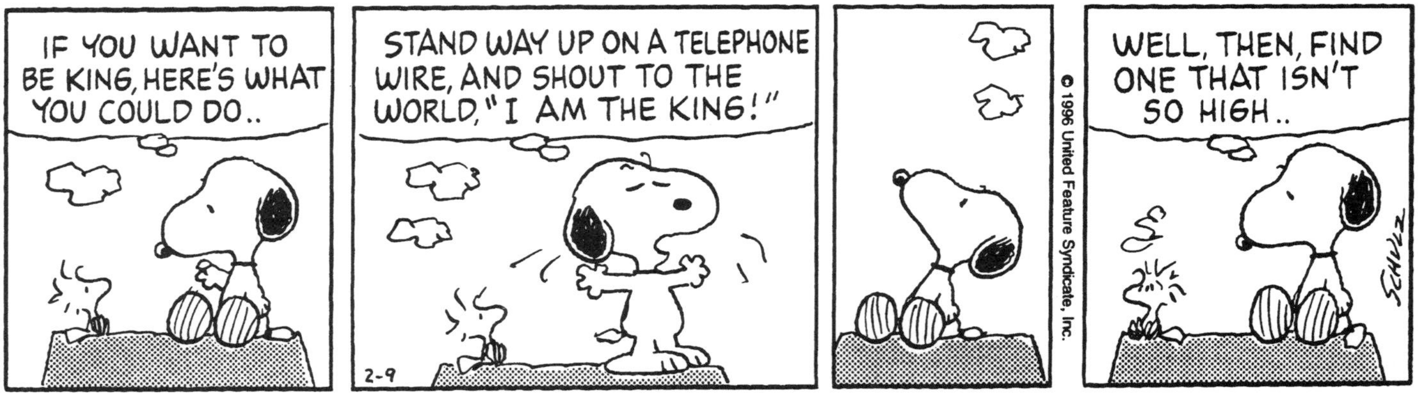
IF YOU WANT TO BE KING, HERE'S WHAT YOU COULD DO..
STAND WAY UP ON A TELEPHONE WIRE, AND SHOUT TO THE WORLD, "I AM THE KING!"
2-9
© 1996 United Feature Syndicate, Inc.
WELL, THEN, FIND ONE THAT ISN'T SO HIGH..
SCHULZ

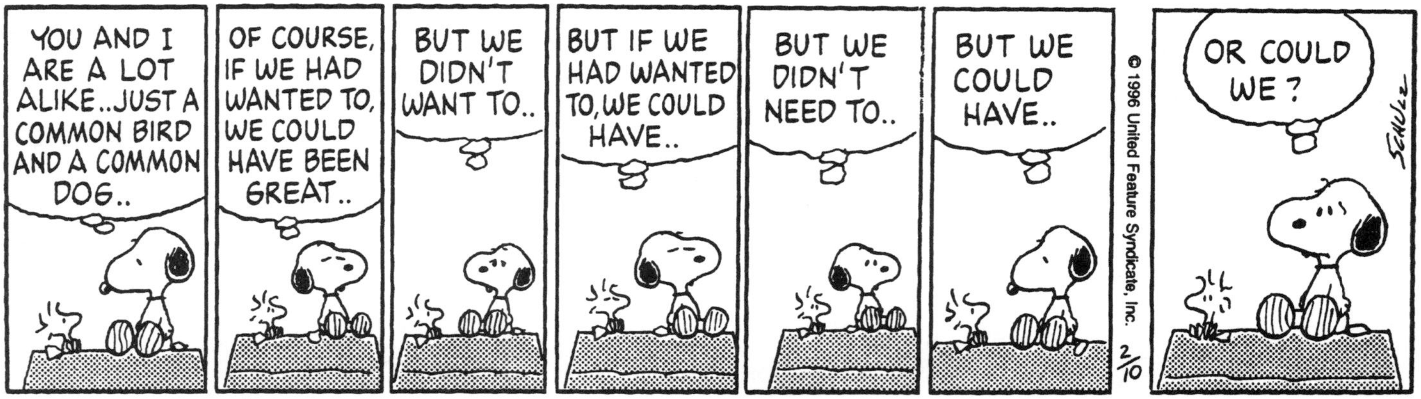
YOU AND I ARE A LOT ALIKE..JUST A COMMON BIRD AND A COMMON DOG..
OF COURSE, IF WE HAD WANTED TO, WE COULD HAVE BEEN GREAT..
BUT WE DIDN'T WANT TO..
BUT IF WE HAD WANTED TO, WE COULD HAVE..
BUT WE DIDN'T NEED TO..
BUT WE COULD HAVE..
© 1996 United Feature Syndicate, Inc.
2/10
OR COULD WE?
SCHULZ

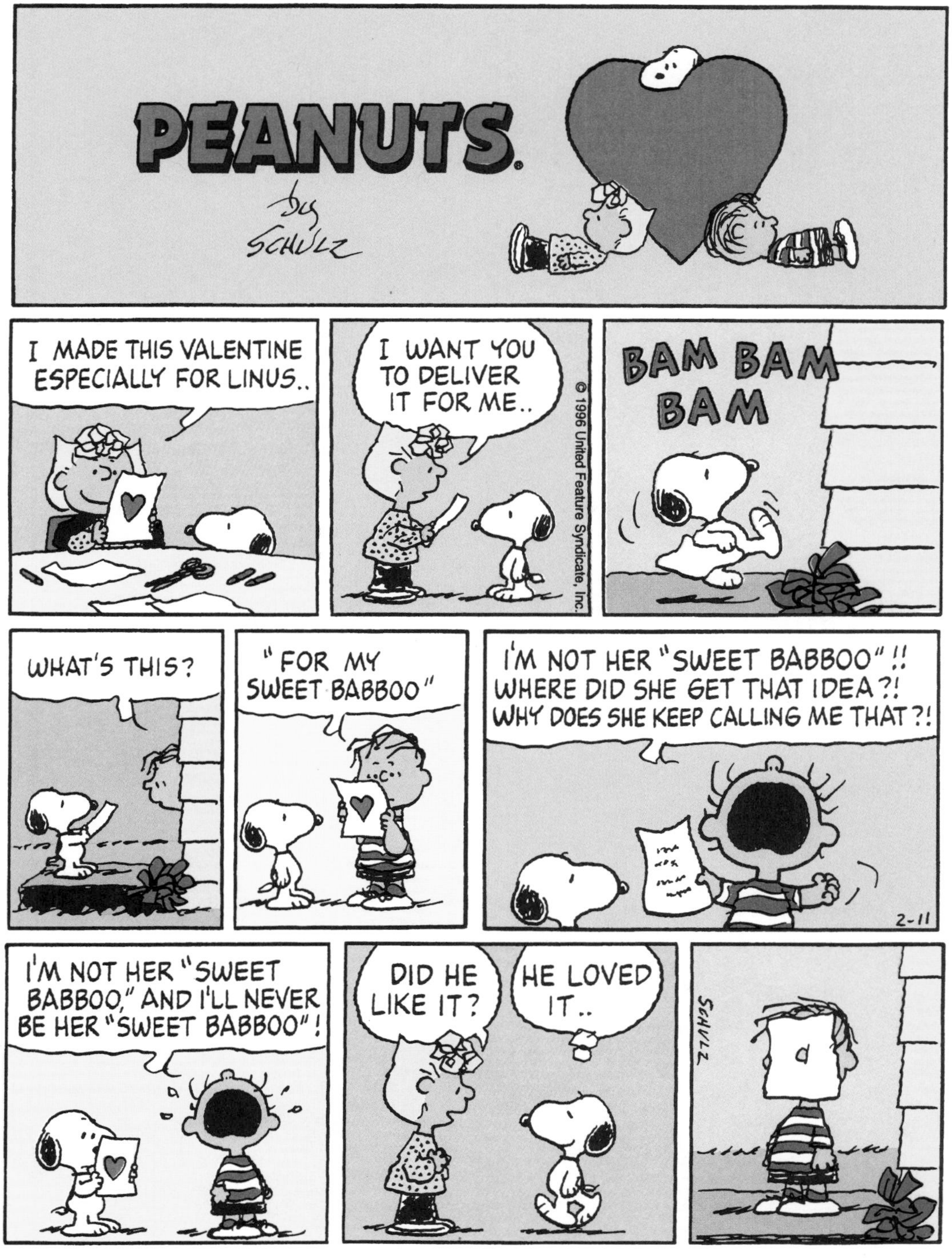
PEANUTS
by SCHULZ
I MADE THIS VALENTINE ESPECIALLY FOR LINUS..
I WANT YOU TO DELIVER IT FOR ME..
© 1996 United Feature Syndicate, Inc.
BAM BAM BAM
WHAT'S THIS?
"FOR MY SWEET BABBOO"
I'M NOT HER "SWEET BABBOO"!! WHERE DID SHE GET THAT IDEA?! WHY DOES SHE KEEP CALLING ME THAT?!
2-11
I'M NOT HER "SWEET BABBOO," AND I'LL NEVER BE HER "SWEET BABBOO"!
DID HE LIKE IT?
HE LOVED IT..
SCHULZ

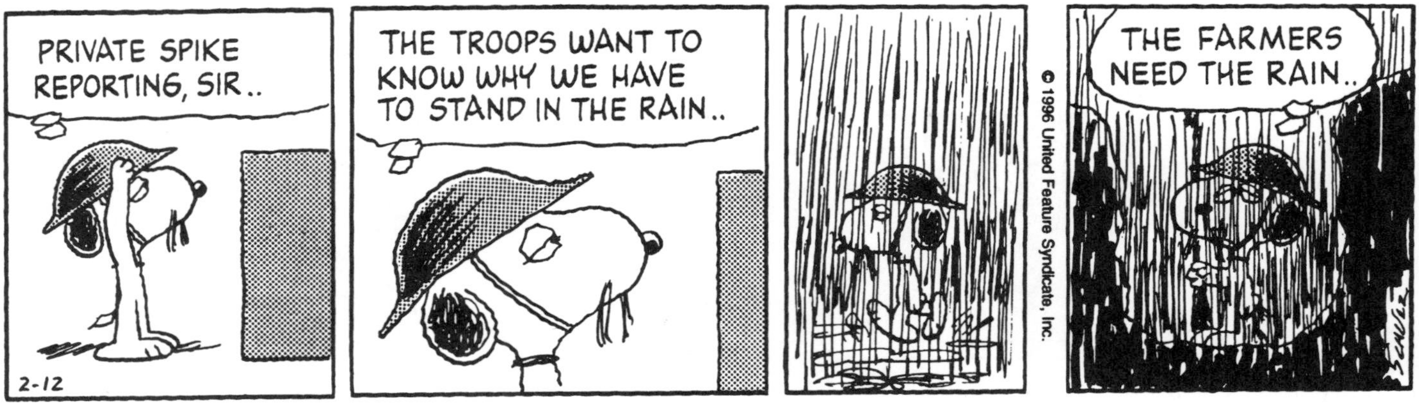
PRIVATE SPIKE REPORTING, SIR..
THE TROOPS WANT TO KNOW WHY WE HAVE TO STAND IN THE RAIN..
THE FARMERS NEED THE RAIN..
2-12
© 1996 United Feature Syndicate, Inc.
SCHULZ

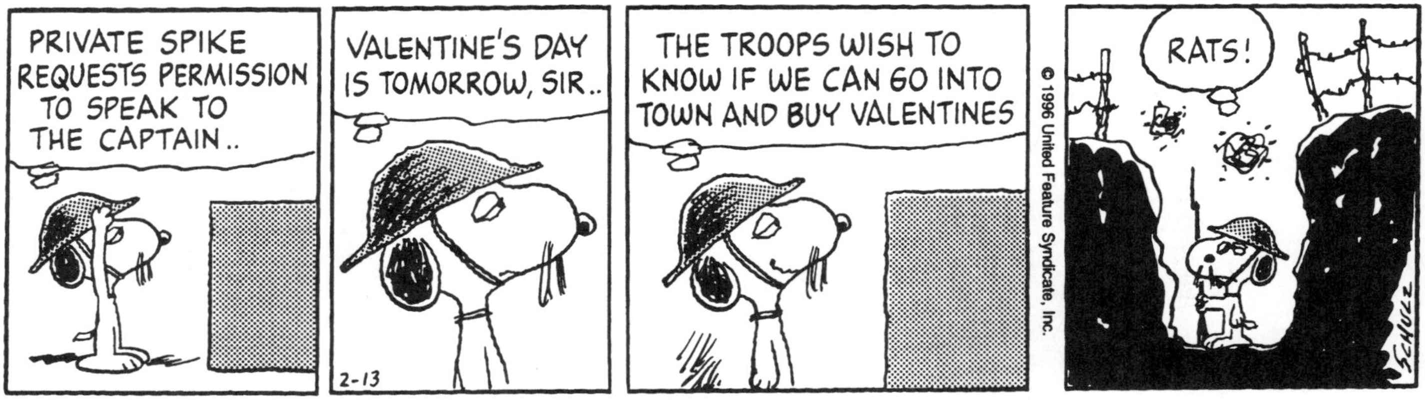
PRIVATE SPIKE REQUESTS PERMISSION TO SPEAK TO THE CAPTAIN..
VALENTINE'S DAY IS TOMORROW, SIR..
THE TROOPS WISH TO KNOW IF WE CAN GO INTO TOWN AND BUY VALENTINES
RATS!
2-13
© 1996 United Feature Syndicate, Inc.
SCHULZ

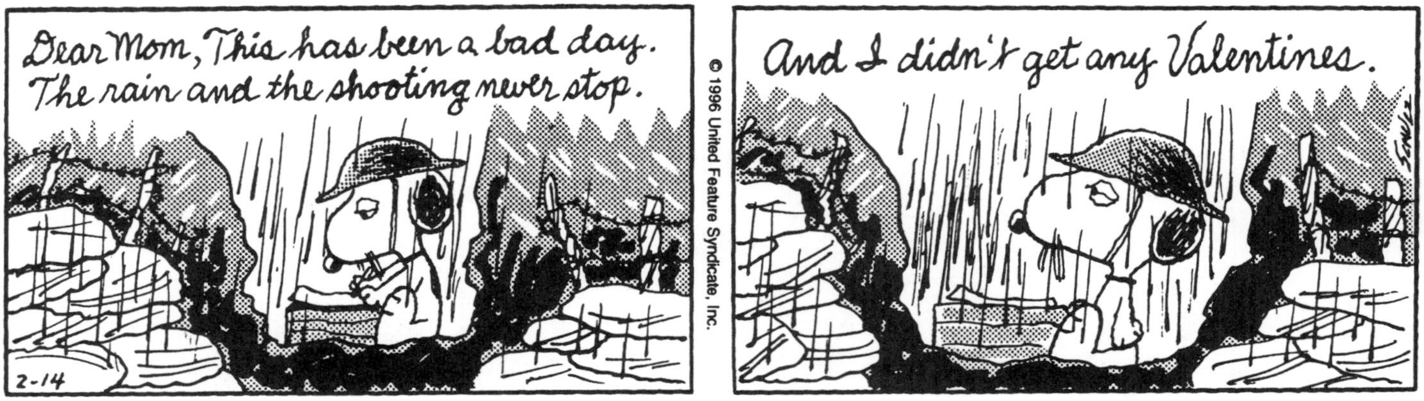
Dear Mom, This has been a bad day. The rain and the shooting never stop.
And I didn't get any Valentines.
2-14
© 1996 United Feature Syndicate, Inc.
SCHULZ

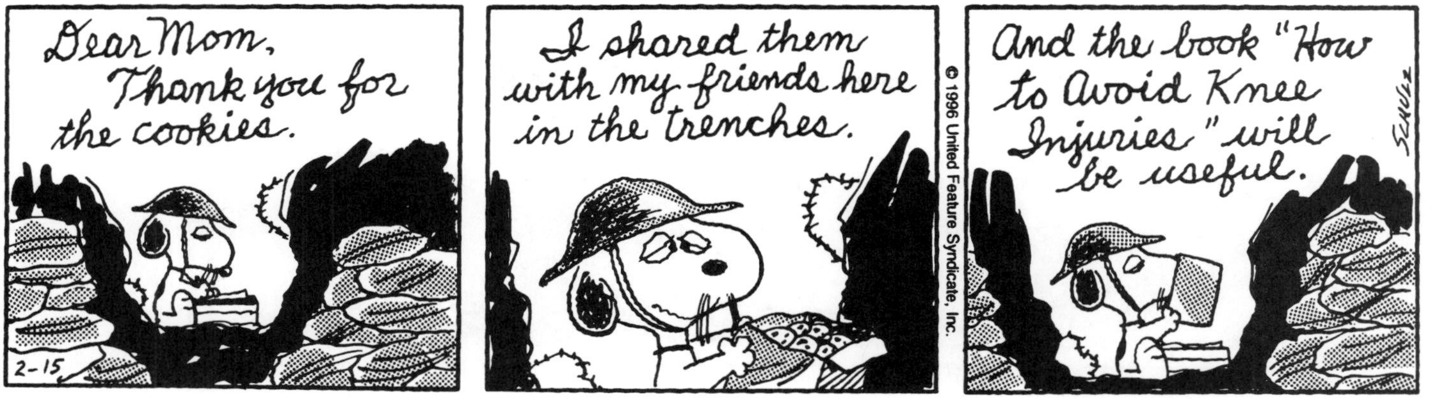
Dear Mom,
Thank you for the cookies.
I shared them with my friends here in the trenches.
And the book "How to Avoid Knee Injuries" will be useful.
© 1996 United Feature Syndicate, Inc.
2-15

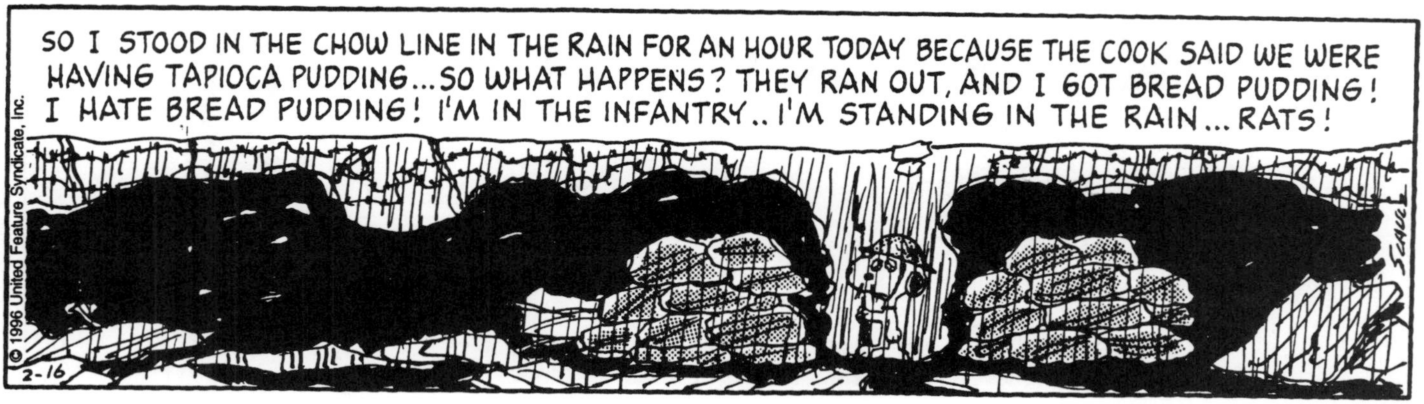
SO I STOOD IN THE CHOW LINE IN THE RAIN FOR AN HOUR TODAY BECAUSE THE COOK SAID WE WERE HAVING TAPIOCA PUDDING...SO WHAT HAPPENS? THEY RAN OUT, AND I GOT BREAD PUDDING! I HATE BREAD PUDDING! I'M IN THE INFANTRY.. I'M STANDING IN THE RAIN... RATS!
© 1996 United Feature Syndicate, Inc.
2-16

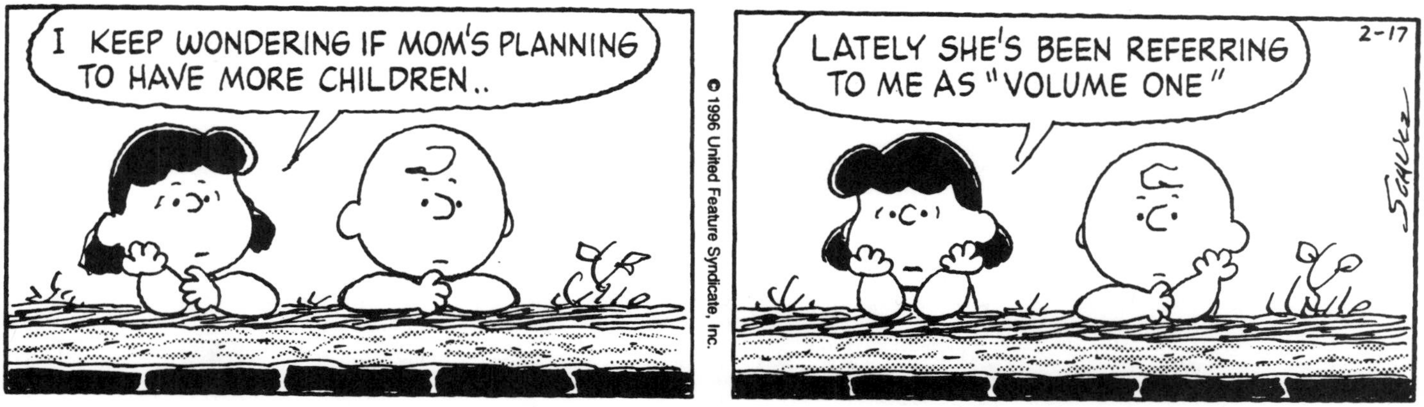
I KEEP WONDERING IF MOM'S PLANNING TO HAVE MORE CHILDREN..
LATELY SHE'S BEEN REFERRING TO ME AS "VOLUME ONE"
© 1996 United Feature Syndicate, Inc.
2-17

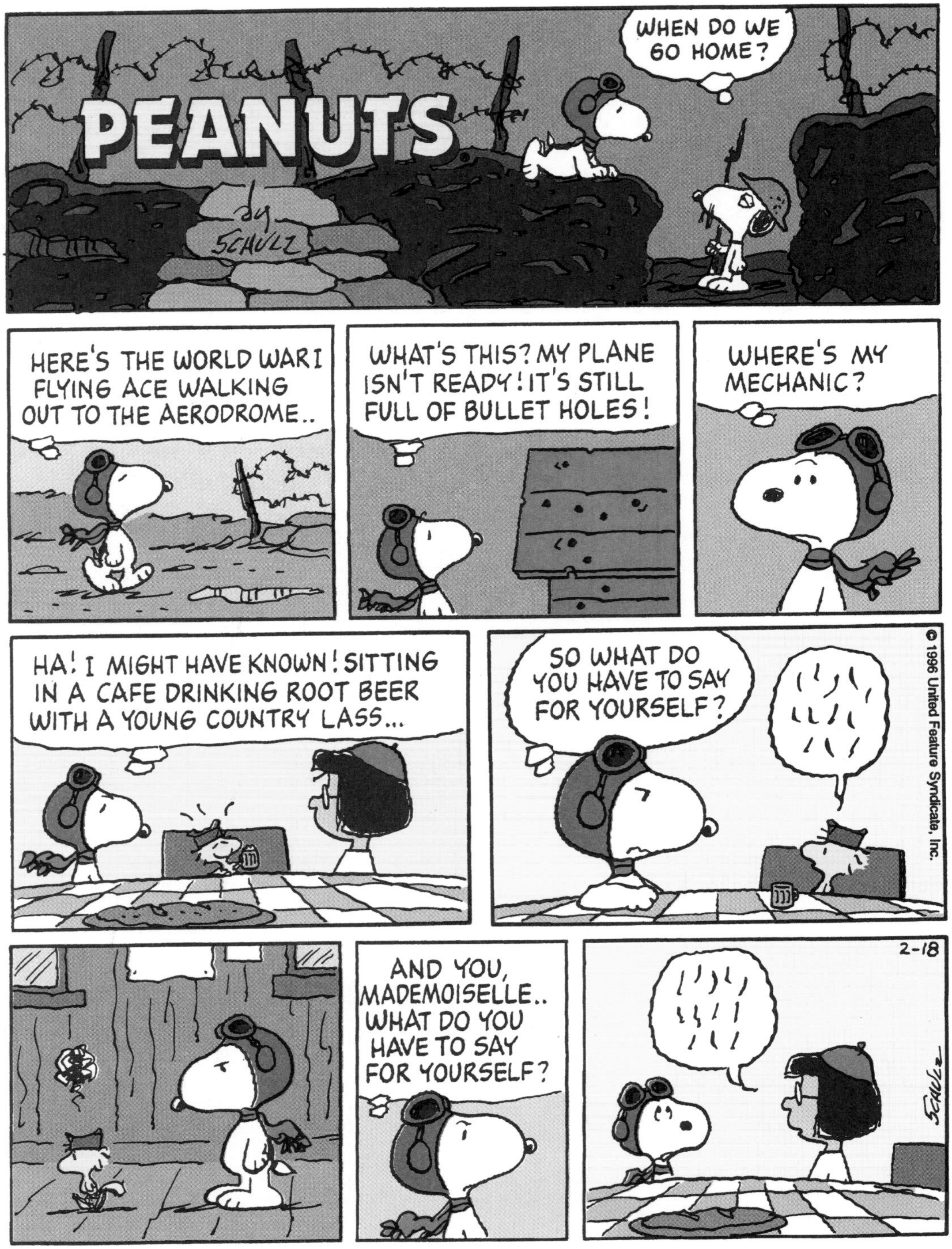
WHEN DO WE GO HOME?
PEANUTS
by SCHULZ
HERE'S THE WORLD WAR I FLYING ACE WALKING OUT TO THE AERODROME..
WHAT'S THIS? MY PLANE ISN'T READY! IT'S STILL FULL OF BULLET HOLES!
WHERE'S MY MECHANIC?
HA! I MIGHT HAVE KNOWN! SITTING IN A CAFE DRINKING ROOT BEER WITH A YOUNG COUNTRY LASS...
SO WHAT DO YOU HAVE TO SAY FOR YOURSELF?
© 1996 United Feature Syndicate, Inc.
AND YOU, MADEMOISELLE.. WHAT DO YOU HAVE TO SAY FOR YOURSELF?
2-18
SCHULZ

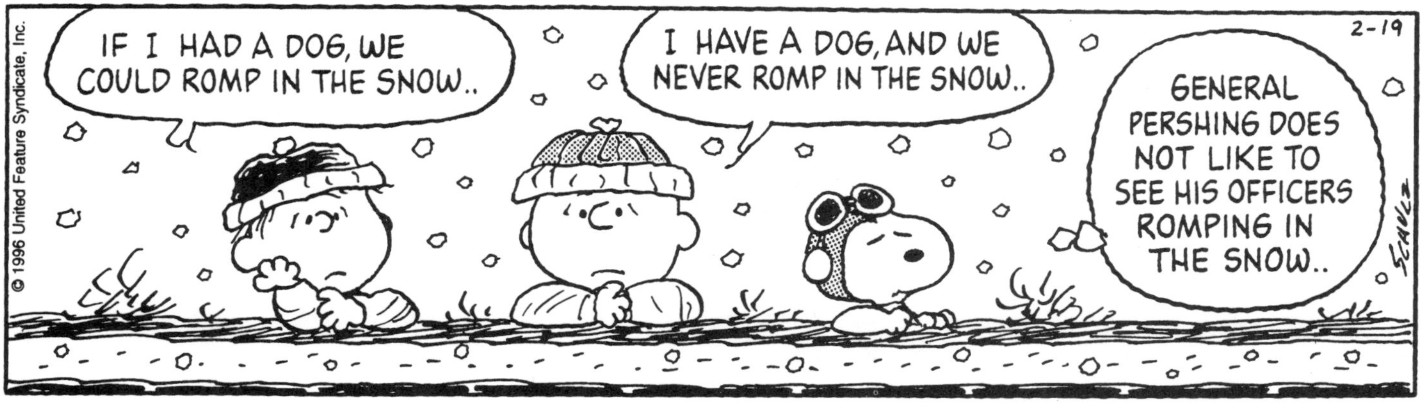
© 1996 United Feature Syndicate, Inc.
2-19
IF I HAD A DOG, WE COULD ROMP IN THE SNOW..
I HAVE A DOG, AND WE NEVER ROMP IN THE SNOW..
GENERAL PERSHING DOES NOT LIKE TO SEE HIS OFFICERS ROMPING IN THE SNOW..
SCHULZ

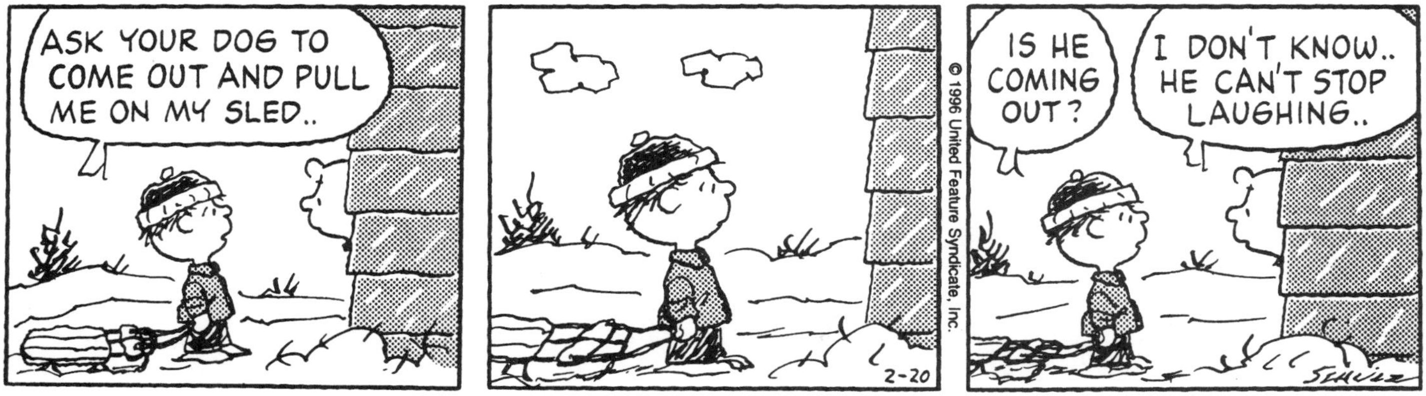
ASK YOUR DOG TO COME OUT AND PULL ME ON MY SLED..
© 1996 United Feature Syndicate, Inc.
2-20
IS HE COMING OUT?
I DON'T KNOW.. HE CAN'T STOP LAUGHING..
SCHULZ

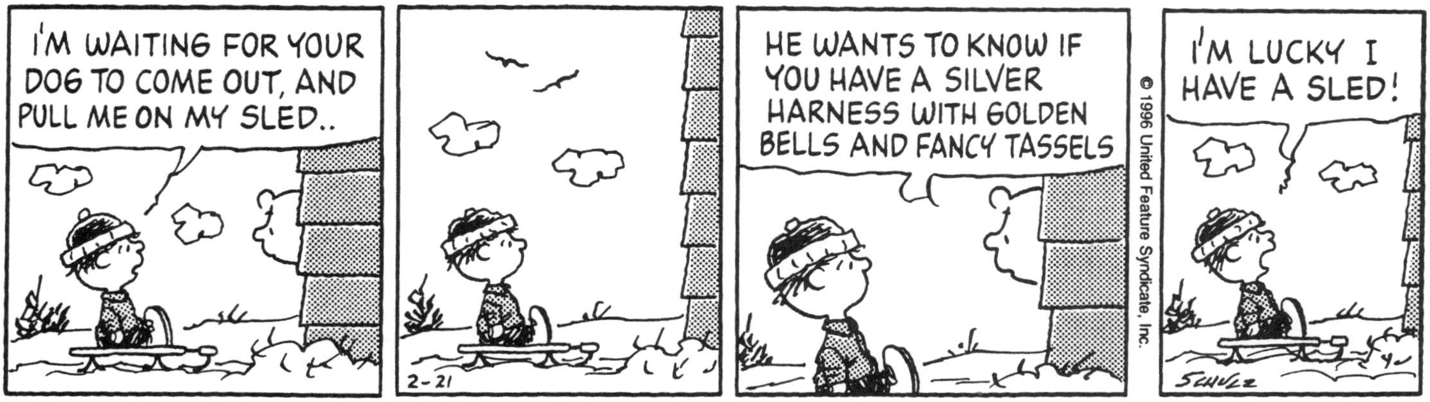
I'M WAITING FOR YOUR DOG TO COME OUT, AND PULL ME ON MY SLED..
2-21
HE WANTS TO KNOW IF YOU HAVE A SILVER HARNESS WITH GOLDEN BELLS AND FANCY TASSELS
© 1996 United Feature Syndicate, Inc.
I'M LUCKY I HAVE A SLED!
SCHULZ

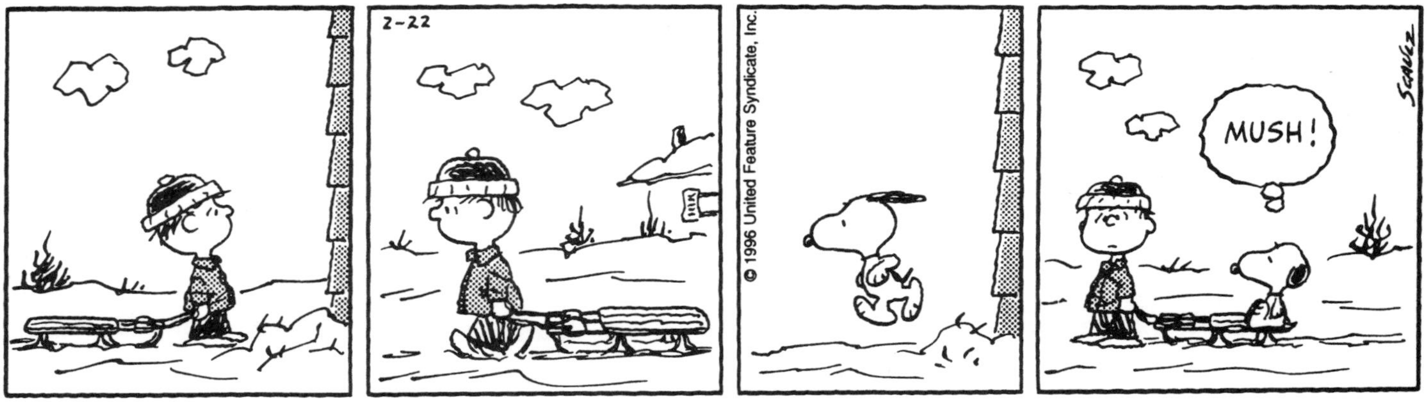
2-22
© 1996 United Feature Syndicate, Inc.
MUSH!
SCHULZ

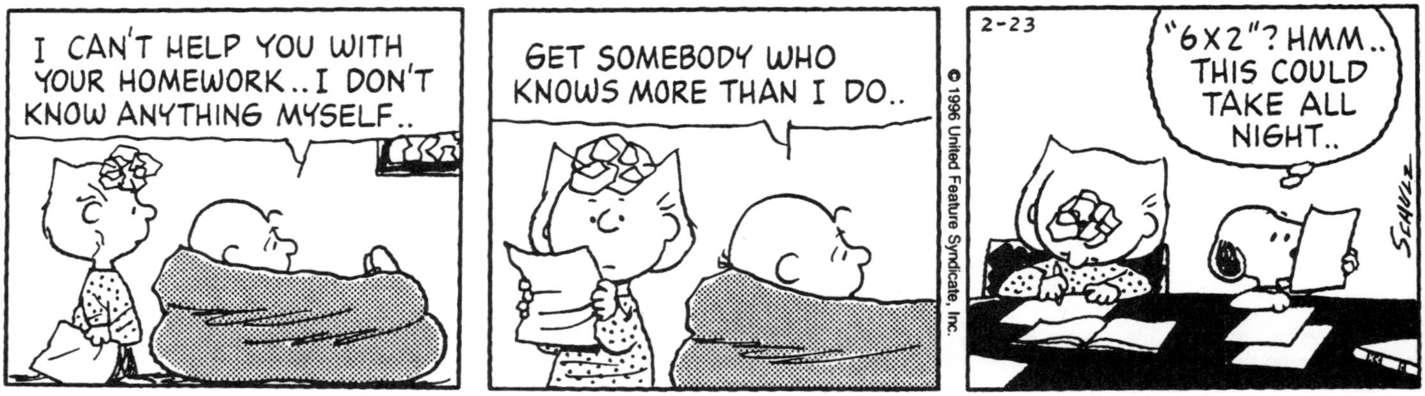
I CAN'T HELP YOU WITH YOUR HOMEWORK..I DON'T KNOW ANYTHING MYSELF..
GET SOMEBODY WHO KNOWS MORE THAN I DO..
© 1996 United Feature Syndicate, Inc.
2-23
"6X2"? HMM.. THIS COULD TAKE ALL NIGHT..
SCHULZ

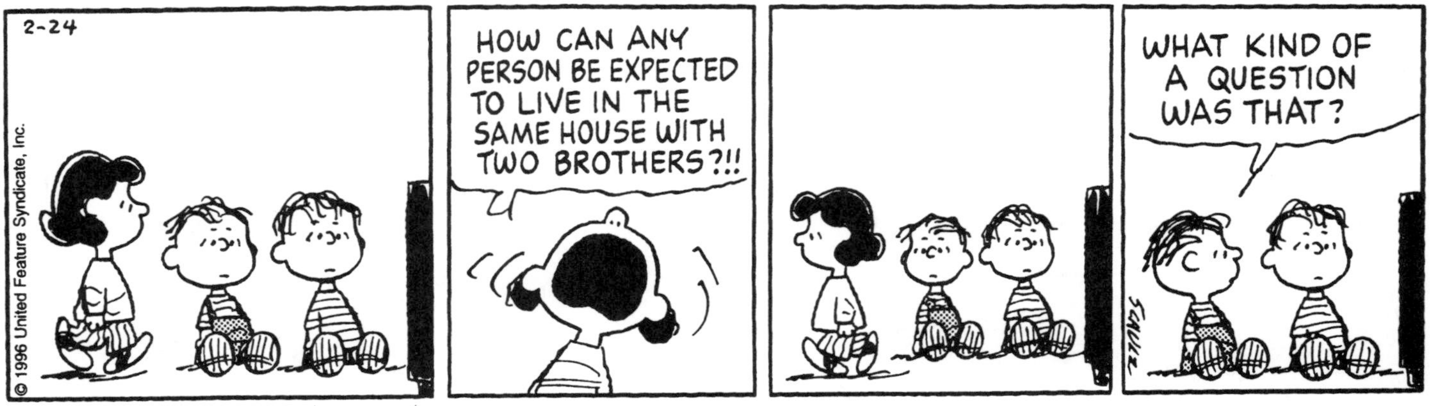
2-24
© 1996 United Feature Syndicate, Inc.
HOW CAN ANY PERSON BE EXPECTED TO LIVE IN THE SAME HOUSE WITH TWO BROTHERS?!!
WHAT KIND OF A QUESTION WAS THAT?
SCHULZ

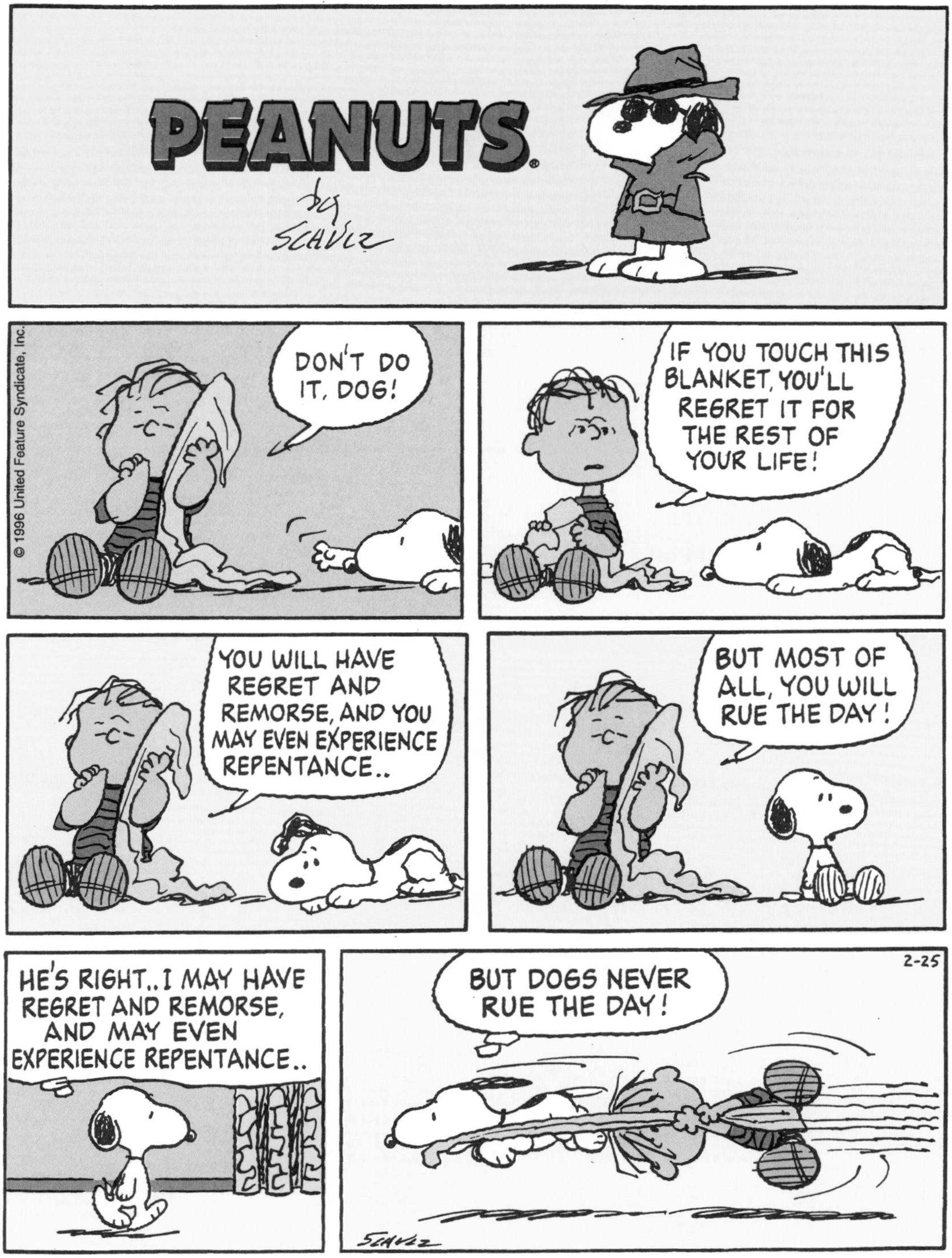

PEANUTS
by SCHULZ
© 1996 United Feature Syndicate, Inc.
DON'T DO IT, DOG!
IF YOU TOUCH THIS BLANKET, YOU'LL REGRET IT FOR THE REST OF YOUR LIFE!
YOU WILL HAVE REGRET AND REMORSE, AND YOU MAY EVEN EXPERIENCE REPENTANCE..
BUT MOST OF ALL, YOU WILL RUE THE DAY!
HE'S RIGHT..I MAY HAVE REGRET AND REMORSE, AND MAY EVEN EXPERIENCE REPENTANCE..
2-25
BUT DOGS NEVER RUE THE DAY!
SCHULZ

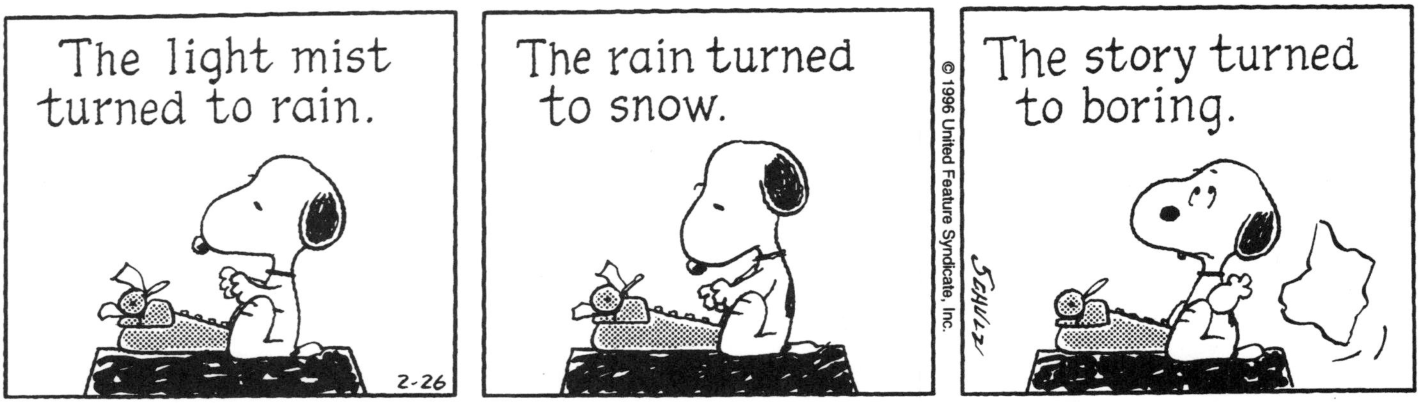
The light mist turned to rain.
2-26
The rain turned to snow.
© 1996 United Feature Syndicate, Inc.
The story turned to boring.
SCHULZ

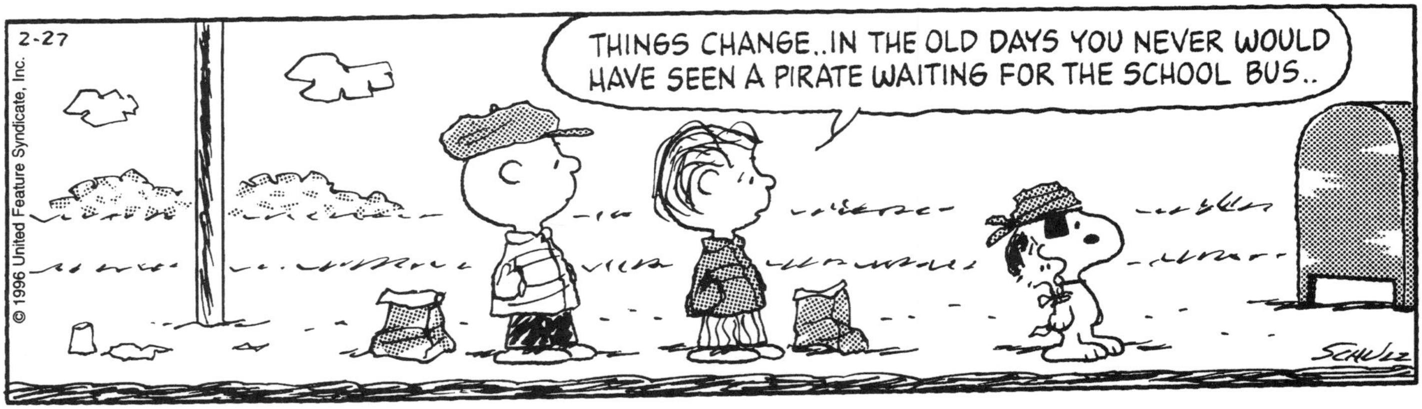
2-27
© 1996 United Feature Syndicate, Inc.
THINGS CHANGE..IN THE OLD DAYS YOU NEVER WOULD HAVE SEEN A PIRATE WAITING FOR THE SCHOOL BUS..
SCHULZ

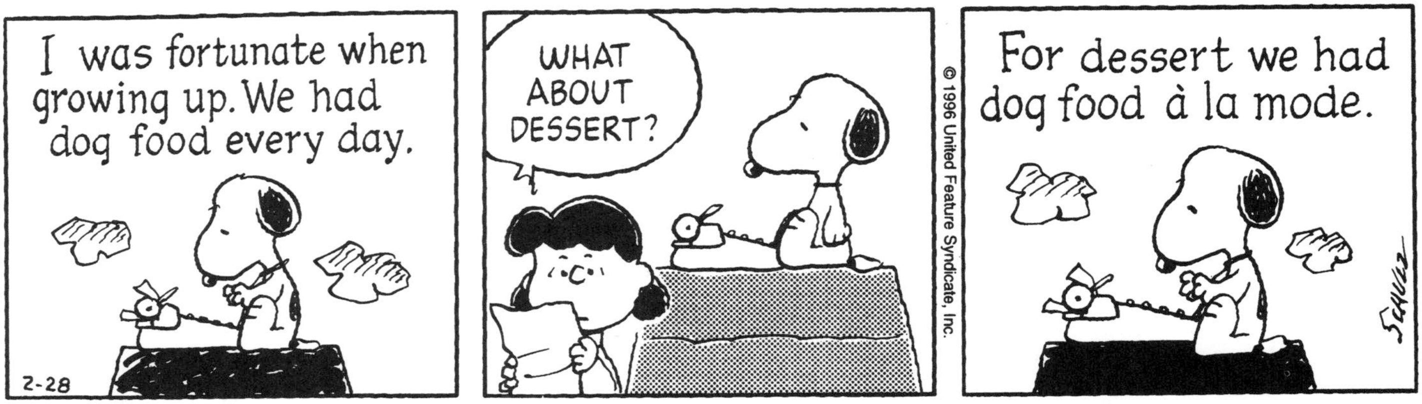
I was fortunate when growing up. We had dog food every day.
2-28
WHAT ABOUT DESSERT?
© 1996 United Feature Syndicate, Inc.
For dessert we had dog food à la mode.
SCHULZ

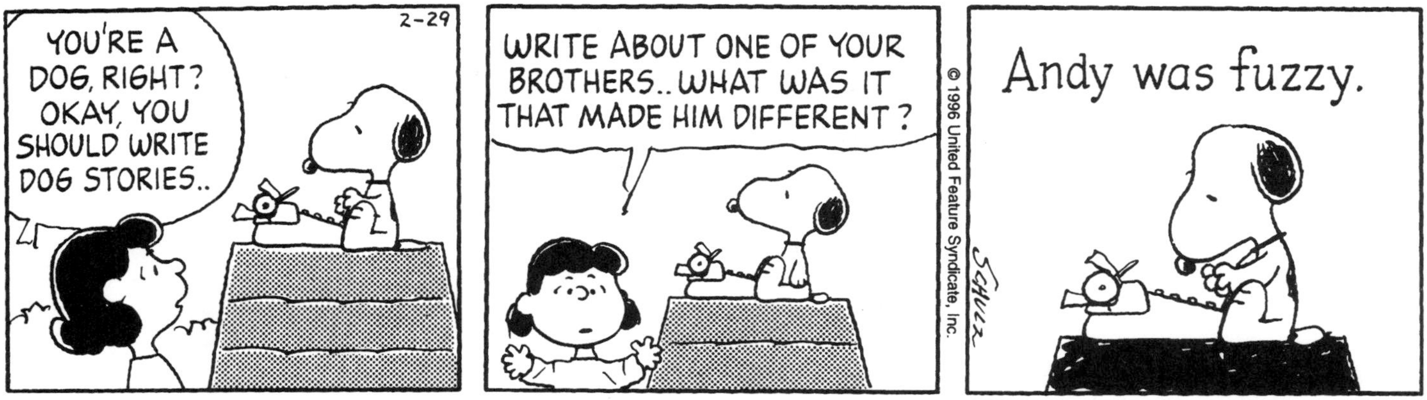
2-29
YOU'RE A DOG, RIGHT? OKAY, YOU SHOULD WRITE DOG STORIES..
WRITE ABOUT ONE OF YOUR BROTHERS.. WHAT WAS IT THAT MADE HIM DIFFERENT?
© 1996 United Feature Syndicate, Inc.
Andy was fuzzy.
SCHULZ

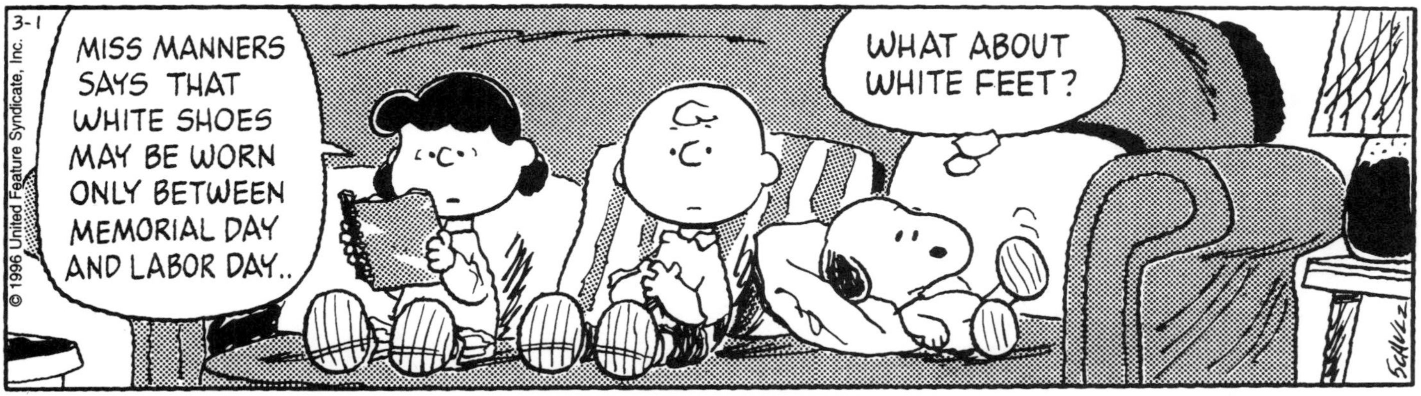
3-1
© 1996 United Feature Syndicate, Inc.
MISS MANNERS SAYS THAT WHITE SHOES MAY BE WORN ONLY BETWEEN MEMORIAL DAY AND LABOR DAY..
WHAT ABOUT WHITE FEET?
SCHULZ

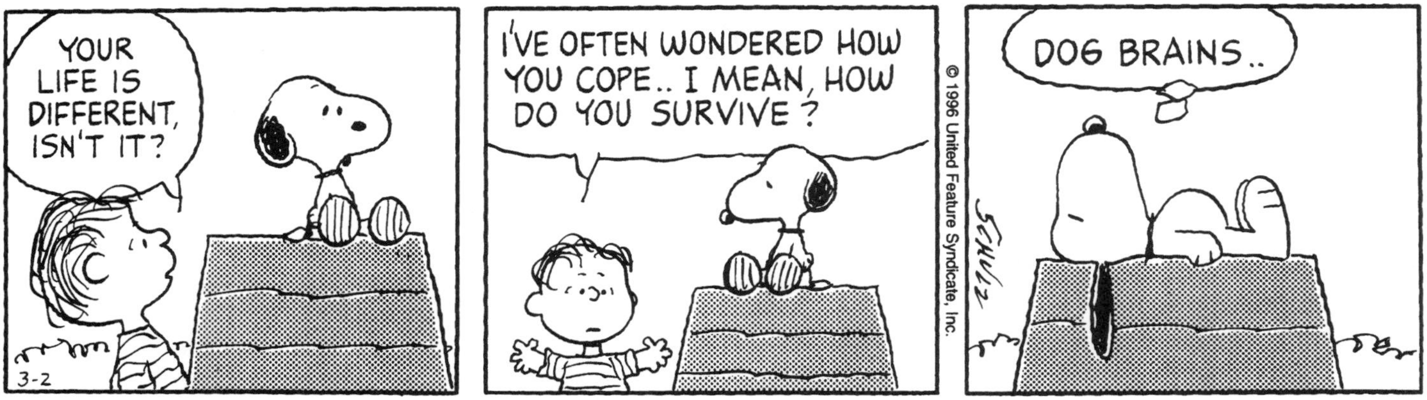
YOUR LIFE IS DIFFERENT, ISN'T IT?
3-2
I'VE OFTEN WONDERED HOW YOU COPE.. I MEAN, HOW DO YOU SURVIVE?
© 1996 United Feature Syndicate, Inc.
SCHULZ
DOG BRAINS..

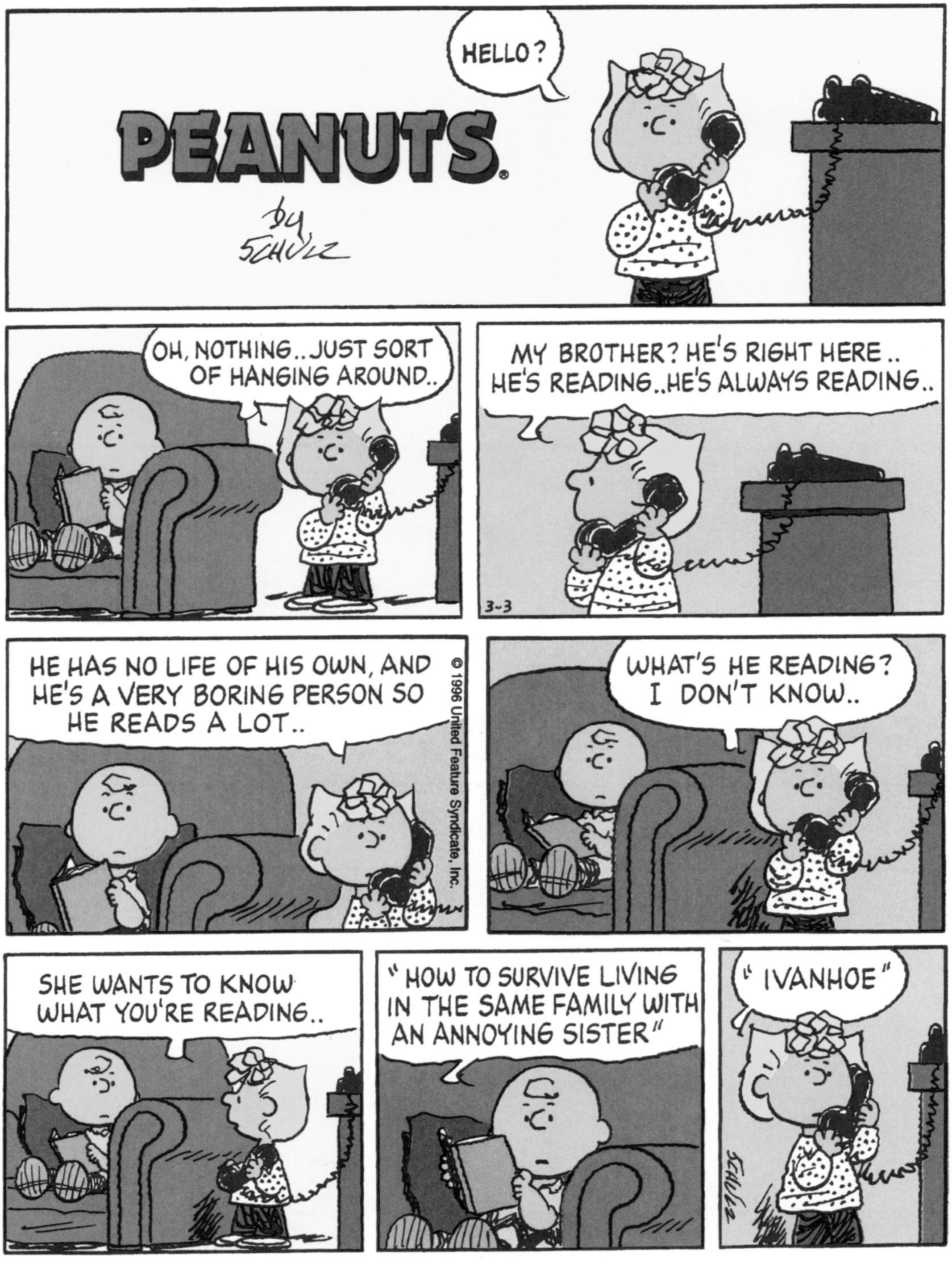
HELLO?
PEANUTS
by SCHULZ
OH, NOTHING.. JUST SORT OF HANGING AROUND..
MY BROTHER? HE'S RIGHT HERE.. HE'S READING..HE'S ALWAYS READING..
3-3
HE HAS NO LIFE OF HIS OWN, AND HE'S A VERY BORING PERSON SO HE READS A LOT..
© 1996 United Feature Syndicate, Inc.
WHAT'S HE READING? I DON'T KNOW..
SHE WANTS TO KNOW WHAT YOU'RE READING..
"HOW TO SURVIVE LIVING IN THE SAME FAMILY WITH AN ANNOYING SISTER"
"IVANHOE"
SCHULZ

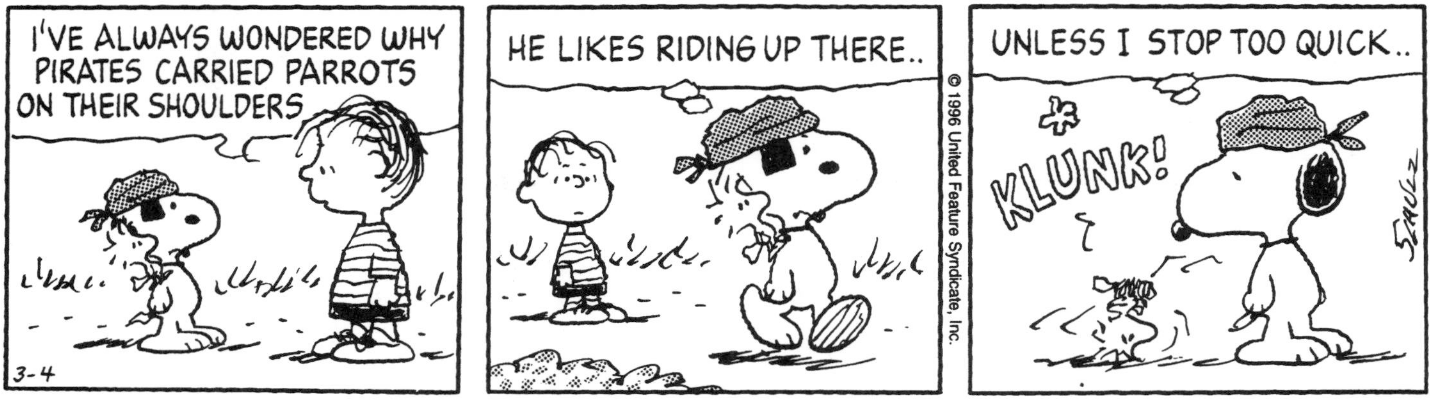
I'VE ALWAYS WONDERED WHY PIRATES CARRIED PARROTS ON THEIR SHOULDERS
3-4
HE LIKES RIDING UP THERE..
© 1996 United Feature Syndicate, Inc.
UNLESS I STOP TOO QUICK..
KLUNK!
SCHULZ

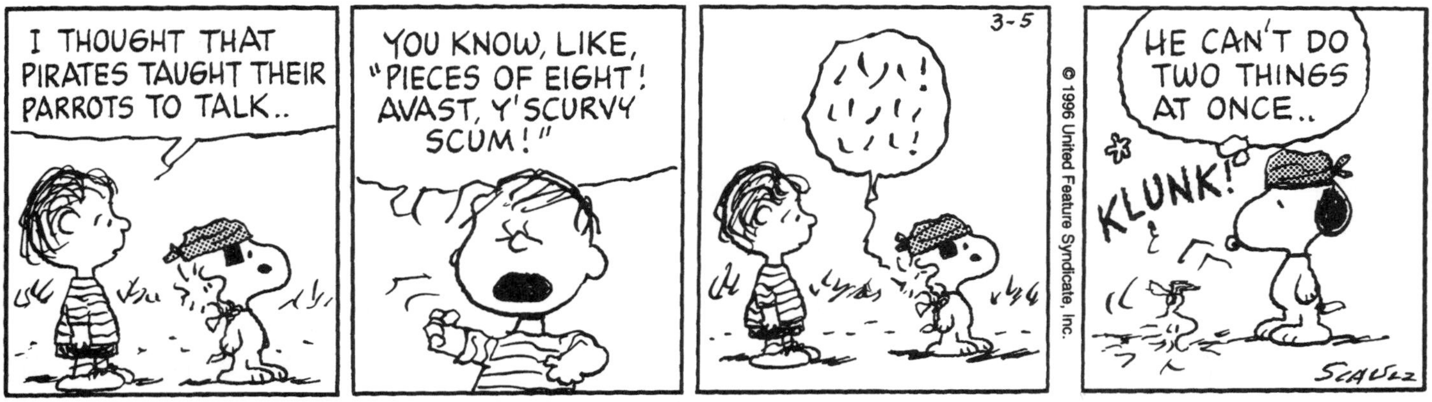
I THOUGHT THAT PIRATES TAUGHT THEIR PARROTS TO TALK..
YOU KNOW, LIKE, "PIECES OF EIGHT! AVAST, Y'SCURVY SCUM!"
3-5
© 1996 United Feature Syndicate, Inc.
HE CAN'T DO TWO THINGS AT ONCE..
KLUNK!
SCHULZ

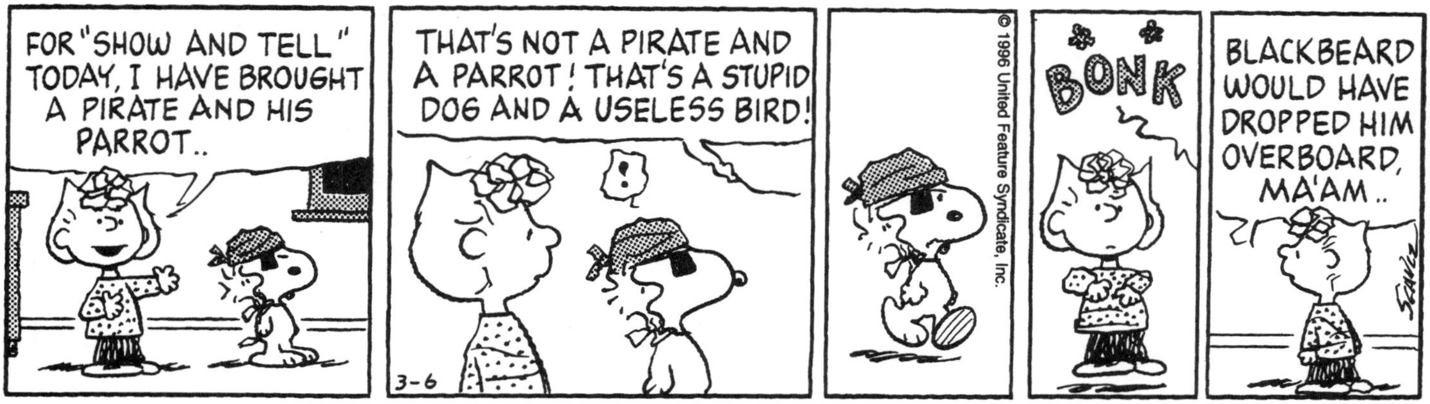
FOR "SHOW AND TELL" TODAY, I HAVE BROUGHT A PIRATE AND HIS PARROT..
THAT'S NOT A PIRATE AND A PARROT! THAT'S A STUPID DOG AND A USELESS BIRD!
3-6
© 1996 United Feature Syndicate, Inc.
BONK
BLACKBEARD WOULD HAVE DROPPED HIM OVERBOARD, MA'AM..
SCHULZ

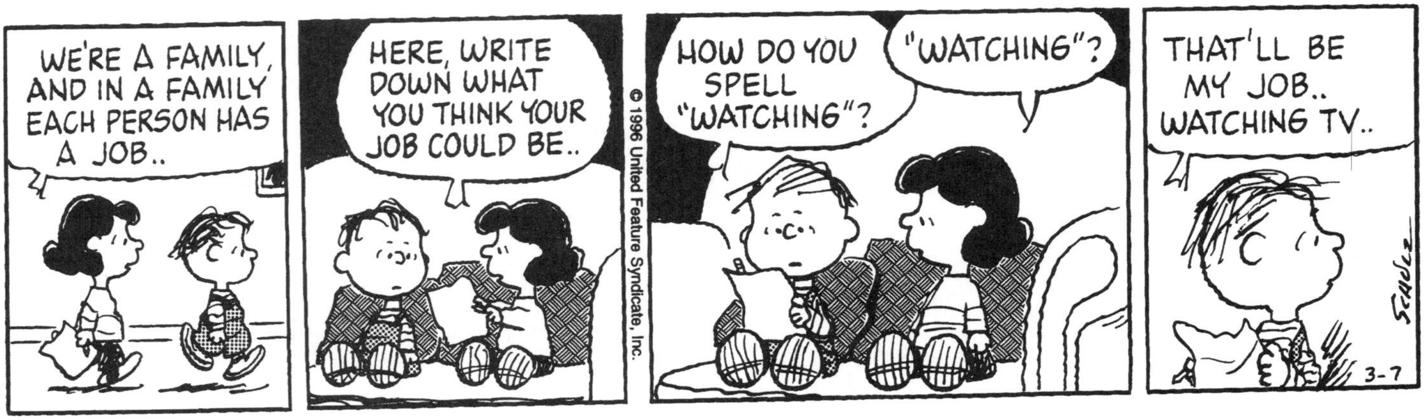
WE'RE A FAMILY, AND IN A FAMILY EACH PERSON HAS A JOB..
HERE, WRITE DOWN WHAT YOU THINK YOUR JOB COULD BE..
© 1996 United Feature Syndicate, Inc.
HOW DO YOU SPELL "WATCHING"?
"WATCHING"?
THAT'LL BE MY JOB.. WATCHING TV..
SCHULZ
3-7

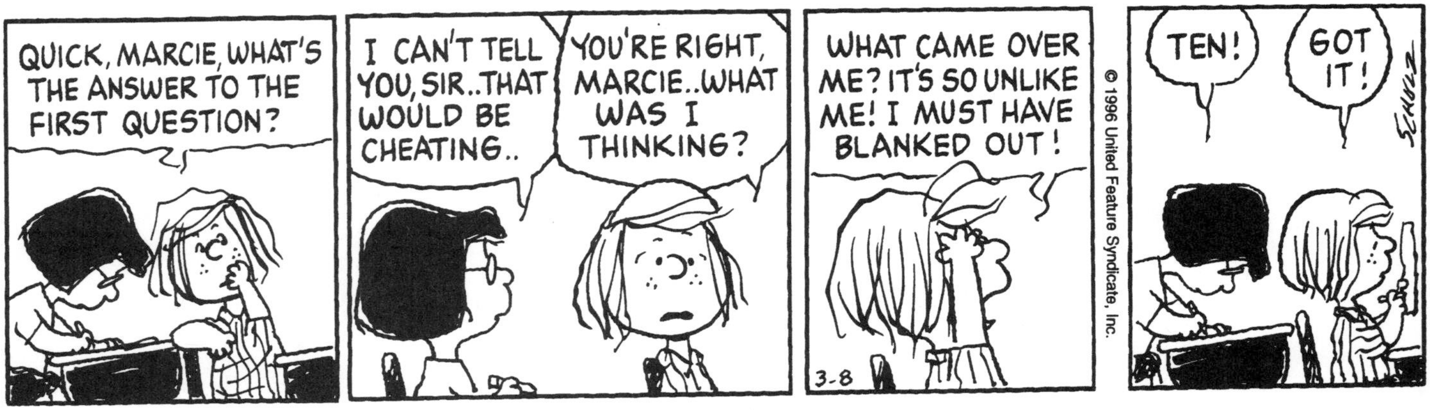
QUICK, MARCIE, WHAT'S THE ANSWER TO THE FIRST QUESTION?
I CAN'T TELL YOU, SIR..THAT WOULD BE CHEATING..
YOU'RE RIGHT, MARCIE..WHAT WAS I THINKING?
WHAT CAME OVER ME? IT'S SO UNLIKE ME! I MUST HAVE BLANKED OUT!
3-8
© 1996 United Feature Syndicate, Inc.
TEN!
GOT IT!
SCHULZ

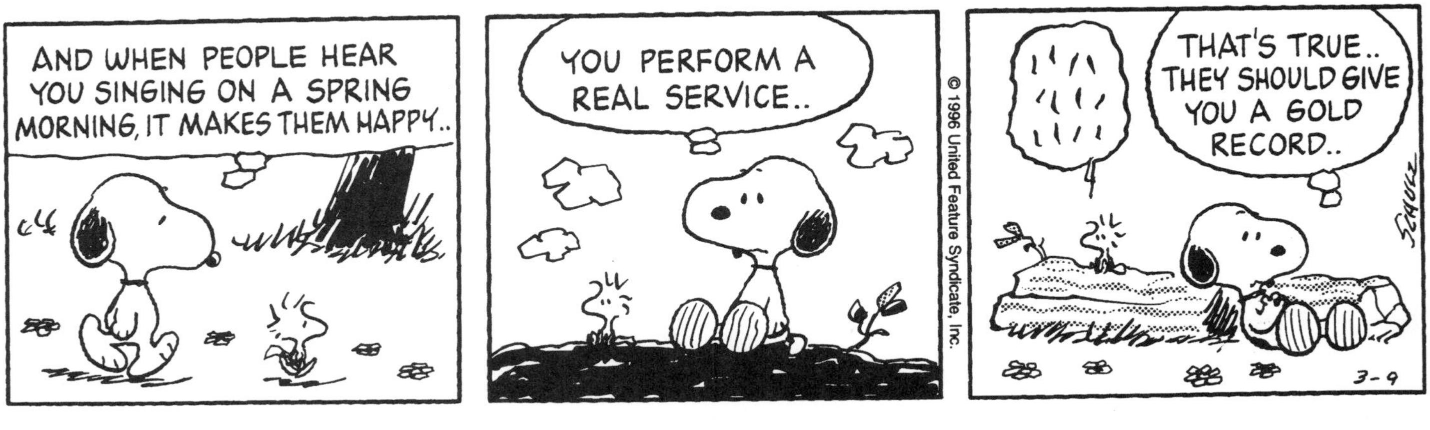
AND WHEN PEOPLE HEAR YOU SINGING ON A SPRING MORNING, IT MAKES THEM HAPPY..
YOU PERFORM A REAL SERVICE..
© 1996 United Feature Syndicate, Inc.
THAT'S TRUE.. THEY SHOULD GIVE YOU A GOLD RECORD..
SCHULZ
3-9

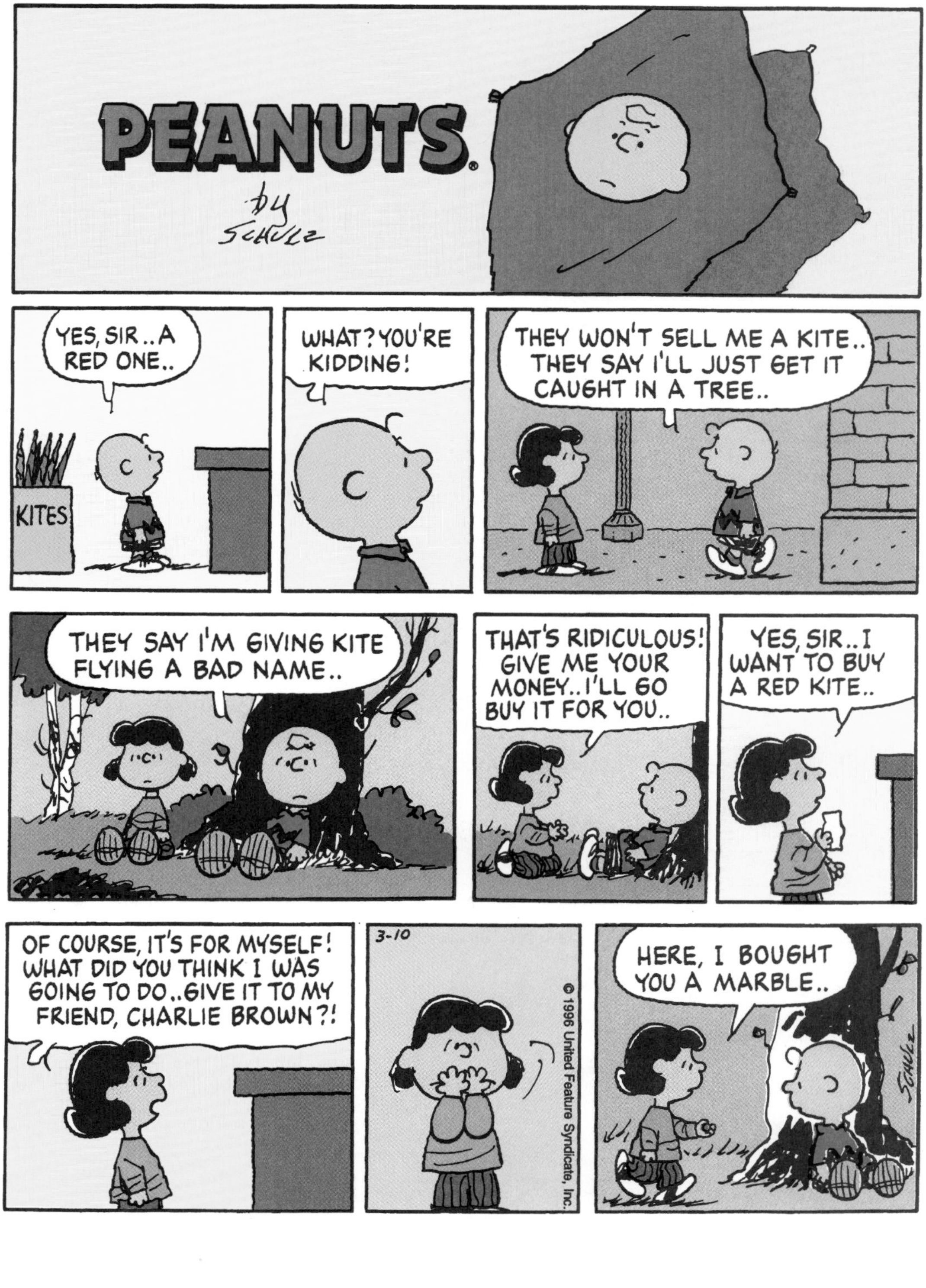

PEANUTS
by Schulz
YES, SIR..A RED ONE..
KITES
WHAT? YOU'RE KIDDING!
THEY WON'T SELL ME A KITE.. THEY SAY I'LL JUST GET IT CAUGHT IN A TREE..
THEY SAY I'M GIVING KITE FLYING A BAD NAME..
THAT'S RIDICULOUS! GIVE ME YOUR MONEY..I'LL GO BUY IT FOR YOU..
YES, SIR..I WANT TO BUY A RED KITE..
OF COURSE, IT'S FOR MYSELF! WHAT DID YOU THINK I WAS GOING TO DO..GIVE IT TO MY FRIEND, CHARLIE BROWN?!
3-10
© 1996 United Feature Syndicate, Inc.
HERE, I BOUGHT YOU A MARBLE..
SCHULZ

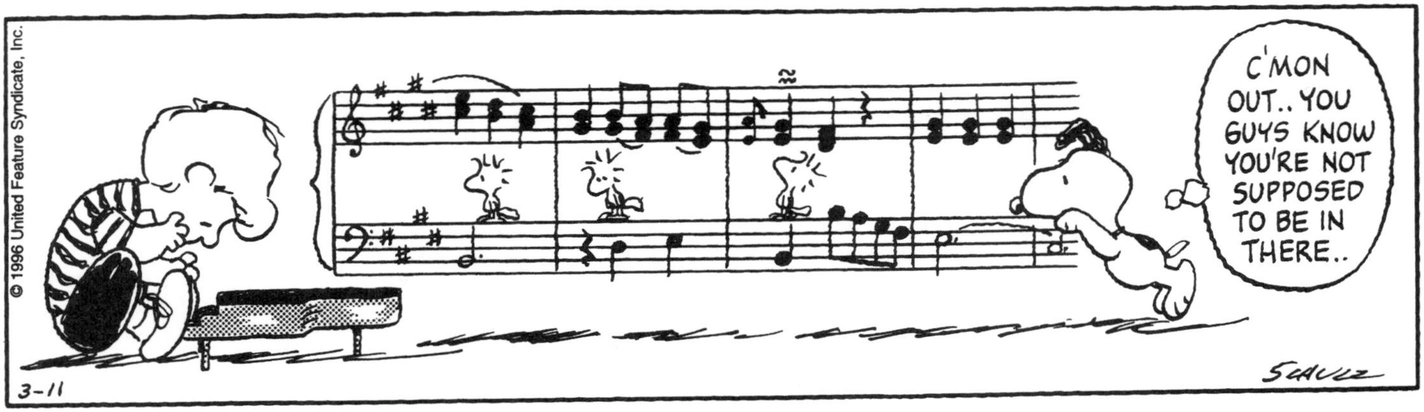
© 1996 United Feature Syndicate, Inc.
C'MON OUT.. YOU GUYS KNOW YOU'RE NOT SUPPOSED TO BE IN THERE..
3-11

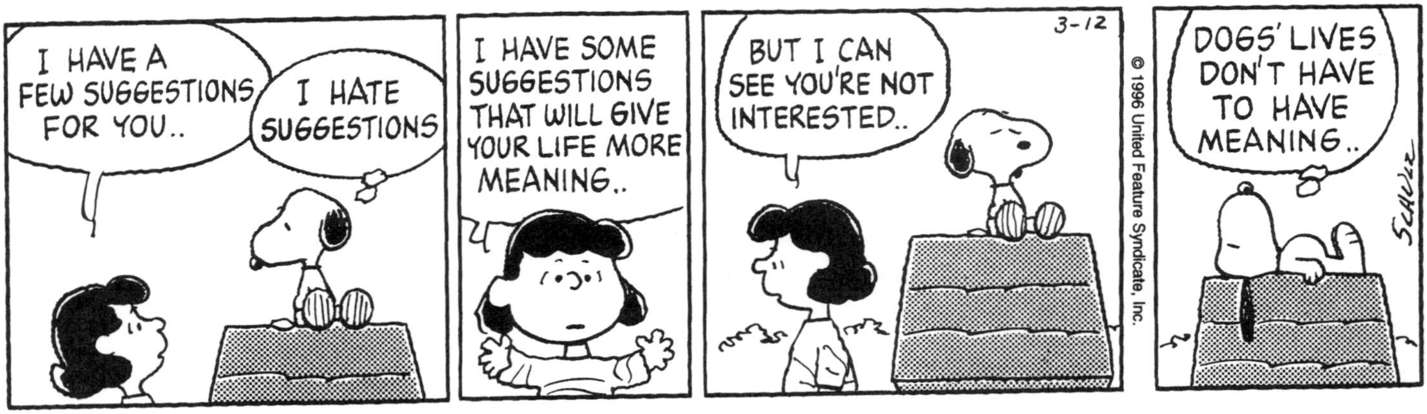
I HAVE A FEW SUGGESTIONS FOR YOU..
I HATE SUGGESTIONS
I HAVE SOME SUGGESTIONS THAT WILL GIVE YOUR LIFE MORE MEANING..
BUT I CAN SEE YOU'RE NOT INTERESTED..
3-12
© 1996 United Feature Syndicate, Inc.
DOGS' LIVES DON'T HAVE TO HAVE MEANING..

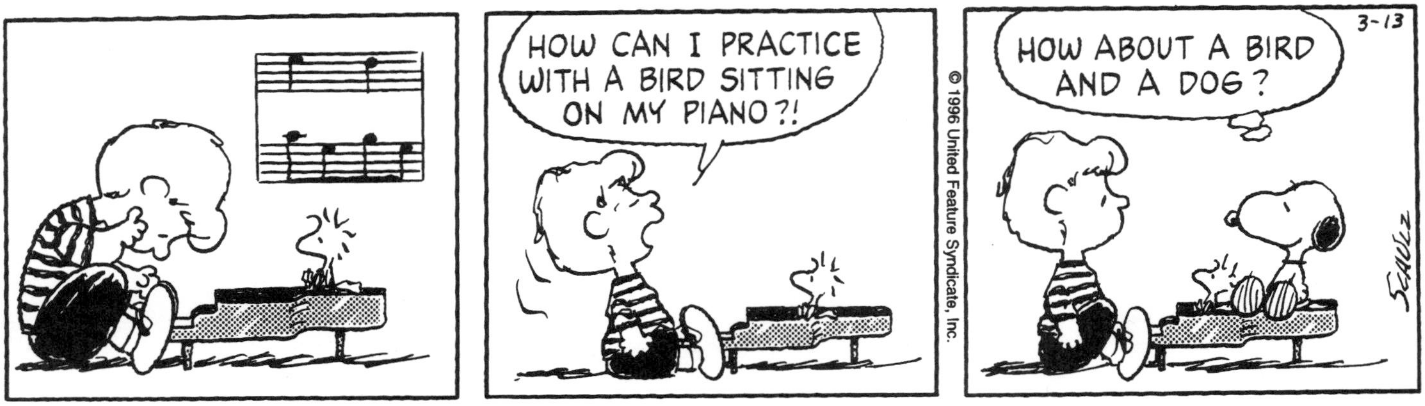
HOW CAN I PRACTICE WITH A BIRD SITTING ON MY PIANO?!
© 1996 United Feature Syndicate, Inc.
HOW ABOUT A BIRD AND A DOG?
3-13

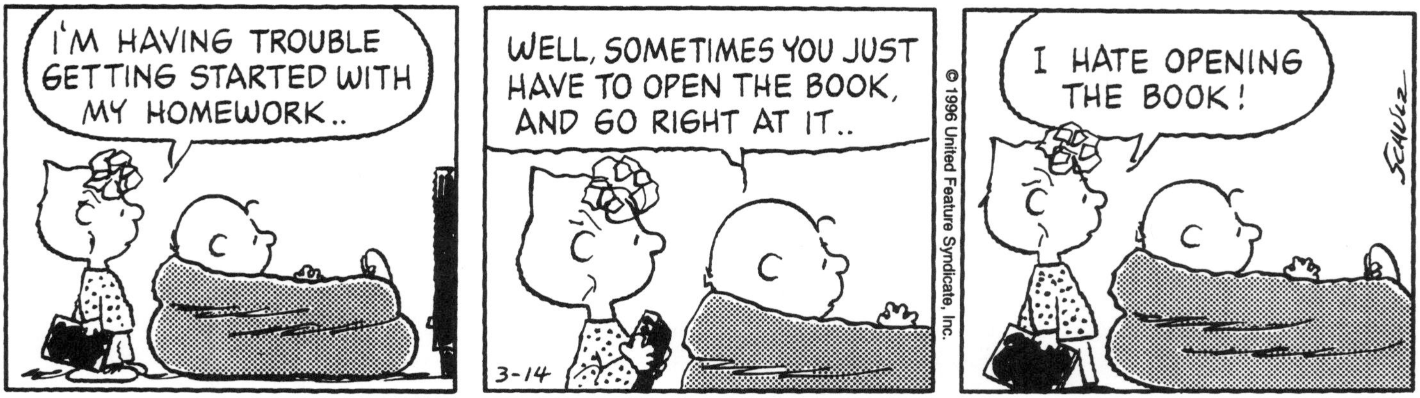
I'M HAVING TROUBLE GETTING STARTED WITH MY HOMEWORK..
WELL, SOMETIMES YOU JUST HAVE TO OPEN THE BOOK, AND GO RIGHT AT IT..
3-14
© 1996 United Feature Syndicate, Inc.
I HATE OPENING THE BOOK!
SCHULZ

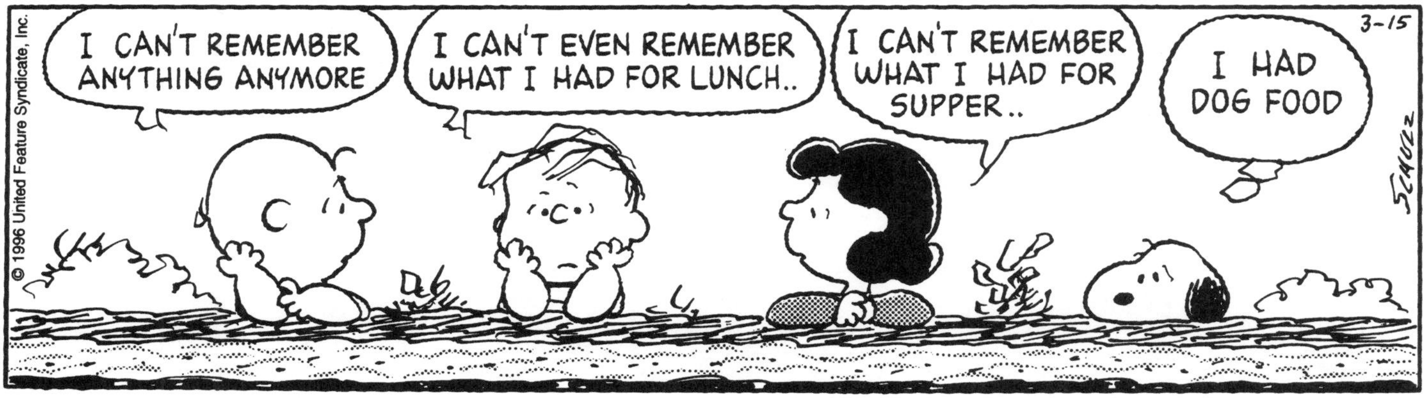
© 1996 United Feature Syndicate, Inc.
I CAN'T REMEMBER ANYTHING ANYMORE
I CAN'T EVEN REMEMBER WHAT I HAD FOR LUNCH..
I CAN'T REMEMBER WHAT I HAD FOR SUPPER..
3-15
I HAD DOG FOOD
SCHULZ

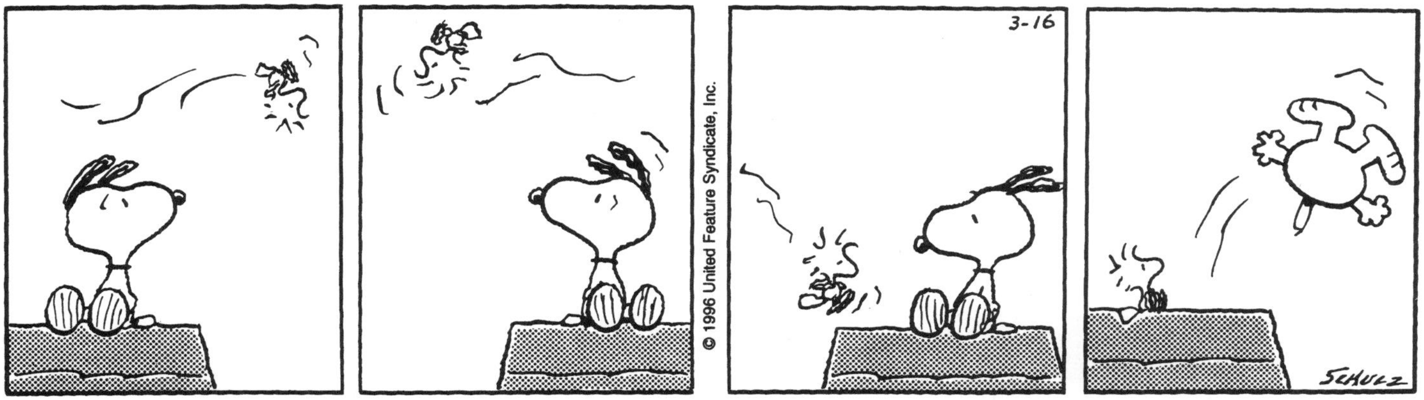
© 1996 United Feature Syndicate, Inc.
3-16
SCHULZ

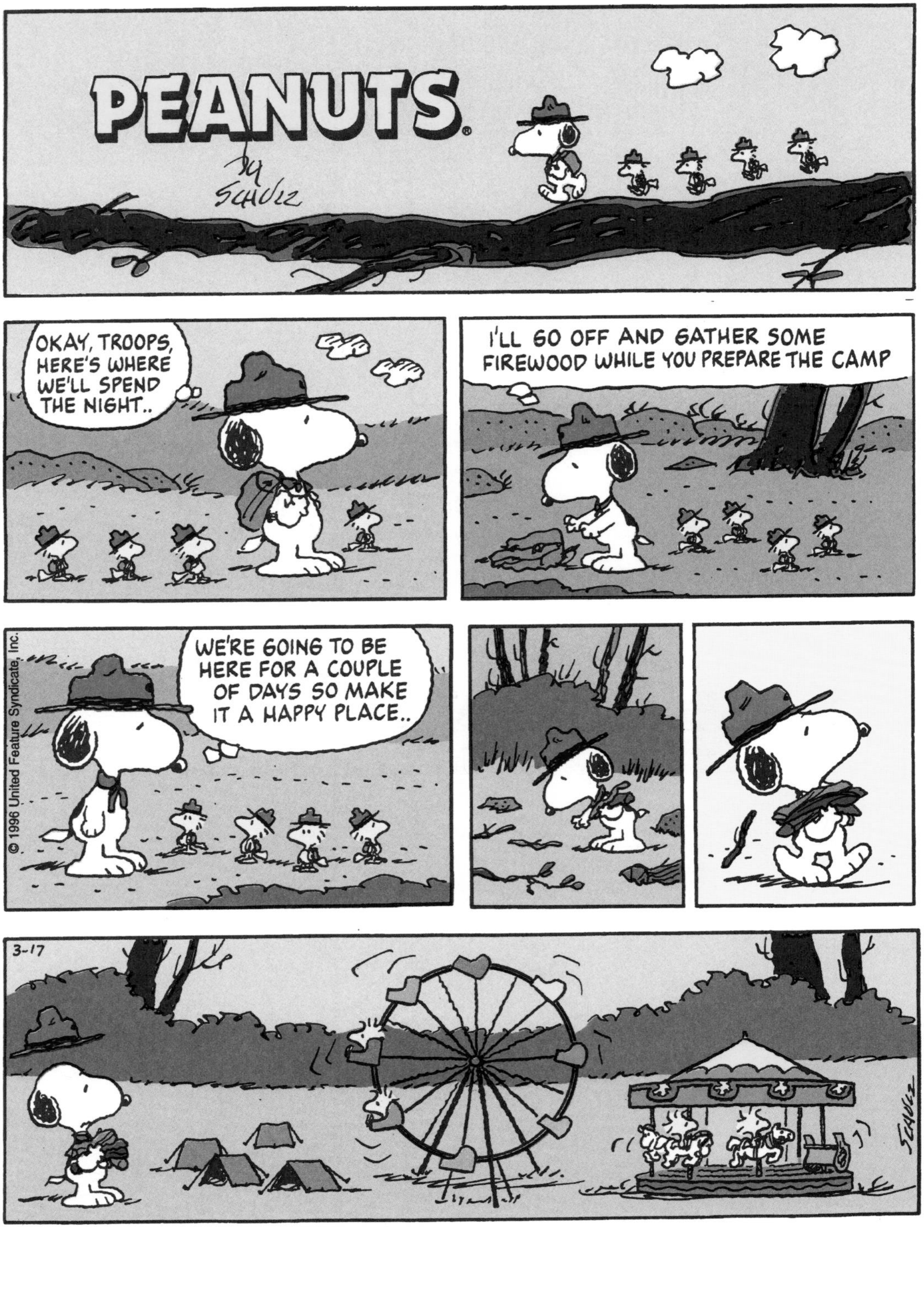
PEANUTS
SCHULZ
OKAY, TROOPS, HERE'S WHERE WE'LL SPEND THE NIGHT..
I'LL GO OFF AND GATHER SOME FIREWOOD WHILE YOU PREPARE THE CAMP
© 1996 United Feature Syndicate, Inc.
WE'RE GOING TO BE HERE FOR A COUPLE OF DAYS SO MAKE IT A HAPPY PLACE..
3-17
SCHULZ

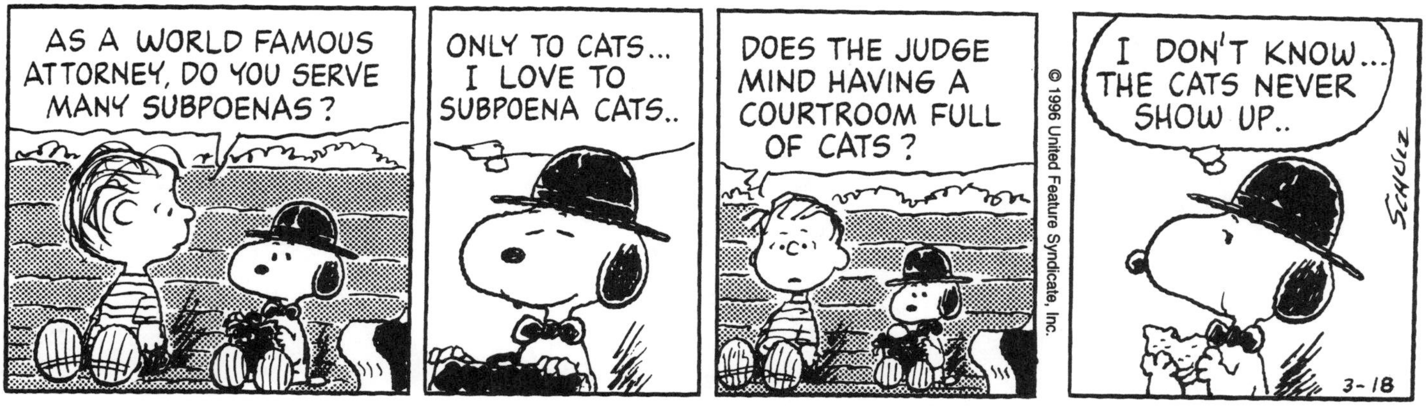
AS A WORLD FAMOUS ATTORNEY, DO YOU SERVE MANY SUBPOENAS?
ONLY TO CATS... I LOVE TO SUBPOENA CATS..
DOES THE JUDGE MIND HAVING A COURTROOM FULL OF CATS?
I DON'T KNOW... THE CATS NEVER SHOW UP..
© 1996 United Feature Syndicate, Inc.
SCHULZ
3-18

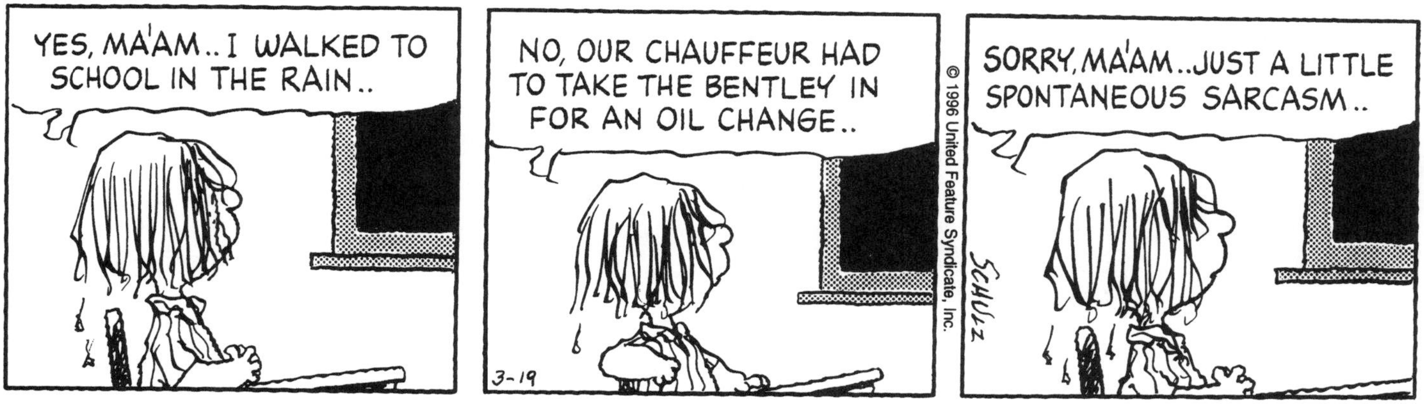
YES, MA'AM.. I WALKED TO SCHOOL IN THE RAIN..
NO, OUR CHAUFFEUR HAD TO TAKE THE BENTLEY IN FOR AN OIL CHANGE..
SORRY, MA'AM..JUST A LITTLE SPONTANEOUS SARCASM..
3-19
© 1996 United Feature Syndicate, Inc.
SCHULZ

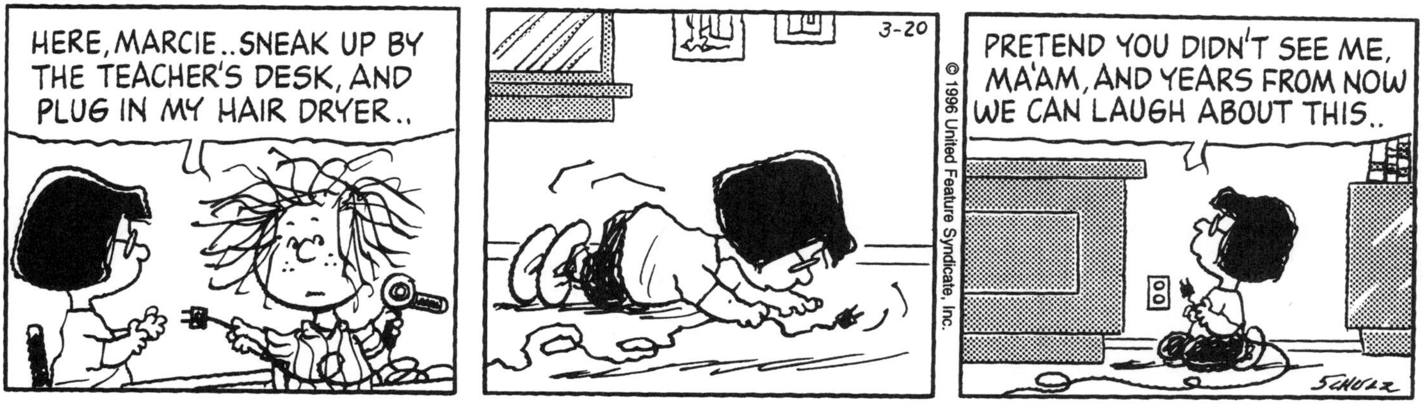
HERE, MARCIE..SNEAK UP BY THE TEACHER'S DESK, AND PLUG IN MY HAIR DRYER..
3-20
© 1996 United Feature Syndicate, Inc.
PRETEND YOU DIDN'T SEE ME, MA'AM, AND YEARS FROM NOW WE CAN LAUGH ABOUT THIS..
SCHULZ

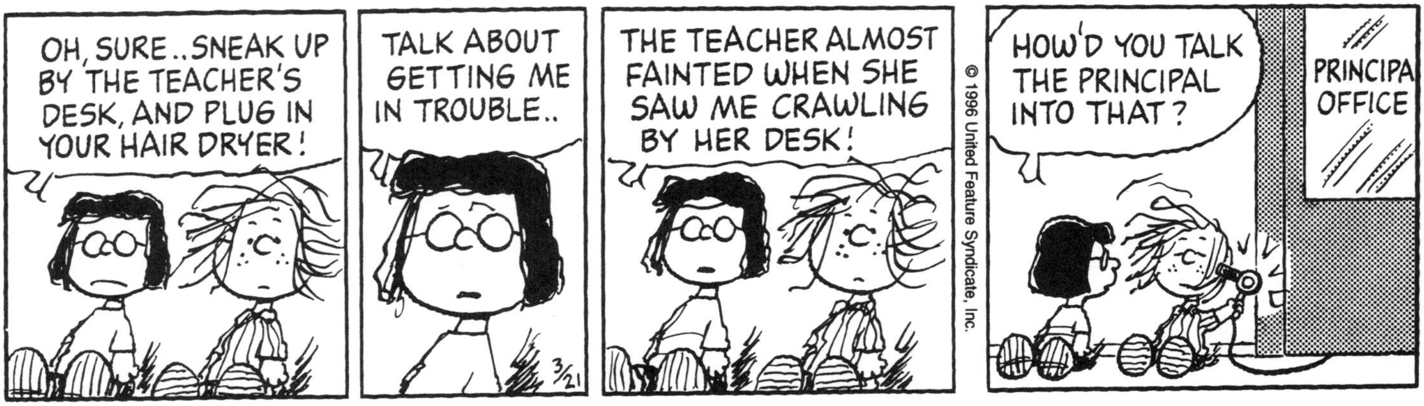
OH, SURE..SNEAK UP BY THE TEACHER'S DESK, AND PLUG IN YOUR HAIR DRYER!
TALK ABOUT GETTING ME IN TROUBLE..
3/21
THE TEACHER ALMOST FAINTED WHEN SHE SAW ME CRAWLING BY HER DESK!
© 1996 United Feature Syndicate, Inc.
HOW'D YOU TALK THE PRINCIPAL INTO THAT?
PRINCIPA OFFICE

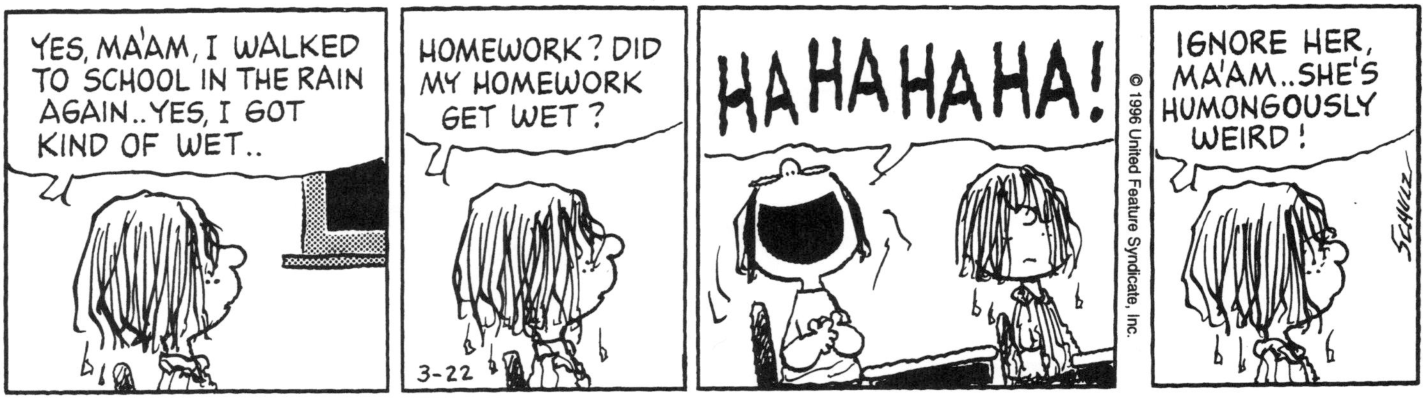
YES, MA'AM, I WALKED TO SCHOOL IN THE RAIN AGAIN..YES, I GOT KIND OF WET..
HOMEWORK? DID MY HOMEWORK GET WET?
3-22
HAHAHAHA!
© 1996 United Feature Syndicate, Inc.
IGNORE HER, MA'AM..SHE'S HUMONGOUSLY WEIRD!
SCHULZ

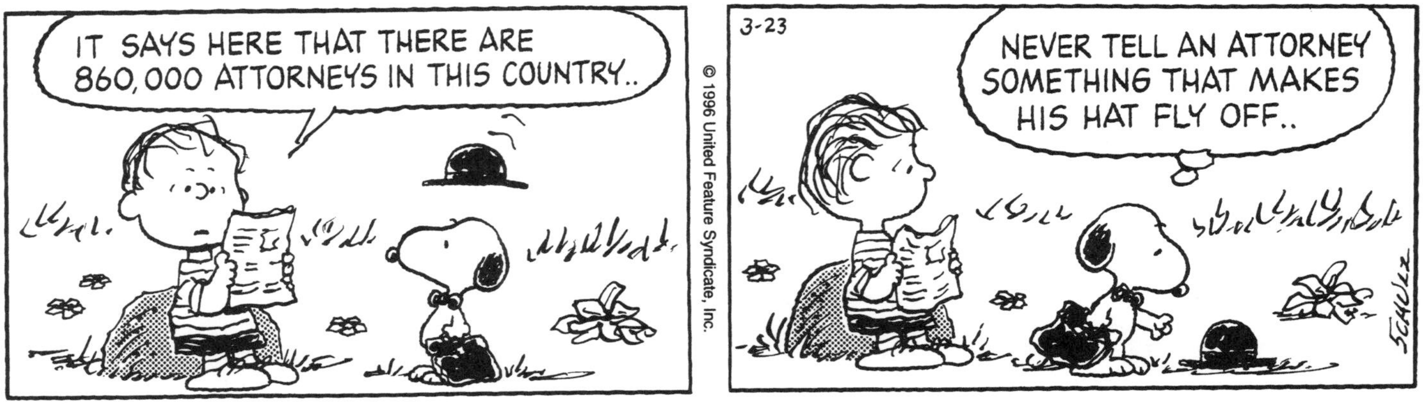
IT SAYS HERE THAT THERE ARE 860,000 ATTORNEYS IN THIS COUNTRY..
© 1996 United Feature Syndicate, Inc.
3-23
NEVER TELL AN ATTORNEY SOMETHING THAT MAKES HIS HAT FLY OFF..
SCHULZ

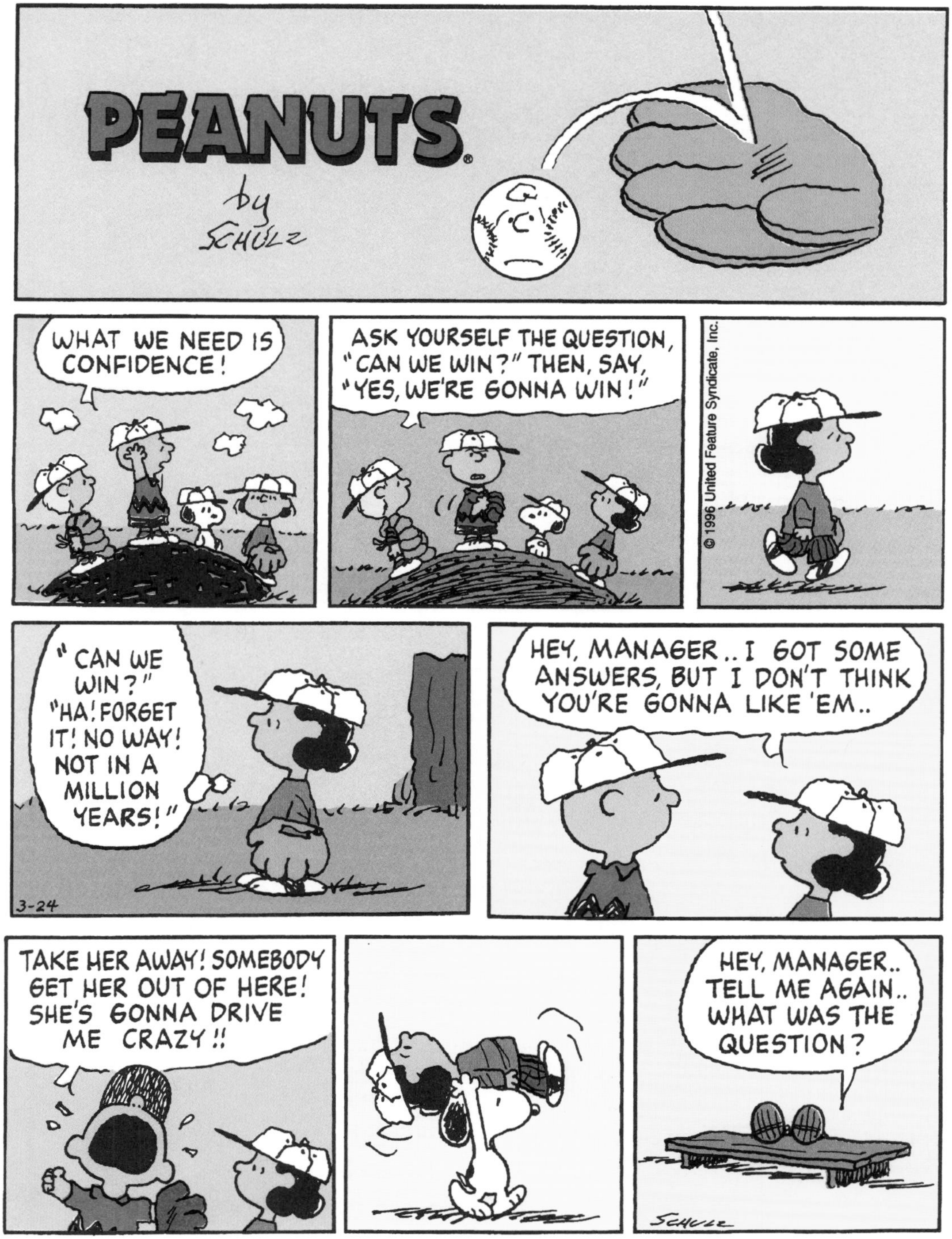
PEANUTS®
by SCHULZ
WHAT WE NEED IS CONFIDENCE!
ASK YOURSELF THE QUESTION, "CAN WE WIN?" THEN, SAY, "YES, WE'RE GONNA WIN!"
© 1996 United Feature Syndicate, Inc.
"CAN WE WIN?" "HA! FORGET IT! NO WAY! NOT IN A MILLION YEARS!"
3-24
HEY, MANAGER.. I GOT SOME ANSWERS, BUT I DON'T THINK YOU'RE GONNA LIKE 'EM..
TAKE HER AWAY! SOMEBODY GET HER OUT OF HERE! SHE'S GONNA DRIVE ME CRAZY!!
HEY, MANAGER.. TELL ME AGAIN.. WHAT WAS THE QUESTION?
SCHULZ

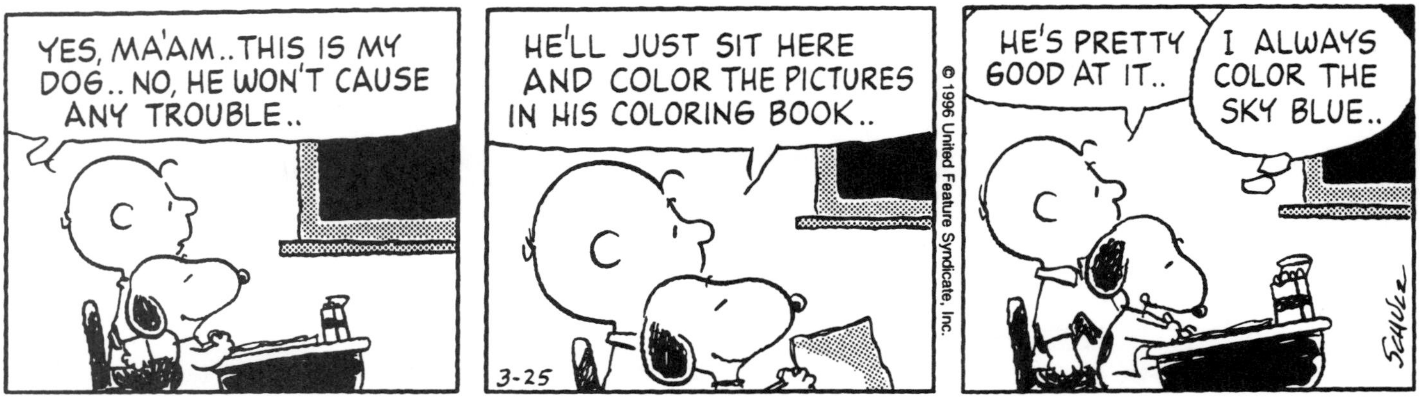
YES, MA'AM.. THIS IS MY DOG.. NO, HE WON'T CAUSE ANY TROUBLE..
HE'LL JUST SIT HERE AND COLOR THE PICTURES IN HIS COLORING BOOK..
3-25
© 1996 United Feature Syndicate, Inc.
HE'S PRETTY GOOD AT IT..
I ALWAYS COLOR THE SKY BLUE..
SCHULZ

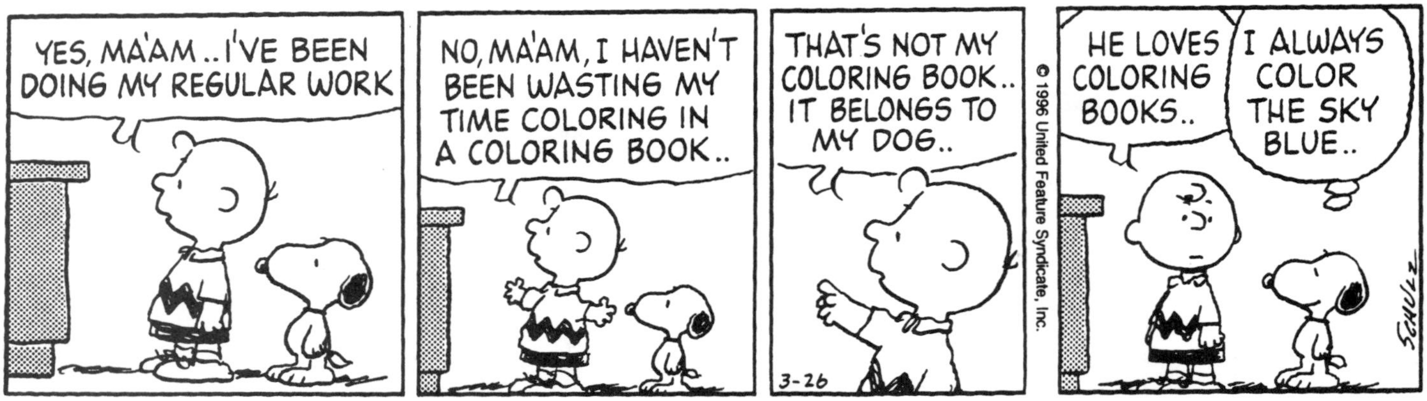
YES, MA'AM.. I'VE BEEN DOING MY REGULAR WORK
NO, MA'AM, I HAVEN'T BEEN WASTING MY TIME COLORING IN A COLORING BOOK..
THAT'S NOT MY COLORING BOOK.. IT BELONGS TO MY DOG..
3-26
© 1996 United Feature Syndicate, Inc.
HE LOVES COLORING BOOKS..
I ALWAYS COLOR THE SKY BLUE..
SCHULZ

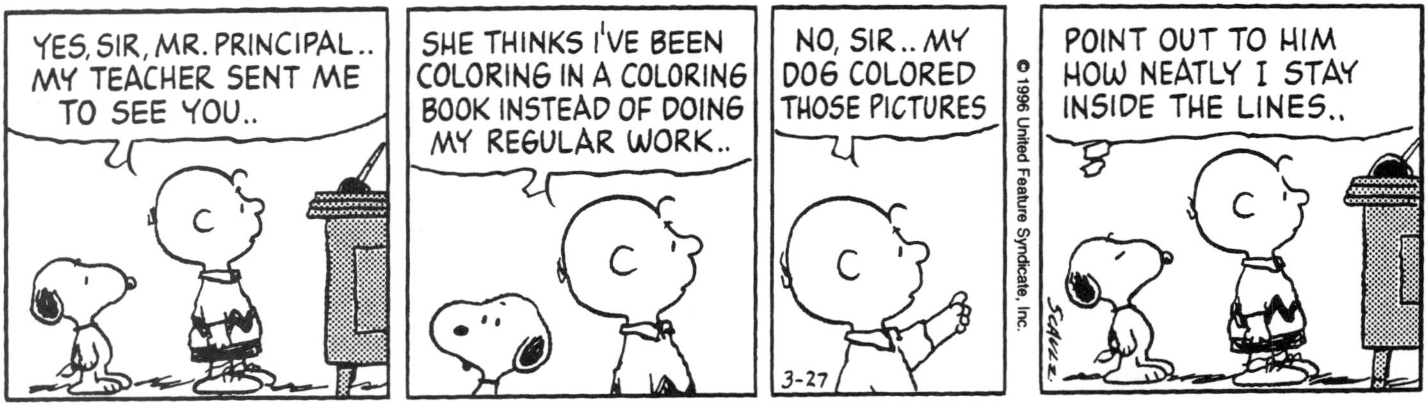
YES, SIR, MR. PRINCIPAL.. MY TEACHER SENT ME TO SEE YOU..
SHE THINKS I'VE BEEN COLORING IN A COLORING BOOK INSTEAD OF DOING MY REGULAR WORK..
NO, SIR.. MY DOG COLORED THOSE PICTURES
3-27
© 1996 United Feature Syndicate, Inc.
POINT OUT TO HIM HOW NEATLY I STAY INSIDE THE LINES..
SCHULZ

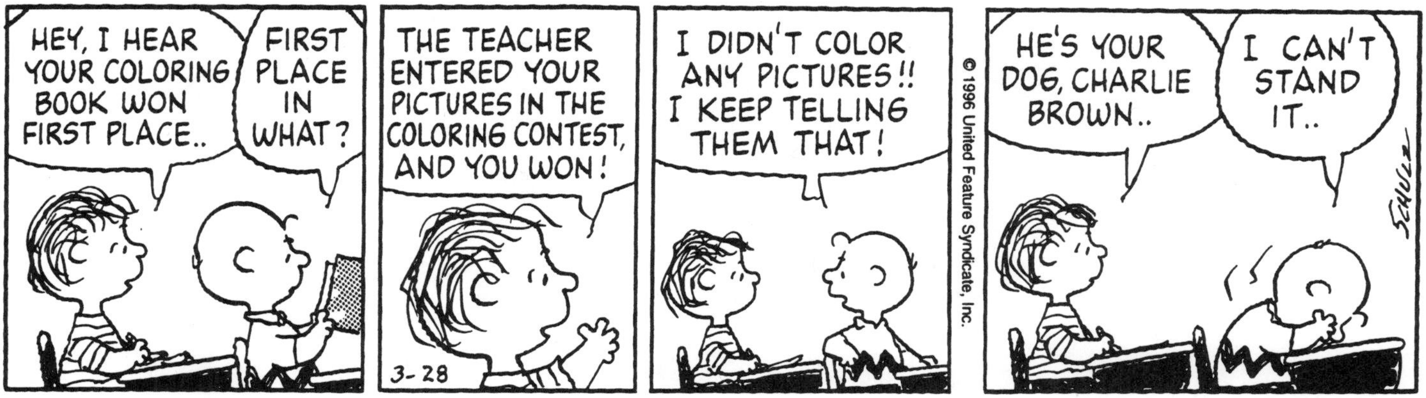
HEY, I HEAR YOUR COLORING BOOK WON FIRST PLACE..
FIRST PLACE IN WHAT?
THE TEACHER ENTERED YOUR PICTURES IN THE COLORING CONTEST, AND YOU WON!
3-28
I DIDN'T COLOR ANY PICTURES!! I KEEP TELLING THEM THAT!
© 1996 United Feature Syndicate, Inc.
HE'S YOUR DOG, CHARLIE BROWN..
I CAN'T STAND IT..
SCHULZ

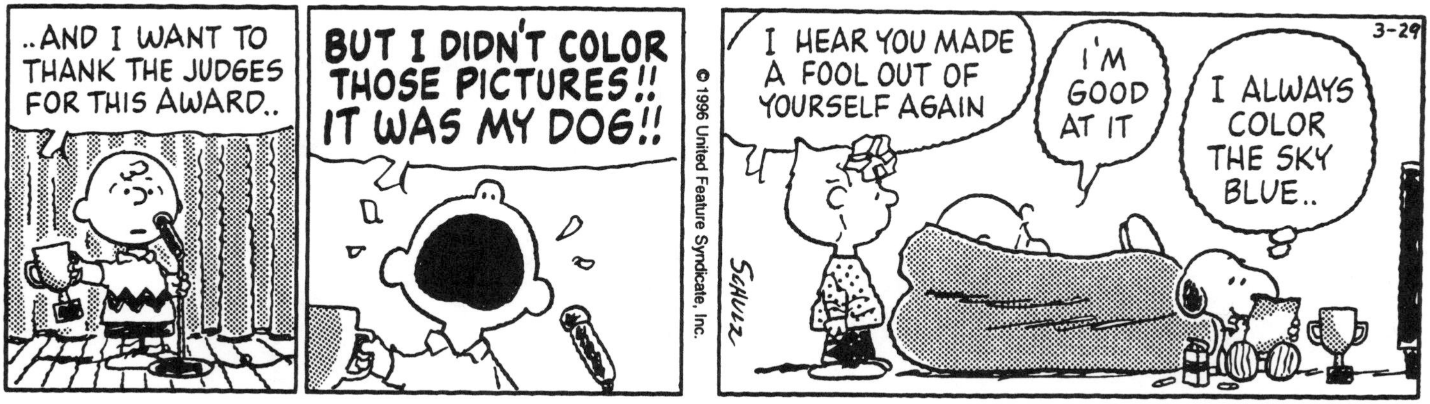
..AND I WANT TO THANK THE JUDGES FOR THIS AWARD..
BUT I DIDN'T COLOR THOSE PICTURES!! IT WAS MY DOG!!
© 1996 United Feature Syndicate, Inc.
SCHULZ
3-29
I HEAR YOU MADE A FOOL OUT OF YOURSELF AGAIN
I'M GOOD AT IT
I ALWAYS COLOR THE SKY BLUE..

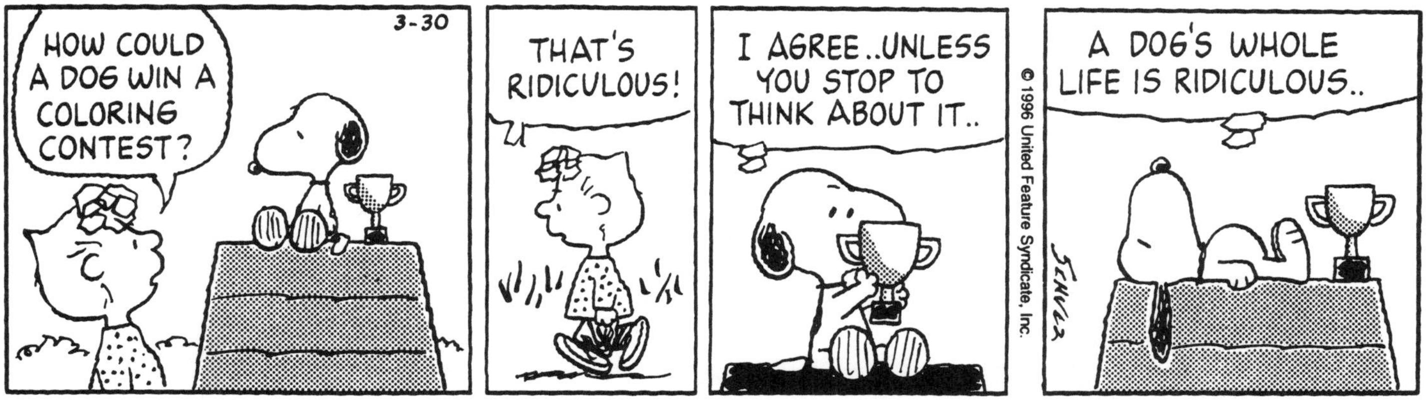
3-30
HOW COULD A DOG WIN A COLORING CONTEST?
THAT'S RIDICULOUS!
I AGREE..UNLESS YOU STOP TO THINK ABOUT IT..
© 1996 United Feature Syndicate, Inc.
SCHULZ
A DOG'S WHOLE LIFE IS RIDICULOUS..

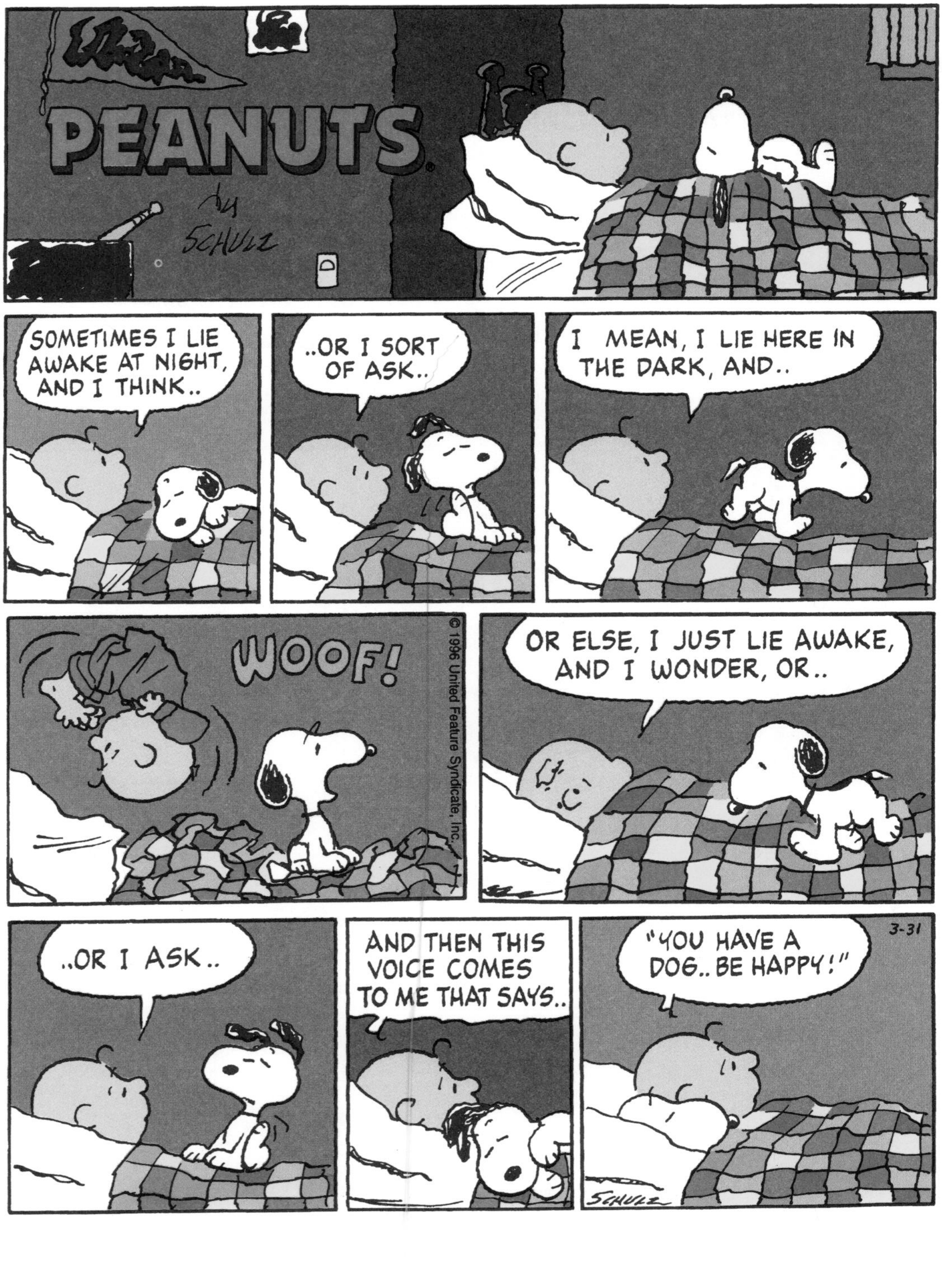
PEANUTS
by SCHULZ
SOMETIMES I LIE AWAKE AT NIGHT, AND I THINK..
..OR I SORT OF ASK..
I MEAN, I LIE HERE IN THE DARK, AND..
WOOF!
© 1996 United Feature Syndicate, Inc.
OR ELSE, I JUST LIE AWAKE, AND I WONDER, OR..
..OR I ASK..
AND THEN THIS VOICE COMES TO ME THAT SAYS..
3-31
"YOU HAVE A DOG.. BE HAPPY!"
SCHULZ

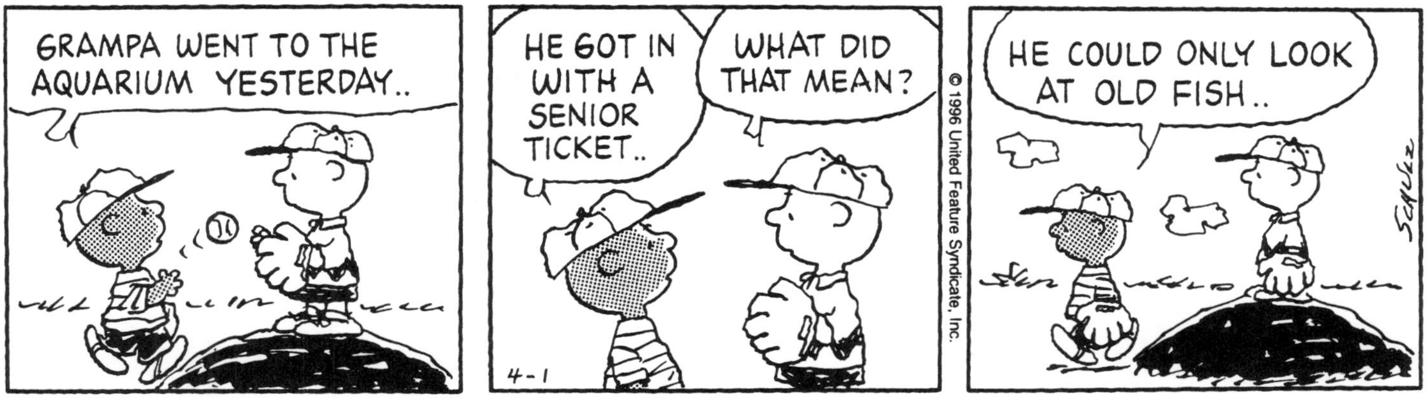
GRAMPA WENT TO THE AQUARIUM YESTERDAY..
HE GOT IN WITH A SENIOR TICKET..
WHAT DID THAT MEAN?
HE COULD ONLY LOOK AT OLD FISH..

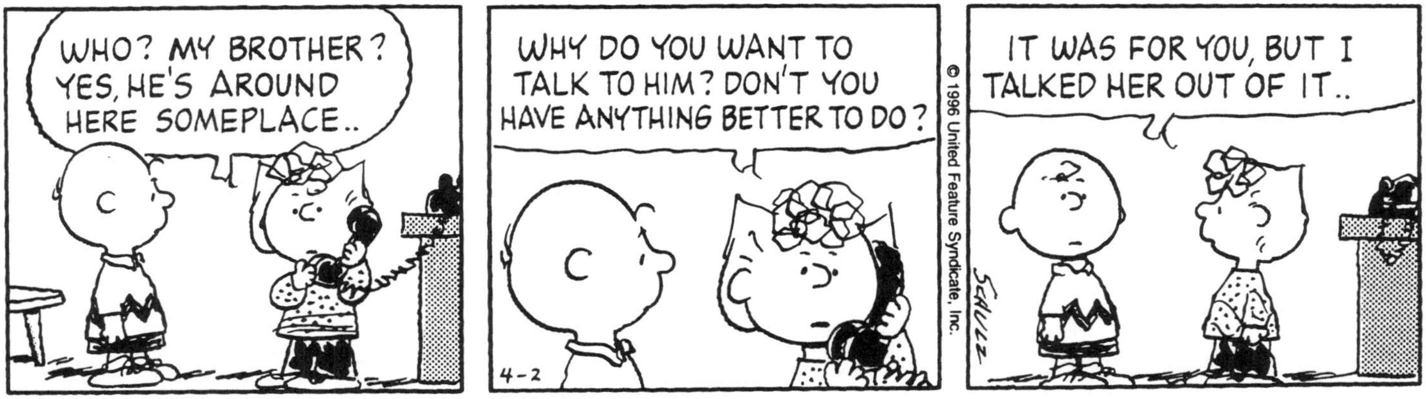
WHO? MY BROTHER? YES, HE'S AROUND HERE SOMEPLACE..
WHY DO YOU WANT TO TALK TO HIM? DON'T YOU HAVE ANYTHING BETTER TO DO?
IT WAS FOR YOU, BUT I TALKED HER OUT OF IT..

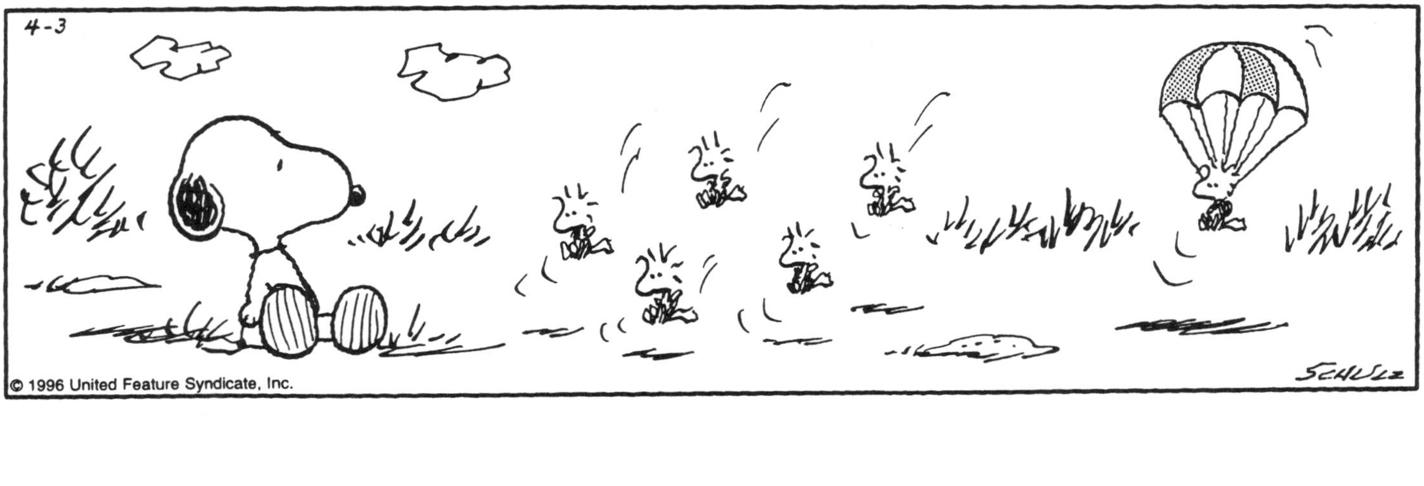

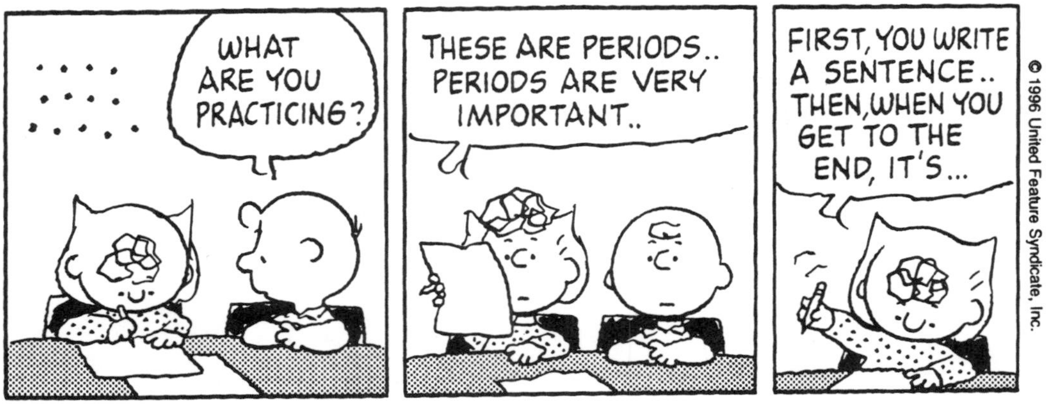
WHAT ARE YOU PRACTICING?
THESE ARE PERIODS.. PERIODS ARE VERY IMPORTANT..
FIRST, YOU WRITE A SENTENCE.. THEN, WHEN YOU GET TO THE END, IT'S...
© 1996 United Feature Syndicate, Inc.
4-4
PERIOD!
SCHULZ

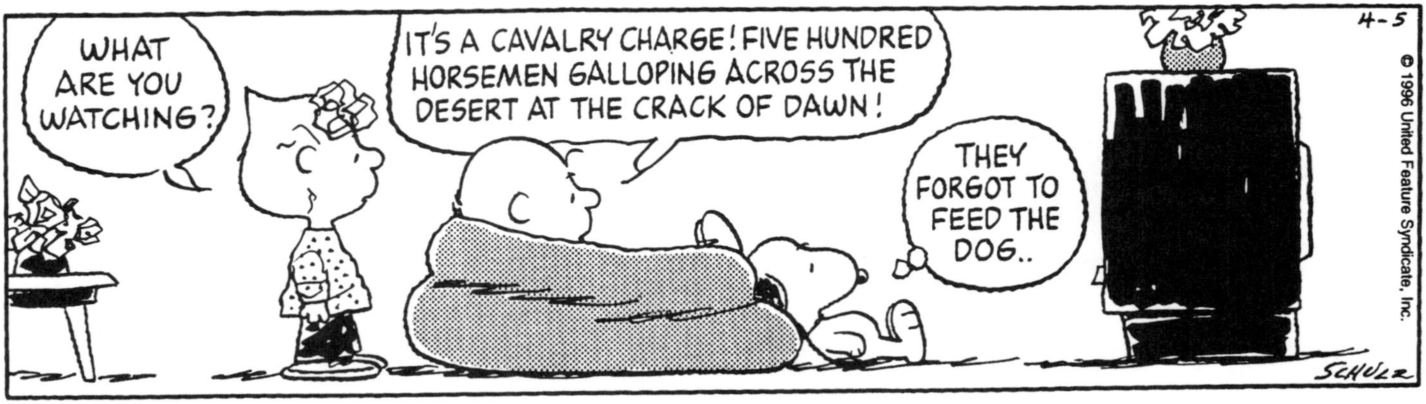
WHAT ARE YOU WATCHING?
IT'S A CAVALRY CHARGE! FIVE HUNDRED HORSEMEN GALLOPING ACROSS THE DESERT AT THE CRACK OF DAWN!
THEY FORGOT TO FEED THE DOG..
4-5
© 1996 United Feature Syndicate, Inc.
SCHULZ

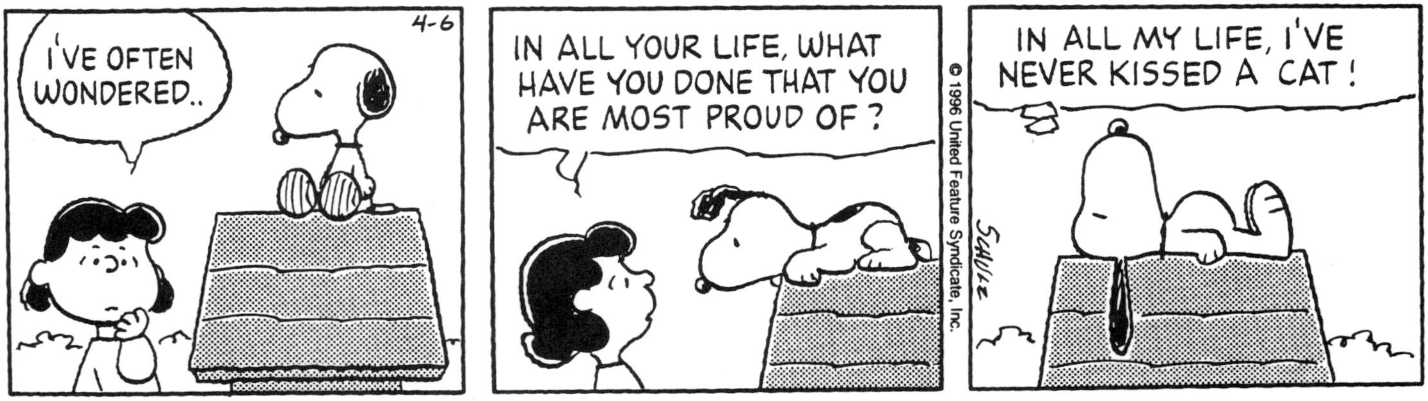
4-6
I'VE OFTEN WONDERED..
IN ALL YOUR LIFE, WHAT HAVE YOU DONE THAT YOU ARE MOST PROUD OF?
© 1996 United Feature Syndicate, Inc.
SCHULZ
IN ALL MY LIFE, I'VE NEVER KISSED A CAT!

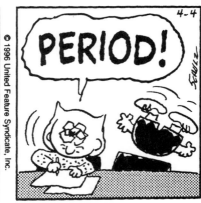

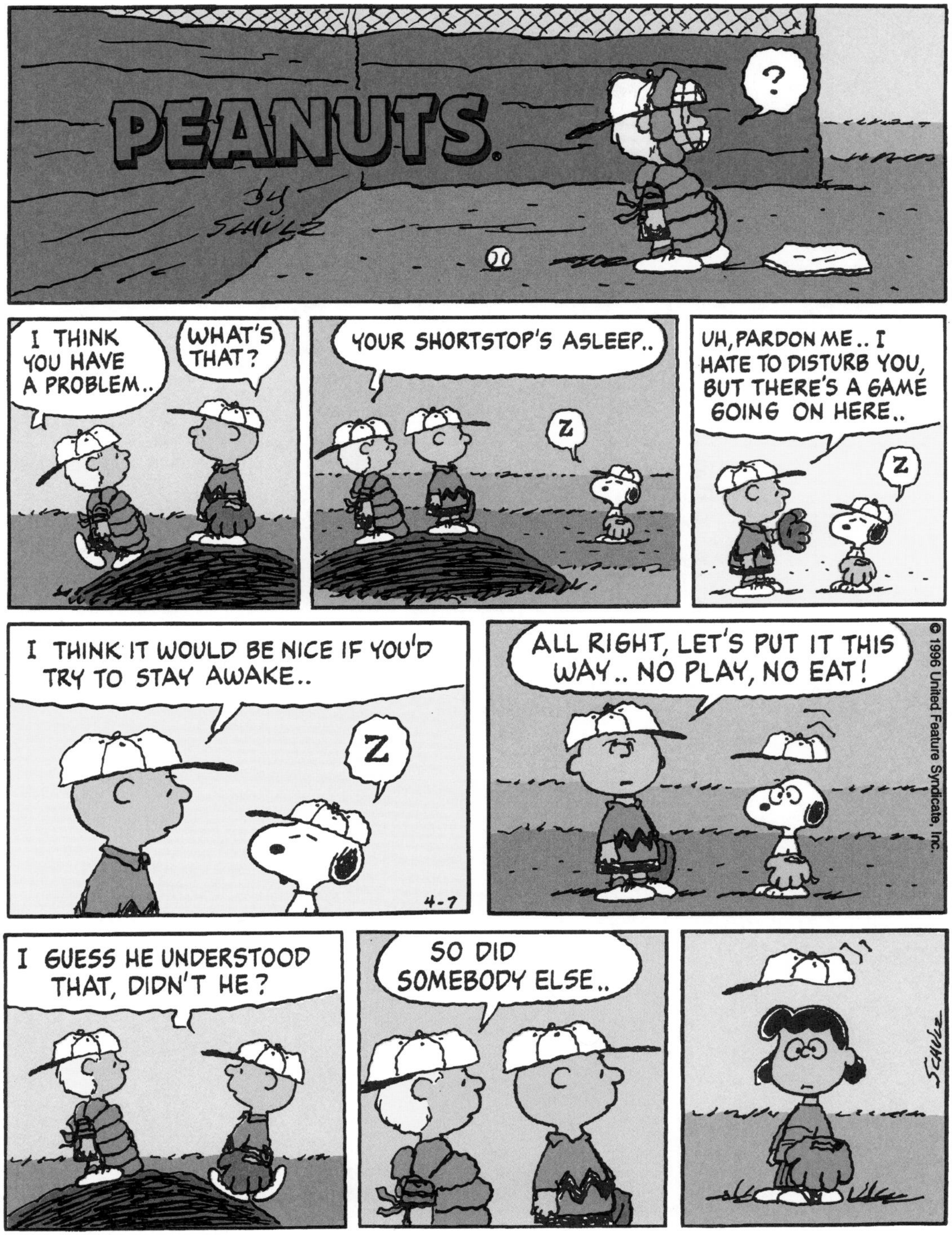
PEANUTS
by SCHULZ
?
I THINK YOU HAVE A PROBLEM..
WHAT'S THAT?
YOUR SHORTSTOP'S ASLEEP..
Z
UH, PARDON ME.. I HATE TO DISTURB YOU, BUT THERE'S A GAME GOING ON HERE..
Z
I THINK IT WOULD BE NICE IF YOU'D TRY TO STAY AWAKE..
Z
4-7
ALL RIGHT, LET'S PUT IT THIS WAY.. NO PLAY, NO EAT!
© 1996 United Feature Syndicate, Inc.
I GUESS HE UNDERSTOOD THAT, DIDN'T HE?
SO DID SOMEBODY ELSE..
SCHULZ

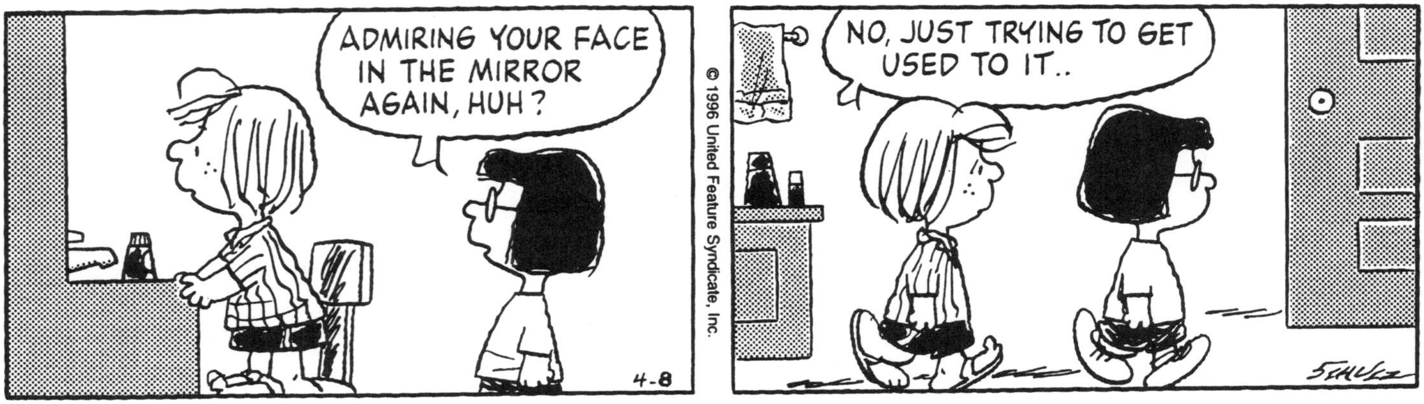
ADMIRING YOUR FACE IN THE MIRROR AGAIN, HUH?
© 1996 United Feature Syndicate, Inc.
NO, JUST TRYING TO GET USED TO IT..

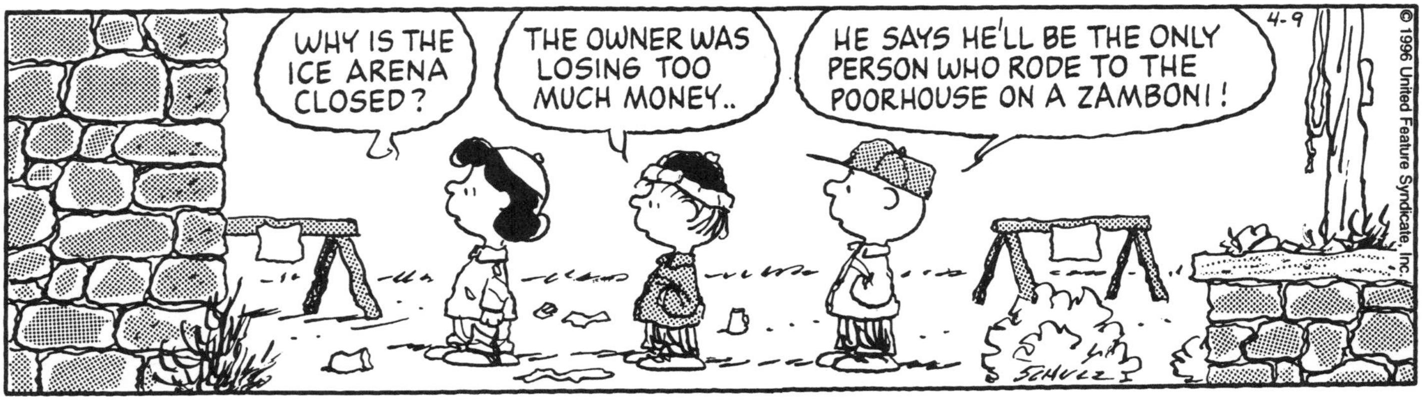
WHY IS THE ICE ARENA CLOSED?
THE OWNER WAS LOSING TOO MUCH MONEY..
HE SAYS HE'LL BE THE ONLY PERSON WHO RODE TO THE POORHOUSE ON A ZAMBONI!
© 1996 United Feature Syndicate, Inc.

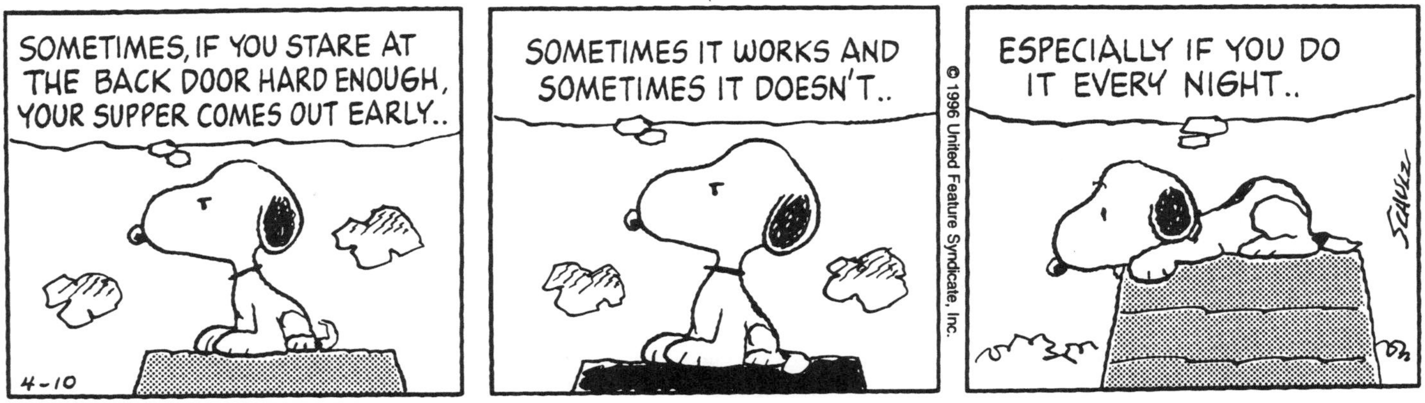
SOMETIMES, IF YOU STARE AT THE BACK DOOR HARD ENOUGH, YOUR SUPPER COMES OUT EARLY..
SOMETIMES IT WORKS AND SOMETIMES IT DOESN'T..
© 1996 United Feature Syndicate, Inc.
ESPECIALLY IF YOU DO IT EVERY NIGHT..

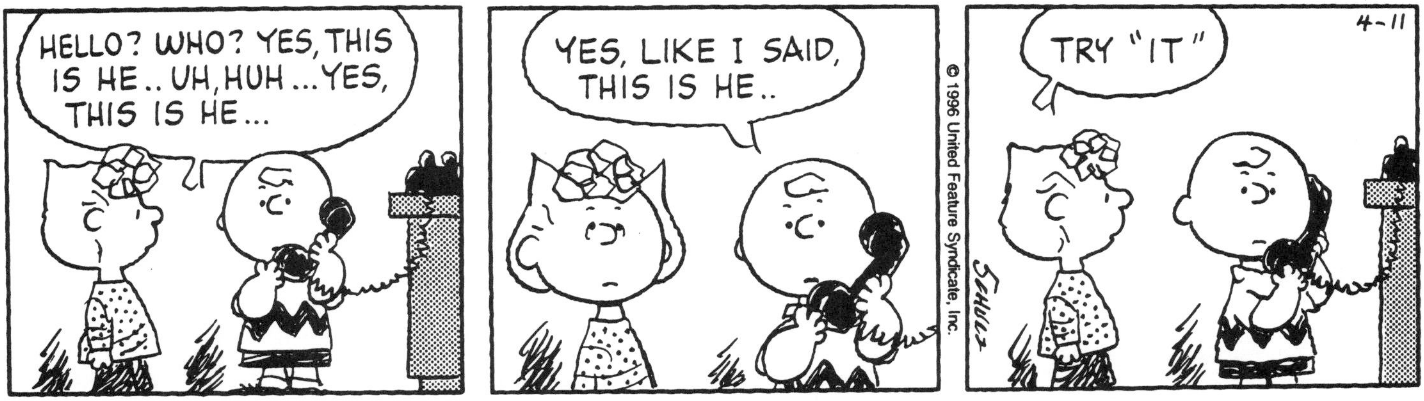
HELLO? WHO? YES, THIS IS HE.. UH, HUH ... YES, THIS IS HE...
YES, LIKE I SAID, THIS IS HE..
© 1996 United Feature Syndicate, Inc.
4-11
TRY "IT"

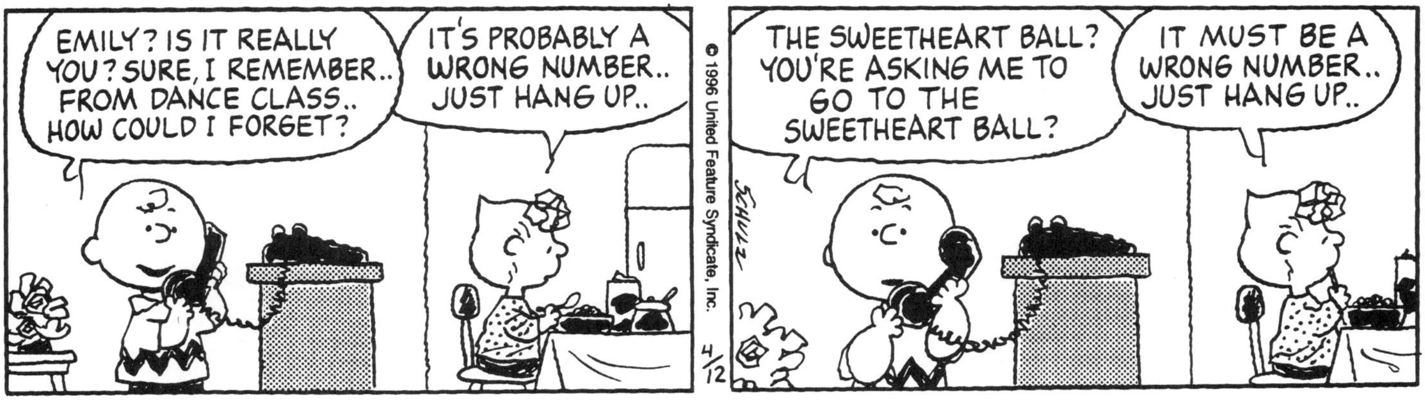
EMILY? IS IT REALLY YOU? SURE, I REMEMBER.. FROM DANCE CLASS.. HOW COULD I FORGET?
IT'S PROBABLY A WRONG NUMBER.. JUST HANG UP..
© 1996 United Feature Syndicate, Inc.
4/12
THE SWEETHEART BALL? YOU'RE ASKING ME TO GO TO THE SWEETHEART BALL?
IT MUST BE A WRONG NUMBER.. JUST HANG UP..

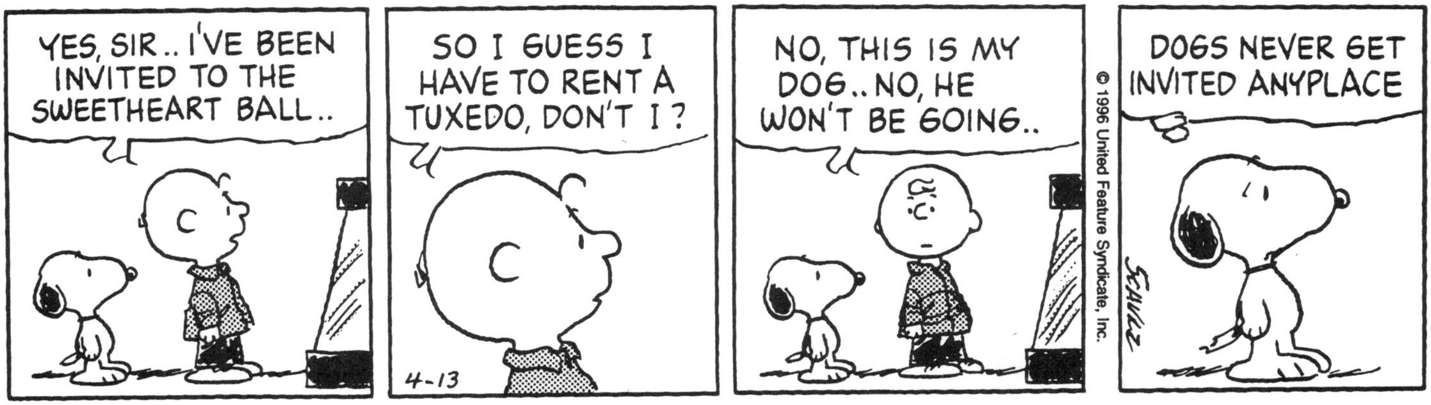
YES, SIR.. I'VE BEEN INVITED TO THE SWEETHEART BALL..
SO I GUESS I HAVE TO RENT A TUXEDO, DON'T I?
4-13
NO, THIS IS MY DOG.. NO, HE WON'T BE GOING..
© 1996 United Feature Syndicate, Inc.
DOGS NEVER GET INVITED ANYPLACE

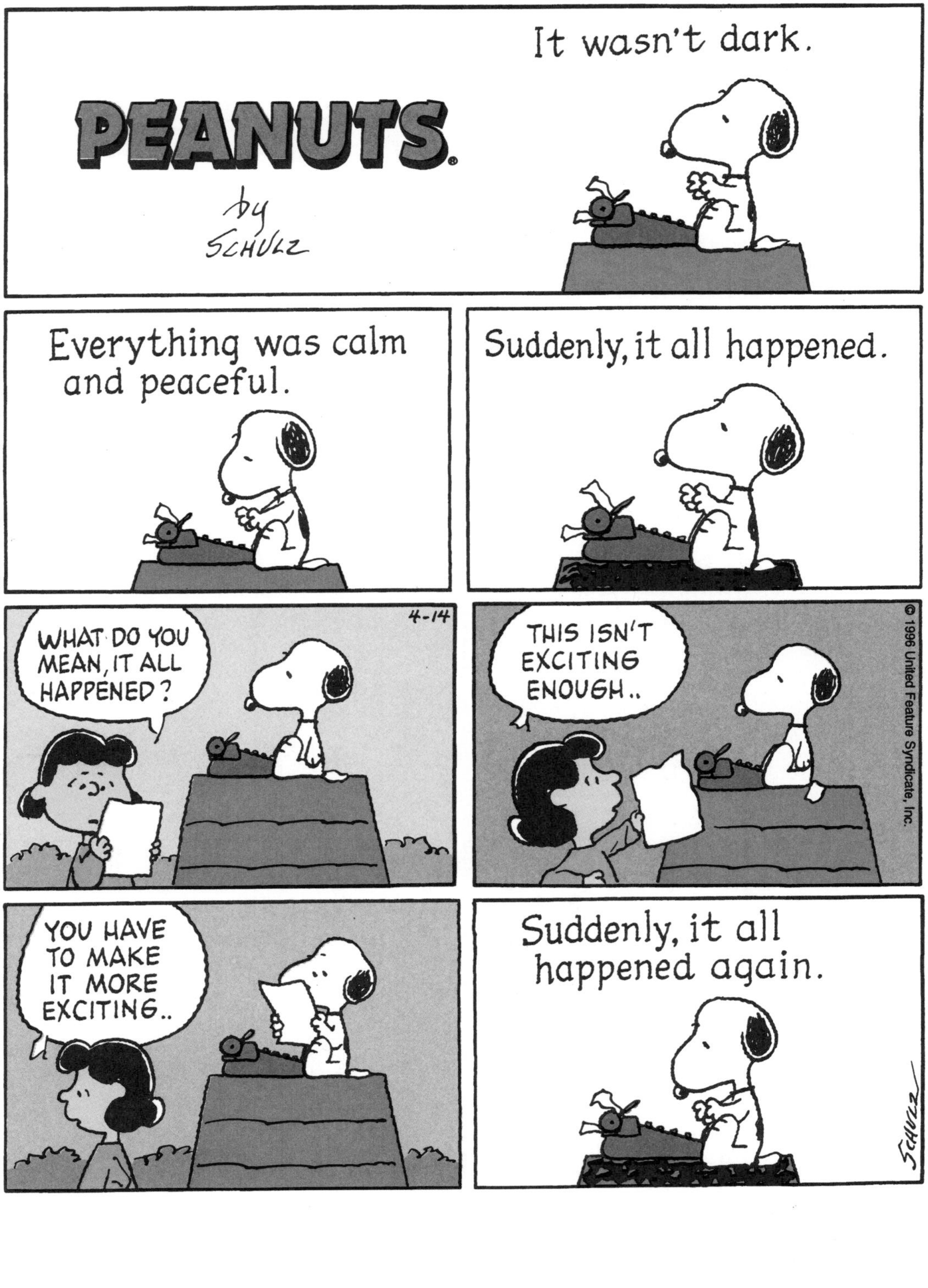

PEANUTS
by SCHULZ
It wasn't dark.
Everything was calm and peaceful.
Suddenly, it all happened.
4-14
WHAT DO YOU MEAN, IT ALL HAPPENED?
THIS ISN'T EXCITING ENOUGH..
© 1996 United Feature Syndicate, Inc.
YOU HAVE TO MAKE IT MORE EXCITING..
Suddenly, it all happened again.
SCHULZ

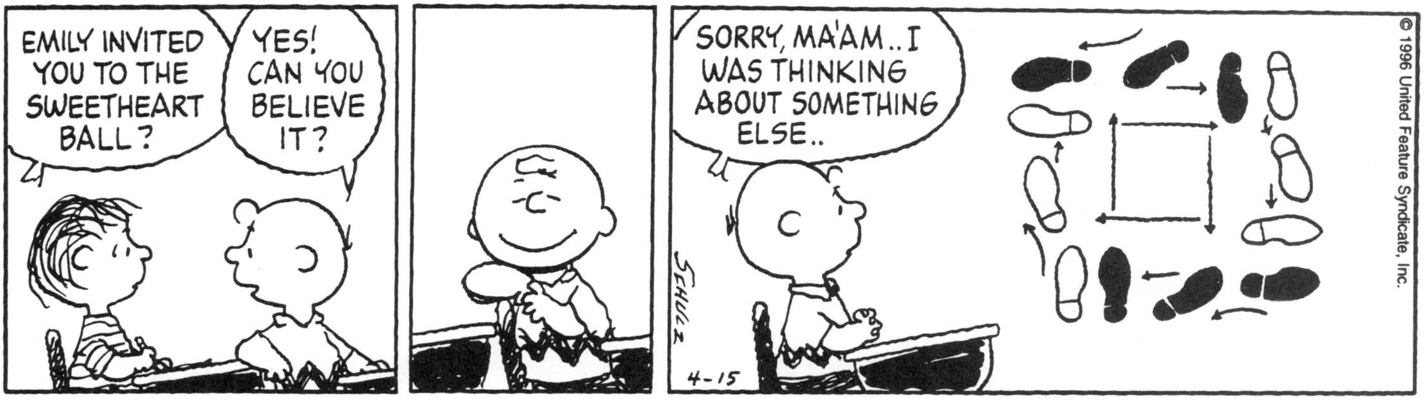
EMILY INVITED YOU TO THE SWEETHEART BALL?
YES! CAN YOU BELIEVE IT?
SORRY, MA'AM.. I WAS THINKING ABOUT SOMETHING ELSE..
© 1996 United Feature Syndicate, Inc.

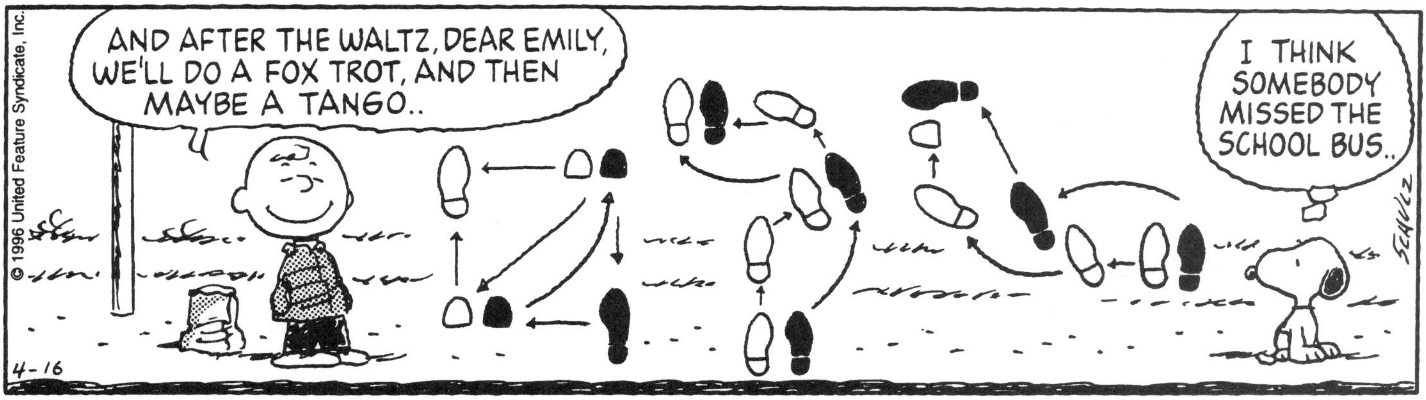
AND AFTER THE WALTZ, DEAR EMILY, WE'LL DO A FOX TROT, AND THEN MAYBE A TANGO..
I THINK SOMEBODY MISSED THE SCHOOL BUS..
© 1996 United Feature Syndicate, Inc.

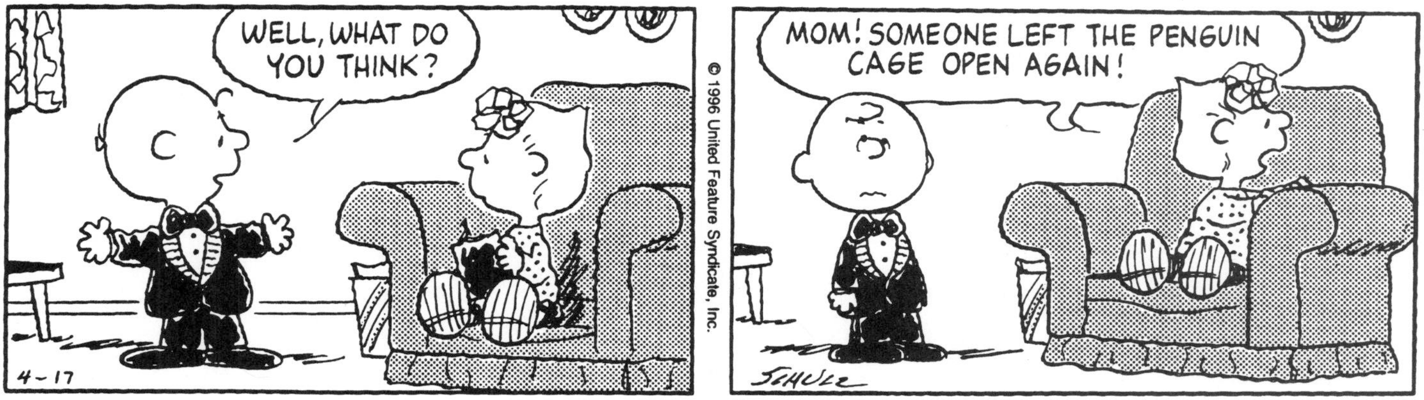
WELL, WHAT DO YOU THINK?
MOM! SOMEONE LEFT THE PENGUIN CAGE OPEN AGAIN!
© 1996 United Feature Syndicate, Inc.

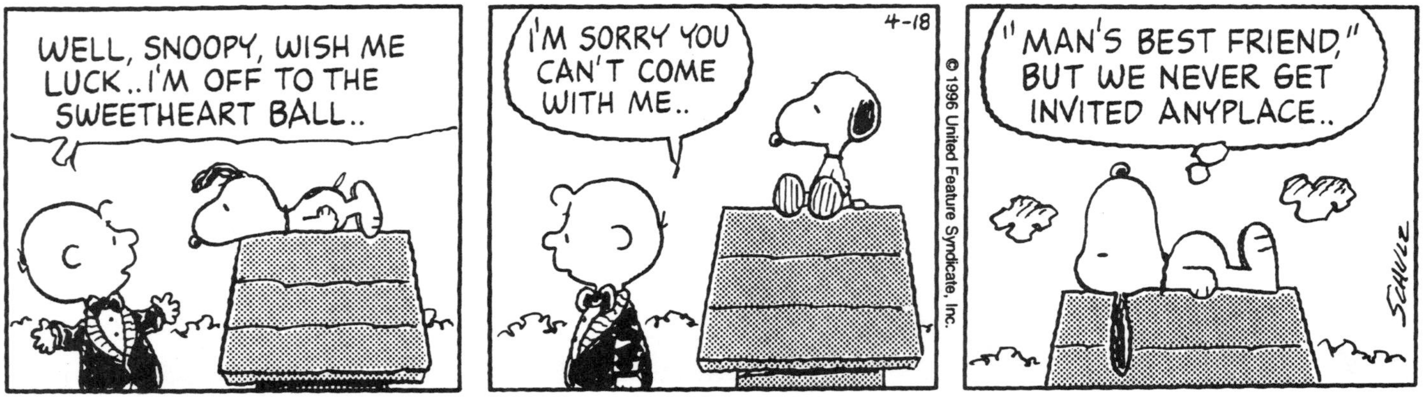
WELL, SNOOPY, WISH ME LUCK..I'M OFF TO THE SWEETHEART BALL..
I'M SORRY YOU CAN'T COME WITH ME..
4-18
© 1996 United Feature Syndicate, Inc.
"MAN'S BEST FRIEND," BUT WE NEVER GET INVITED ANYPLACE..
SCHULZ

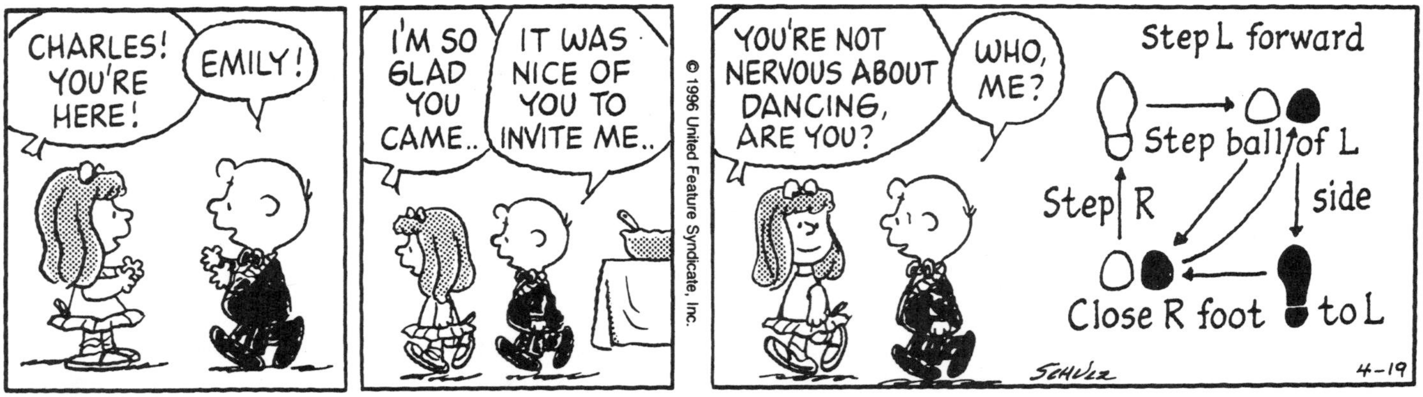
CHARLES! YOU'RE HERE!
EMILY!
© 1996 United Feature Syndicate, Inc.
I'M SO GLAD YOU CAME..
IT WAS NICE OF YOU TO INVITE ME..
YOU'RE NOT NERVOUS ABOUT DANCING, ARE YOU?
WHO, ME?
Step L forward
Step ball of L
Step R
side
Close R foot
to L
SCHULZ
4-19

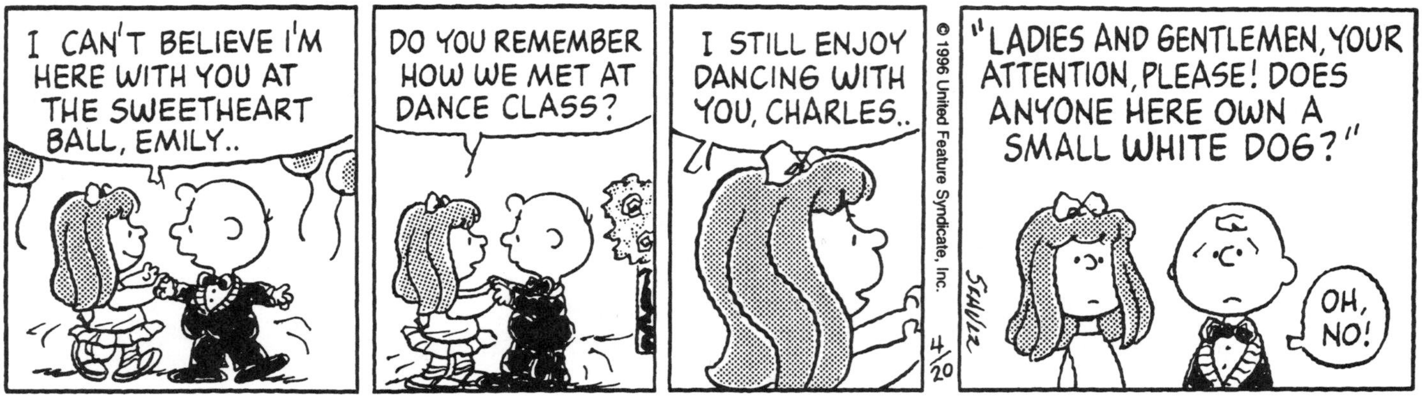
I CAN'T BELIEVE I'M HERE WITH YOU AT THE SWEETHEART BALL, EMILY..
DO YOU REMEMBER HOW WE MET AT DANCE CLASS?
I STILL ENJOY DANCING WITH YOU, CHARLES..
4/20
© 1996 United Feature Syndicate, Inc.
SCHULZ
"LADIES AND GENTLEMEN, YOUR ATTENTION, PLEASE! DOES ANYONE HERE OWN A SMALL WHITE DOG?"
OH, NO!

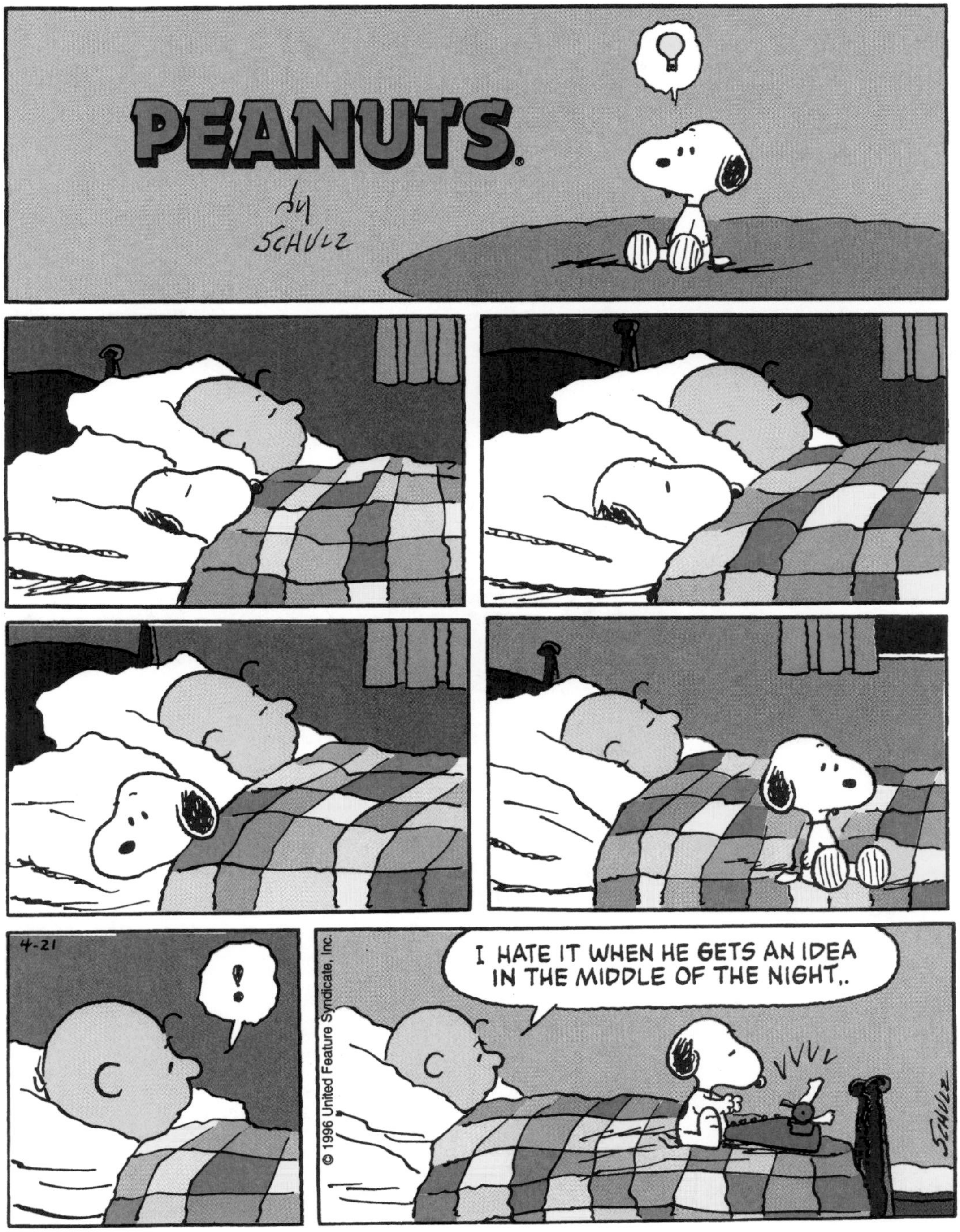
PEANUTS
by SCHULZ
4-21
!
I HATE IT WHEN HE GETS AN IDEA IN THE MIDDLE OF THE NIGHT..
VVVL
SCHULZ
© 1996 United Feature Syndicate, Inc.

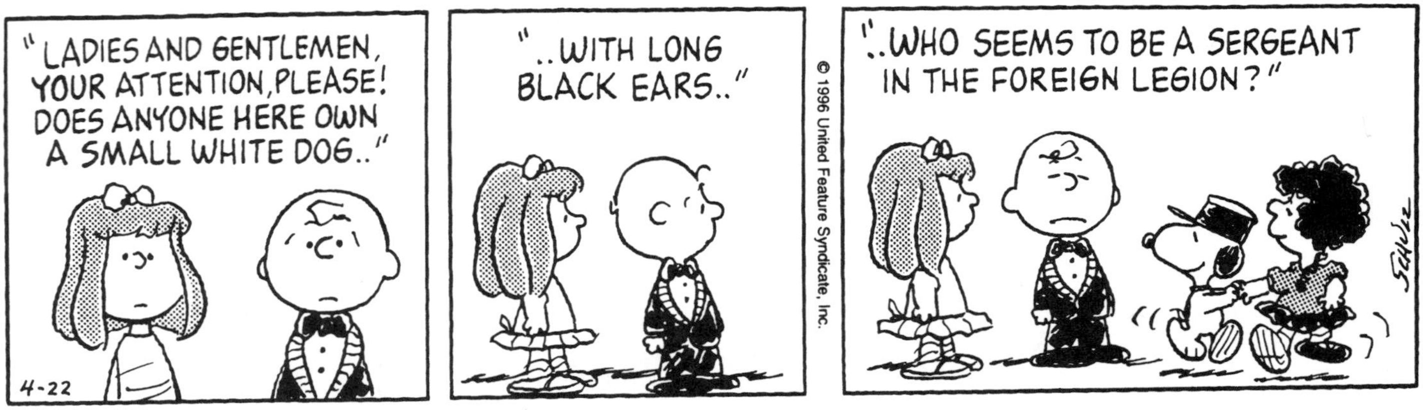
"LADIES AND GENTLEMEN, YOUR ATTENTION, PLEASE! DOES ANYONE HERE OWN A SMALL WHITE DOG.."
4-22
"..WITH LONG BLACK EARS.."
© 1996 United Feature Syndicate, Inc.
"..WHO SEEMS TO BE A SERGEANT IN THE FOREIGN LEGION?"
SCHULZ

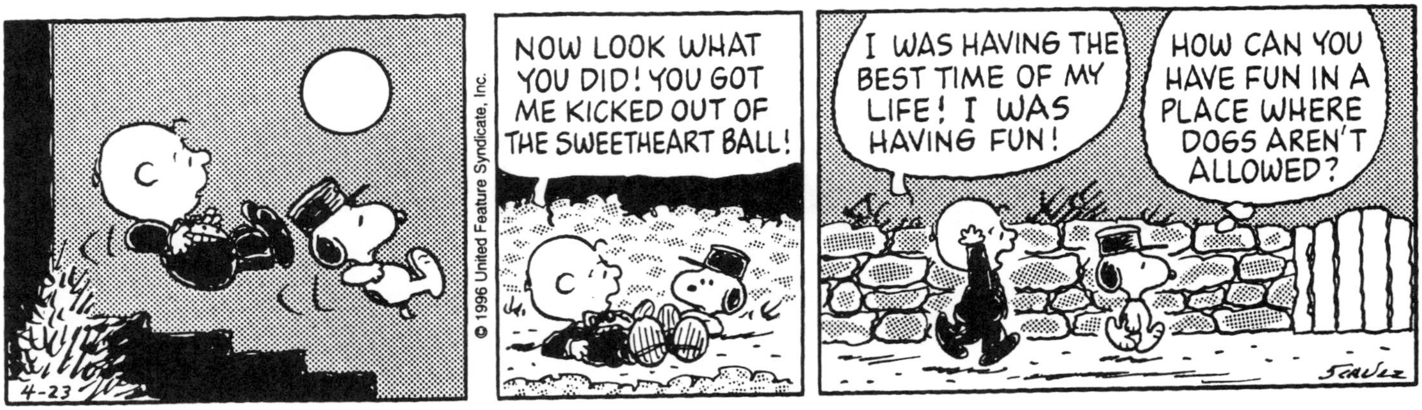
4-23
© 1996 United Feature Syndicate, Inc.
NOW LOOK WHAT YOU DID! YOU GOT ME KICKED OUT OF THE SWEETHEART BALL!
I WAS HAVING THE BEST TIME OF MY LIFE! I WAS HAVING FUN!
HOW CAN YOU HAVE FUN IN A PLACE WHERE DOGS AREN'T ALLOWED?
SCHULZ

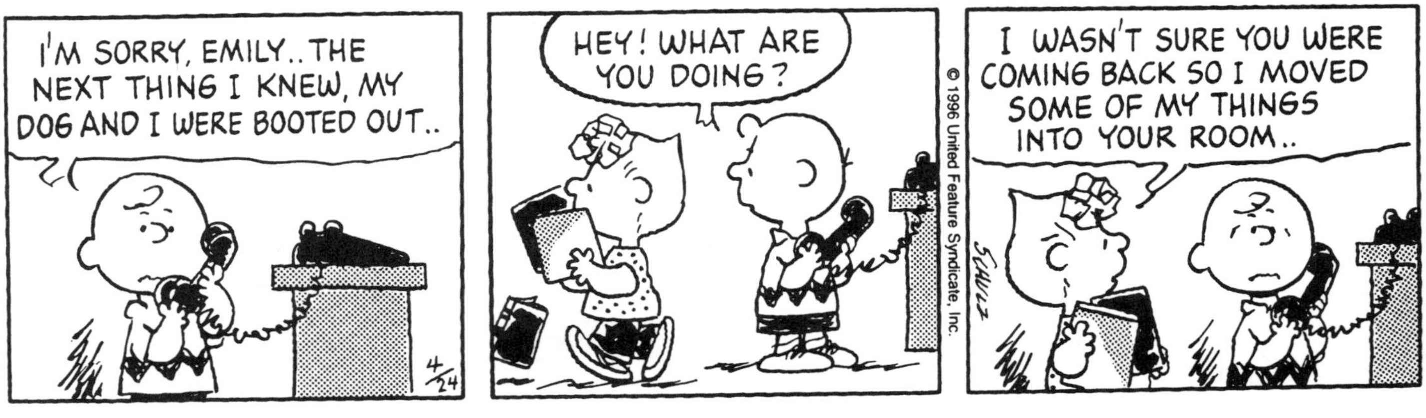
I'M SORRY, EMILY.. THE NEXT THING I KNEW, MY DOG AND I WERE BOOTED OUT..
4/24
HEY! WHAT ARE YOU DOING?
© 1996 United Feature Syndicate, Inc.
SCHULZ
I WASN'T SURE YOU WERE COMING BACK SO I MOVED SOME OF MY THINGS INTO YOUR ROOM..

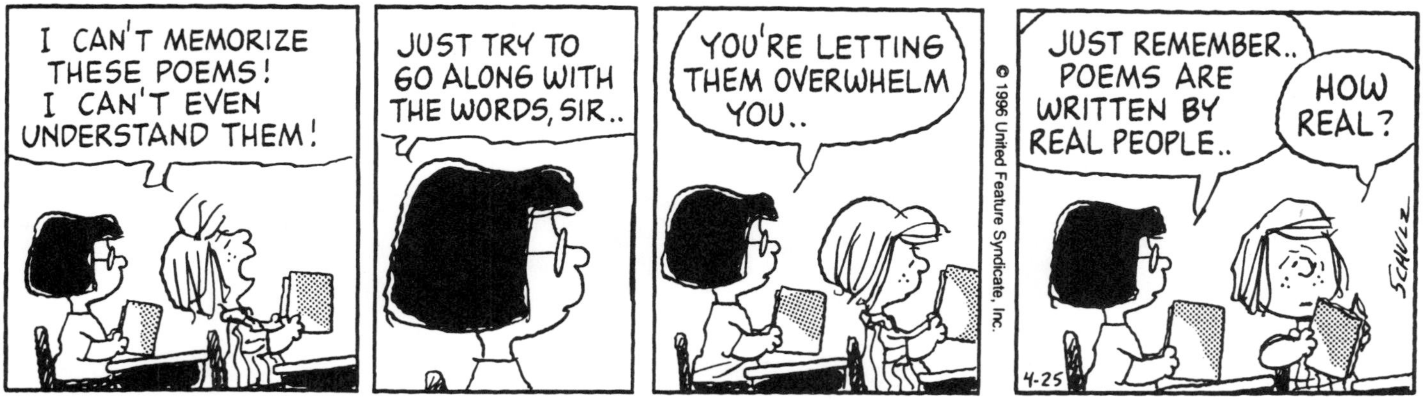
I CAN'T MEMORIZE THESE POEMS! I CAN'T EVEN UNDERSTAND THEM!
JUST TRY TO GO ALONG WITH THE WORDS, SIR..
YOU'RE LETTING THEM OVERWHELM YOU..
© 1996 United Feature Syndicate, Inc.
JUST REMEMBER.. POEMS ARE WRITTEN BY REAL PEOPLE..
HOW REAL?
SCHULZ
4-25

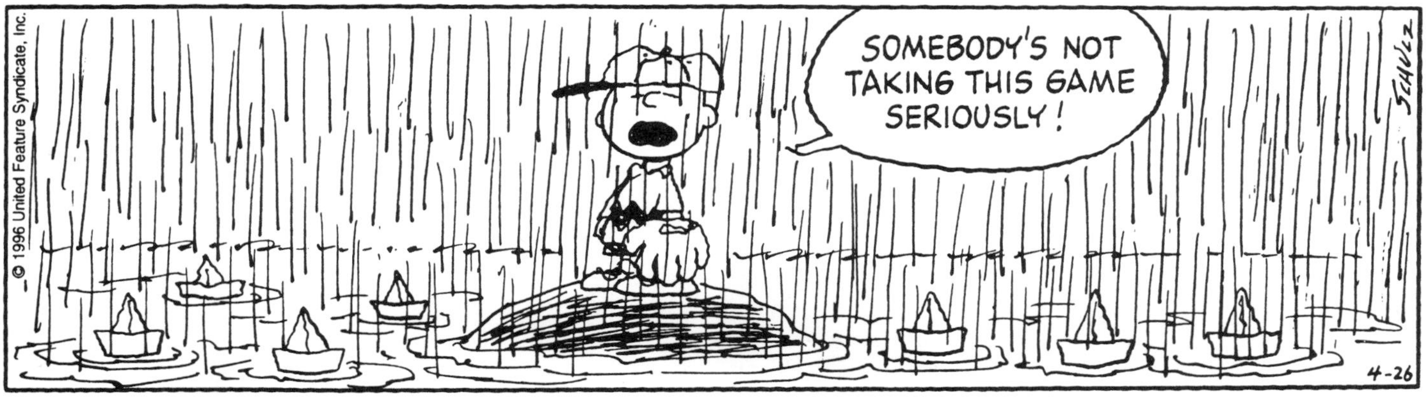
© 1996 United Feature Syndicate, Inc.
SOMEBODY'S NOT TAKING THIS GAME SERIOUSLY!
SCHULZ
4-26

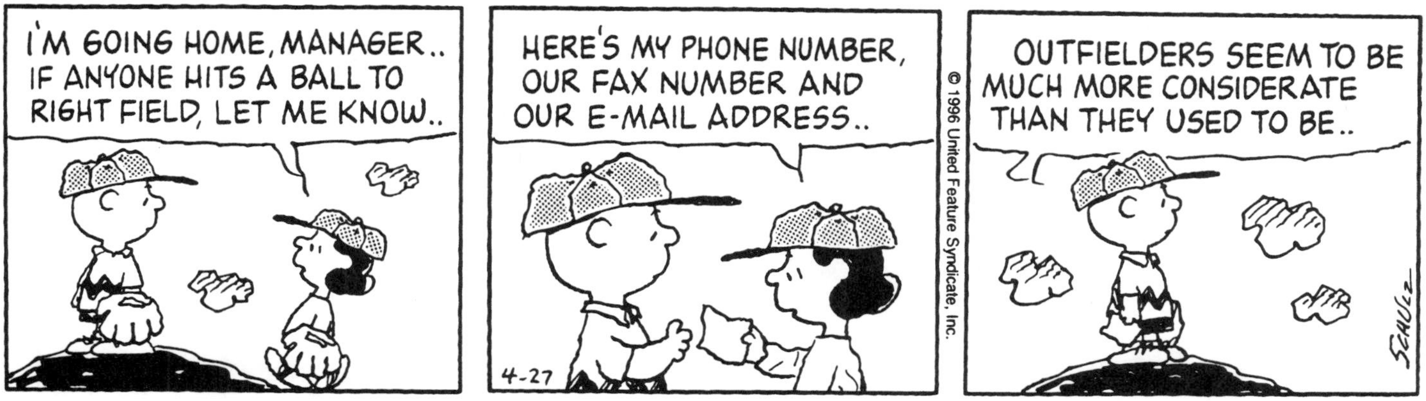
I'M GOING HOME, MANAGER.. IF ANYONE HITS A BALL TO RIGHT FIELD, LET ME KNOW..
HERE'S MY PHONE NUMBER, OUR FAX NUMBER AND OUR E-MAIL ADDRESS..
4-27
© 1996 United Feature Syndicate, Inc.
OUTFIELDERS SEEM TO BE MUCH MORE CONSIDERATE THAN THEY USED TO BE..
SCHULZ

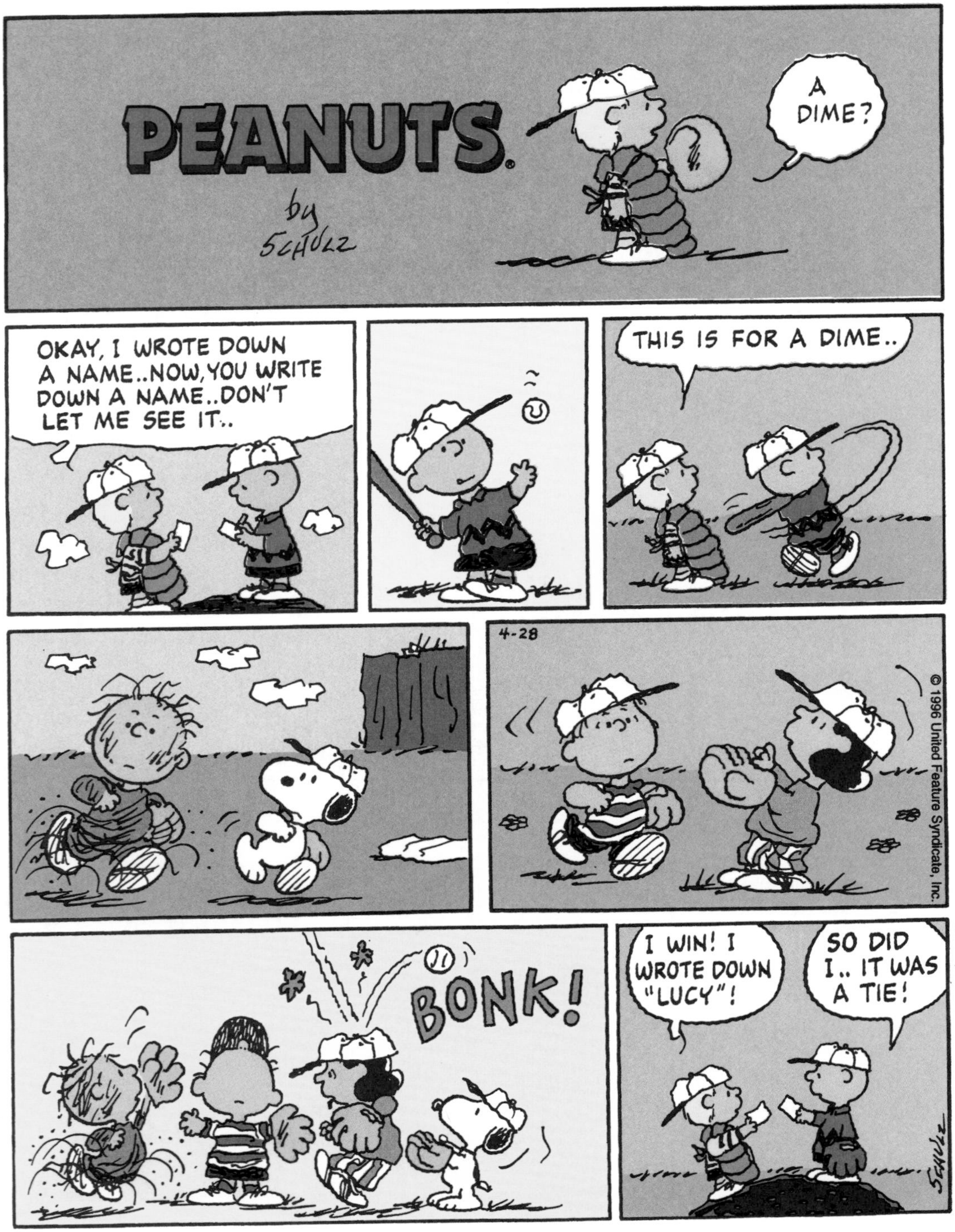
PEANUTS
by SCHULZ
A DIME?
OKAY, I WROTE DOWN A NAME..NOW, YOU WRITE DOWN A NAME..DON'T LET ME SEE IT..
THIS IS FOR A DIME..
4-28
© 1996 United Feature Syndicate, Inc.
BONK!
I WIN! I WROTE DOWN "LUCY"!
SO DID I.. IT WAS A TIE!

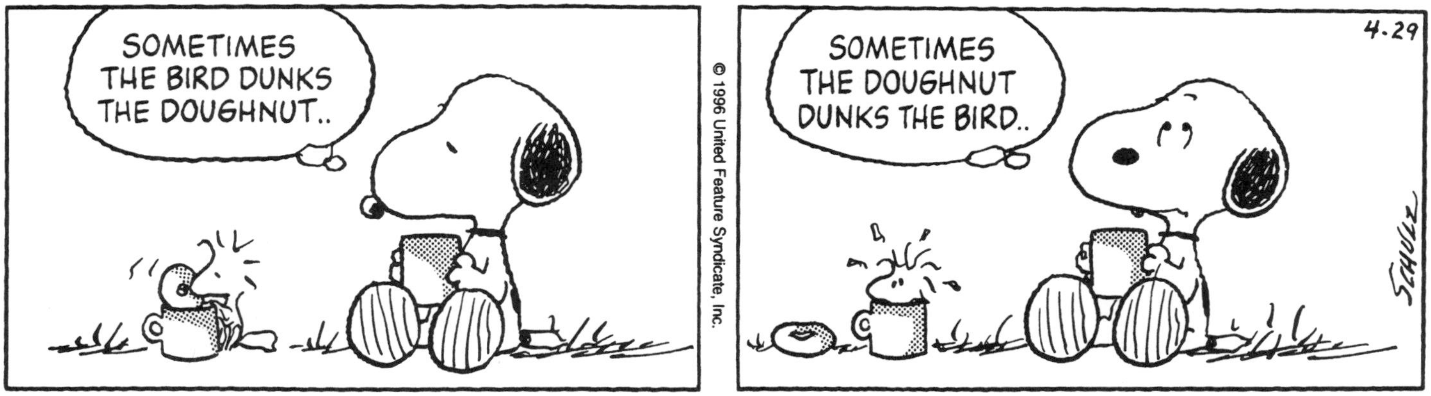
SOMETIMES THE BIRD DUNKS THE DOUGHNUT..
© 1996 United Feature Syndicate, Inc.
4-29
SOMETIMES THE DOUGHNUT DUNKS THE BIRD..
SCHULZ

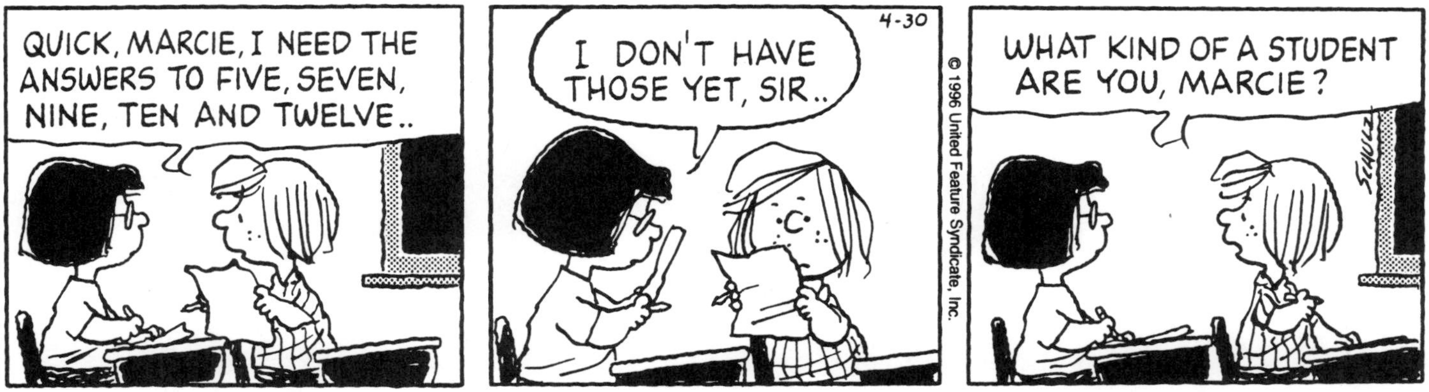
QUICK, MARCIE, I NEED THE ANSWERS TO FIVE, SEVEN, NINE, TEN AND TWELVE..
4-30
I DON'T HAVE THOSE YET, SIR..
© 1996 United Feature Syndicate, Inc.
WHAT KIND OF A STUDENT ARE YOU, MARCIE?
SCHULZ

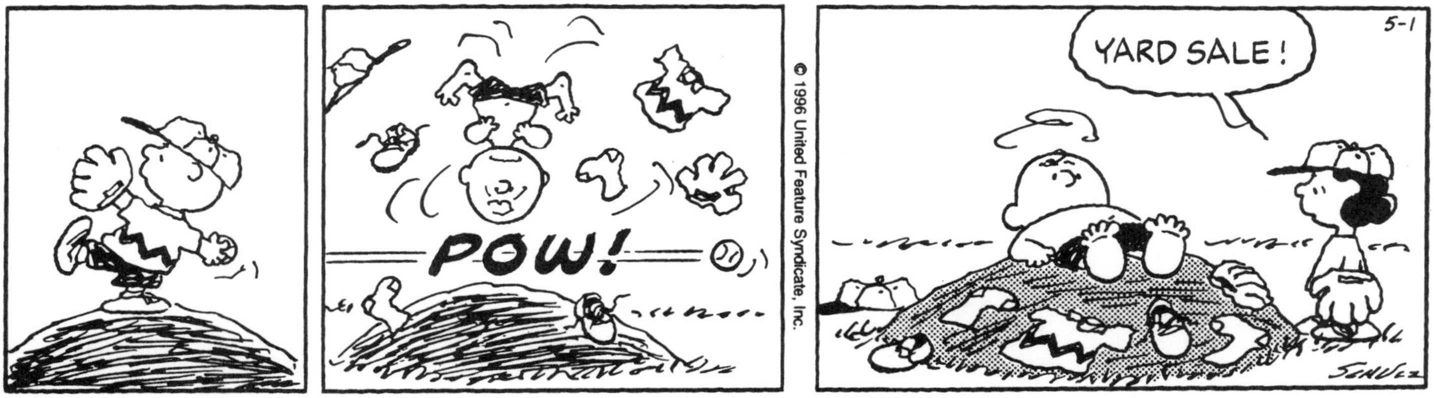
POW!
© 1996 United Feature Syndicate, Inc.
5-1
YARD SALE!
SCHULZ

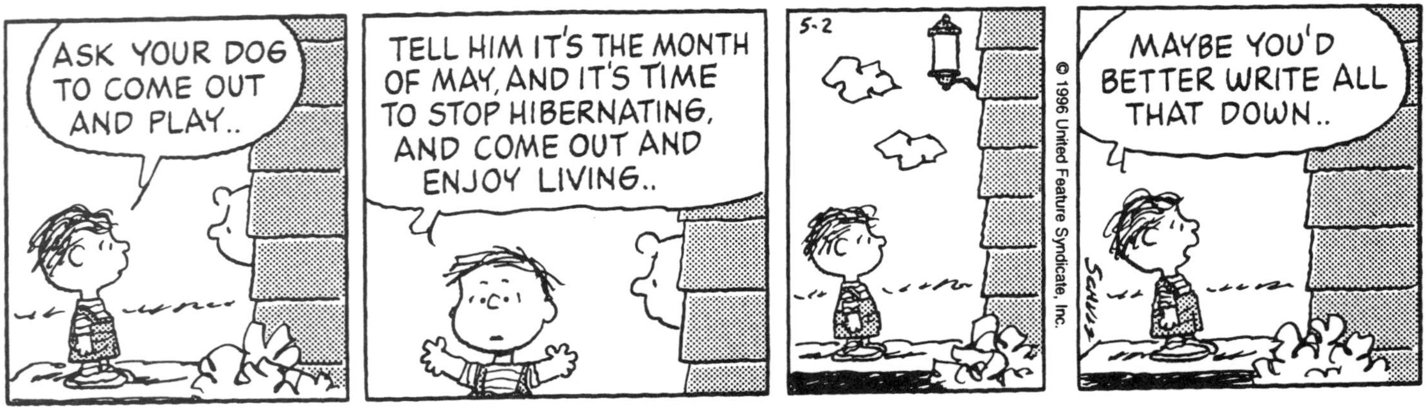
ASK YOUR DOG TO COME OUT AND PLAY..
TELL HIM IT'S THE MONTH OF MAY, AND IT'S TIME TO STOP HIBERNATING, AND COME OUT AND ENJOY LIVING..
5-2
© 1996 United Feature Syndicate, Inc.
MAYBE YOU'D BETTER WRITE ALL THAT DOWN..
SCHULZ

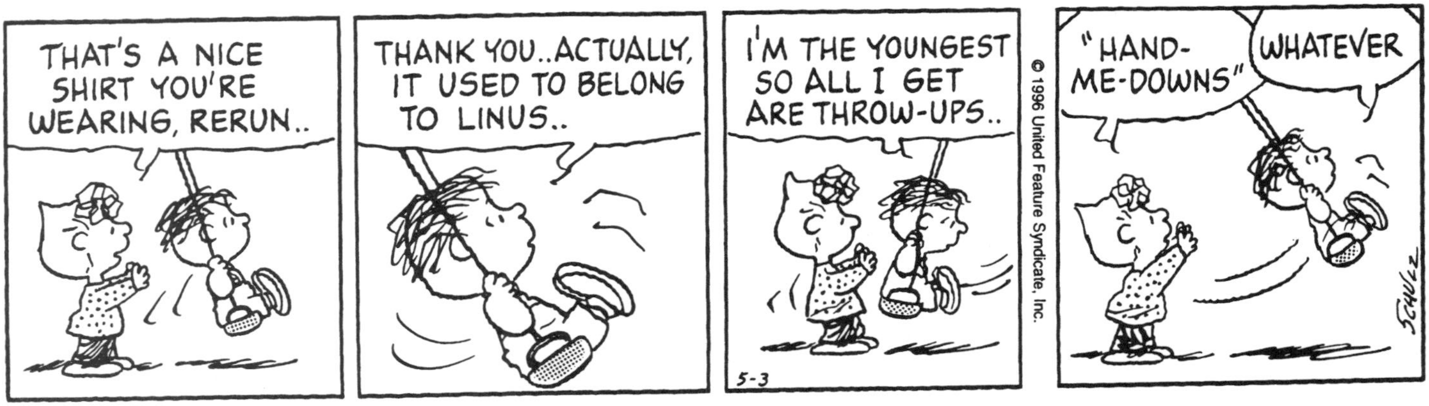
THAT'S A NICE SHIRT YOU'RE WEARING, RERUN..
THANK YOU..ACTUALLY, IT USED TO BELONG TO LINUS..
I'M THE YOUNGEST SO ALL I GET ARE THROW-UPS..
5-3
© 1996 United Feature Syndicate, Inc.
"HAND-ME-DOWNS"
WHATEVER
SCHULZ

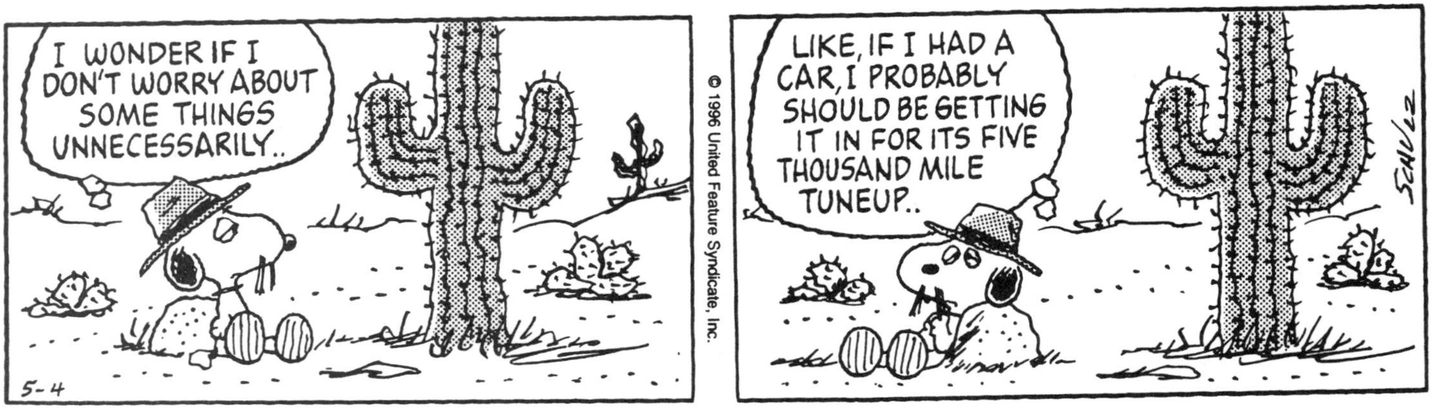
I WONDER IF I DON'T WORRY ABOUT SOME THINGS UNNECESSARILY..
5-4
© 1996 United Feature Syndicate, Inc.
LIKE, IF I HAD A CAR, I PROBABLY SHOULD BE GETTING IT IN FOR ITS FIVE THOUSAND MILE TUNEUP..
SCHULZ

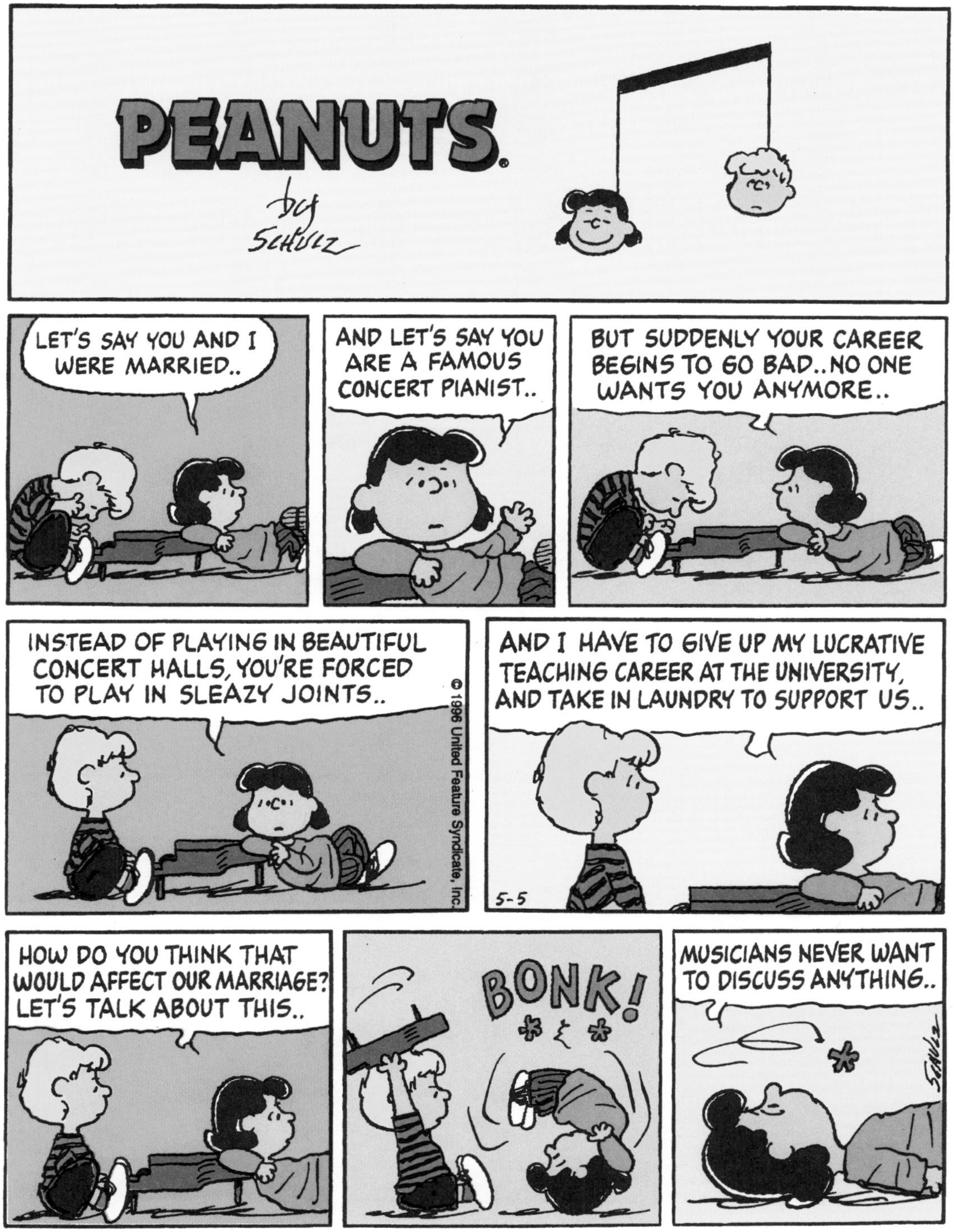
PEANUTS
by SCHULZ
LET'S SAY YOU AND I WERE MARRIED..
AND LET'S SAY YOU ARE A FAMOUS CONCERT PIANIST..
BUT SUDDENLY YOUR CAREER BEGINS TO GO BAD..NO ONE WANTS YOU ANYMORE..
INSTEAD OF PLAYING IN BEAUTIFUL CONCERT HALLS, YOU'RE FORCED TO PLAY IN SLEAZY JOINTS..
© 1996 United Feature Syndicate, Inc.
AND I HAVE TO GIVE UP MY LUCRATIVE TEACHING CAREER AT THE UNIVERSITY, AND TAKE IN LAUNDRY TO SUPPORT US..
5-5
HOW DO YOU THINK THAT WOULD AFFECT OUR MARRIAGE? LET'S TALK ABOUT THIS..
BONK!
MUSICIANS NEVER WANT TO DISCUSS ANYTHING..
SCHULZ

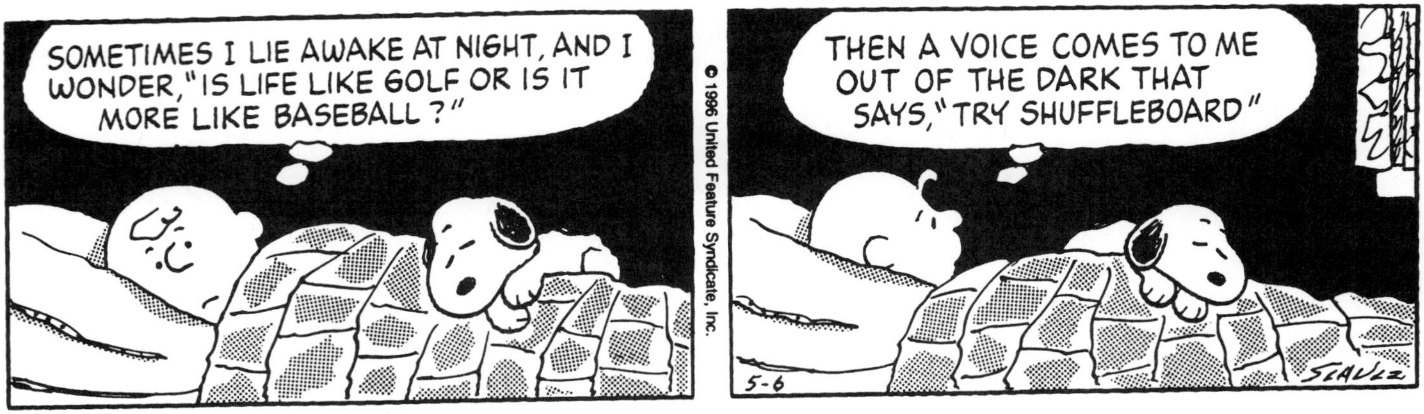
SOMETIMES I LIE AWAKE AT NIGHT, AND I WONDER, "IS LIFE LIKE GOLF OR IS IT MORE LIKE BASEBALL ?"
© 1996 United Feature Syndicate, Inc.
THEN A VOICE COMES TO ME OUT OF THE DARK THAT SAYS, "TRY SHUFFLEBOARD"
5-6
SCHULZ

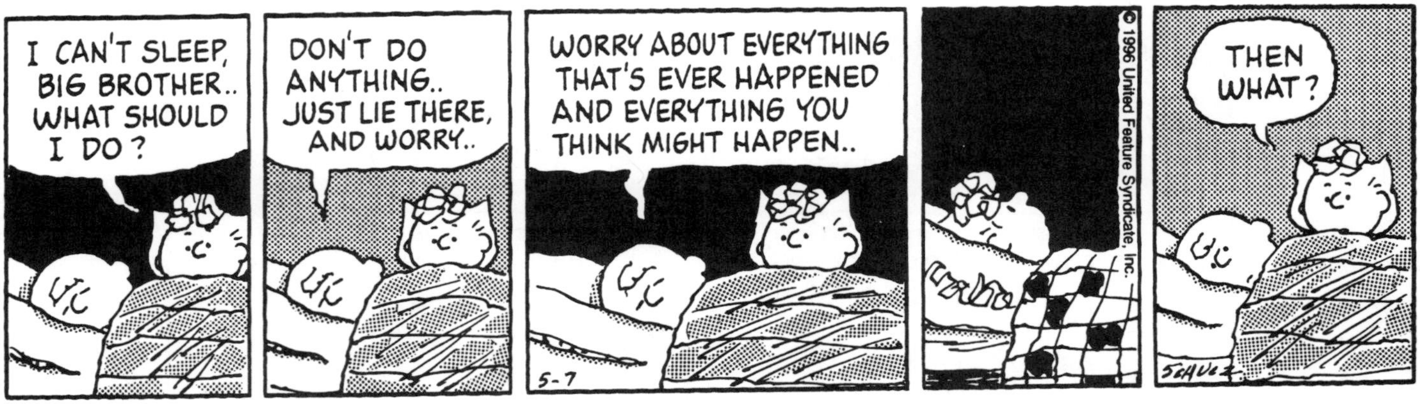
I CAN'T SLEEP, BIG BROTHER.. WHAT SHOULD I DO ?
DON'T DO ANYTHING.. JUST LIE THERE, AND WORRY..
WORRY ABOUT EVERYTHING THAT'S EVER HAPPENED AND EVERYTHING YOU THINK MIGHT HAPPEN..
5-7
© 1996 United Feature Syndicate, Inc.
THEN WHAT ?
SCHULZ

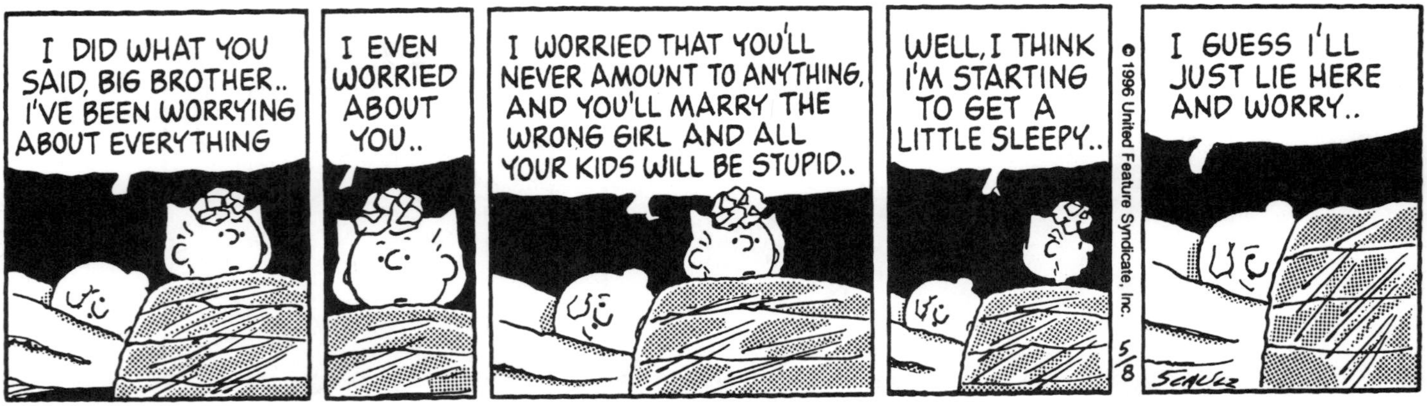
I DID WHAT YOU SAID, BIG BROTHER.. I'VE BEEN WORRYING ABOUT EVERYTHING
I EVEN WORRIED ABOUT YOU..
I WORRIED THAT YOU'LL NEVER AMOUNT TO ANYTHING, AND YOU'LL MARRY THE WRONG GIRL AND ALL YOUR KIDS WILL BE STUPID..
WELL, I THINK I'M STARTING TO GET A LITTLE SLEEPY..
© 1996 United Feature Syndicate, Inc.
5/8
I GUESS I'LL JUST LIE HERE AND WORRY..
SCHULZ

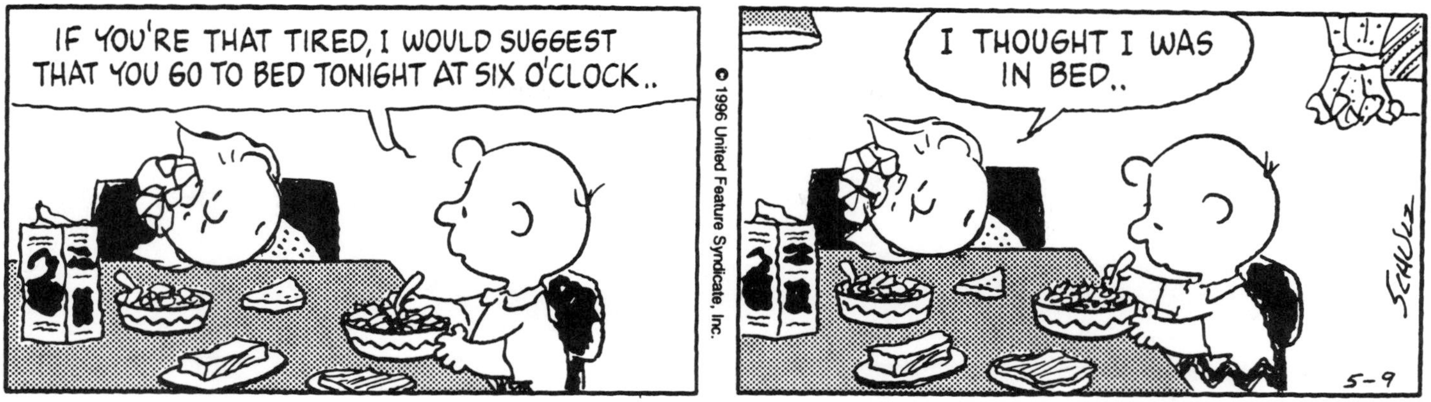
IF YOU'RE THAT TIRED, I WOULD SUGGEST THAT YOU GO TO BED TONIGHT AT SIX O'CLOCK..
© 1996 United Feature Syndicate, Inc.
I THOUGHT I WAS IN BED..
SCHULZ
5-9

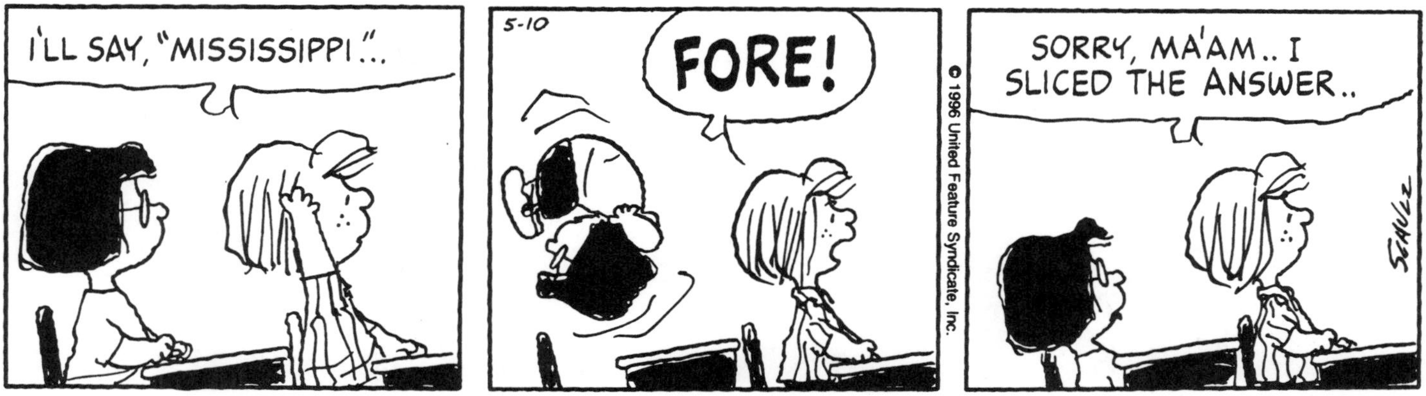
I'LL SAY, "MISSISSIPPI."..
5-10
FORE!
© 1996 United Feature Syndicate, Inc.
SORRY, MA'AM.. I SLICED THE ANSWER..
SCHULZ

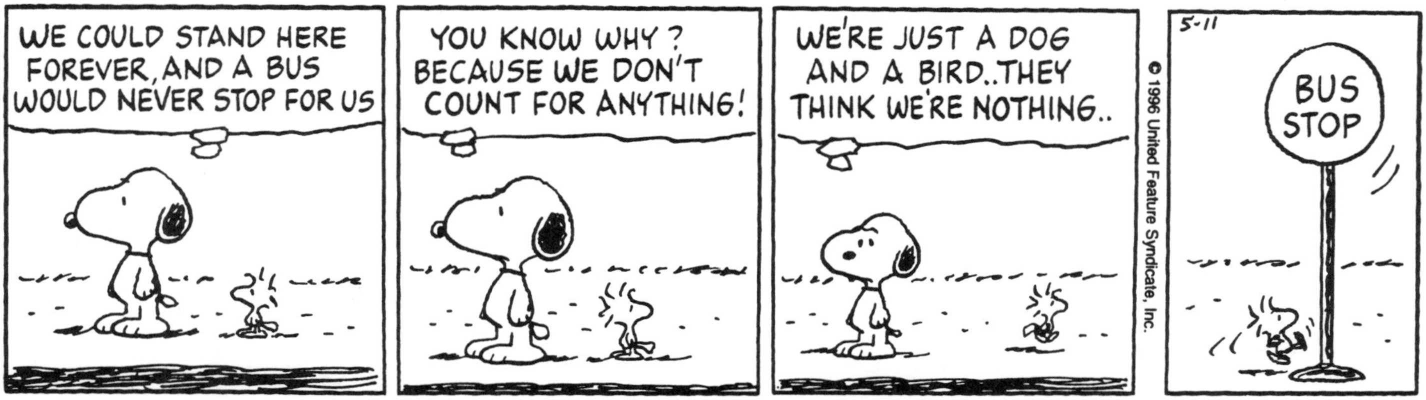
WE COULD STAND HERE FOREVER, AND A BUS WOULD NEVER STOP FOR US
YOU KNOW WHY? BECAUSE WE DON'T COUNT FOR ANYTHING!
WE'RE JUST A DOG AND A BIRD..THEY THINK WE'RE NOTHING..
© 1996 United Feature Syndicate, Inc.
5-11
BUS STOP

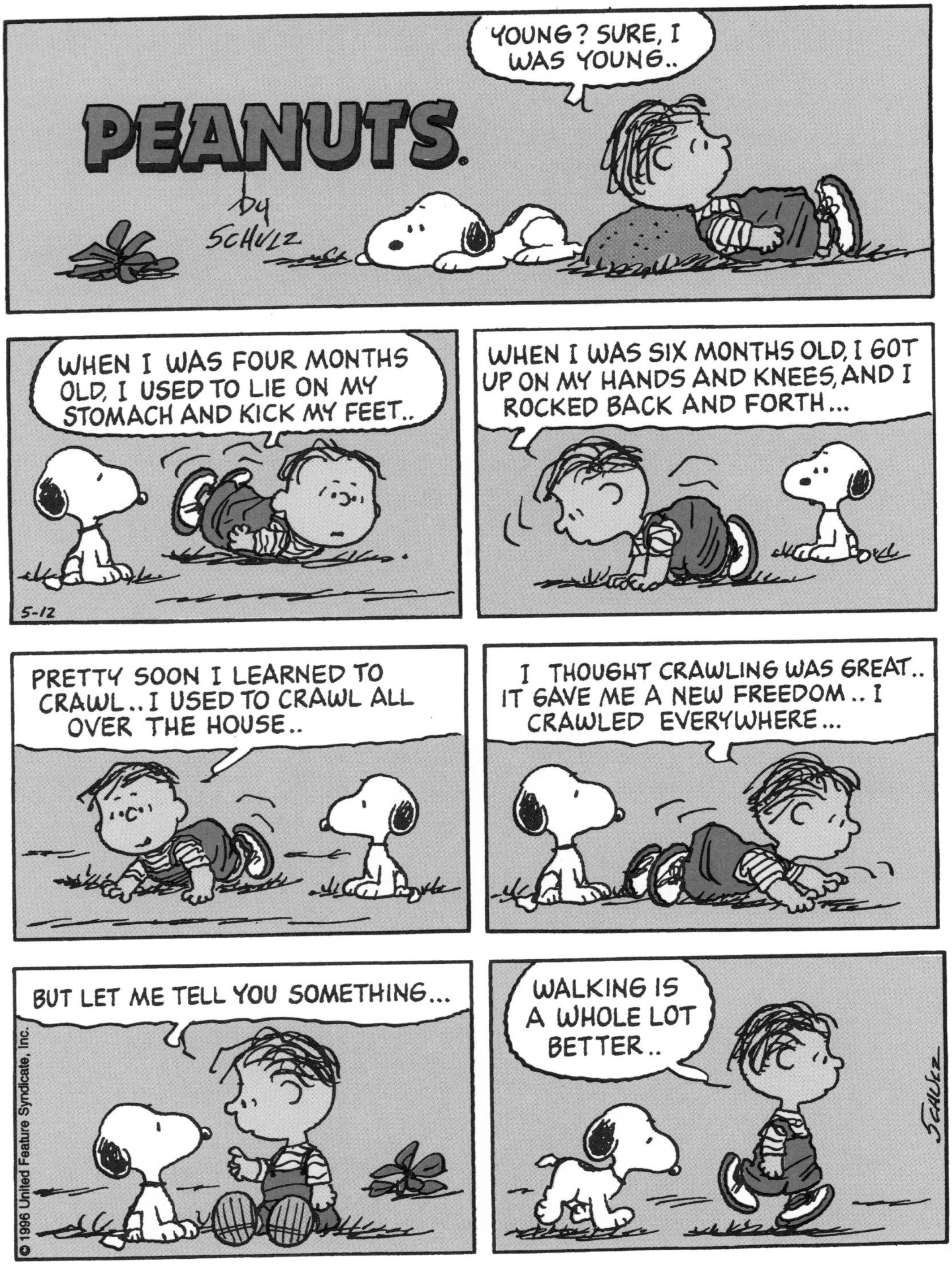
PEANUTS
by SCHULZ
YOUNG? SURE, I WAS YOUNG..
WHEN I WAS FOUR MONTHS OLD, I USED TO LIE ON MY STOMACH AND KICK MY FEET..
5-12
WHEN I WAS SIX MONTHS OLD, I GOT UP ON MY HANDS AND KNEES, AND I ROCKED BACK AND FORTH...
PRETTY SOON I LEARNED TO CRAWL.. I USED TO CRAWL ALL OVER THE HOUSE..
I THOUGHT CRAWLING WAS GREAT.. IT GAVE ME A NEW FREEDOM.. I CRAWLED EVERYWHERE...
BUT LET ME TELL YOU SOMETHING...
© 1996 United Feature Syndicate, Inc.
WALKING IS A WHOLE LOT BETTER..
SCHULZ

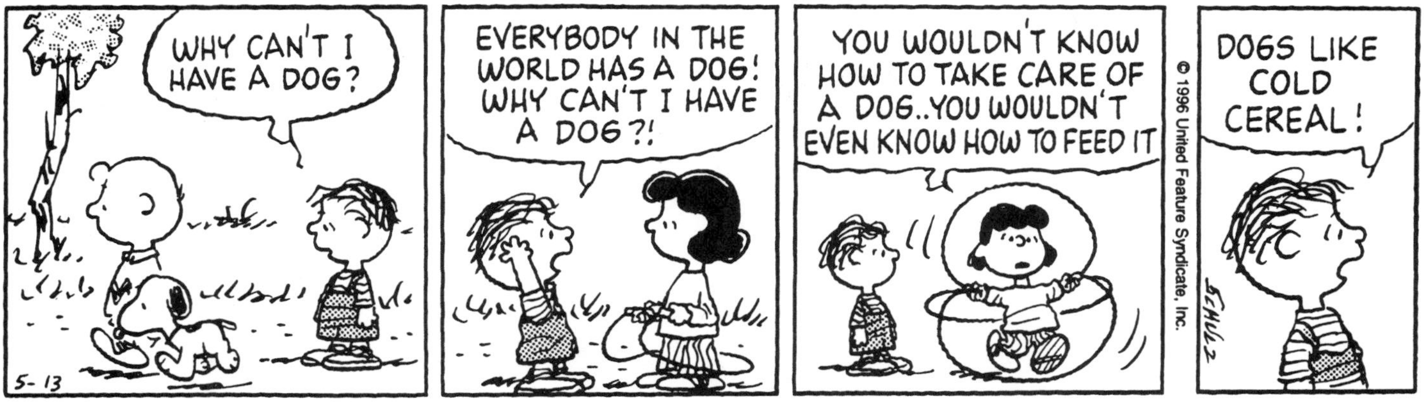
5-13
WHY CAN'T I HAVE A DOG?
EVERYBODY IN THE WORLD HAS A DOG! WHY CAN'T I HAVE A DOG?!
YOU WOULDN'T KNOW HOW TO TAKE CARE OF A DOG..YOU WOULDN'T EVEN KNOW HOW TO FEED IT
© 1996 United Feature Syndicate, Inc.
DOGS LIKE COLD CEREAL!
SCHULZ

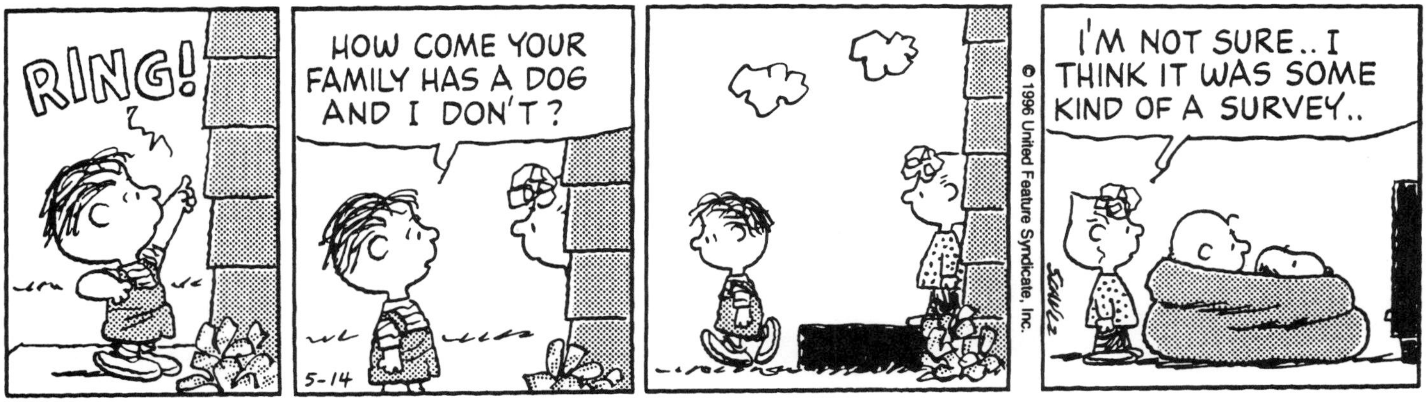
RING!
5-14
HOW COME YOUR FAMILY HAS A DOG AND I DON'T?
© 1996 United Feature Syndicate, Inc.
I'M NOT SURE.. I THINK IT WAS SOME KIND OF A SURVEY..
SCHULZ

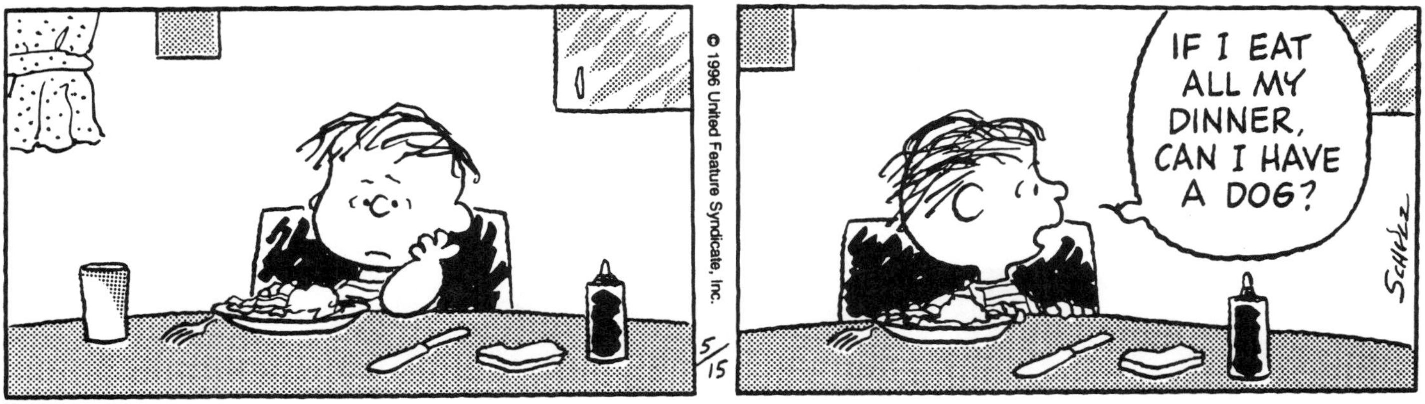
© 1996 United Feature Syndicate, Inc.
5/15
IF I EAT ALL MY DINNER, CAN I HAVE A DOG?
SCHULZ

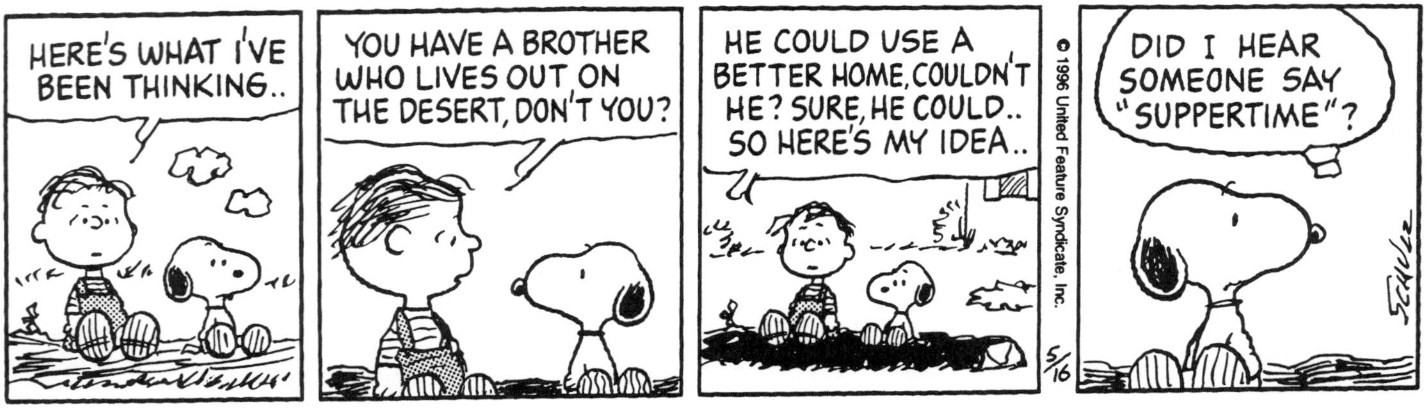
HERE'S WHAT I'VE BEEN THINKING..
YOU HAVE A BROTHER WHO LIVES OUT ON THE DESERT, DON'T YOU?
HE COULD USE A BETTER HOME, COULDN'T HE? SURE, HE COULD.. SO HERE'S MY IDEA..
© 1996 United Feature Syndicate, Inc.
5/16
DID I HEAR SOMEONE SAY "SUPPERTIME"?
SCHULZ

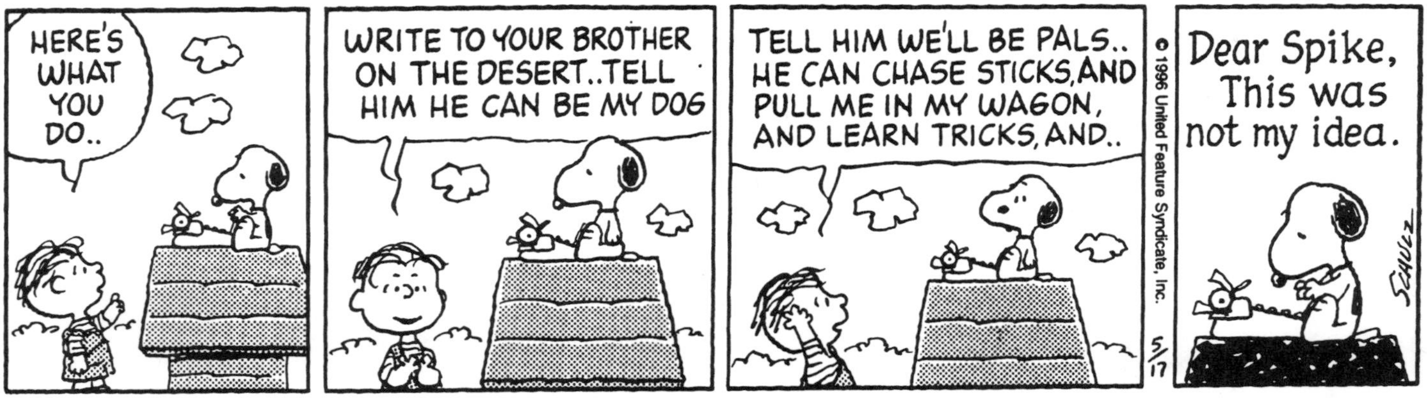
HERE'S WHAT YOU DO..
WRITE TO YOUR BROTHER ON THE DESERT..TELL HIM HE CAN BE MY DOG
TELL HIM WE'LL BE PALS.. HE CAN CHASE STICKS, AND PULL ME IN MY WAGON, AND LEARN TRICKS, AND..
© 1996 United Feature Syndicate, Inc.
5/17
Dear Spike,
This was not my idea.
SCHULZ

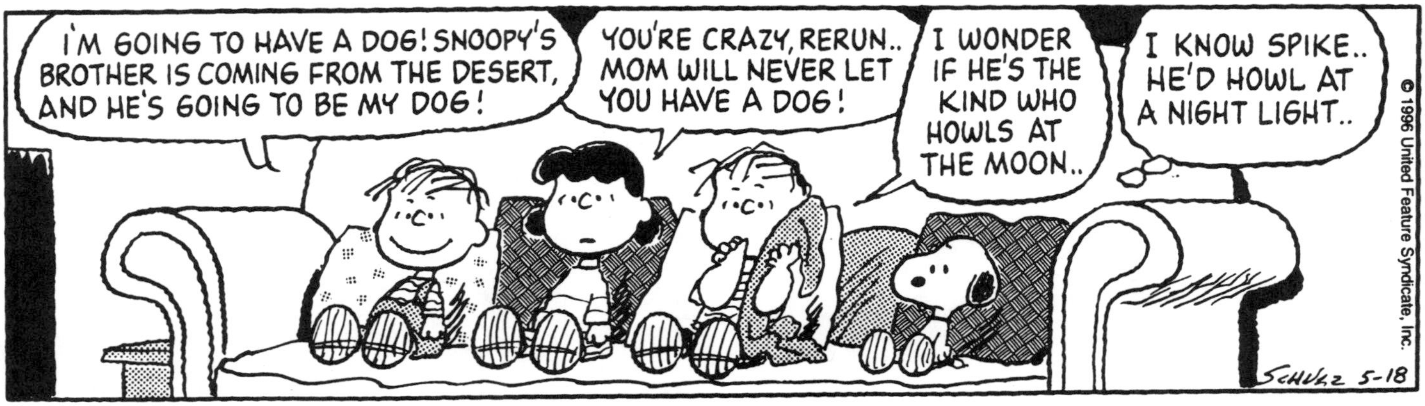
I'M GOING TO HAVE A DOG! SNOOPY'S BROTHER IS COMING FROM THE DESERT, AND HE'S GOING TO BE MY DOG!
YOU'RE CRAZY, RERUN.. MOM WILL NEVER LET YOU HAVE A DOG!
I WONDER IF HE'S THE KIND WHO HOWLS AT THE MOON..
I KNOW SPIKE.. HE'D HOWL AT A NIGHT LIGHT..
© 1996 United Feature Syndicate, Inc.
SCHULZ 5-18

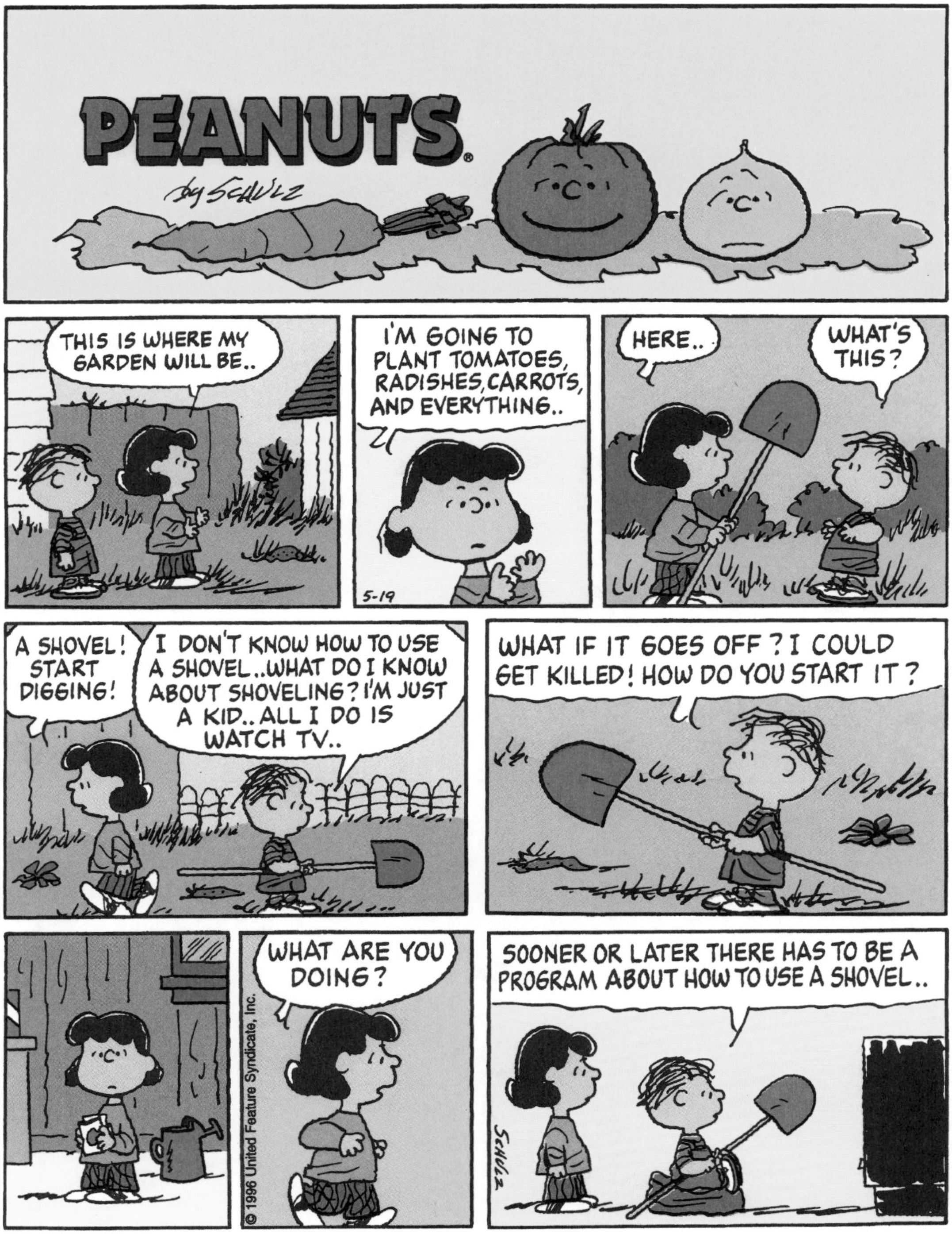
PEANUTS
by SCHULZ
THIS IS WHERE MY GARDEN WILL BE..
I'M GOING TO PLANT TOMATOES, RADISHES, CARROTS, AND EVERYTHING..
5-19
HERE..
WHAT'S THIS?
A SHOVEL! START DIGGING!
I DON'T KNOW HOW TO USE A SHOVEL..WHAT DO I KNOW ABOUT SHOVELING? I'M JUST A KID..ALL I DO IS WATCH TV..
WHAT IF IT GOES OFF? I COULD GET KILLED! HOW DO YOU START IT?
WHAT ARE YOU DOING?
© 1996 United Feature Syndicate, Inc.
SOONER OR LATER THERE HAS TO BE A PROGRAM ABOUT HOW TO USE A SHOVEL..
SCHULZ

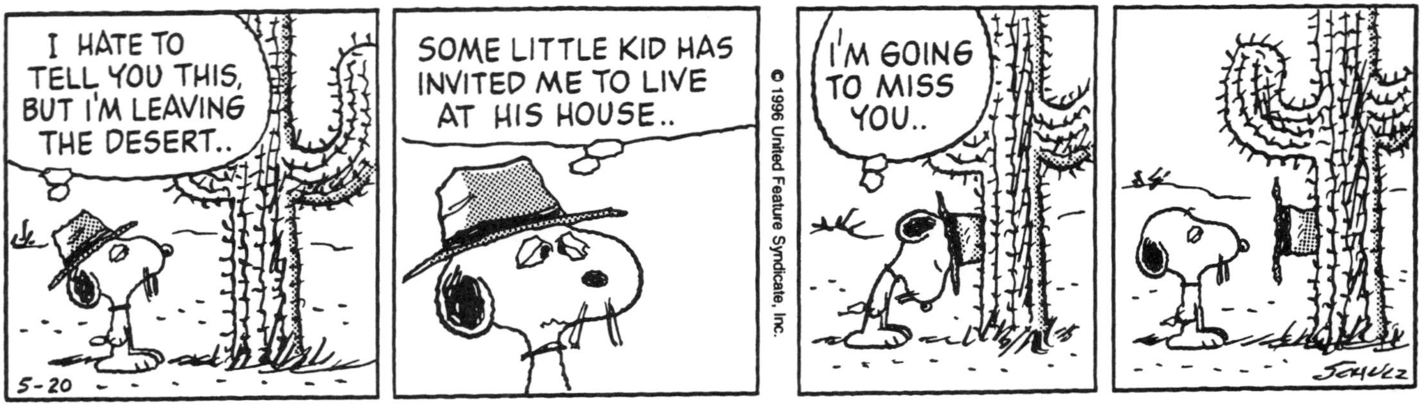
I HATE TO TELL YOU THIS, BUT I'M LEAVING THE DESERT..
5-20
SOME LITTLE KID HAS INVITED ME TO LIVE AT HIS HOUSE..
© 1996 United Feature Syndicate, Inc.
I'M GOING TO MISS YOU..
SCHULZ

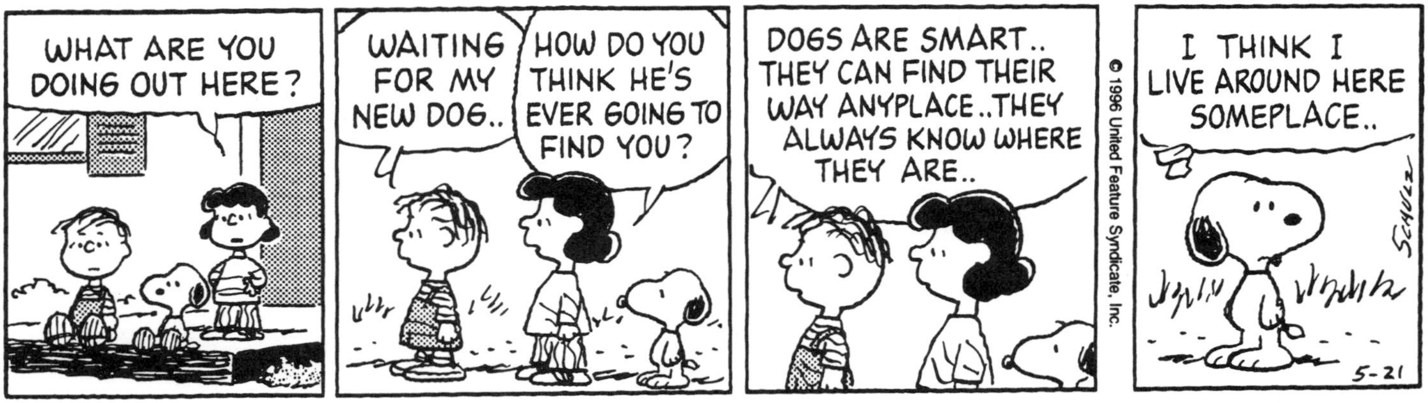
WHAT ARE YOU DOING OUT HERE?
WAITING FOR MY NEW DOG..
HOW DO YOU THINK HE'S EVER GOING TO FIND YOU?
DOGS ARE SMART.. THEY CAN FIND THEIR WAY ANYPLACE..THEY ALWAYS KNOW WHERE THEY ARE..
© 1996 United Feature Syndicate, Inc.
I THINK I LIVE AROUND HERE SOMEPLACE..
SCHULZ
5-21

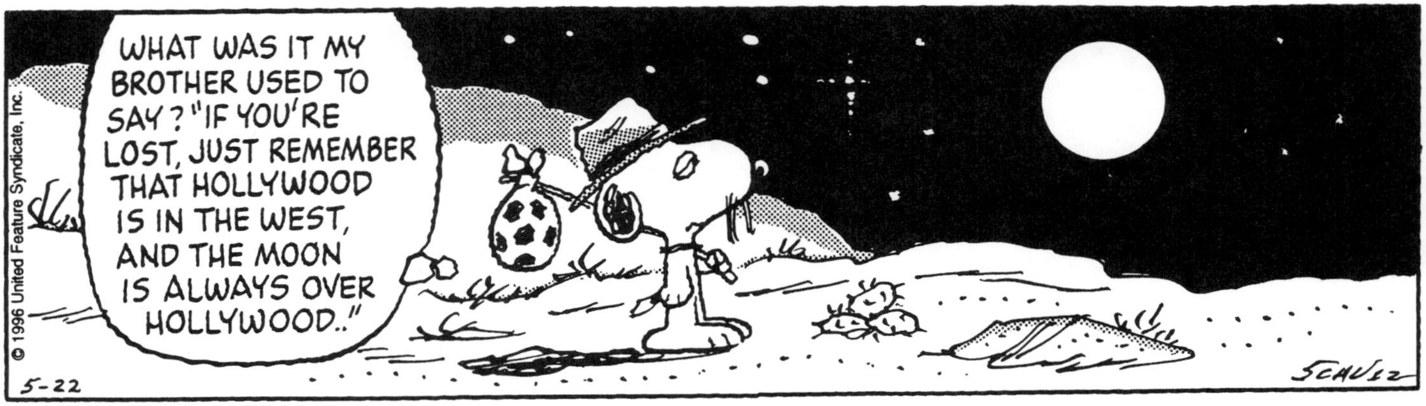
WHAT WAS IT MY BROTHER USED TO SAY? "IF YOU'RE LOST, JUST REMEMBER THAT HOLLYWOOD IS IN THE WEST, AND THE MOON IS ALWAYS OVER HOLLYWOOD.."
© 1996 United Feature Syndicate, Inc.
5-22
SCHULZ

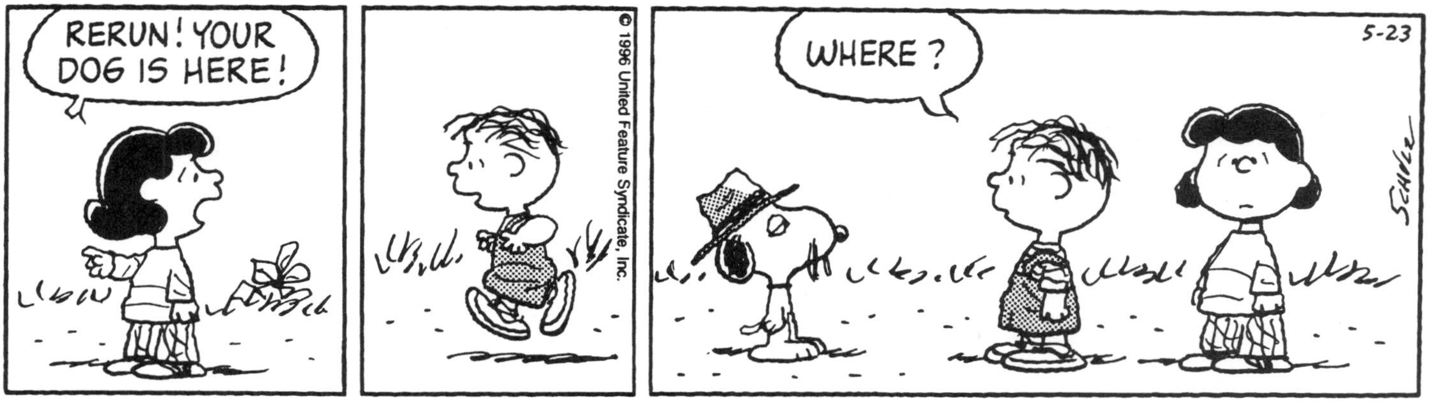
RERUN! YOUR DOG IS HERE!
© 1996 United Feature Syndicate, Inc.
WHERE?
5-23
SCHULZ

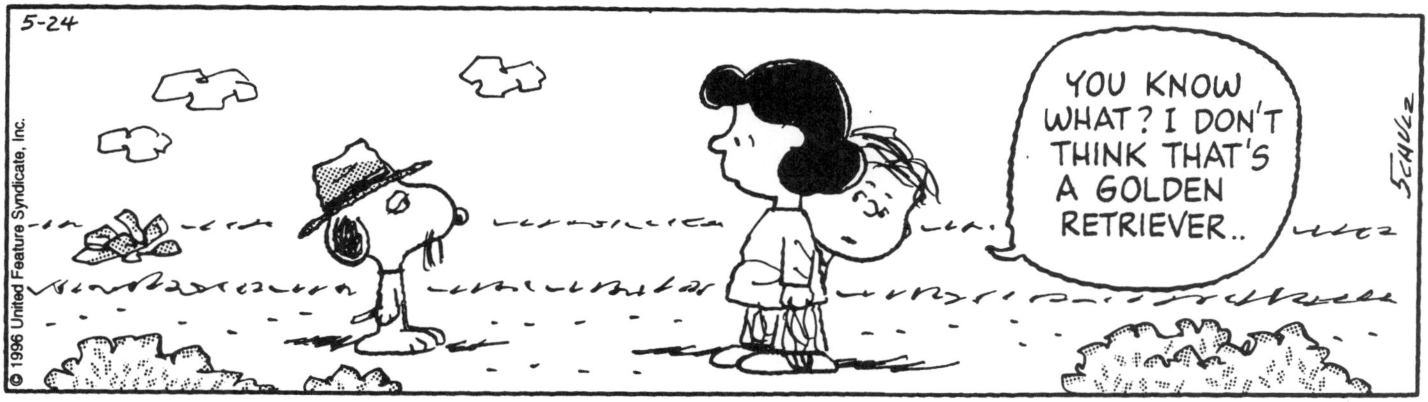
5-24
© 1996 United Feature Syndicate, Inc.
YOU KNOW WHAT? I DON'T THINK THAT'S A GOLDEN RETRIEVER..
SCHULZ

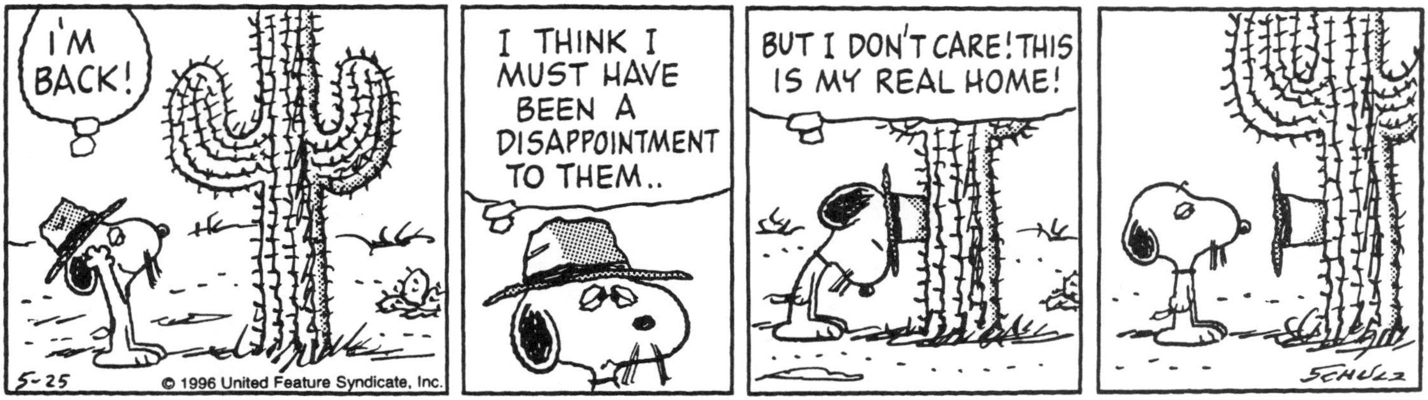
I'M BACK!
5-25
© 1996 United Feature Syndicate, Inc.
I THINK I MUST HAVE BEEN A DISAPPOINTMENT TO THEM..
BUT I DON'T CARE! THIS IS MY REAL HOME!
SCHULZ

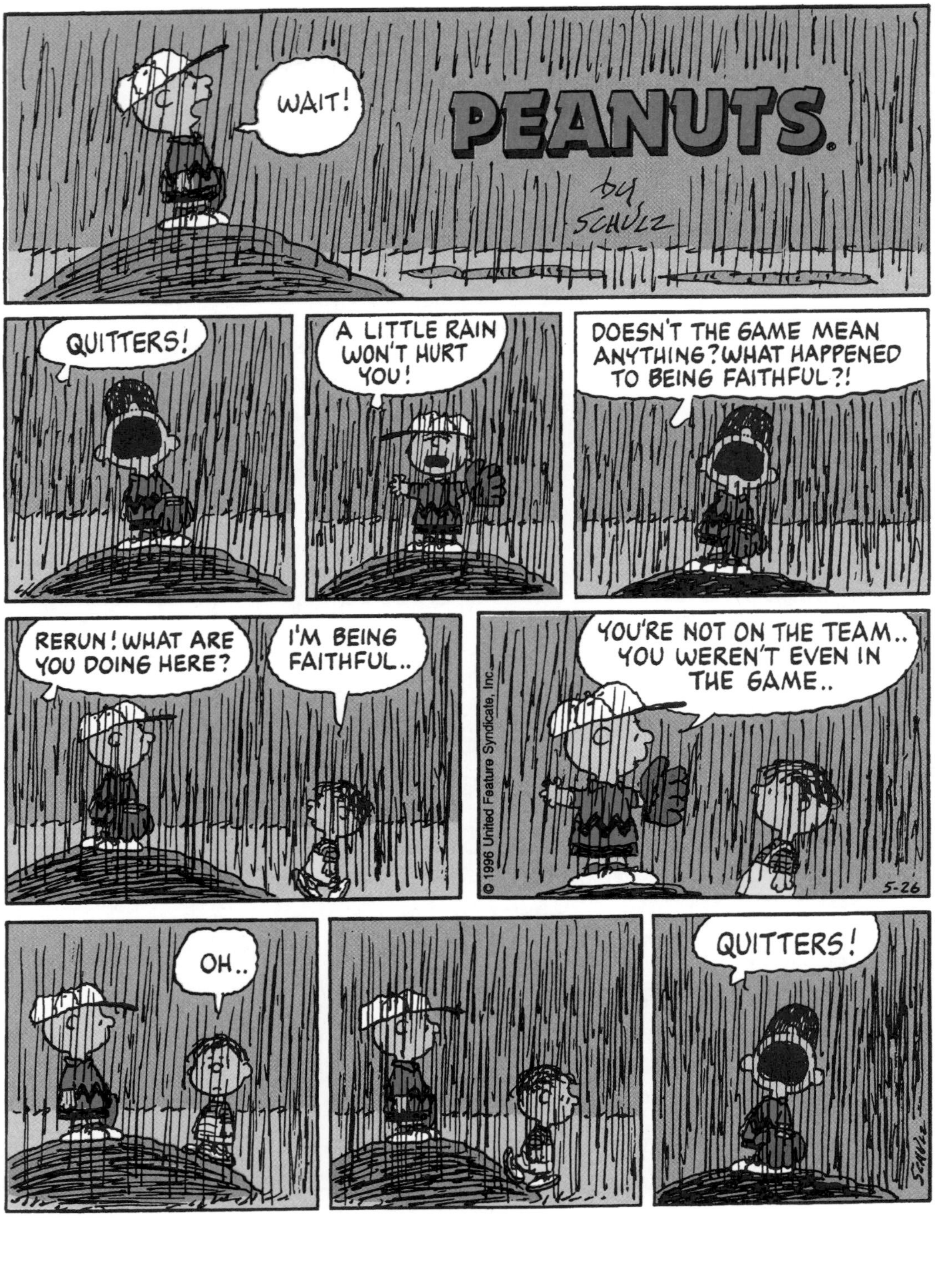
WAIT!
PEANUTS
by SCHULZ
QUITTERS!
A LITTLE RAIN WON'T HURT YOU!
DOESN'T THE GAME MEAN ANYTHING? WHAT HAPPENED TO BEING FAITHFUL?!
RERUN! WHAT ARE YOU DOING HERE?
I'M BEING FAITHFUL..
© 1996 United Feature Syndicate, Inc.
YOU'RE NOT ON THE TEAM.. YOU WEREN'T EVEN IN THE GAME..
5-26
OH..
QUITTERS!

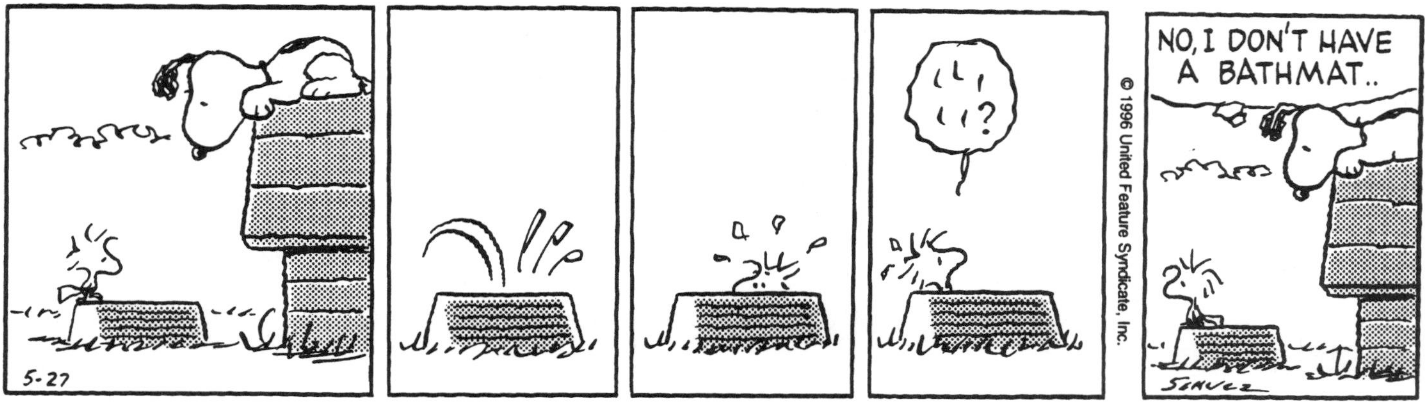
5-27
NO, I DON'T HAVE A BATHMAT..
© 1996 United Feature Syndicate, Inc.
SCHULZ

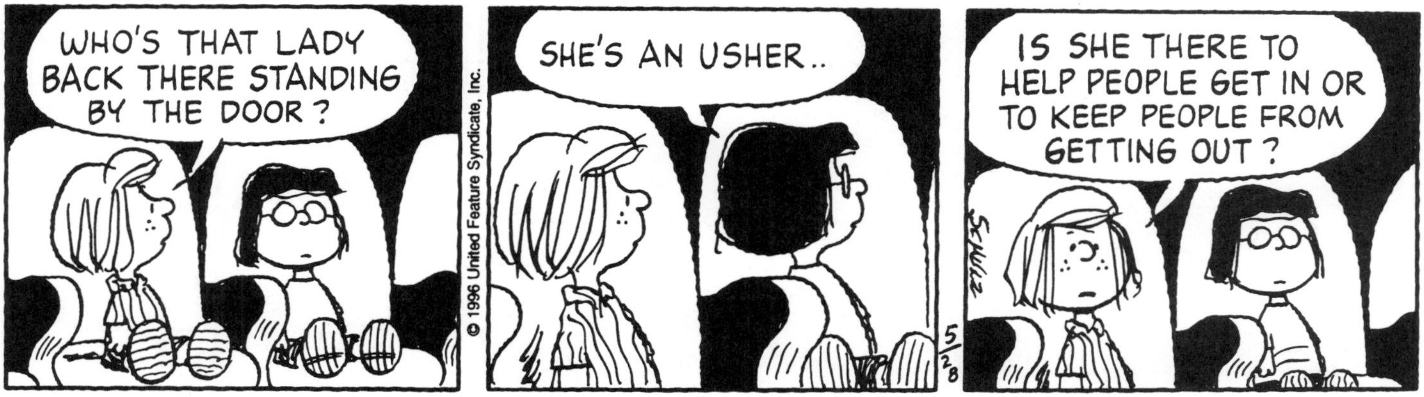
WHO'S THAT LADY BACK THERE STANDING BY THE DOOR ?
© 1996 United Feature Syndicate, Inc.
SHE'S AN USHER..
5/28
IS SHE THERE TO HELP PEOPLE GET IN OR TO KEEP PEOPLE FROM GETTING OUT ?
SCHULZ

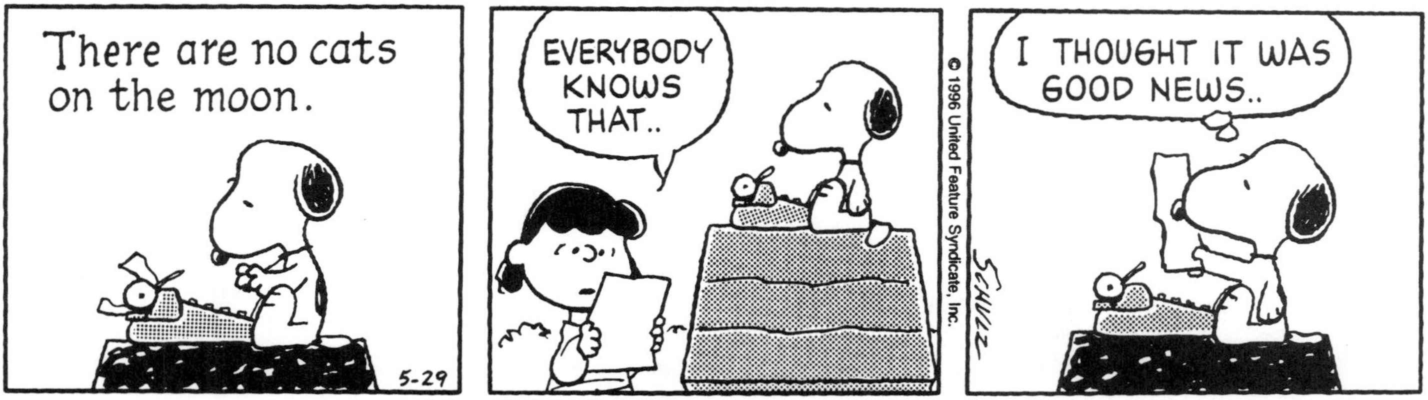
There are no cats on the moon.
5-29
EVERYBODY KNOWS THAT..
© 1996 United Feature Syndicate, Inc.
SCHULZ
I THOUGHT IT WAS GOOD NEWS..

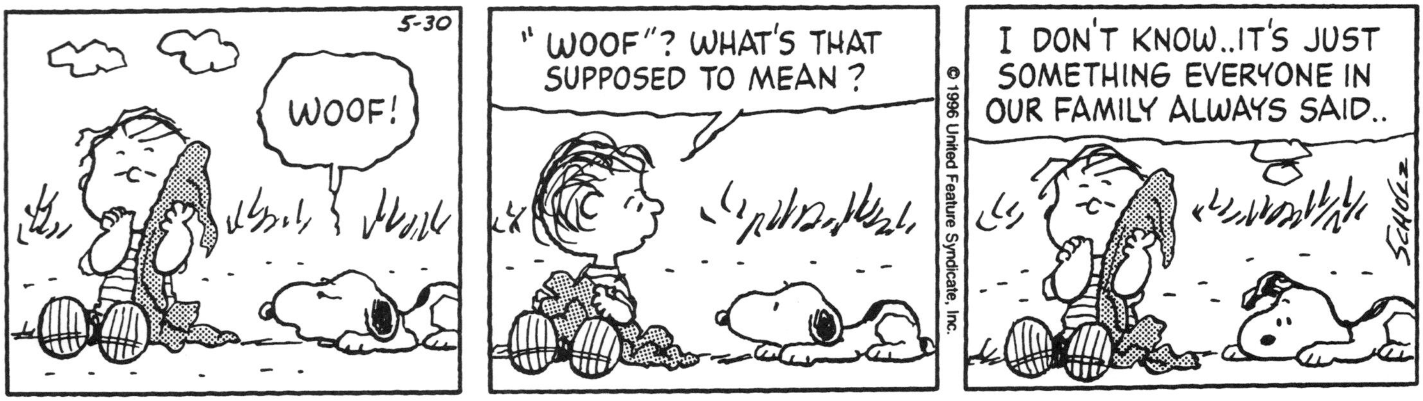
5-30
WOOF!
" WOOF"? WHAT'S THAT SUPPOSED TO MEAN ?
© 1996 United Feature Syndicate, Inc.
I DON'T KNOW..IT'S JUST SOMETHING EVERYONE IN OUR FAMILY ALWAYS SAID..
SCHULZ

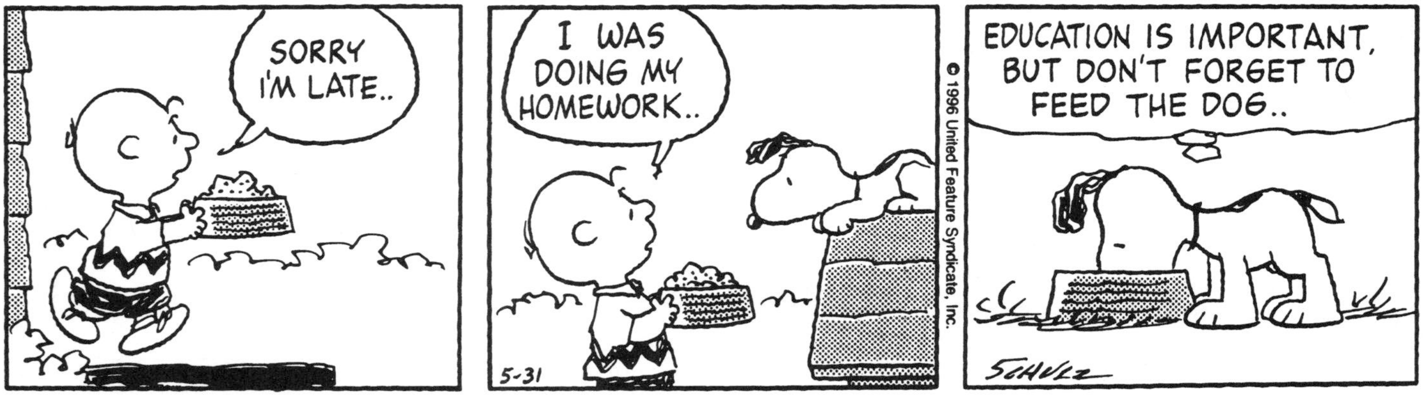
SORRY I'M LATE..
I WAS DOING MY HOMEWORK..
5-31
© 1996 United Feature Syndicate, Inc.
EDUCATION IS IMPORTANT, BUT DON'T FORGET TO FEED THE DOG..
SCHULZ

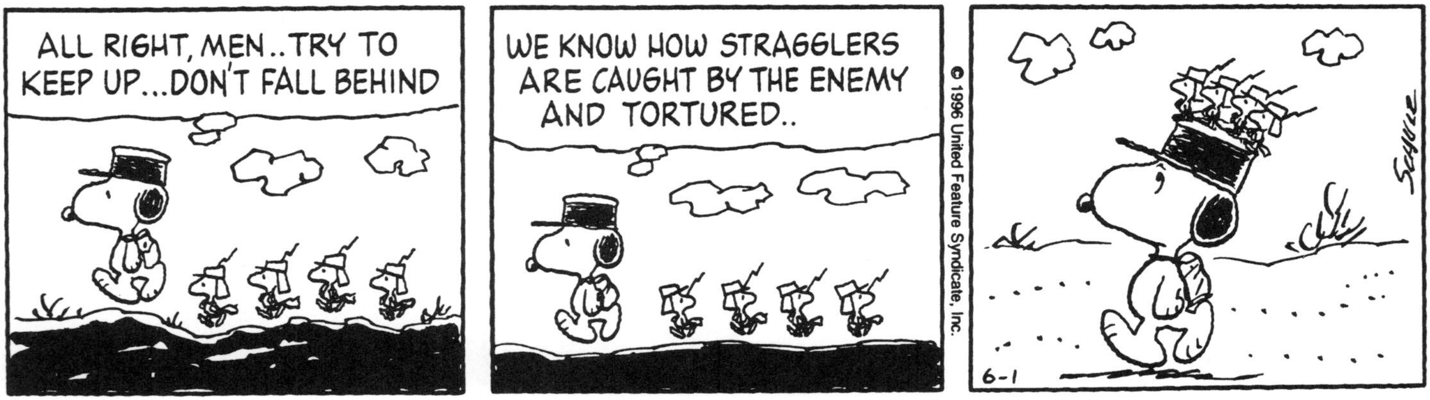
ALL RIGHT, MEN..TRY TO KEEP UP...DON'T FALL BEHIND
WE KNOW HOW STRAGGLERS ARE CAUGHT BY THE ENEMY AND TORTURED..
© 1996 United Feature Syndicate, Inc.
SCHULZ
6-1

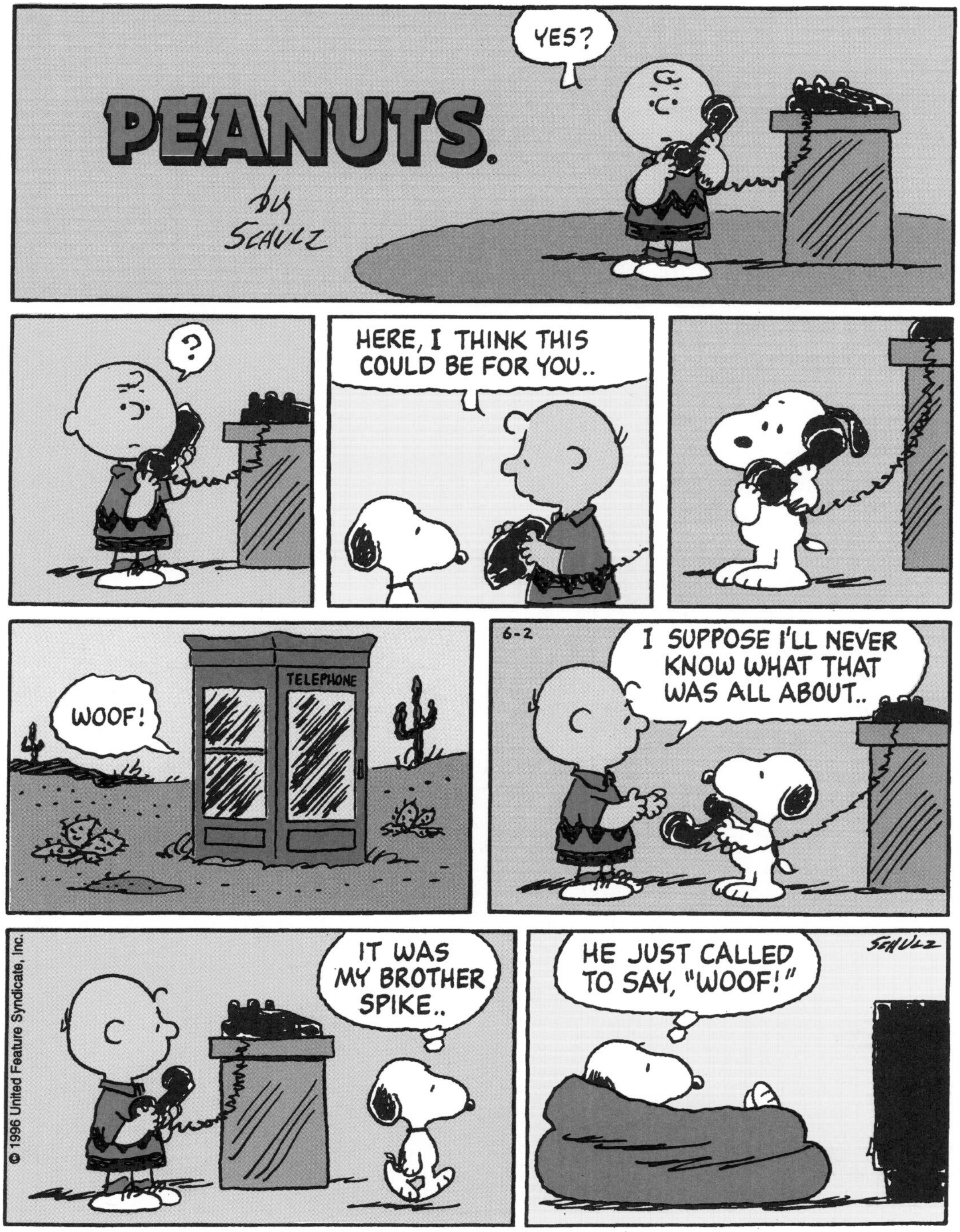
PEANUTS.
by SCHULZ
YES?
?
HERE, I THINK THIS COULD BE FOR YOU..
WOOF!
TELEPHONE
6-2
I SUPPOSE I'LL NEVER KNOW WHAT THAT WAS ALL ABOUT..
© 1996 United Feature Syndicate, Inc.
IT WAS MY BROTHER SPIKE..
SCHULZ
HE JUST CALLED TO SAY, "WOOF!"

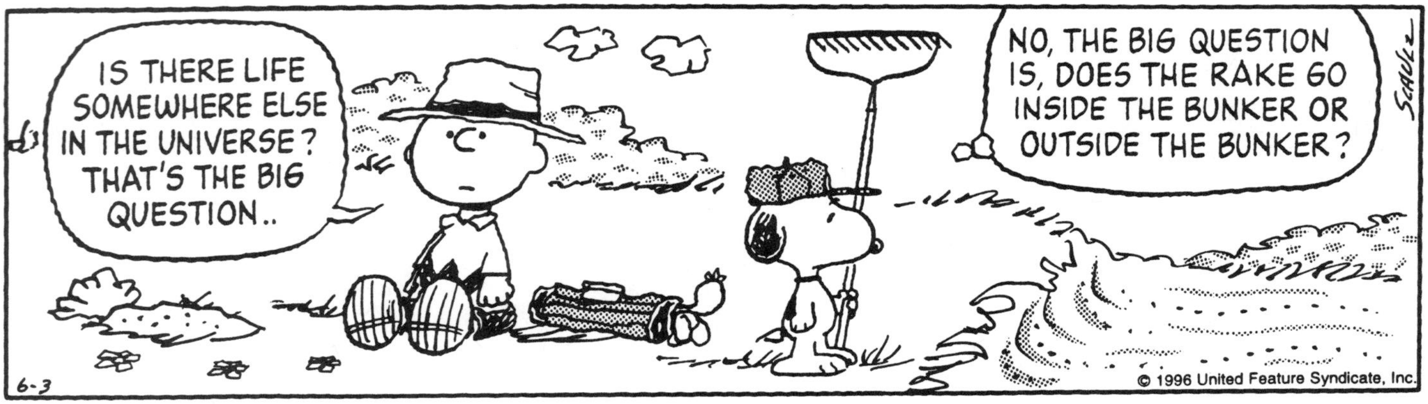
IS THERE LIFE SOMEWHERE ELSE IN THE UNIVERSE? THAT'S THE BIG QUESTION..
NO, THE BIG QUESTION IS, DOES THE RAKE GO INSIDE THE BUNKER OR OUTSIDE THE BUNKER?
SCHULZ
6-3
© 1996 United Feature Syndicate, Inc.

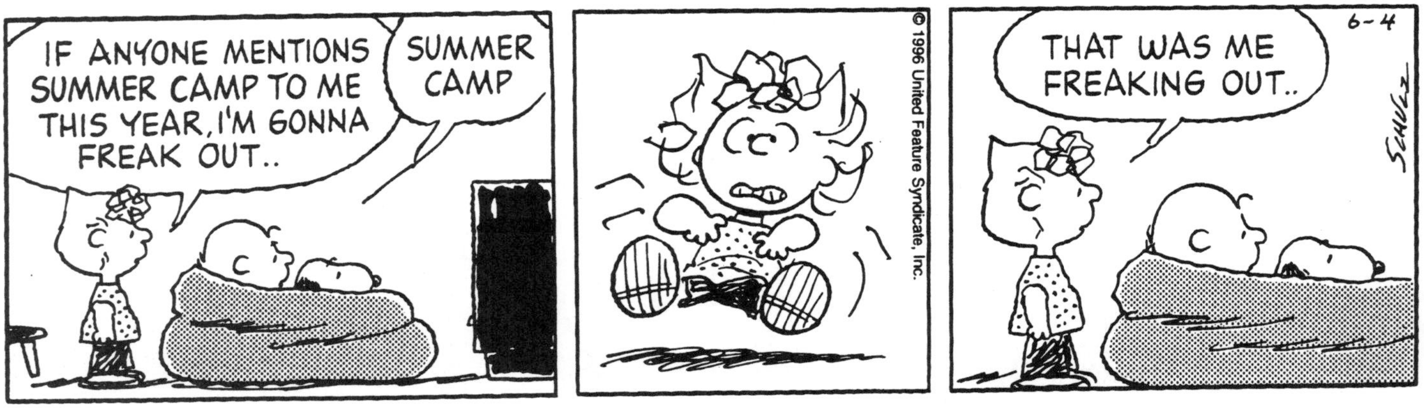
IF ANYONE MENTIONS SUMMER CAMP TO ME THIS YEAR, I'M GONNA FREAK OUT..
SUMMER CAMP
© 1996 United Feature Syndicate, Inc.
THAT WAS ME FREAKING OUT..
6-4
SCHULZ

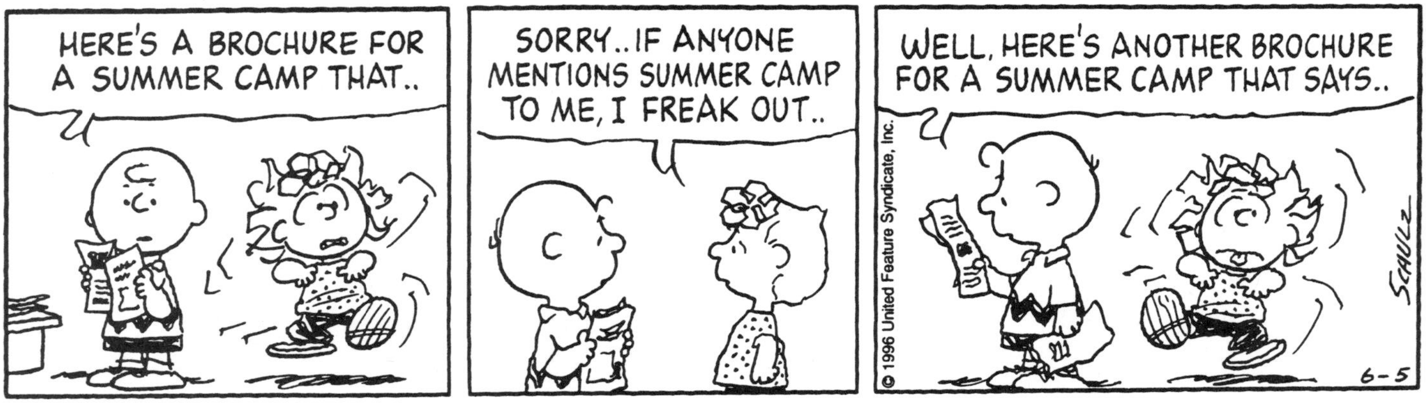
HERE'S A BROCHURE FOR A SUMMER CAMP THAT..
SORRY.. IF ANYONE MENTIONS SUMMER CAMP TO ME, I FREAK OUT..
© 1996 United Feature Syndicate, Inc.
WELL, HERE'S ANOTHER BROCHURE FOR A SUMMER CAMP THAT SAYS..
SCHULZ
6-5

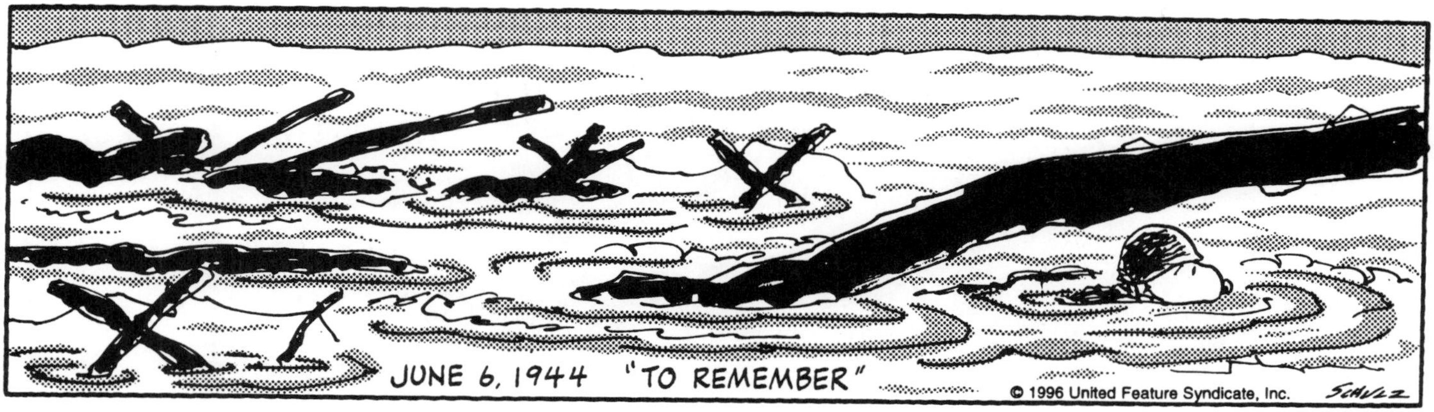
JUNE 6, 1944 "TO REMEMBER"
© 1996 United Feature Syndicate, Inc.
SCHULZ

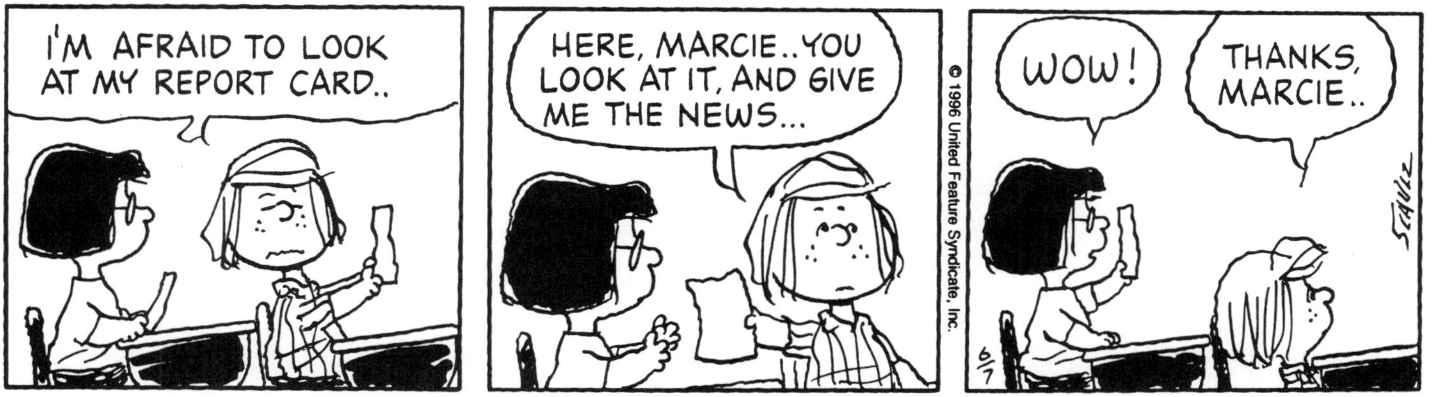
I'M AFRAID TO LOOK AT MY REPORT CARD..
HERE, MARCIE..YOU LOOK AT IT, AND GIVE ME THE NEWS...
© 1996 United Feature Syndicate, Inc.
WOW!
THANKS, MARCIE..
SCHULZ
6/7

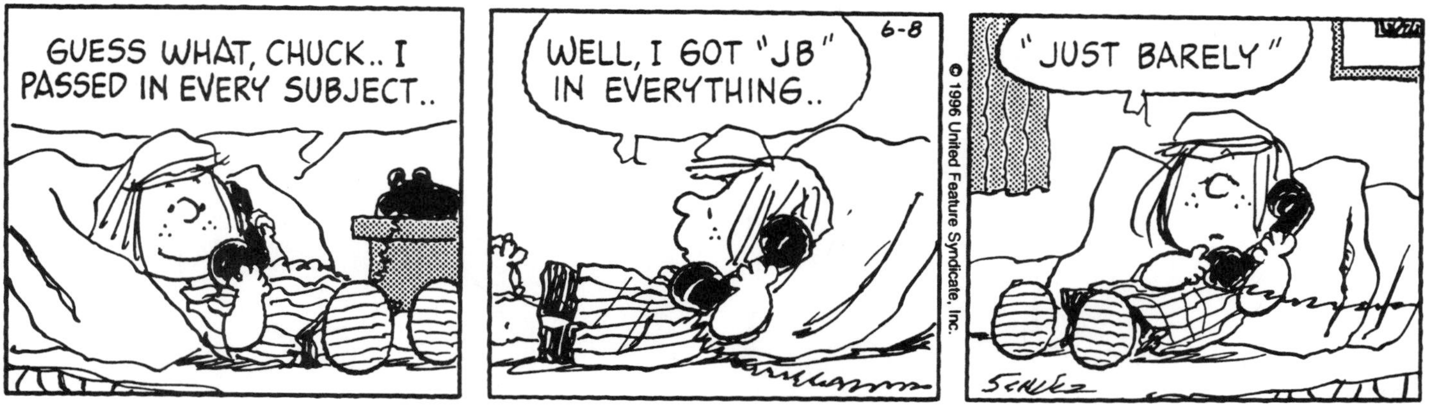
GUESS WHAT, CHUCK.. I PASSED IN EVERY SUBJECT..
6-8
WELL, I GOT "JB" IN EVERYTHING..
© 1996 United Feature Syndicate, Inc.
"JUST BARELY"
SCHULZ

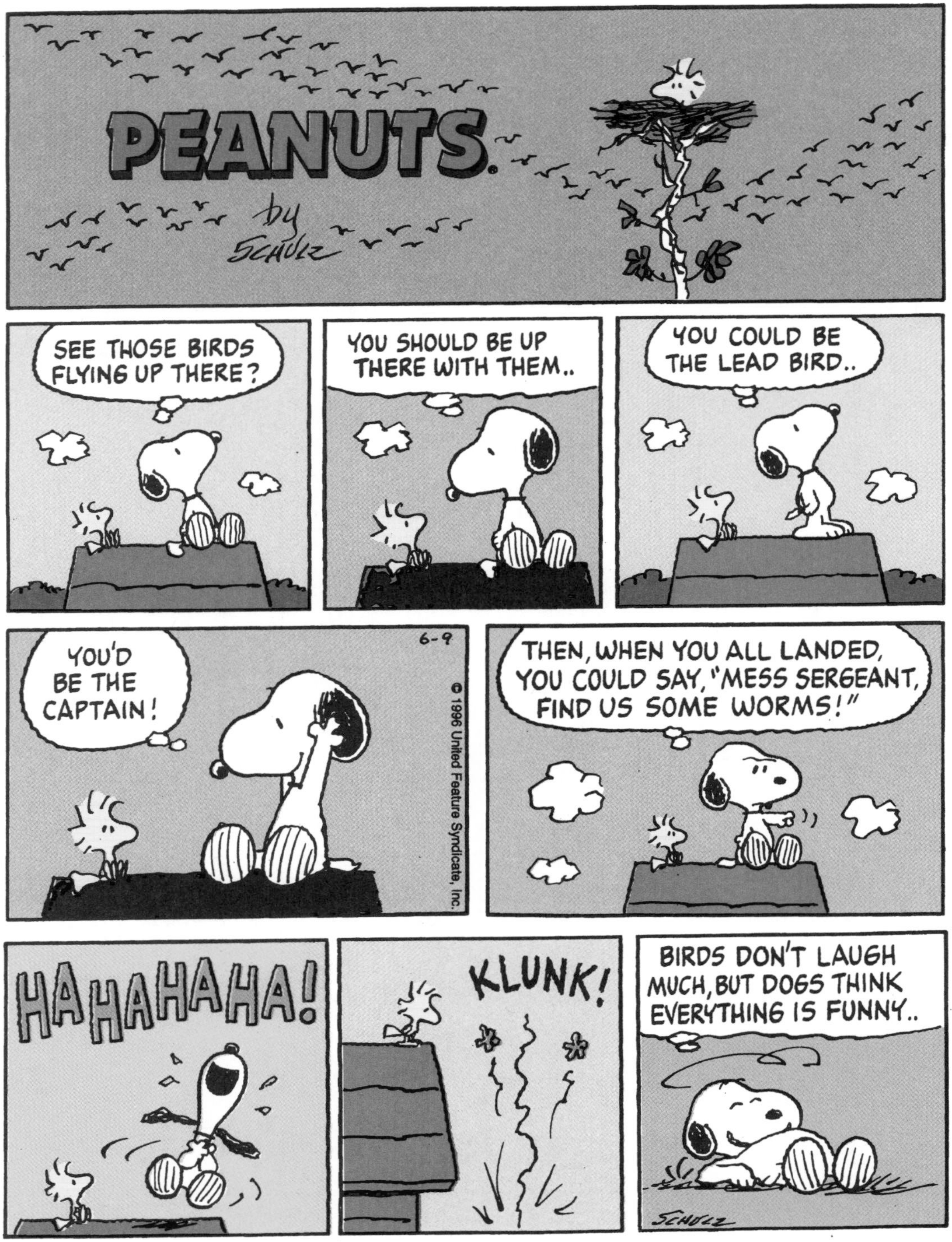
PEANUTS
by SCHULZ
SEE THOSE BIRDS FLYING UP THERE?
YOU SHOULD BE UP THERE WITH THEM..
YOU COULD BE THE LEAD BIRD..
6-9
YOU'D BE THE CAPTAIN!
© 1996 United Feature Syndicate, Inc.
THEN, WHEN YOU ALL LANDED, YOU COULD SAY, "MESS SERGEANT, FIND US SOME WORMS!"
HAHAHAHAHA!
KLUNK!
BIRDS DON'T LAUGH MUCH, BUT DOGS THINK EVERYTHING IS FUNNY..
SCHULZ

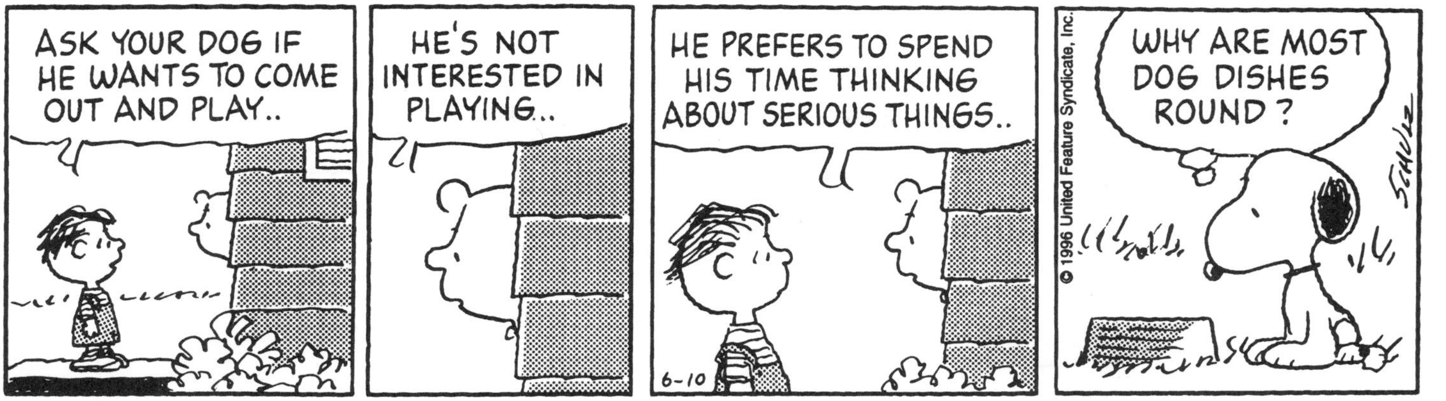
ASK YOUR DOG IF HE WANTS TO COME OUT AND PLAY..
HE'S NOT INTERESTED IN PLAYING..
HE PREFERS TO SPEND HIS TIME THINKING ABOUT SERIOUS THINGS..
6-10
© 1996 United Feature Syndicate, Inc.
WHY ARE MOST DOG DISHES ROUND ?
SCHULZ

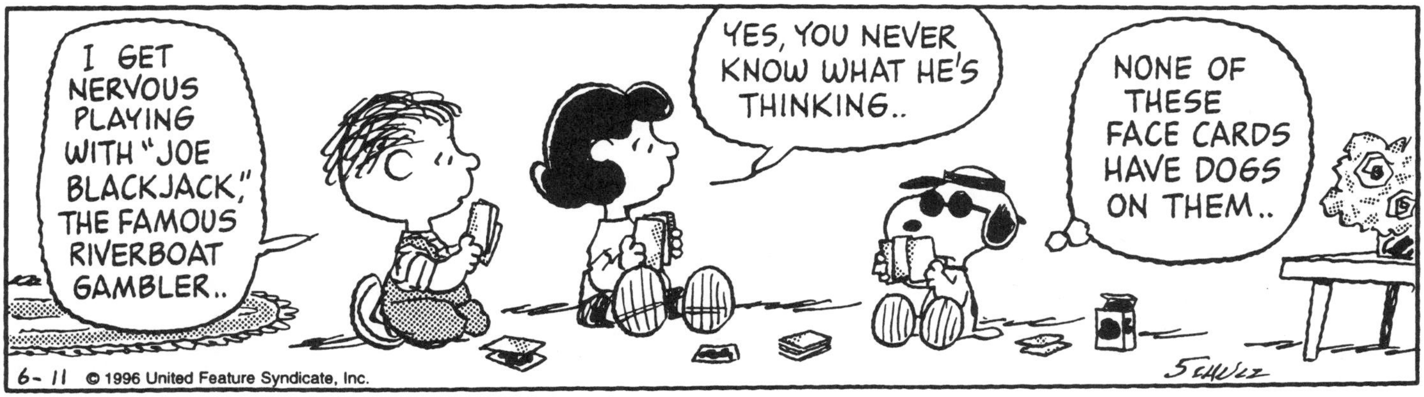
I GET NERVOUS PLAYING WITH "JOE BLACKJACK," THE FAMOUS RIVERBOAT GAMBLER..
YES, YOU NEVER KNOW WHAT HE'S THINKING..
NONE OF THESE FACE CARDS HAVE DOGS ON THEM..
6-11 © 1996 United Feature Syndicate, Inc.
SCHULZ

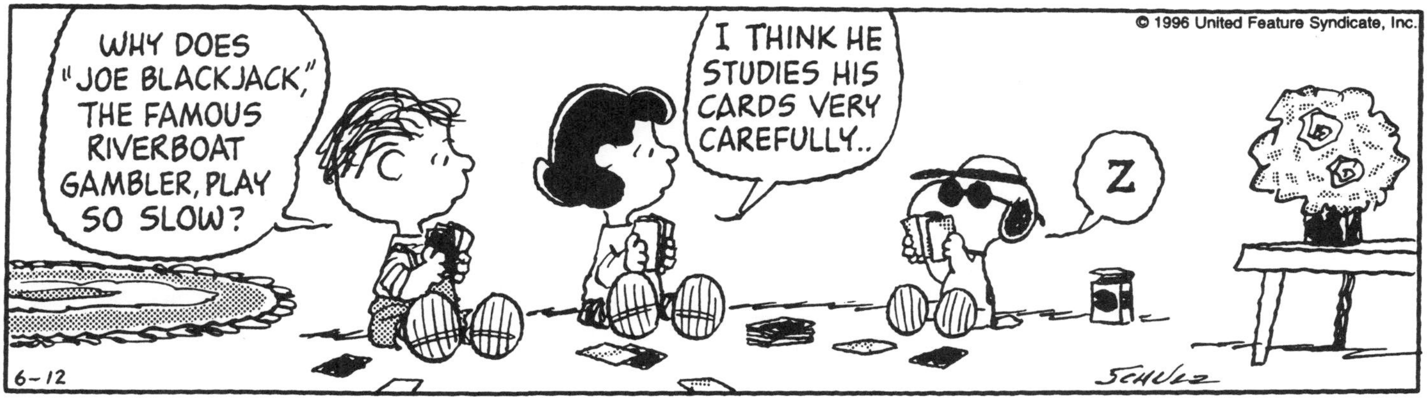
© 1996 United Feature Syndicate, Inc.
WHY DOES "JOE BLACKJACK," THE FAMOUS RIVERBOAT GAMBLER, PLAY SO SLOW?
I THINK HE STUDIES HIS CARDS VERY CAREFULLY..
Z
6-12
SCHULZ

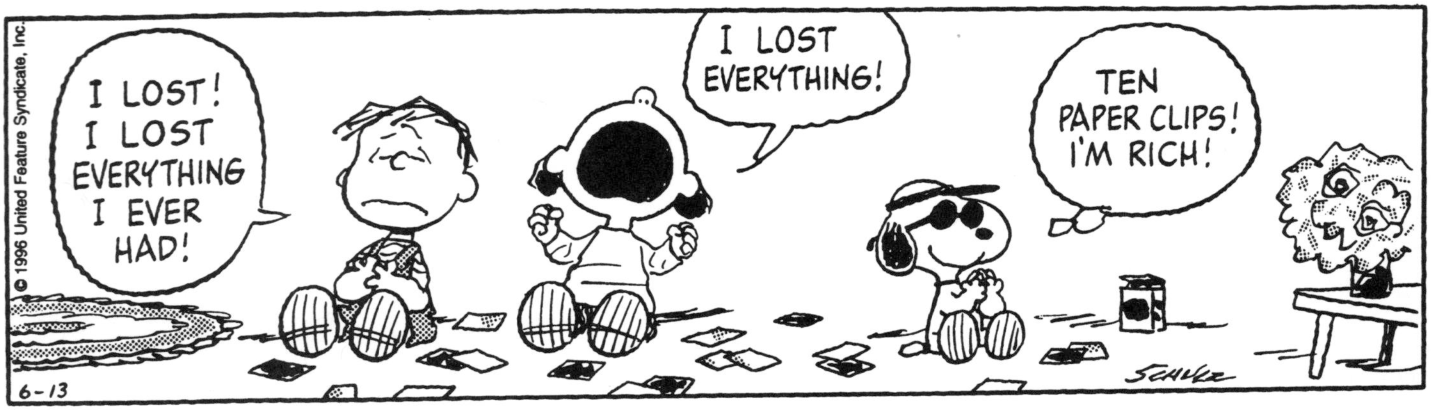
© 1996 United Feature Syndicate, Inc.
I LOST! I LOST EVERYTHING I EVER HAD!
I LOST EVERYTHING!
TEN PAPER CLIPS! I'M RICH!
6-13

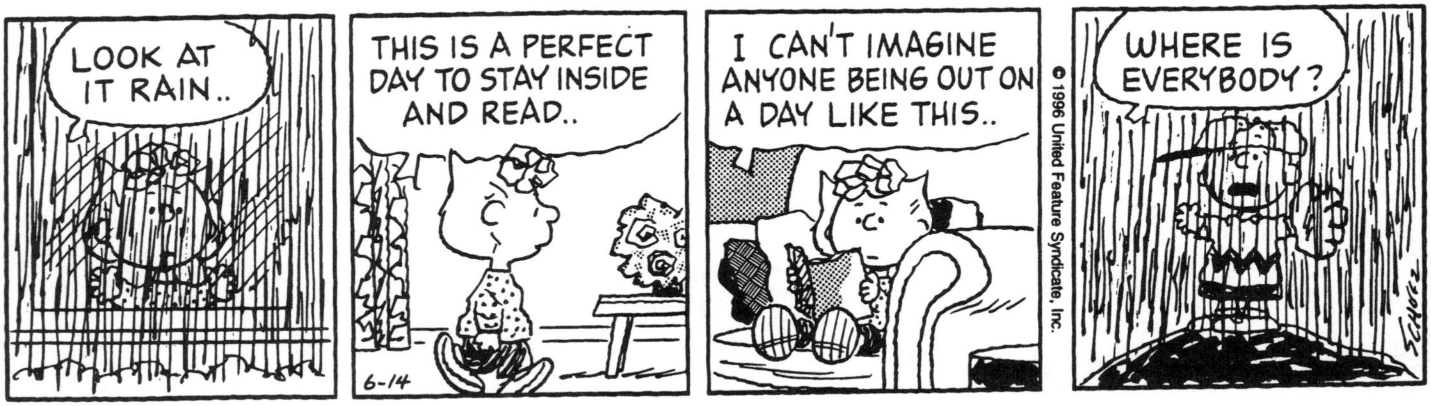
LOOK AT IT RAIN..
THIS IS A PERFECT DAY TO STAY INSIDE AND READ..
6-14
I CAN'T IMAGINE ANYONE BEING OUT ON A DAY LIKE THIS..
© 1996 United Feature Syndicate, Inc.
WHERE IS EVERYBODY?

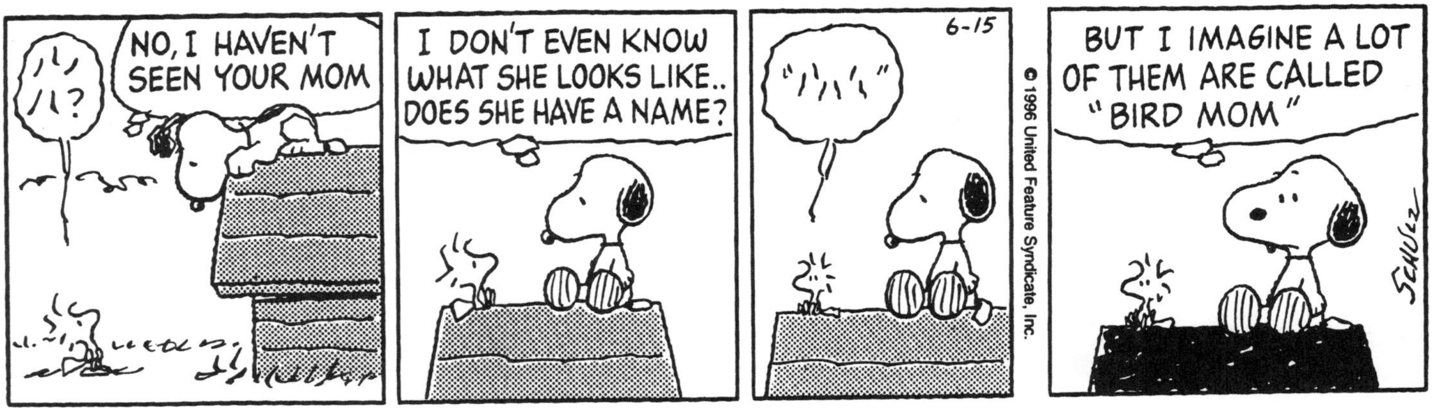
NO, I HAVEN'T SEEN YOUR MOM
I DON'T EVEN KNOW WHAT SHE LOOKS LIKE.. DOES SHE HAVE A NAME?
6-15
© 1996 United Feature Syndicate, Inc.
BUT I IMAGINE A LOT OF THEM ARE CALLED "BIRD MOM"

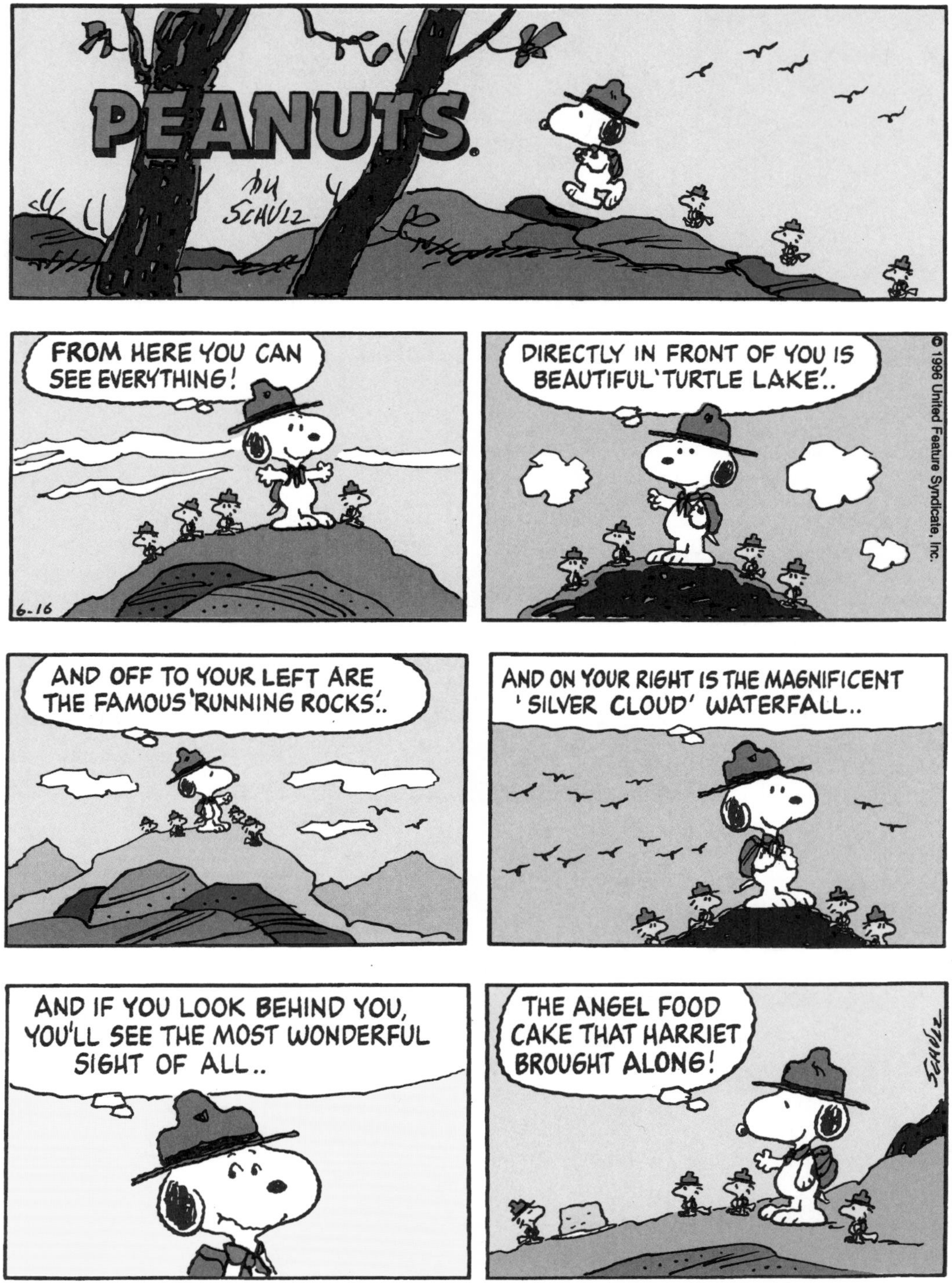
PEANUTS
by SCHULZ
FROM HERE YOU CAN SEE EVERYTHING!
6-16
DIRECTLY IN FRONT OF YOU IS BEAUTIFUL 'TURTLE LAKE'..
© 1996 United Feature Syndicate, Inc.
AND OFF TO YOUR LEFT ARE THE FAMOUS 'RUNNING ROCKS'..
AND ON YOUR RIGHT IS THE MAGNIFICENT 'SILVER CLOUD' WATERFALL..
AND IF YOU LOOK BEHIND YOU, YOU'LL SEE THE MOST WONDERFUL SIGHT OF ALL..
THE ANGEL FOOD CAKE THAT HARRIET BROUGHT ALONG!
SCHULZ

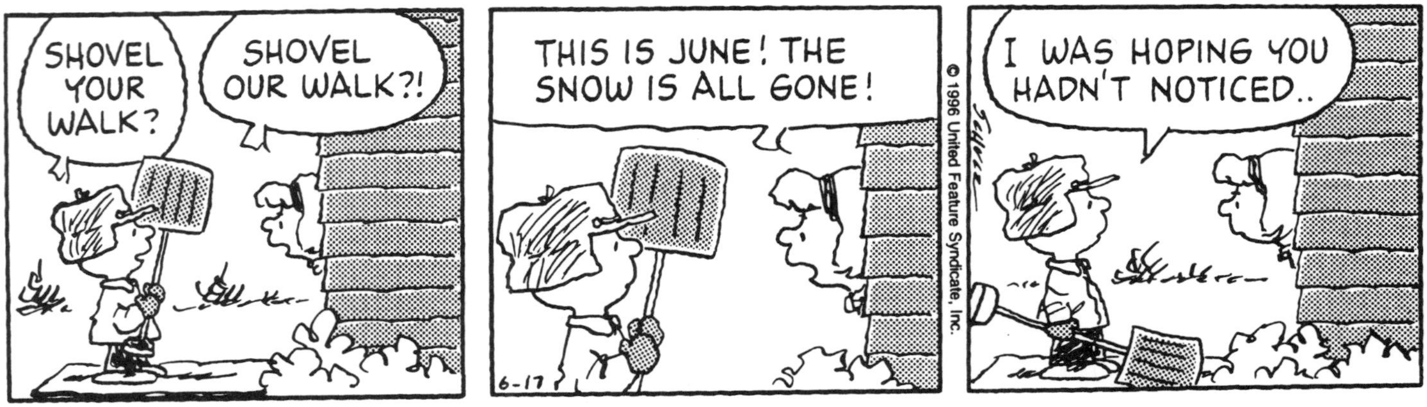
SHOVEL YOUR WALK?
SHOVEL OUR WALK?!
THIS IS JUNE! THE SNOW IS ALL GONE!
I WAS HOPING YOU HADN'T NOTICED..
6-17
© 1996 United Feature Syndicate, Inc.
SCHULZ

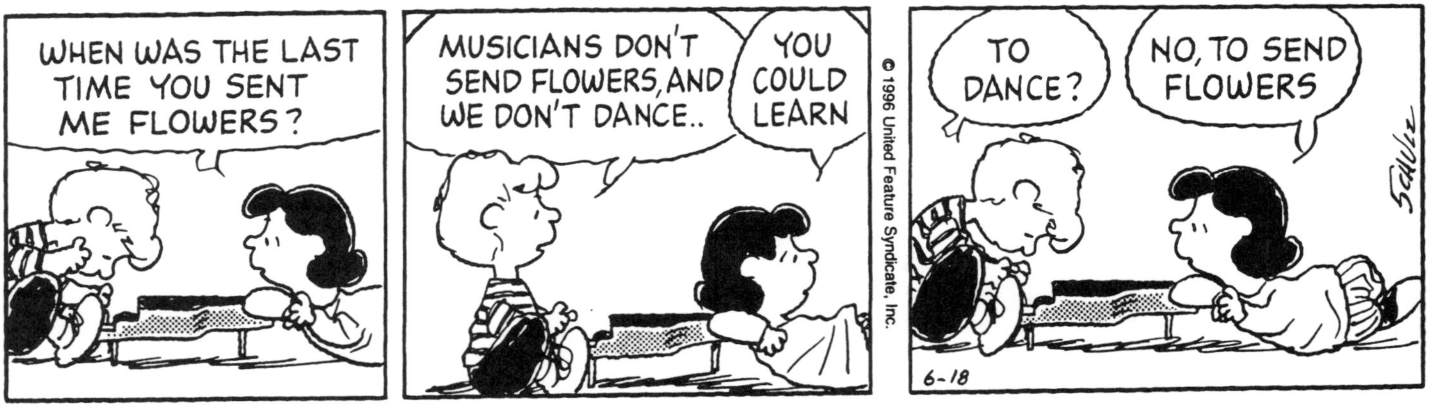
WHEN WAS THE LAST TIME YOU SENT ME FLOWERS?
MUSICIANS DON'T SEND FLOWERS, AND WE DON'T DANCE..
YOU COULD LEARN
TO DANCE?
NO, TO SEND FLOWERS
6-18
© 1996 United Feature Syndicate, Inc.
SCHULZ

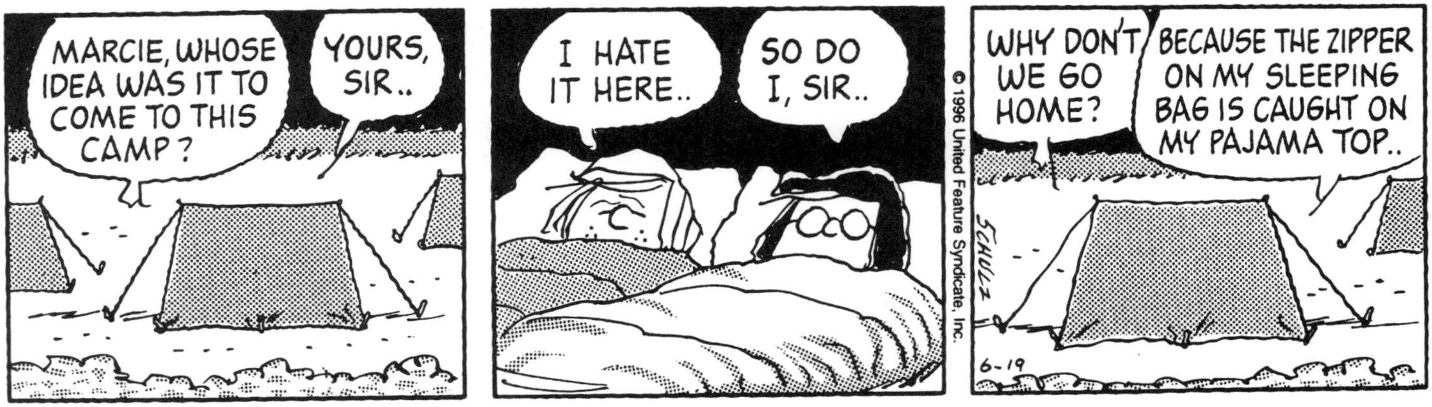
MARCIE, WHOSE IDEA WAS IT TO COME TO THIS CAMP?
YOURS, SIR..
I HATE IT HERE..
SO DO I, SIR..
WHY DON'T WE GO HOME?
BECAUSE THE ZIPPER ON MY SLEEPING BAG IS CAUGHT ON MY PAJAMA TOP..
6-19
© 1996 United Feature Syndicate, Inc.
SCHULZ

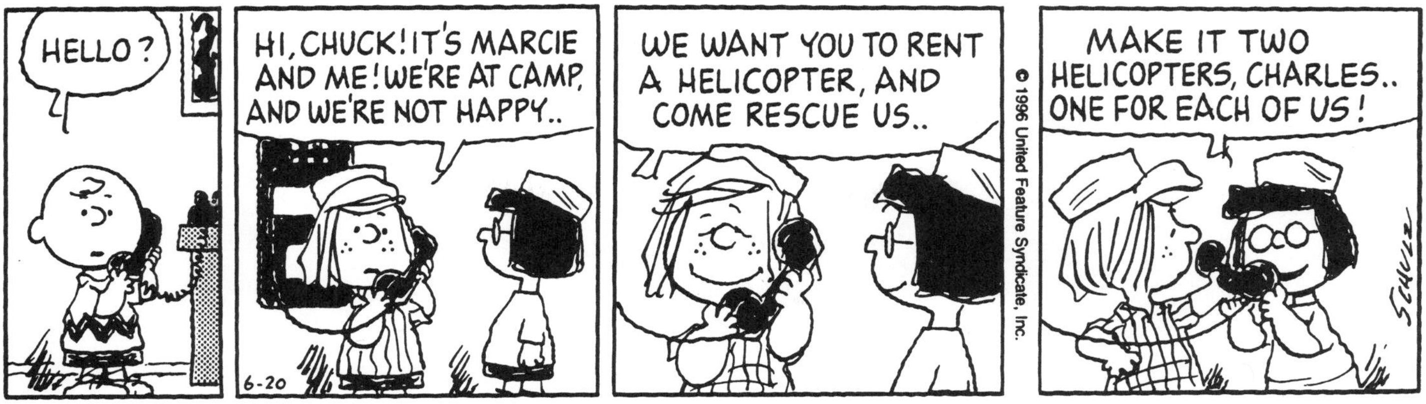
HELLO?
HI, CHUCK! IT'S MARCIE AND ME! WE'RE AT CAMP, AND WE'RE NOT HAPPY..
WE WANT YOU TO RENT A HELICOPTER, AND COME RESCUE US..
MAKE IT TWO HELICOPTERS, CHARLES.. ONE FOR EACH OF US!
6-20
© 1996 United Feature Syndicate, Inc.
SCHULZ

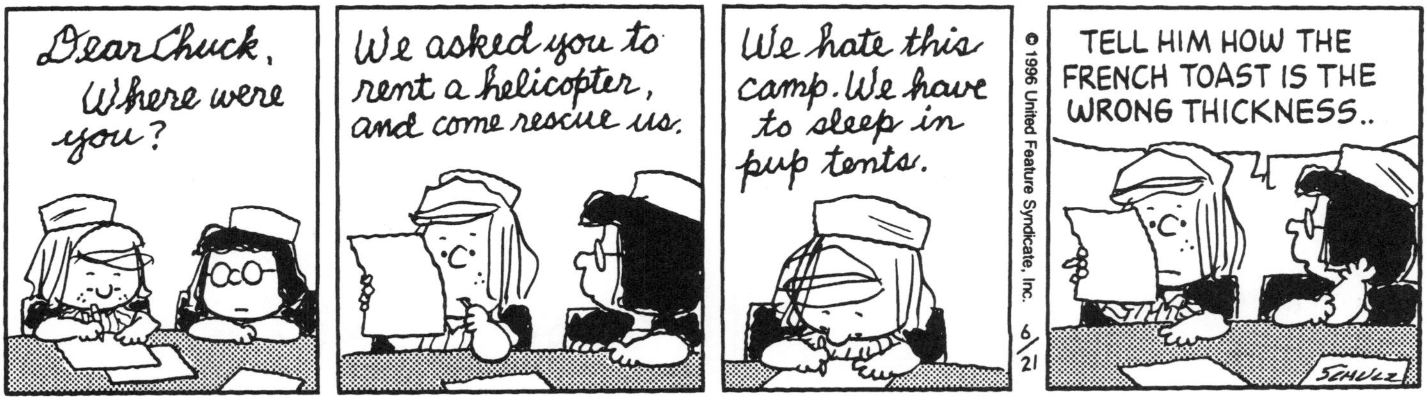
Dear Chuck, Where were you?
We asked you to rent a helicopter, and come rescue us.
We hate this camp. We have to sleep in pup tents.
TELL HIM HOW THE FRENCH TOAST IS THE WRONG THICKNESS..
6/21
© 1996 United Feature Syndicate, Inc.
SCHULZ

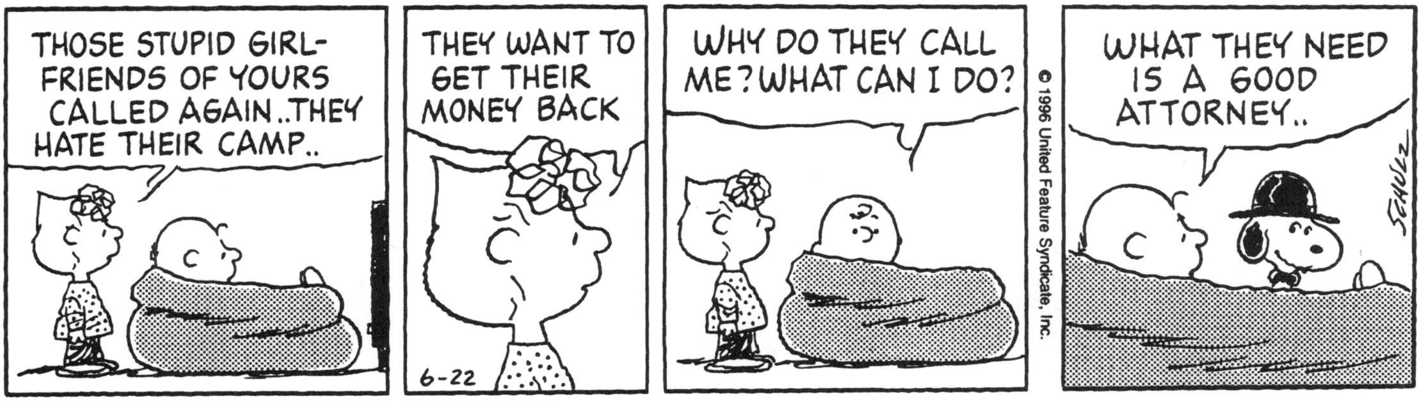
THOSE STUPID GIRL-FRIENDS OF YOURS CALLED AGAIN..THEY HATE THEIR CAMP..
THEY WANT TO GET THEIR MONEY BACK
WHY DO THEY CALL ME? WHAT CAN I DO?
WHAT THEY NEED IS A GOOD ATTORNEY..
6-22
© 1996 United Feature Syndicate, Inc.
SCHULZ

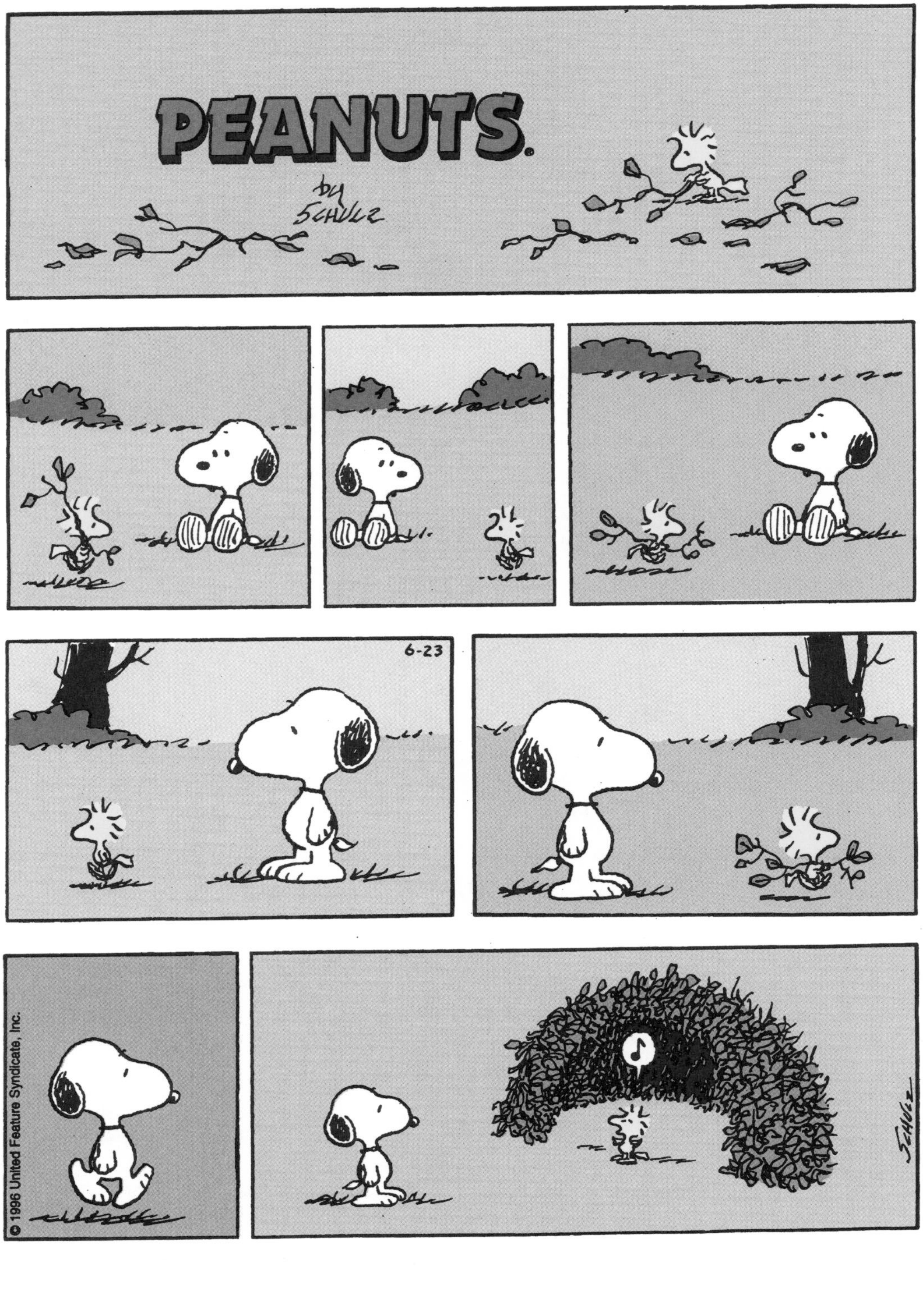
PEANUTS.
by SCHULZ
6-23
© 1996 United Feature Syndicate, Inc.
SCHULZ

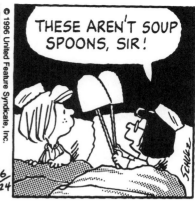

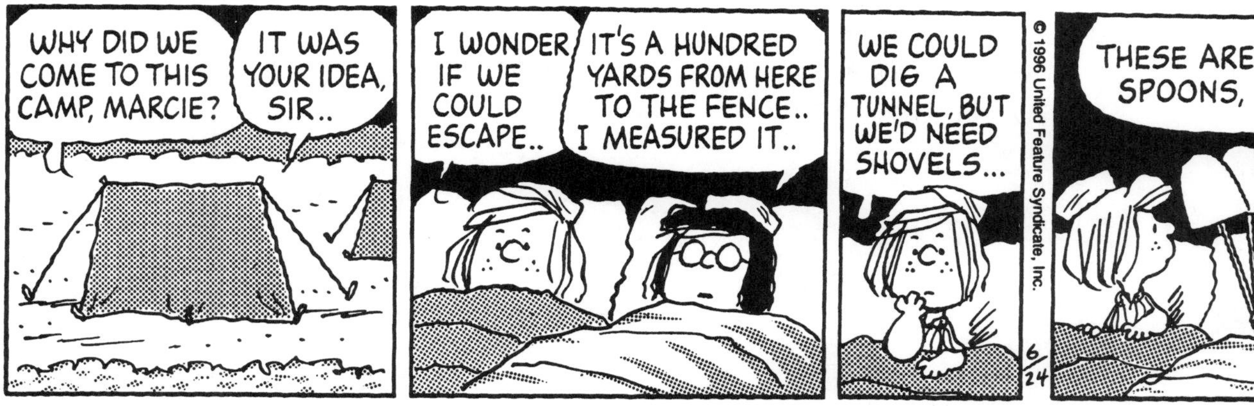
WHY DID WE COME TO THIS CAMP, MARCIE?
IT WAS YOUR IDEA, SIR..
I WONDER IF WE COULD ESCAPE..
IT'S A HUNDRED YARDS FROM HERE TO THE FENCE.. I MEASURED IT..
WE COULD DIG A TUNNEL, BUT WE'D NEED SHOVELS...
© 1996 United Feature Syndicate, Inc.
6/24
THESE AREN'T SOUP SPOONS, SIR!

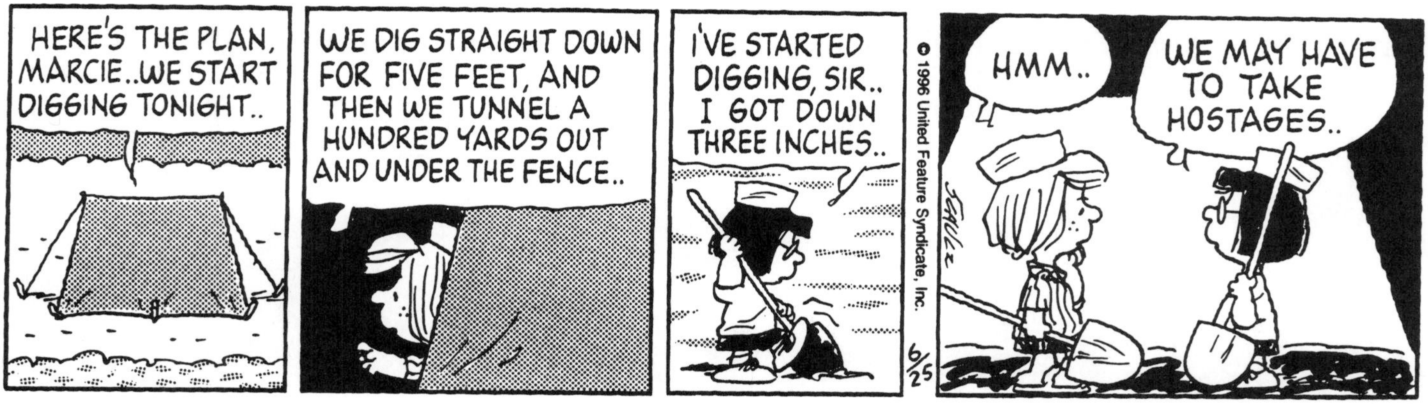
HERE'S THE PLAN, MARCIE..WE START DIGGING TONIGHT..
WE DIG STRAIGHT DOWN FOR FIVE FEET, AND THEN WE TUNNEL A HUNDRED YARDS OUT AND UNDER THE FENCE..
I'VE STARTED DIGGING, SIR.. I GOT DOWN THREE INCHES..
© 1996 United Feature Syndicate, Inc.
6/25
HMM..
WE MAY HAVE TO TAKE HOSTAGES..

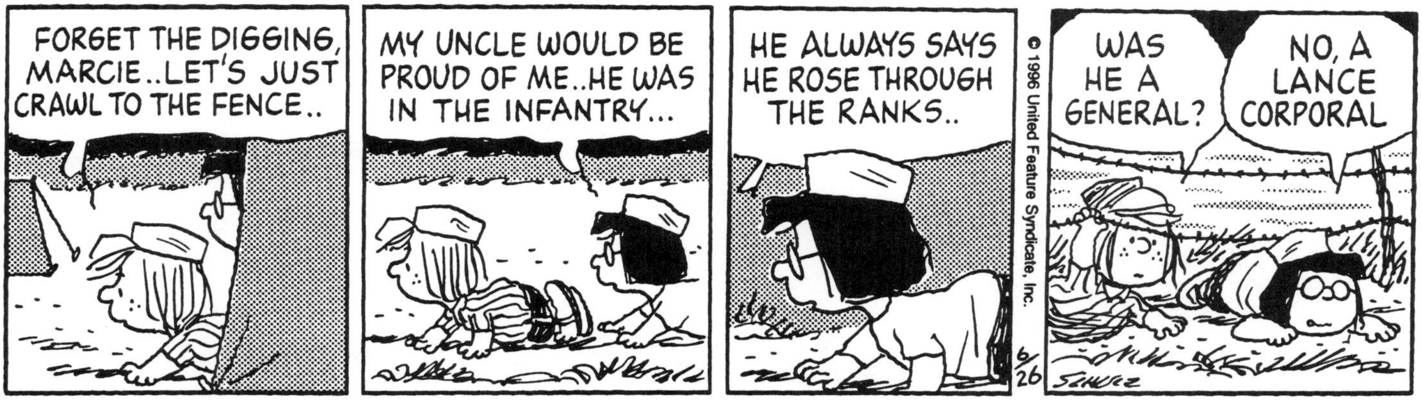
FORGET THE DIGGING, MARCIE..LET'S JUST CRAWL TO THE FENCE..
MY UNCLE WOULD BE PROUD OF ME..HE WAS IN THE INFANTRY...
HE ALWAYS SAYS HE ROSE THROUGH THE RANKS..
© 1996 United Feature Syndicate, Inc.
6/26
WAS HE A GENERAL?
NO, A LANCE CORPORAL

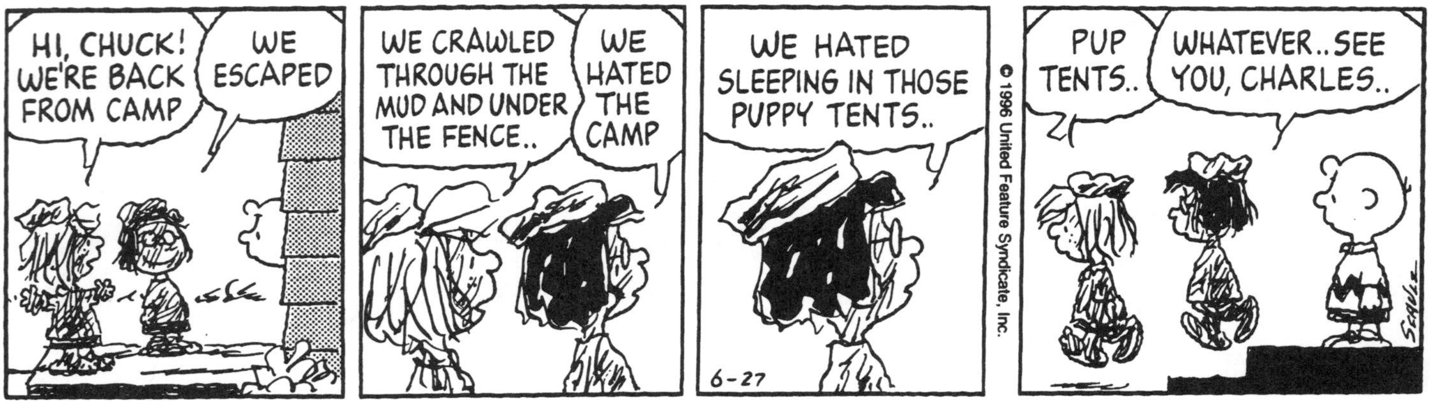
HI, CHUCK! WE'RE BACK FROM CAMP
WE ESCAPED
WE CRAWLED THROUGH THE MUD AND UNDER THE FENCE..
WE HATED THE CAMP
WE HATED SLEEPING IN THOSE PUPPY TENTS..
6-27
© 1996 United Feature Syndicate, Inc.
PUP TENTS..
WHATEVER..SEE YOU, CHARLES..
SCHULZ

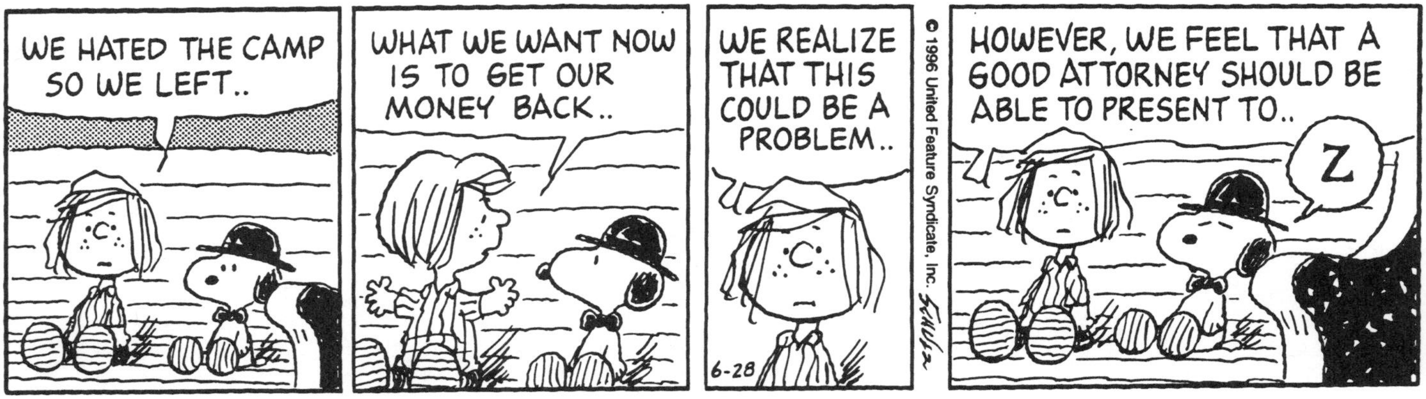
WE HATED THE CAMP SO WE LEFT..
WHAT WE WANT NOW IS TO GET OUR MONEY BACK..
WE REALIZE THAT THIS COULD BE A PROBLEM..
6-28
© 1996 United Feature Syndicate, Inc.
SCHULZ
HOWEVER, WE FEEL THAT A GOOD ATTORNEY SHOULD BE ABLE TO PRESENT TO..
Z

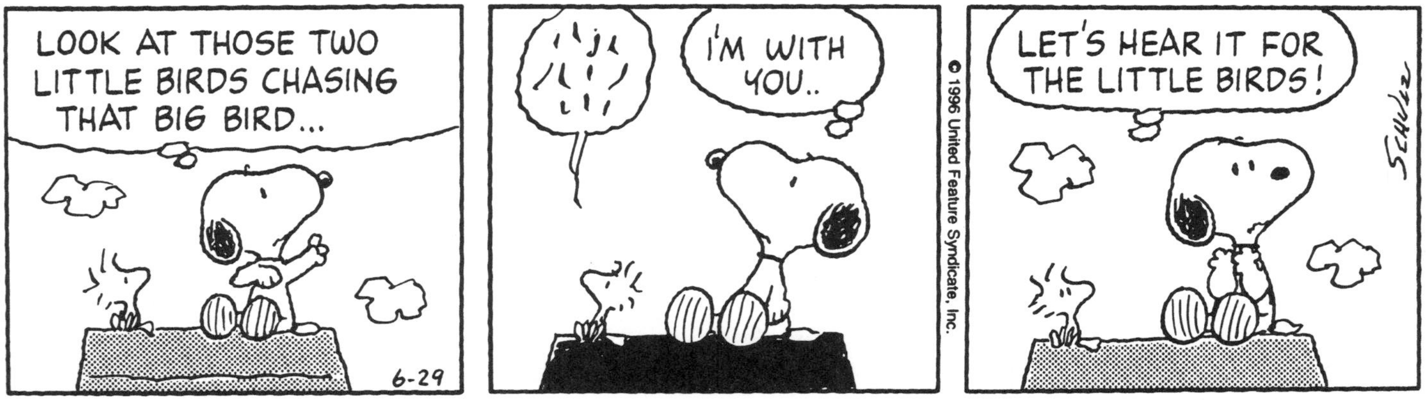
LOOK AT THOSE TWO LITTLE BIRDS CHASING THAT BIG BIRD...
6-29
I'M WITH YOU..
© 1996 United Feature Syndicate, Inc.
LET'S HEAR IT FOR THE LITTLE BIRDS!
SCHULZ

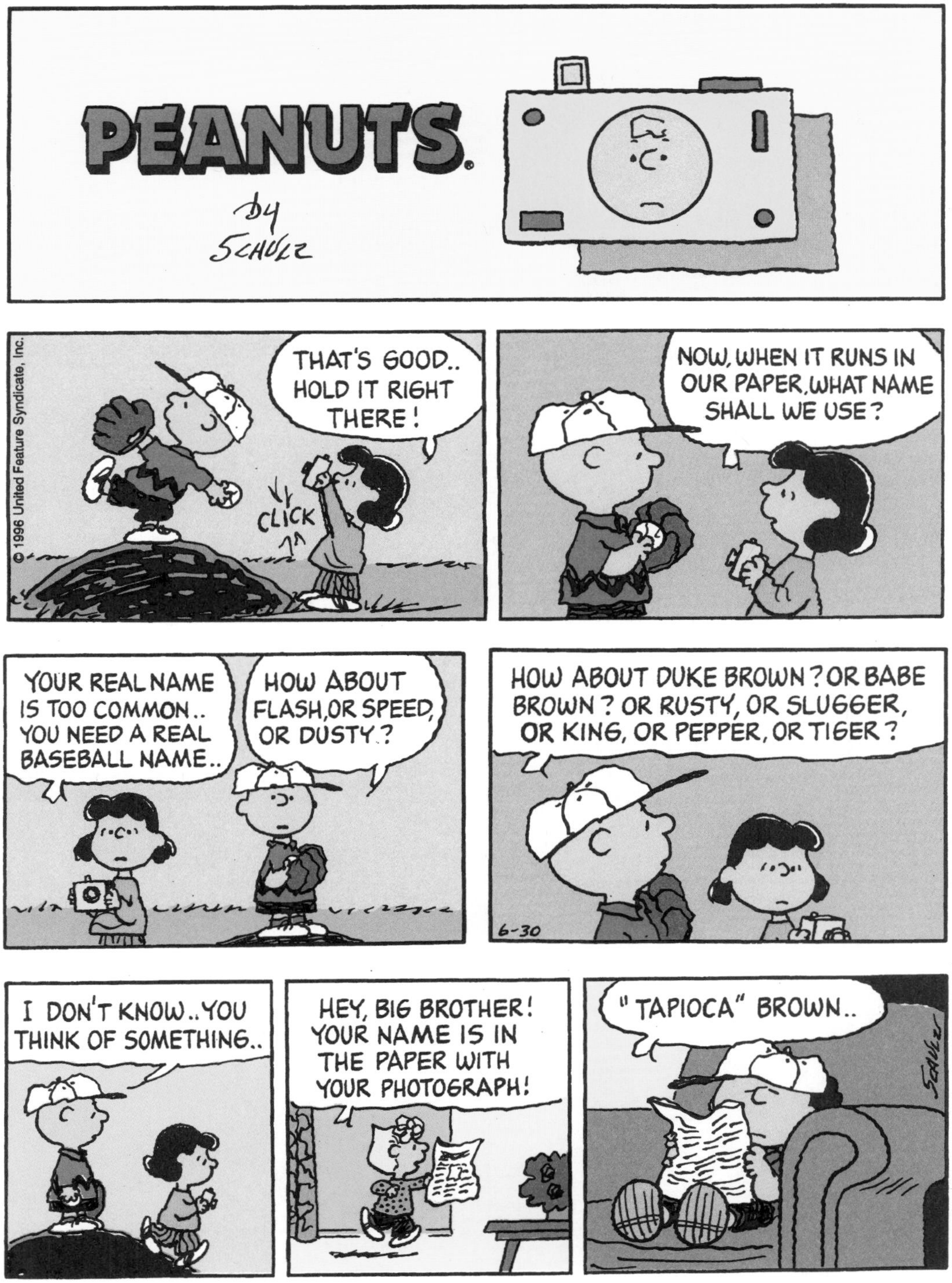
PEANUTS
by SCHULZ
© 1996 United Feature Syndicate, Inc.
THAT'S GOOD.. HOLD IT RIGHT THERE!
CLICK
NOW, WHEN IT RUNS IN OUR PAPER, WHAT NAME SHALL WE USE?
YOUR REAL NAME IS TOO COMMON.. YOU NEED A REAL BASEBALL NAME..
HOW ABOUT FLASH, OR SPEED, OR DUSTY?
HOW ABOUT DUKE BROWN? OR BABE BROWN? OR RUSTY, OR SLUGGER, OR KING, OR PEPPER, OR TIGER?
6-30
I DON'T KNOW.. YOU THINK OF SOMETHING..
HEY, BIG BROTHER! YOUR NAME IS IN THE PAPER WITH YOUR PHOTOGRAPH!
"TAPIOCA" BROWN..
SCHULZ

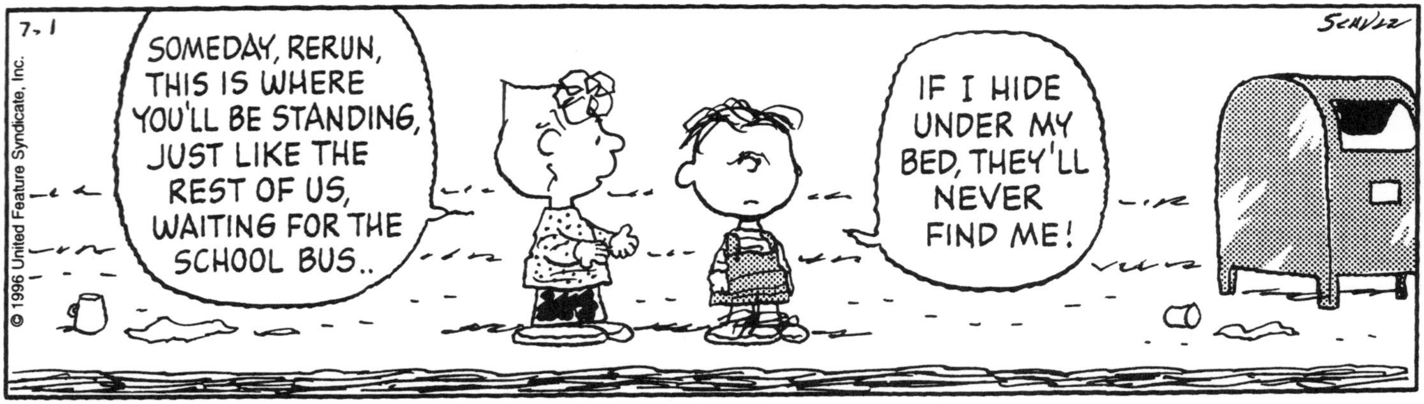
7-1
SOMEDAY, RERUN, THIS IS WHERE YOU'LL BE STANDING, JUST LIKE THE REST OF US, WAITING FOR THE SCHOOL BUS..
IF I HIDE UNDER MY BED, THEY'LL NEVER FIND ME!
© 1996 United Feature Syndicate, Inc.

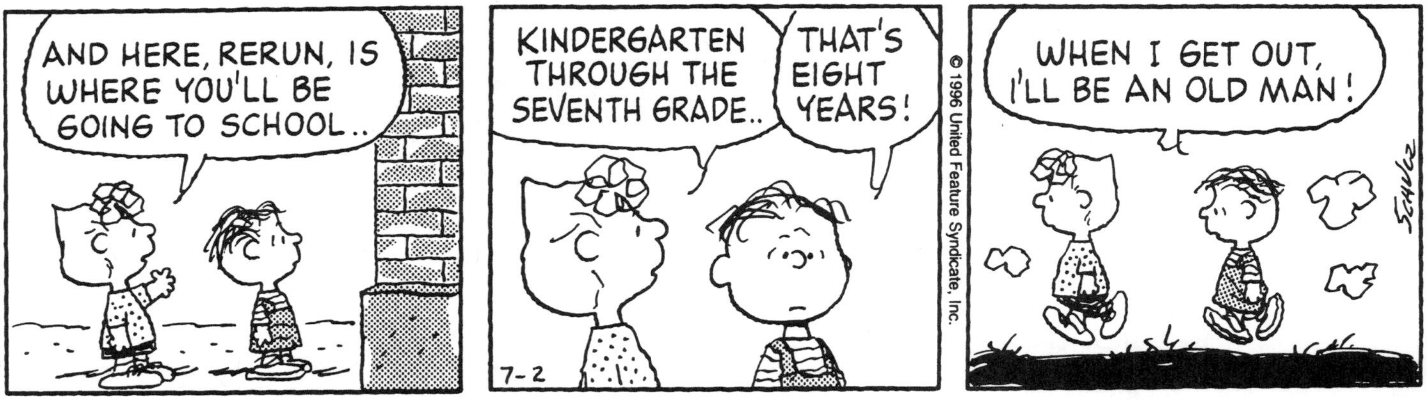
AND HERE, RERUN, IS WHERE YOU'LL BE GOING TO SCHOOL..
KINDERGARTEN THROUGH THE SEVENTH GRADE..
THAT'S EIGHT YEARS!
7-2
© 1996 United Feature Syndicate, Inc.
WHEN I GET OUT, I'LL BE AN OLD MAN!

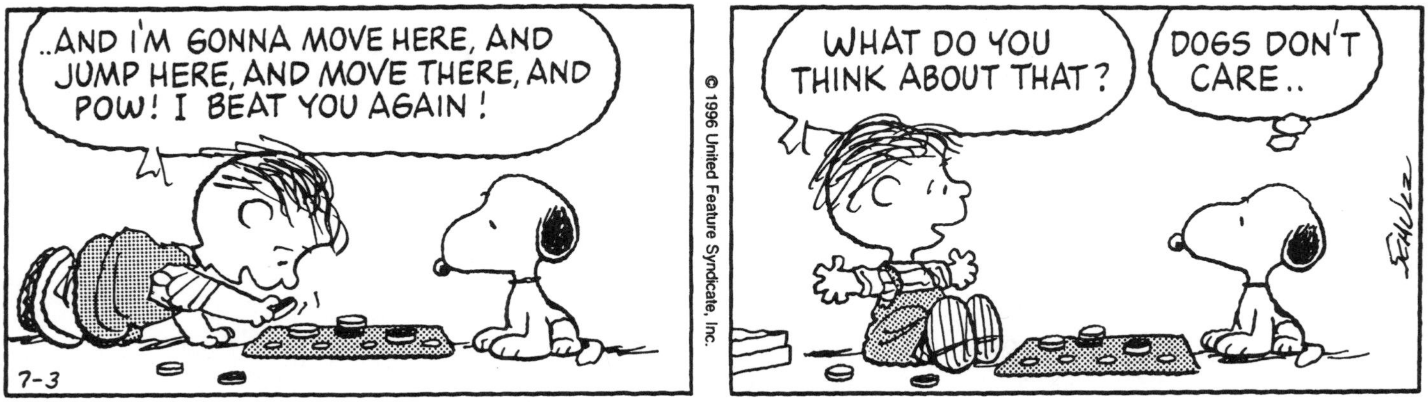
..AND I'M GONNA MOVE HERE, AND JUMP HERE, AND MOVE THERE, AND POW! I BEAT YOU AGAIN!
7-3
© 1996 United Feature Syndicate, Inc.
WHAT DO YOU THINK ABOUT THAT?
DOGS DON'T CARE..

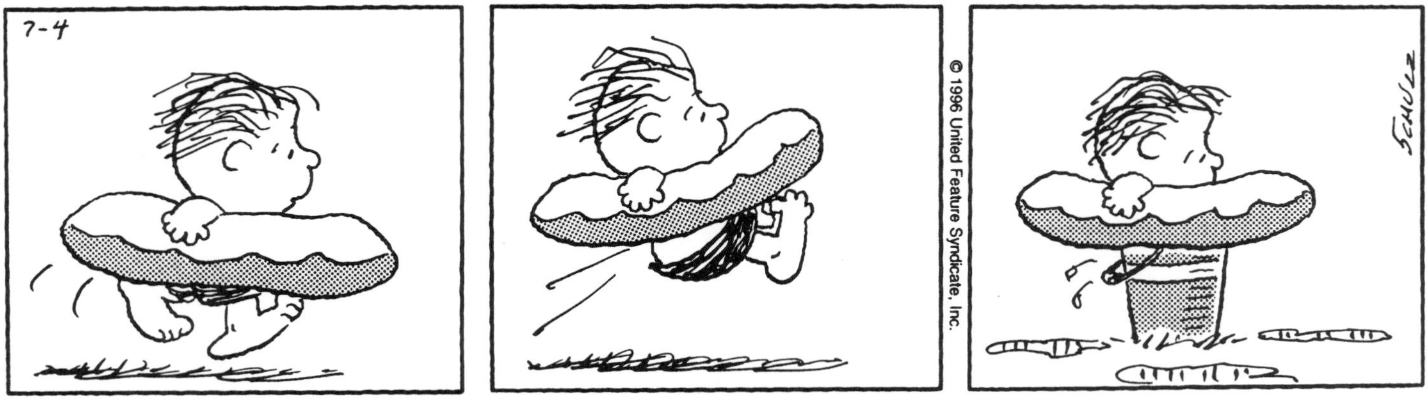
7-4
© 1996 United Feature Syndicate, Inc.
SCHULZ

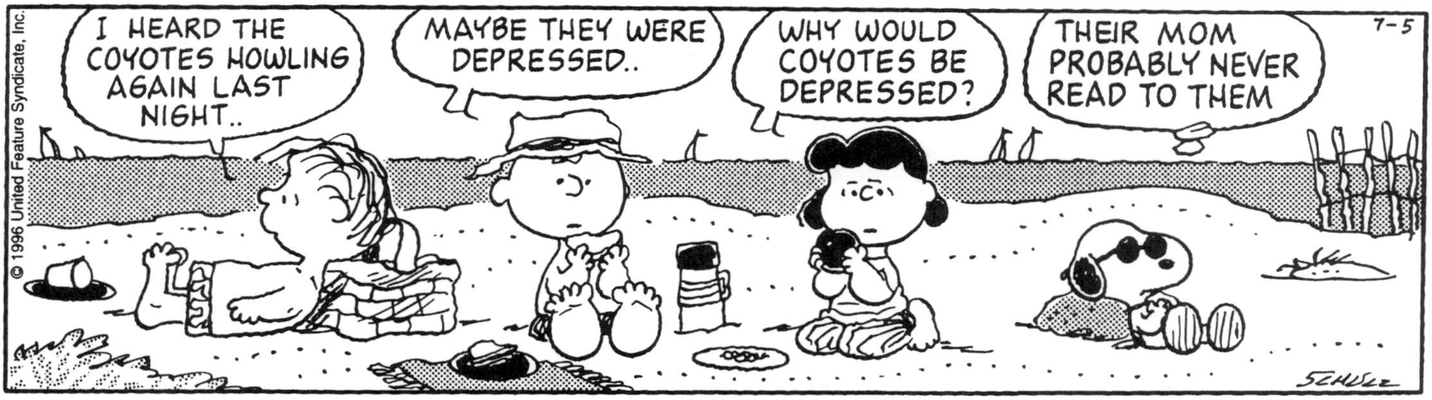
© 1996 United Feature Syndicate, Inc.
I HEARD THE COYOTES HOWLING AGAIN LAST NIGHT..
MAYBE THEY WERE DEPRESSED..
WHY WOULD COYOTES BE DEPRESSED?
THEIR MOM PROBABLY NEVER READ TO THEM
7-5
SCHULZ

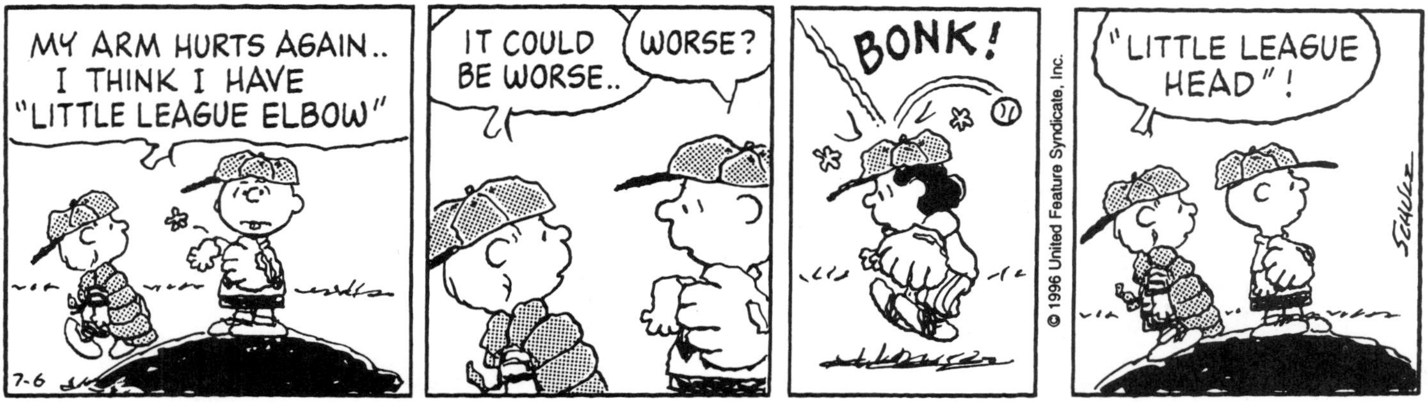
MY ARM HURTS AGAIN.. I THINK I HAVE "LITTLE LEAGUE ELBOW"
7-6
IT COULD BE WORSE..
WORSE?
BONK!
© 1996 United Feature Syndicate, Inc.
"LITTLE LEAGUE HEAD"!
SCHULZ

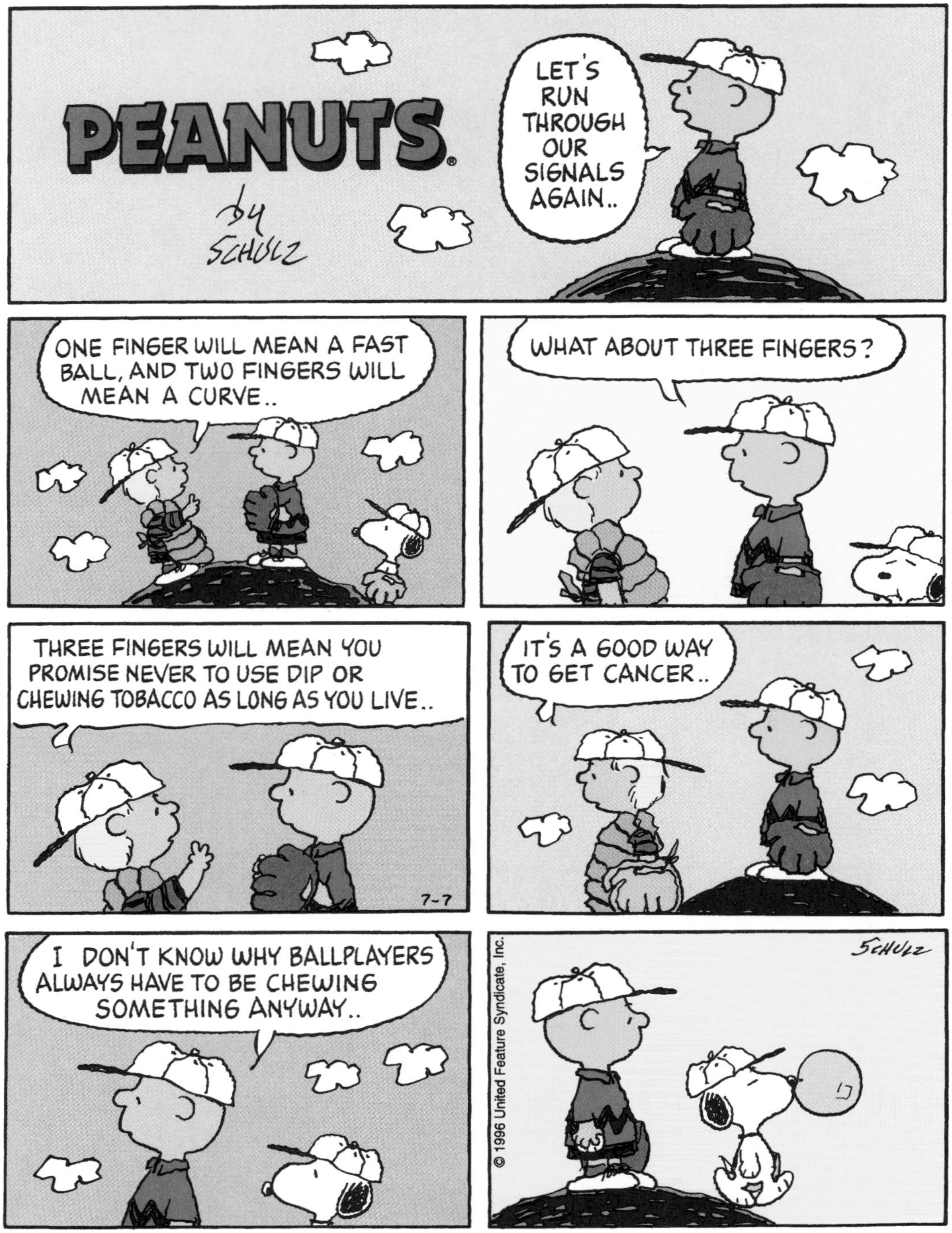
PEANUTS
by SCHULZ
LET'S RUN THROUGH OUR SIGNALS AGAIN..
ONE FINGER WILL MEAN A FAST BALL, AND TWO FINGERS WILL MEAN A CURVE..
WHAT ABOUT THREE FINGERS?
THREE FINGERS WILL MEAN YOU PROMISE NEVER TO USE DIP OR CHEWING TOBACCO AS LONG AS YOU LIVE..
7-7
IT'S A GOOD WAY TO GET CANCER..
I DON'T KNOW WHY BALLPLAYERS ALWAYS HAVE TO BE CHEWING SOMETHING ANYWAY..
SCHULZ
© 1996 United Feature Syndicate, Inc.

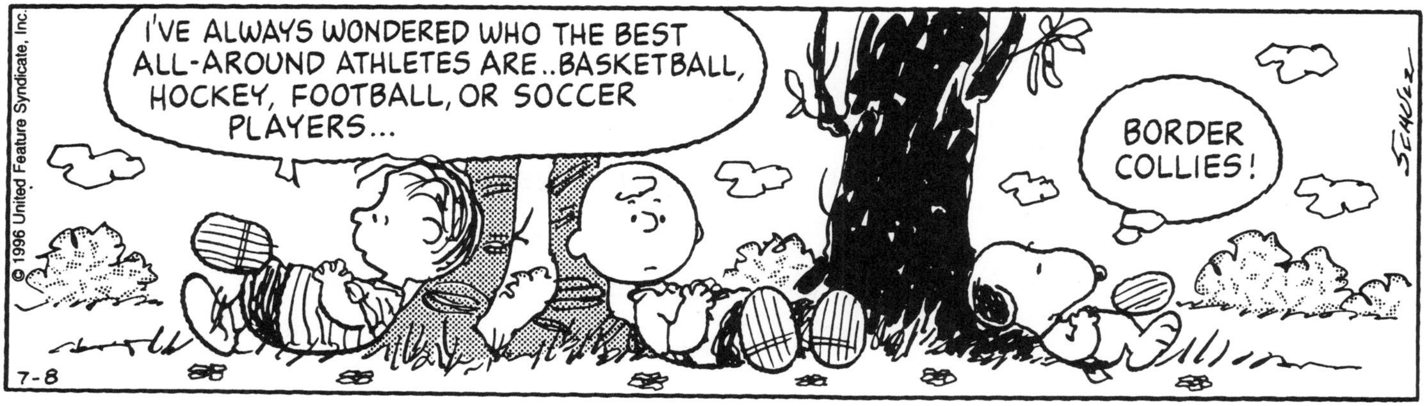
© 1996 United Feature Syndicate, Inc.
I'VE ALWAYS WONDERED WHO THE BEST ALL-AROUND ATHLETES ARE..BASKETBALL, HOCKEY, FOOTBALL, OR SOCCER PLAYERS...
BORDER COLLIES!
SCHULZ
7-8

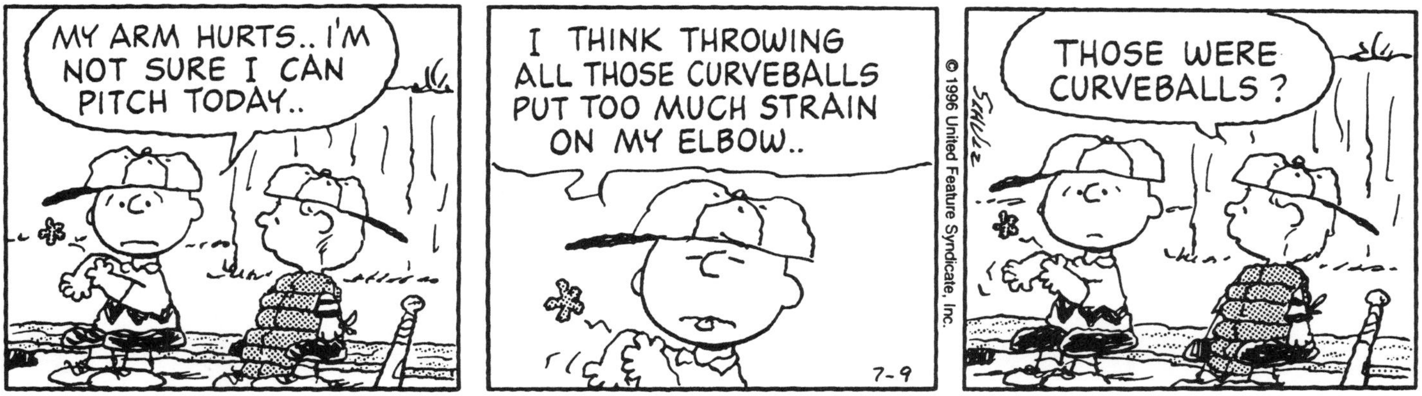
MY ARM HURTS.. I'M NOT SURE I CAN PITCH TODAY..
I THINK THROWING ALL THOSE CURVEBALLS PUT TOO MUCH STRAIN ON MY ELBOW..
7-9
© 1996 United Feature Syndicate, Inc.
SCHULZ
THOSE WERE CURVEBALLS ?

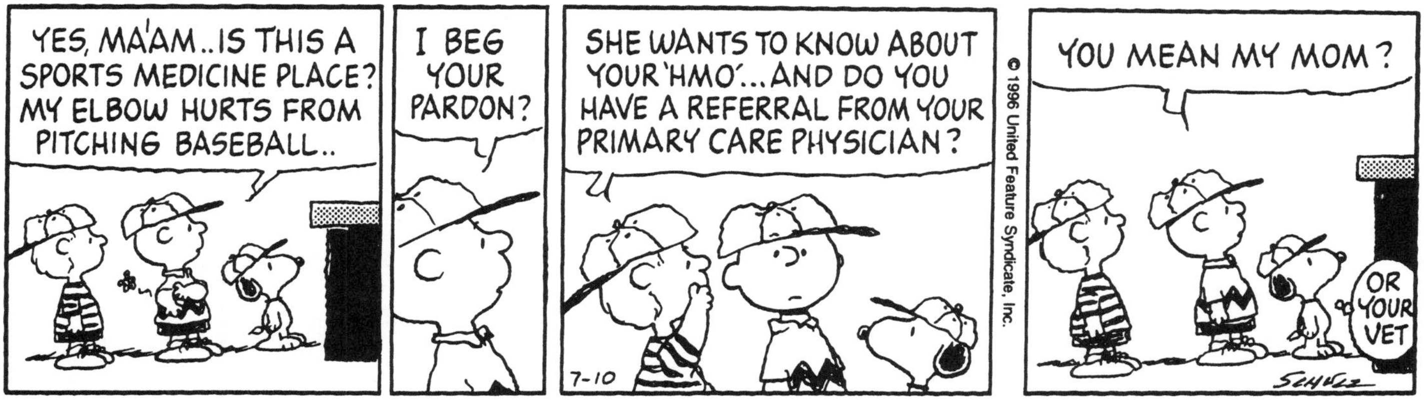
YES, MA'AM..IS THIS A SPORTS MEDICINE PLACE? MY ELBOW HURTS FROM PITCHING BASEBALL..
I BEG YOUR PARDON?
SHE WANTS TO KNOW ABOUT YOUR 'HMO'...AND DO YOU HAVE A REFERRAL FROM YOUR PRIMARY CARE PHYSICIAN?
7-10
© 1996 United Feature Syndicate, Inc.
YOU MEAN MY MOM?
OR YOUR VET
SCHULZ

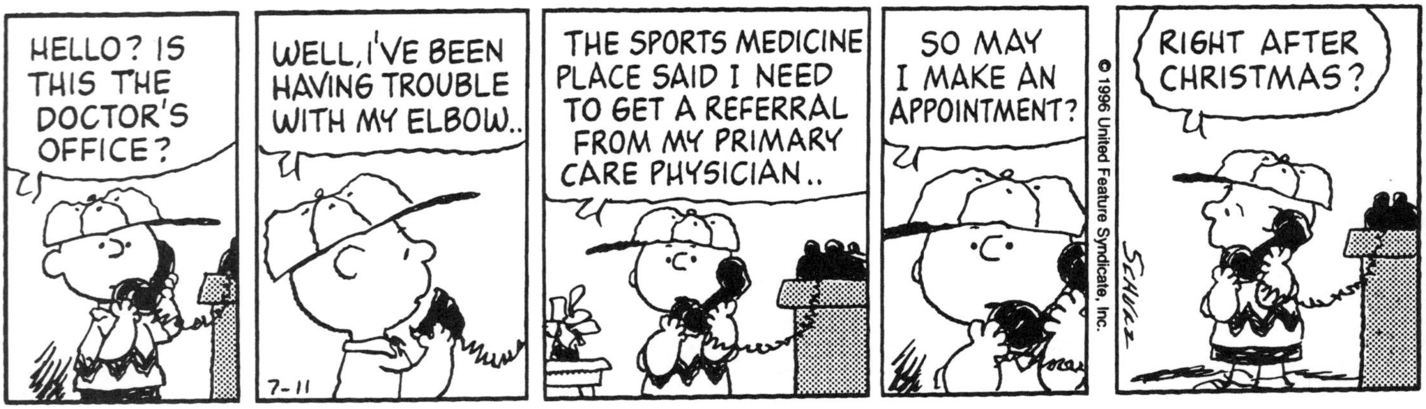
HELLO? IS THIS THE DOCTOR'S OFFICE?
WELL, I'VE BEEN HAVING TROUBLE WITH MY ELBOW..
7-11
THE SPORTS MEDICINE PLACE SAID I NEED TO GET A REFERRAL FROM MY PRIMARY CARE PHYSICIAN..
SO MAY I MAKE AN APPOINTMENT?
© 1996 United Feature Syndicate, Inc.
RIGHT AFTER CHRISTMAS?

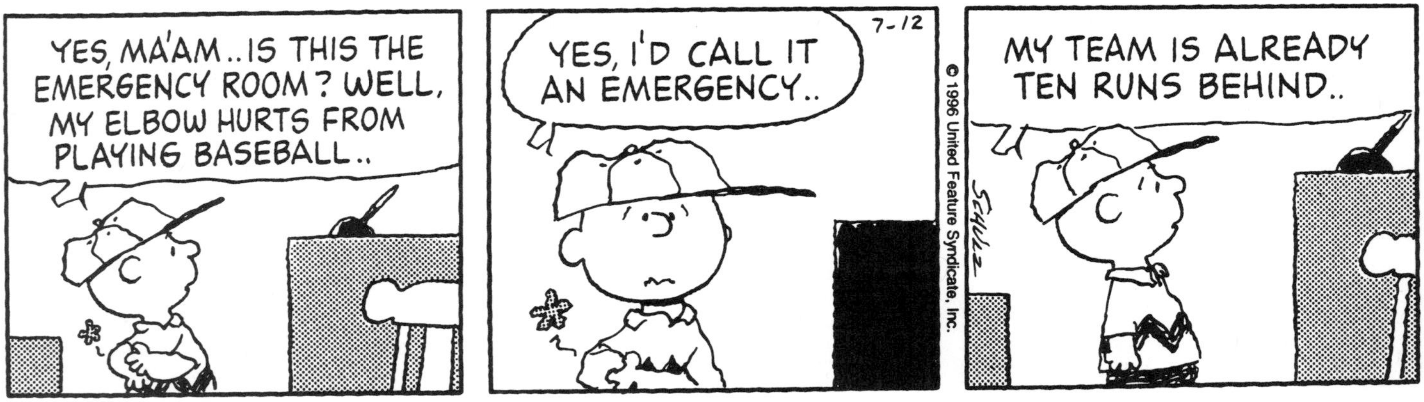
YES, MA'AM..IS THIS THE EMERGENCY ROOM? WELL, MY ELBOW HURTS FROM PLAYING BASEBALL..
7-12
YES, I'D CALL IT AN EMERGENCY..
© 1996 United Feature Syndicate, Inc.
MY TEAM IS ALREADY TEN RUNS BEHIND..

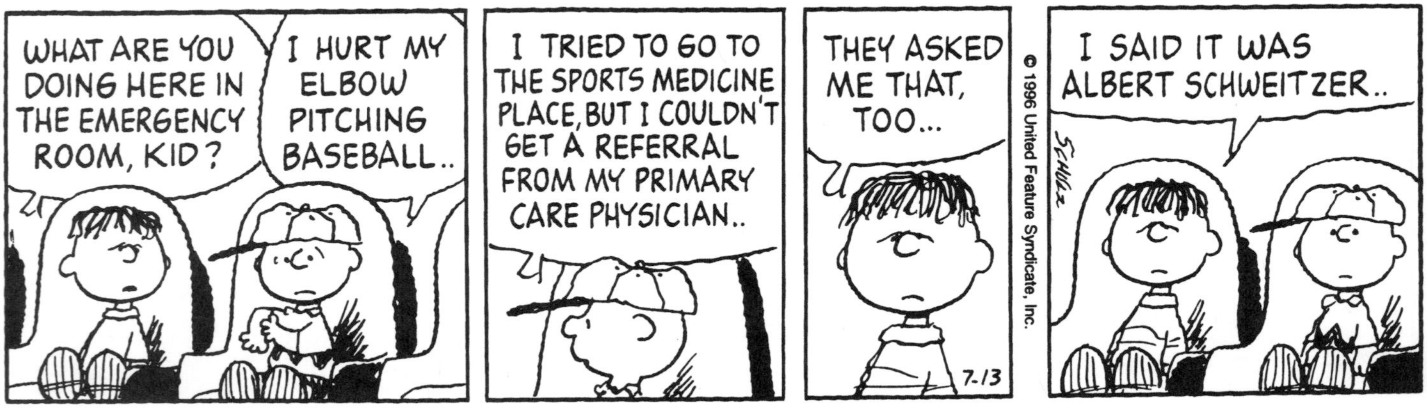
WHAT ARE YOU DOING HERE IN THE EMERGENCY ROOM, KID?
I HURT MY ELBOW PITCHING BASEBALL..
I TRIED TO GO TO THE SPORTS MEDICINE PLACE, BUT I COULDN'T GET A REFERRAL FROM MY PRIMARY CARE PHYSICIAN..
THEY ASKED ME THAT, TOO...
7-13
© 1996 United Feature Syndicate, Inc.
I SAID IT WAS ALBERT SCHWEITZER..

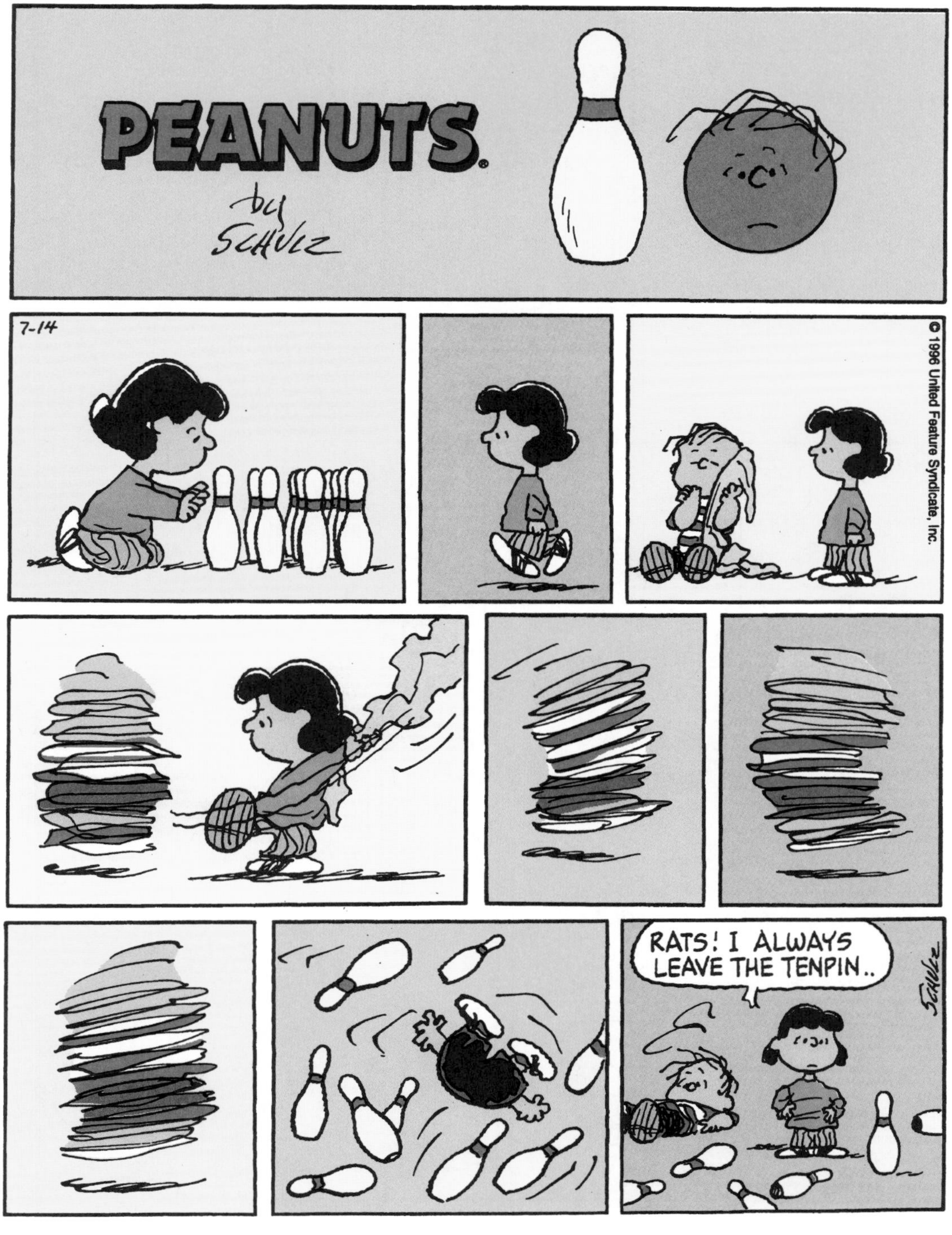
PEANUTS
by SCHULZ
7-14
© 1996 United Feature Syndicate, Inc.
RATS! I ALWAYS LEAVE THE TENPIN..
SCHULZ

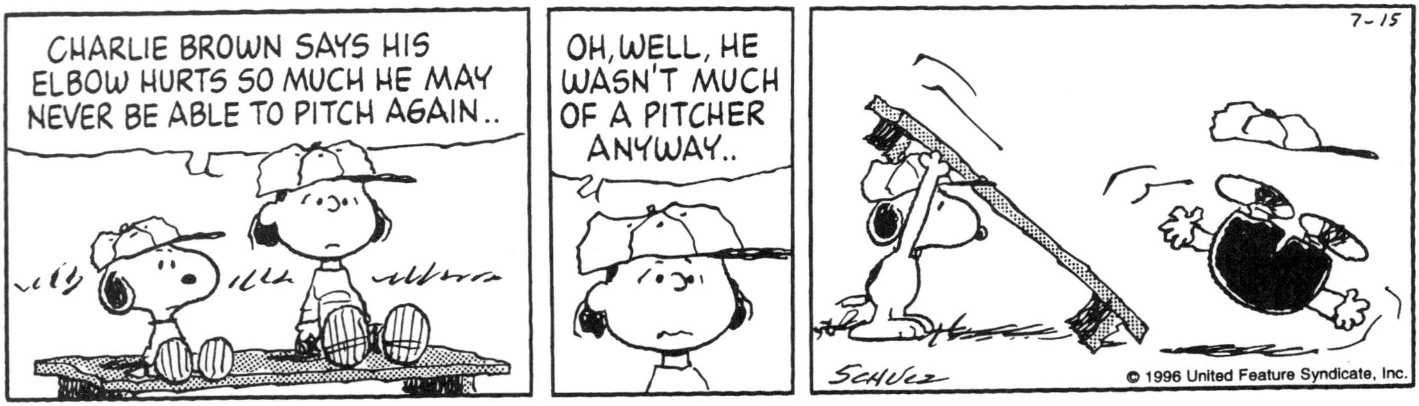

CHARLIE BROWN SAYS HIS ELBOW HURTS SO MUCH HE MAY NEVER BE ABLE TO PITCH AGAIN..
OH, WELL, HE WASN'T MUCH OF A PITCHER ANYWAY..
7-15
SCHULZ
© 1996 United Feature Syndicate, Inc.

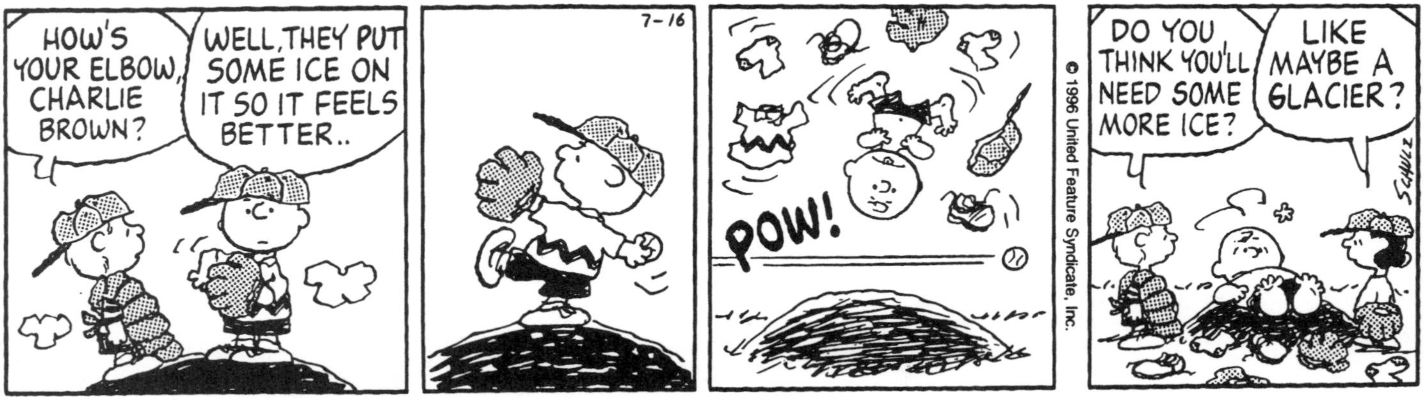

HOW'S YOUR ELBOW, CHARLIE BROWN?
WELL, THEY PUT SOME ICE ON IT SO IT FEELS BETTER..
7-16
POW!
© 1996 United Feature Syndicate, Inc.
DO YOU THINK YOU'LL NEED SOME MORE ICE?
LIKE MAYBE A GLACIER?
SCHULZ

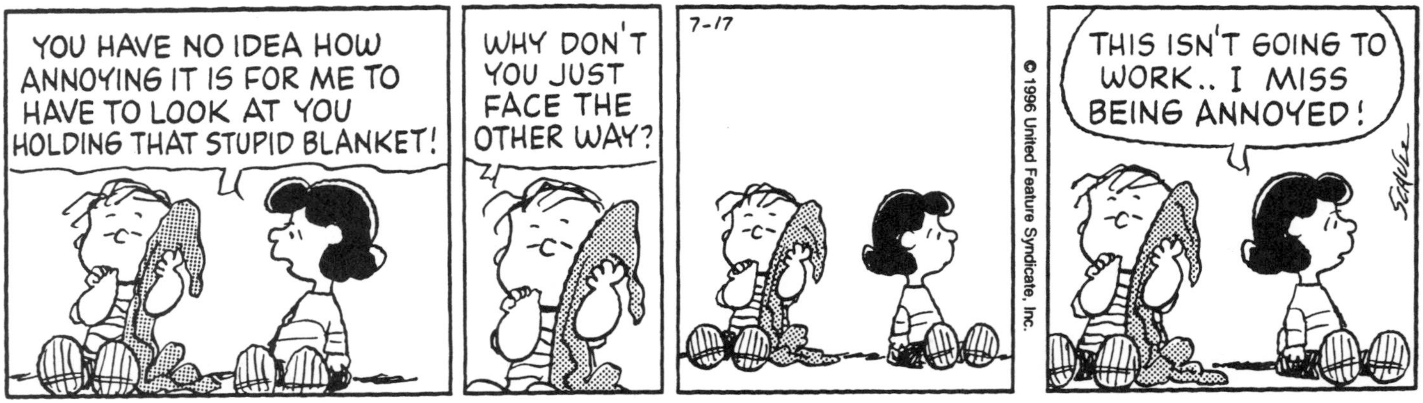

YOU HAVE NO IDEA HOW ANNOYING IT IS FOR ME TO HAVE TO LOOK AT YOU HOLDING THAT STUPID BLANKET!
WHY DON'T YOU JUST FACE THE OTHER WAY?
7-17
© 1996 United Feature Syndicate, Inc.
THIS ISN'T GOING TO WORK.. I MISS BEING ANNOYED!
SCHULZ

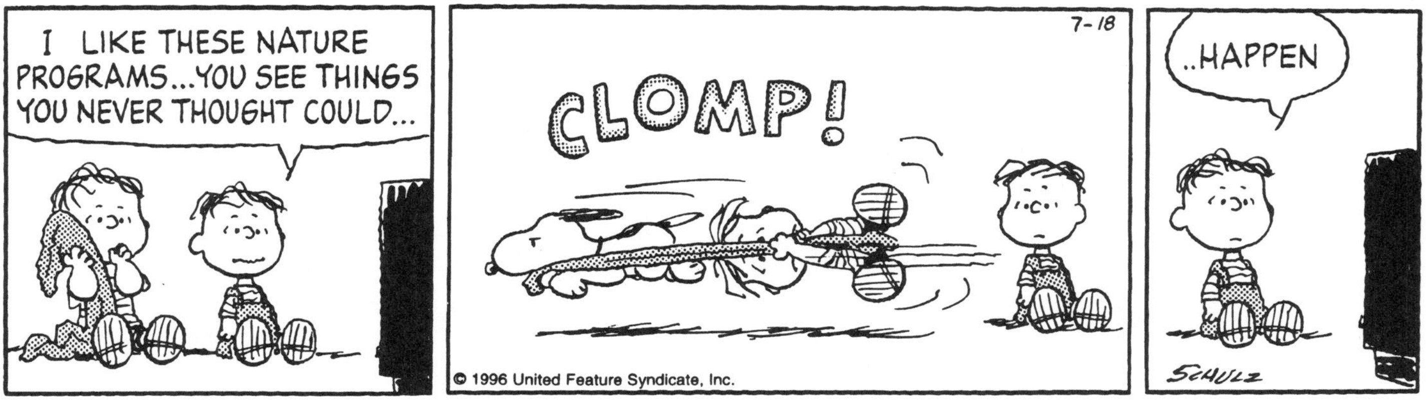
I LIKE THESE NATURE PROGRAMS...YOU SEE THINGS YOU NEVER THOUGHT COULD...
7-18
CLOMP!
© 1996 United Feature Syndicate, Inc.
..HAPPEN
SCHULZ

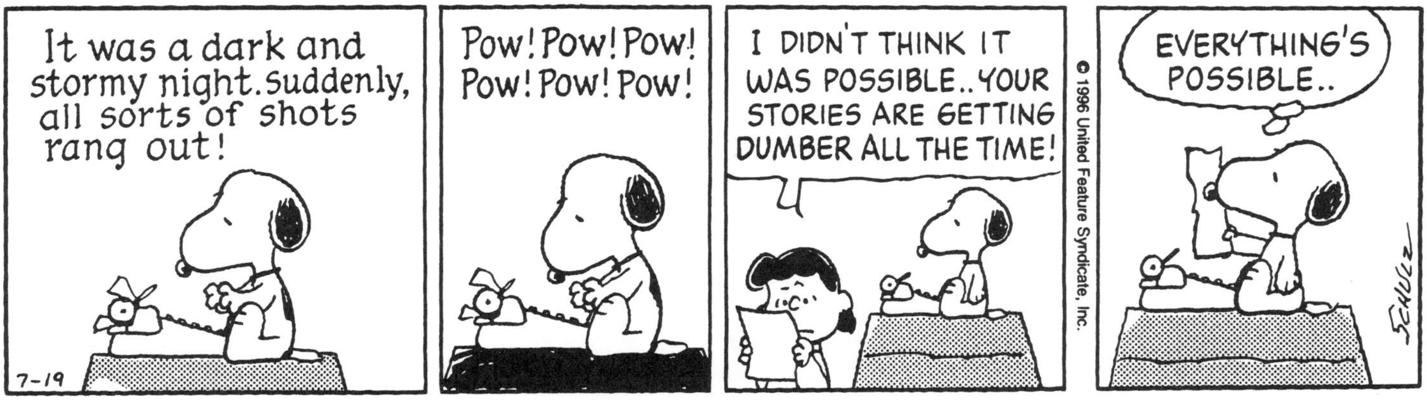
It was a dark and stormy night. Suddenly, all sorts of shots rang out!
7-19
Pow! Pow! Pow! Pow! Pow! Pow!
I DIDN'T THINK IT WAS POSSIBLE..YOUR STORIES ARE GETTING DUMBER ALL THE TIME!
© 1996 United Feature Syndicate, Inc.
EVERYTHING'S POSSIBLE..
SCHULZ

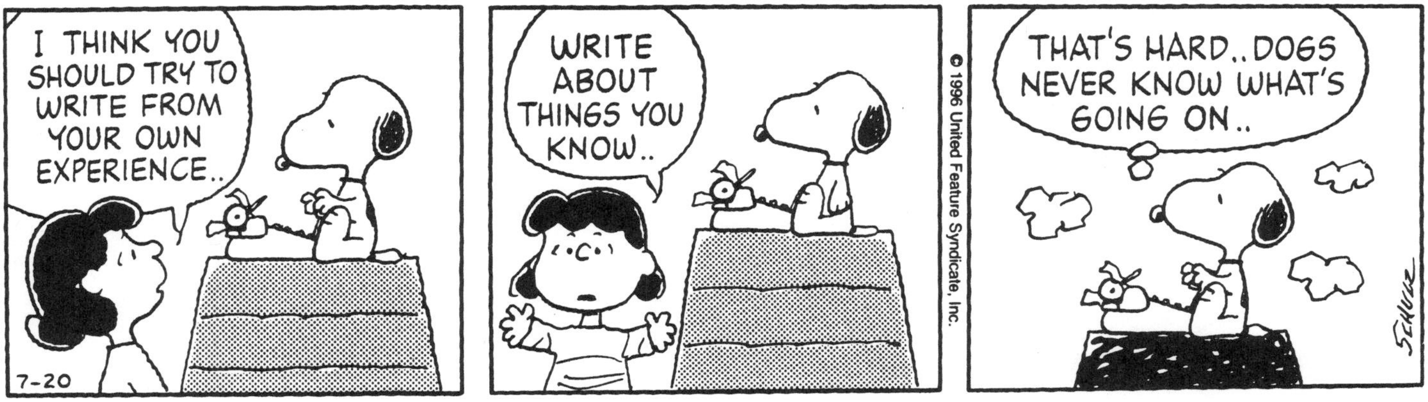
I THINK YOU SHOULD TRY TO WRITE FROM YOUR OWN EXPERIENCE..
7-20
WRITE ABOUT THINGS YOU KNOW..
© 1996 United Feature Syndicate, Inc.
THAT'S HARD..DOGS NEVER KNOW WHAT'S GOING ON..
SCHULZ

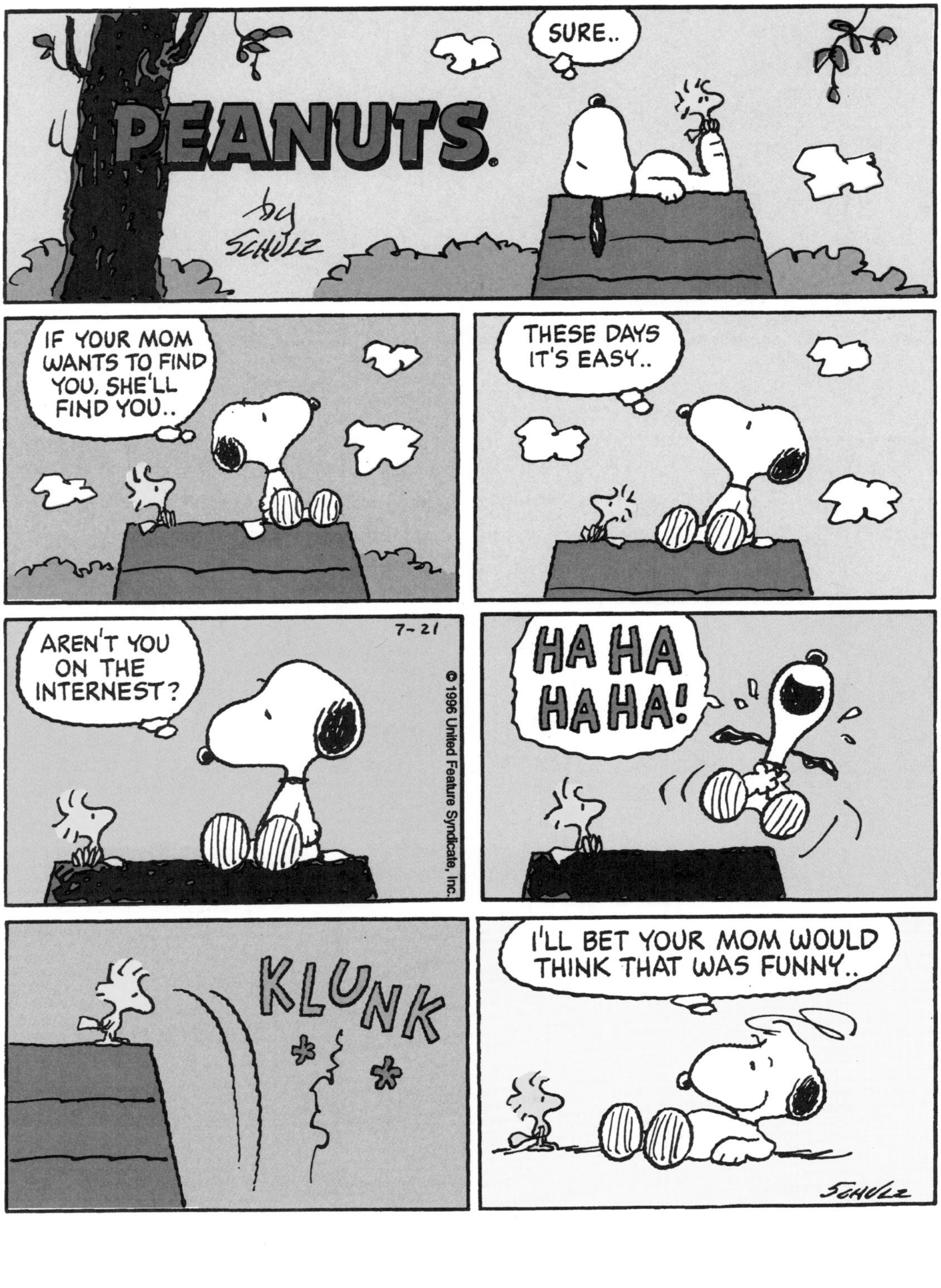
PEANUTS
by SCHULZ
SURE..
IF YOUR MOM WANTS TO FIND YOU, SHE'LL FIND YOU..
THESE DAYS IT'S EASY..
7-21
© 1996 United Feature Syndicate, Inc.
AREN'T YOU ON THE INTERNEST?
HA HA HA HA!
KLUNK
I'LL BET YOUR MOM WOULD THINK THAT WAS FUNNY..
SCHULZ

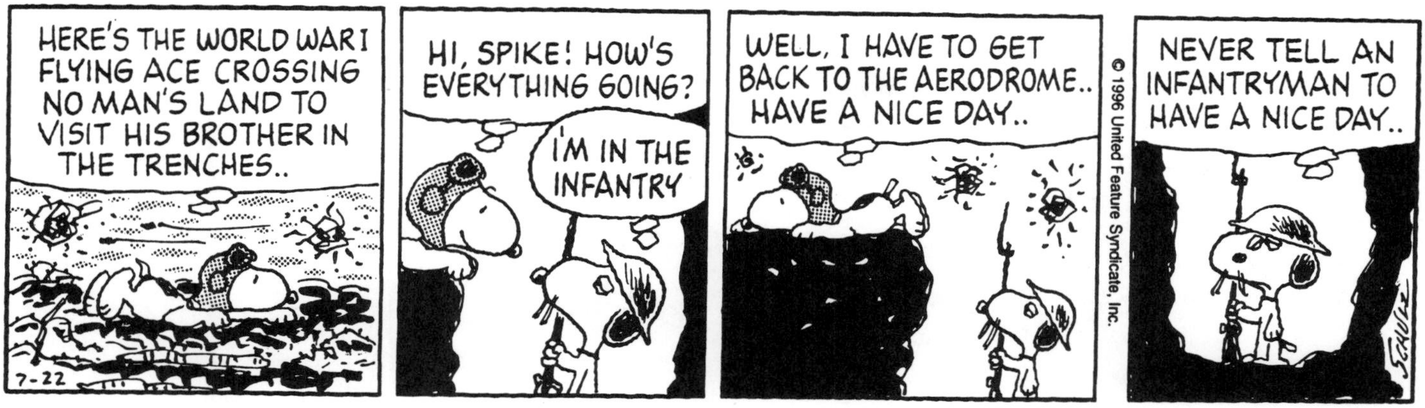
HERE'S THE WORLD WAR I FLYING ACE CROSSING NO MAN'S LAND TO VISIT HIS BROTHER IN THE TRENCHES..
7-22
HI, SPIKE! HOW'S EVERYTHING GOING?
I'M IN THE INFANTRY
WELL, I HAVE TO GET BACK TO THE AERODROME.. HAVE A NICE DAY..
© 1996 United Feature Syndicate, Inc.
NEVER TELL AN INFANTRYMAN TO HAVE A NICE DAY..
SCHULZ

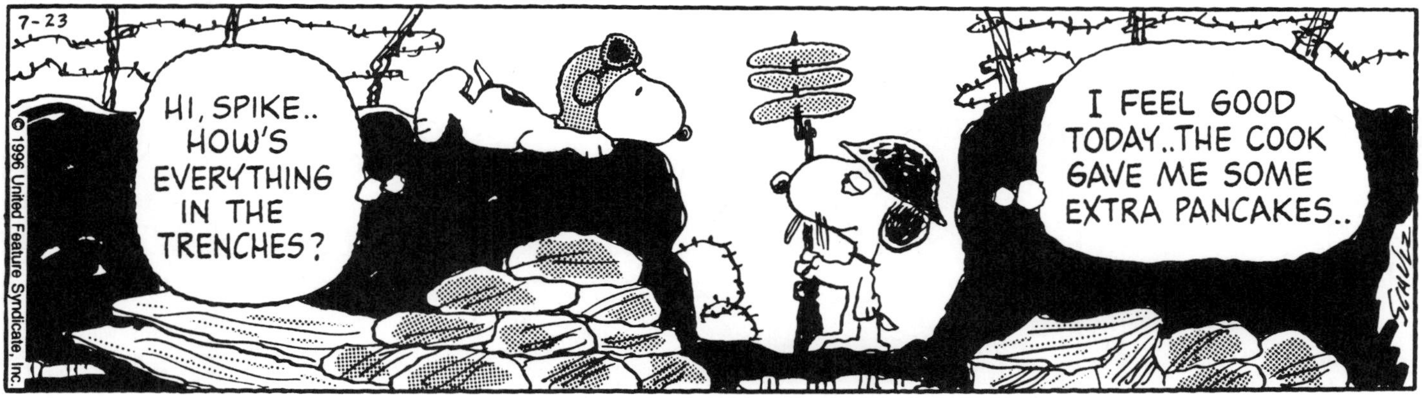
7-23
© 1996 United Feature Syndicate, Inc.
HI, SPIKE.. HOW'S EVERYTHING IN THE TRENCHES?
I FEEL GOOD TODAY..THE COOK GAVE ME SOME EXTRA PANCAKES..
SCHULZ

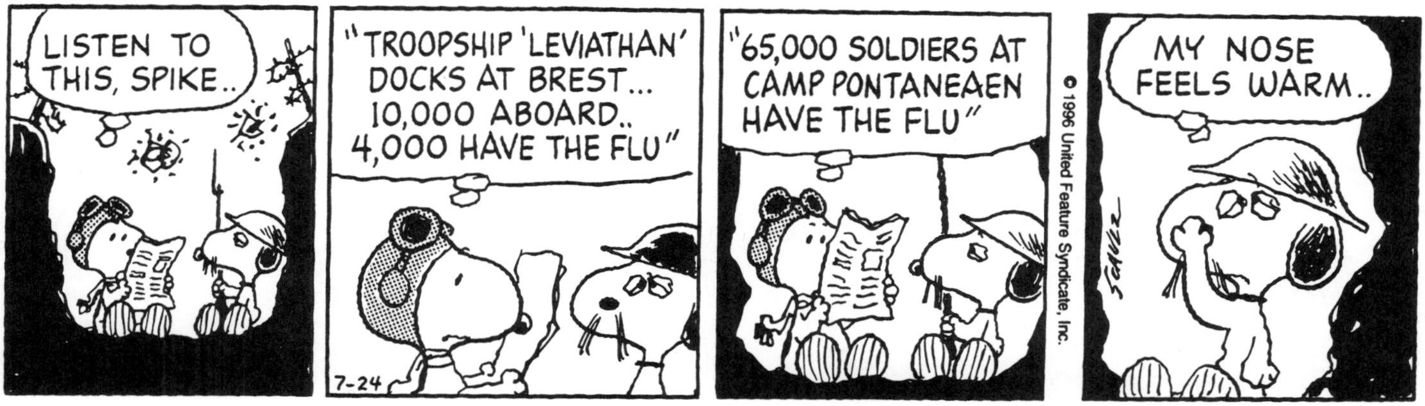
LISTEN TO THIS, SPIKE..
"TROOPSHIP 'LEVIATHAN' DOCKS AT BREST... 10,000 ABOARD.. 4,000 HAVE THE FLU"
7-24
"65,000 SOLDIERS AT CAMP PONTANEAEN HAVE THE FLU"
© 1996 United Feature Syndicate, Inc.
SCHULZ
MY NOSE FEELS WARM..

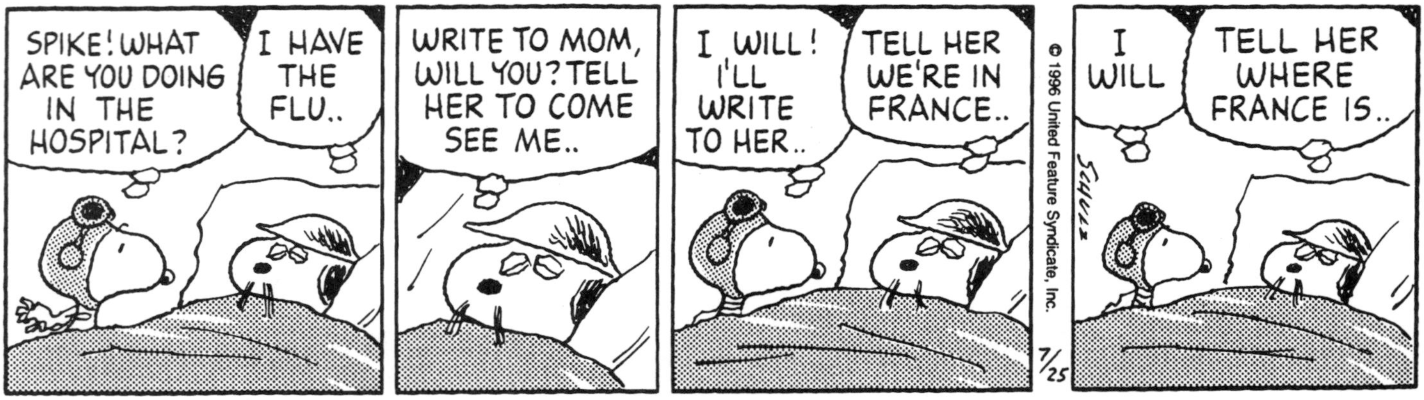
SPIKE! WHAT ARE YOU DOING IN THE HOSPITAL?
I HAVE THE FLU..
WRITE TO MOM, WILL YOU? TELL HER TO COME SEE ME..
I WILL! I'LL WRITE TO HER..
TELL HER WE'RE IN FRANCE..
© 1996 United Feature Syndicate, Inc.
7/25
I WILL
TELL HER WHERE FRANCE IS..

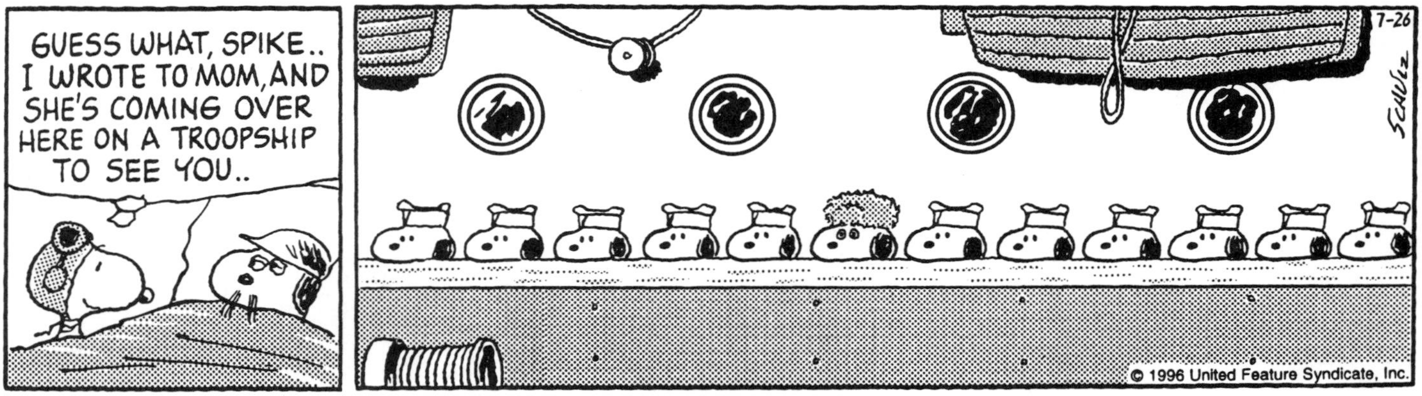
GUESS WHAT, SPIKE.. I WROTE TO MOM, AND SHE'S COMING OVER HERE ON A TROOPSHIP TO SEE YOU..
7-26
© 1996 United Feature Syndicate, Inc.

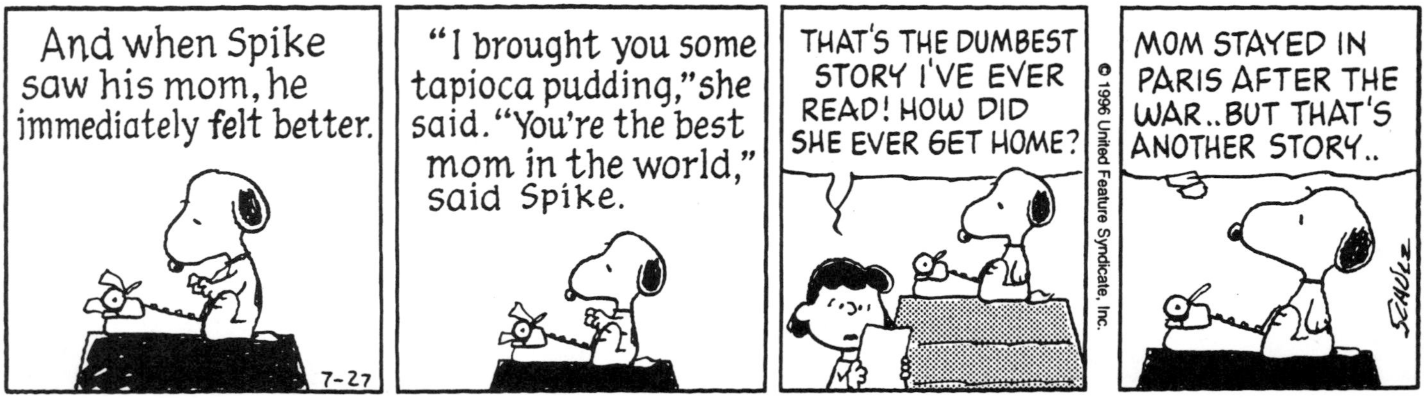
And when Spike saw his mom, he immediately felt better.
7-27
"I brought you some tapioca pudding," she said. "You're the best mom in the world," said Spike.
THAT'S THE DUMBEST STORY I'VE EVER READ! HOW DID SHE EVER GET HOME?
© 1996 United Feature Syndicate, Inc.
MOM STAYED IN PARIS AFTER THE WAR.. BUT THAT'S ANOTHER STORY..

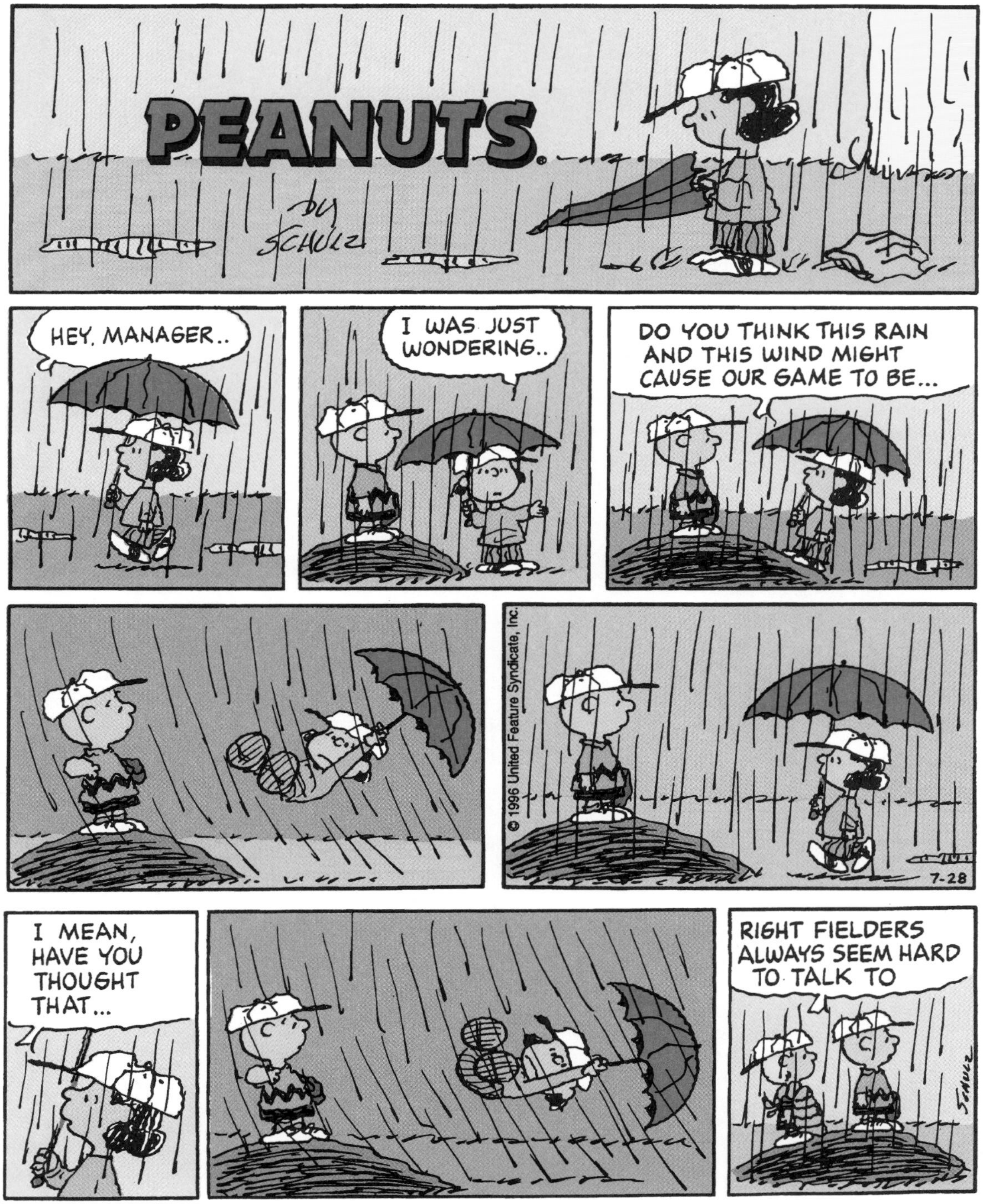
PEANUTS
by SCHULZ
HEY, MANAGER..
I WAS JUST WONDERING..
DO YOU THINK THIS RAIN AND THIS WIND MIGHT CAUSE OUR GAME TO BE...
© 1996 United Feature Syndicate, Inc.
7-28
I MEAN, HAVE YOU THOUGHT THAT...
RIGHT FIELDERS ALWAYS SEEM HARD TO TALK TO
SCHULZ

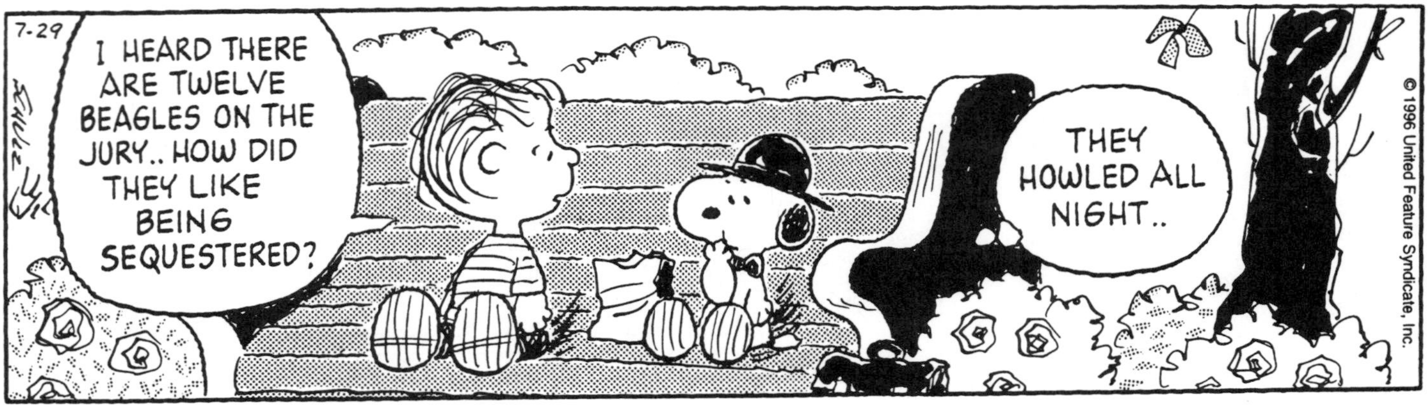
7-29
SCHULZ
I HEARD THERE ARE TWELVE BEAGLES ON THE JURY.. HOW DID THEY LIKE BEING SEQUESTERED?
THEY HOWLED ALL NIGHT..
© 1996 United Feature Syndicate, Inc.

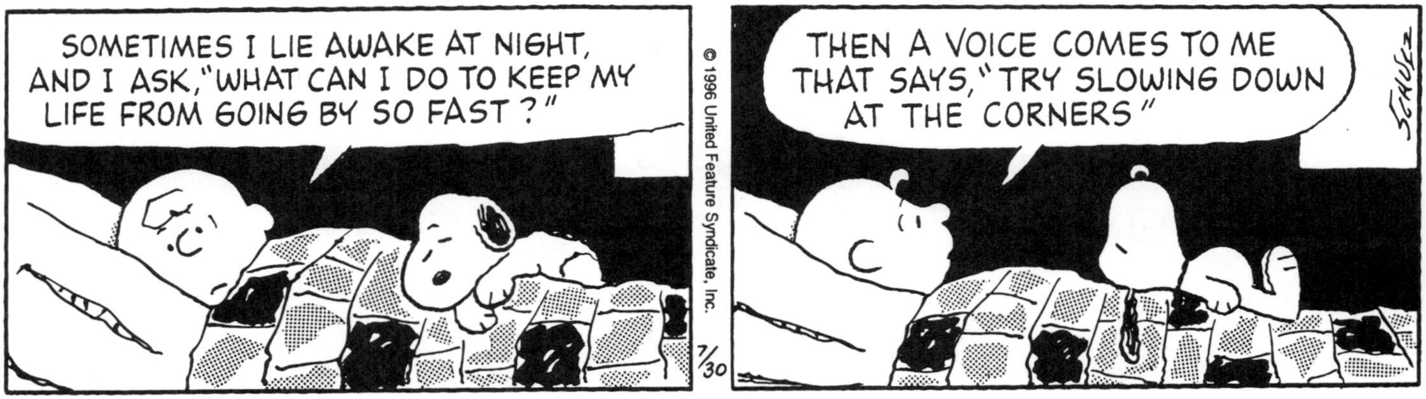
SOMETIMES I LIE AWAKE AT NIGHT, AND I ASK, "WHAT CAN I DO TO KEEP MY LIFE FROM GOING BY SO FAST?"
© 1996 United Feature Syndicate, Inc.
7/30
THEN A VOICE COMES TO ME THAT SAYS, "TRY SLOWING DOWN AT THE CORNERS"
SCHULZ

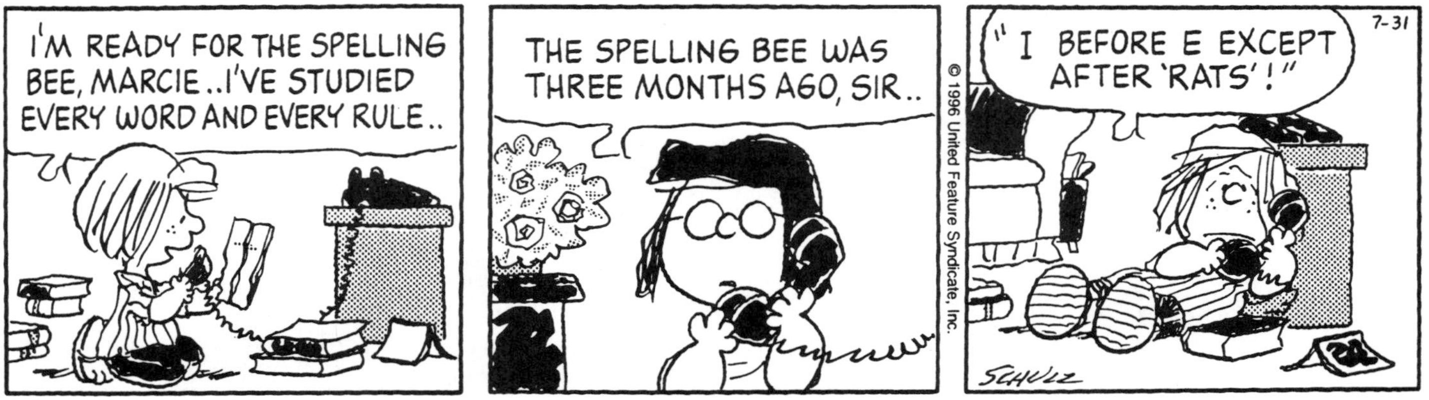
I'M READY FOR THE SPELLING BEE, MARCIE.. I'VE STUDIED EVERY WORD AND EVERY RULE..
THE SPELLING BEE WAS THREE MONTHS AGO, SIR..
© 1996 United Feature Syndicate, Inc.
7-31
"I BEFORE E EXCEPT AFTER 'RATS'!"
SCHULZ

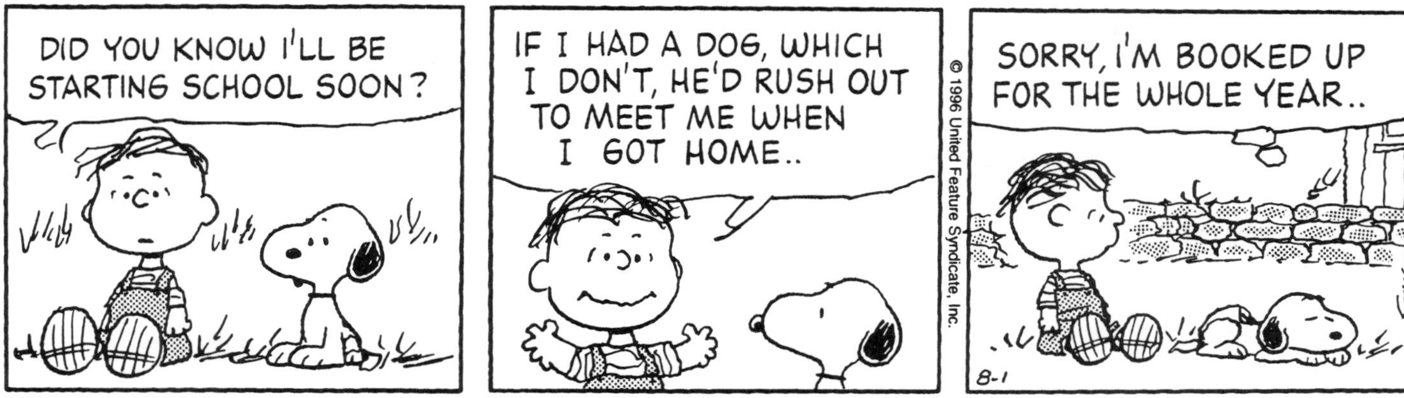
DID YOU KNOW I'LL BE STARTING SCHOOL SOON?
IF I HAD A DOG, WHICH I DON'T, HE'D RUSH OUT TO MEET ME WHEN I GOT HOME..
SORRY, I'M BOOKED UP FOR THE WHOLE YEAR..
SCHULZ
8-1

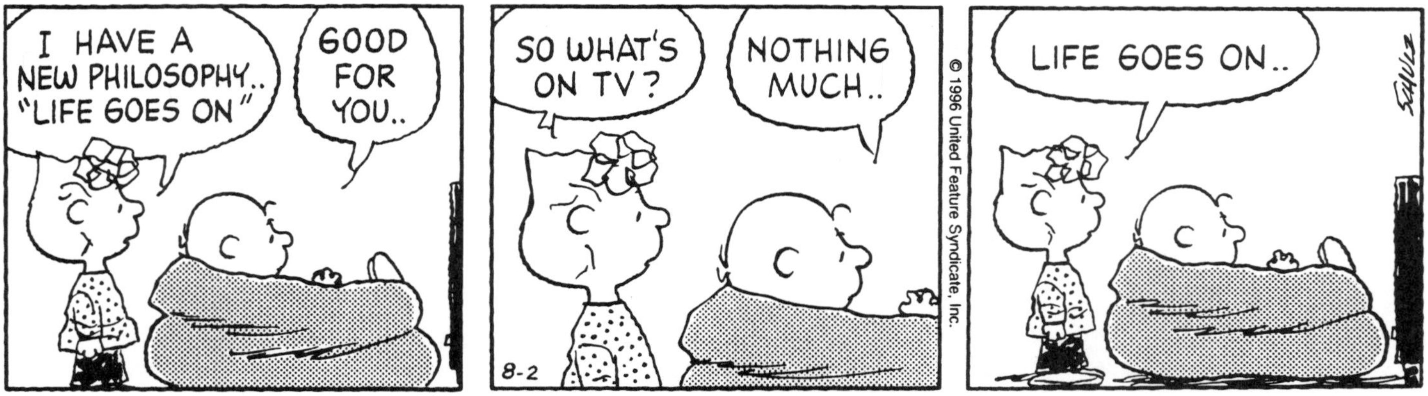
I HAVE A NEW PHILOSOPHY.. "LIFE GOES ON"
GOOD FOR YOU..
SO WHAT'S ON TV?
NOTHING MUCH..
8-2
LIFE GOES ON..
SCHULZ

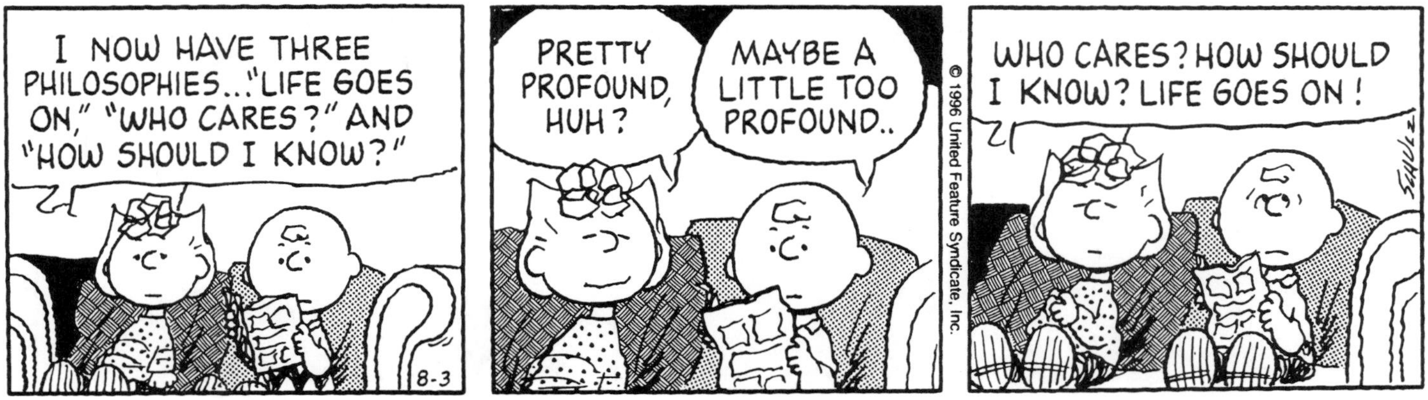
I NOW HAVE THREE PHILOSOPHIES.."LIFE GOES ON," "WHO CARES?" AND "HOW SHOULD I KNOW?"
8-3
PRETTY PROFOUND, HUH?
MAYBE A LITTLE TOO PROFOUND..
WHO CARES? HOW SHOULD I KNOW? LIFE GOES ON!
SCHULZ

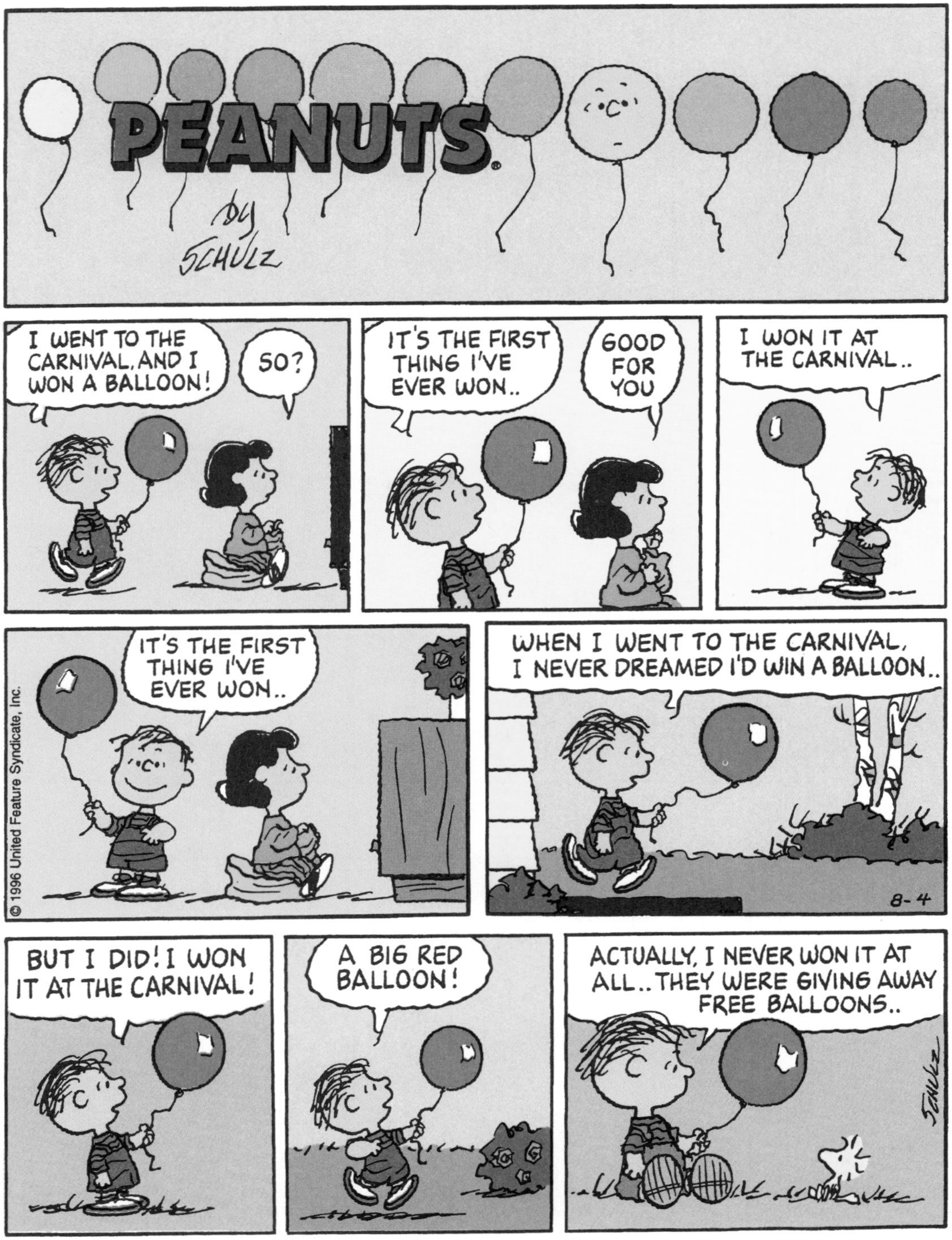
PEANUTS
by SCHULZ
I WENT TO THE CARNIVAL, AND I WON A BALLOON!
SO?
IT'S THE FIRST THING I'VE EVER WON..
GOOD FOR YOU
I WON IT AT THE CARNIVAL..
IT'S THE FIRST THING I'VE EVER WON..
© 1996 United Feature Syndicate, Inc.
WHEN I WENT TO THE CARNIVAL, I NEVER DREAMED I'D WIN A BALLOON..
8-4
BUT I DID! I WON IT AT THE CARNIVAL!
A BIG RED BALLOON!
ACTUALLY, I NEVER WON IT AT ALL.. THEY WERE GIVING AWAY FREE BALLOONS..
SCHULZ

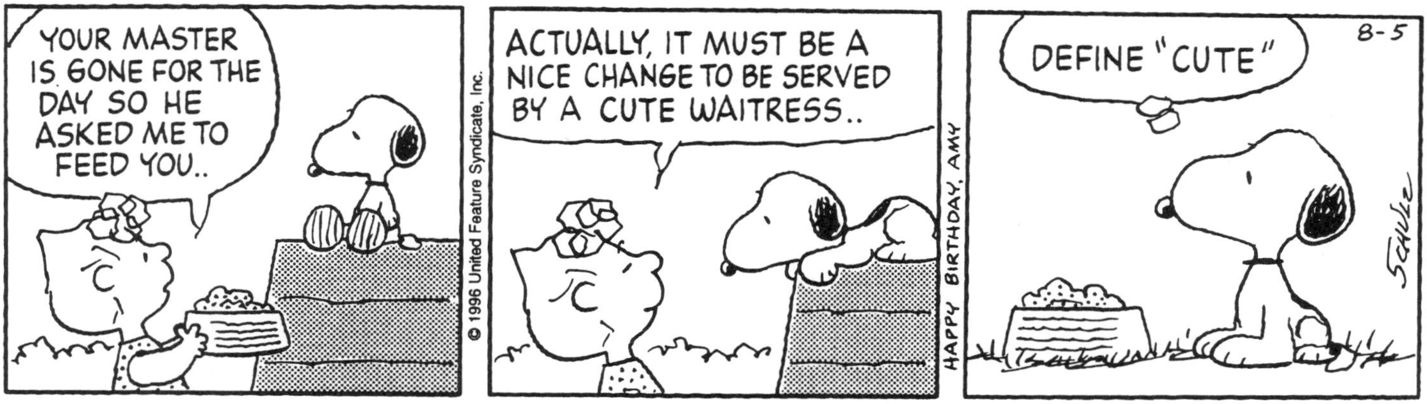
YOUR MASTER IS GONE FOR THE DAY SO HE ASKED ME TO FEED YOU..
© 1996 United Feature Syndicate, Inc.
ACTUALLY, IT MUST BE A NICE CHANGE TO BE SERVED BY A CUTE WAITRESS..
HAPPY BIRTHDAY, AMY
8-5
DEFINE "CUTE"
SCHULZ

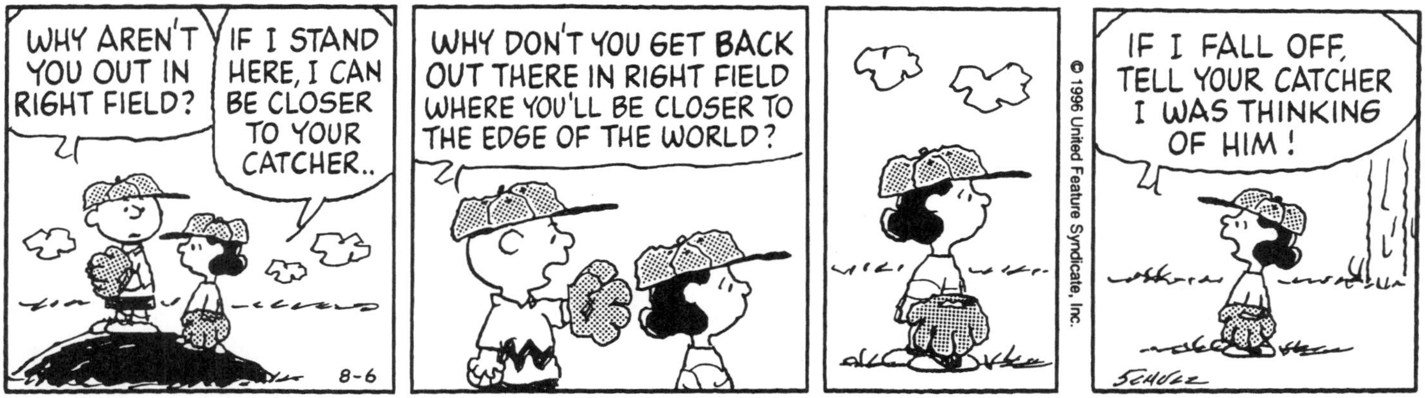
WHY AREN'T YOU OUT IN RIGHT FIELD?
IF I STAND HERE, I CAN BE CLOSER TO YOUR CATCHER..
8-6
WHY DON'T YOU GET BACK OUT THERE IN RIGHT FIELD WHERE YOU'LL BE CLOSER TO THE EDGE OF THE WORLD?
© 1996 United Feature Syndicate, Inc.
IF I FALL OFF, TELL YOUR CATCHER I WAS THINKING OF HIM!
SCHULZ

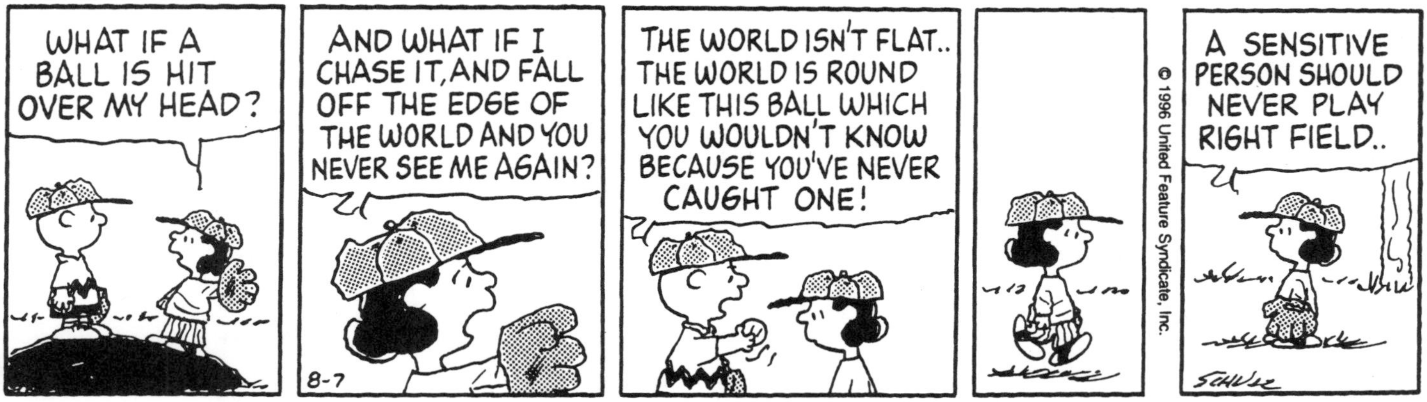
WHAT IF A BALL IS HIT OVER MY HEAD?
AND WHAT IF I CHASE IT, AND FALL OFF THE EDGE OF THE WORLD AND YOU NEVER SEE ME AGAIN?
8-7
THE WORLD ISN'T FLAT.. THE WORLD IS ROUND LIKE THIS BALL WHICH YOU WOULDN'T KNOW BECAUSE YOU'VE NEVER CAUGHT ONE!
© 1996 United Feature Syndicate, Inc.
A SENSITIVE PERSON SHOULD NEVER PLAY RIGHT FIELD..
SCHULZ

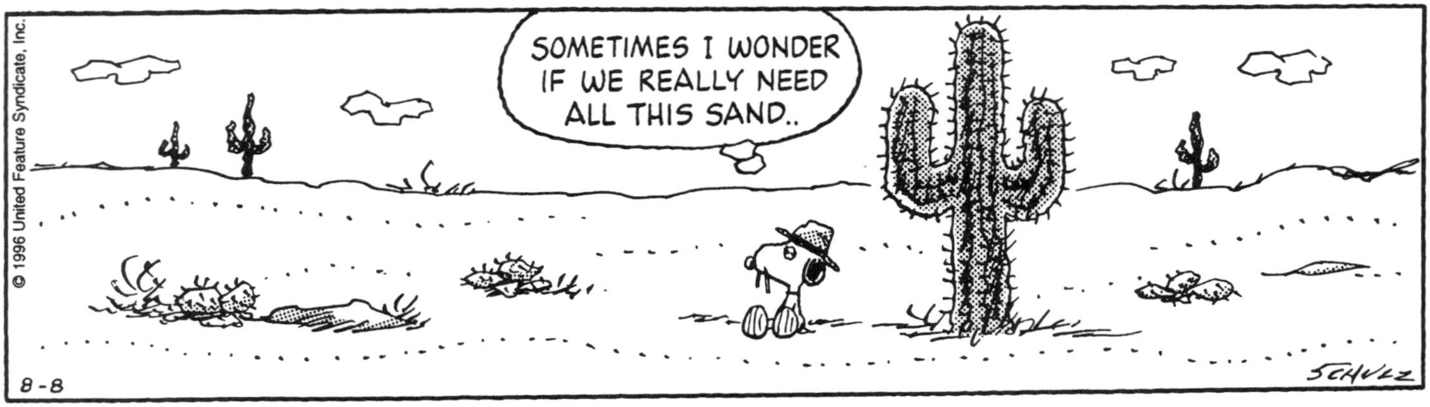
© 1996 United Feature Syndicate, Inc.
SOMETIMES I WONDER IF WE REALLY NEED ALL THIS SAND..
8-8
SCHULZ

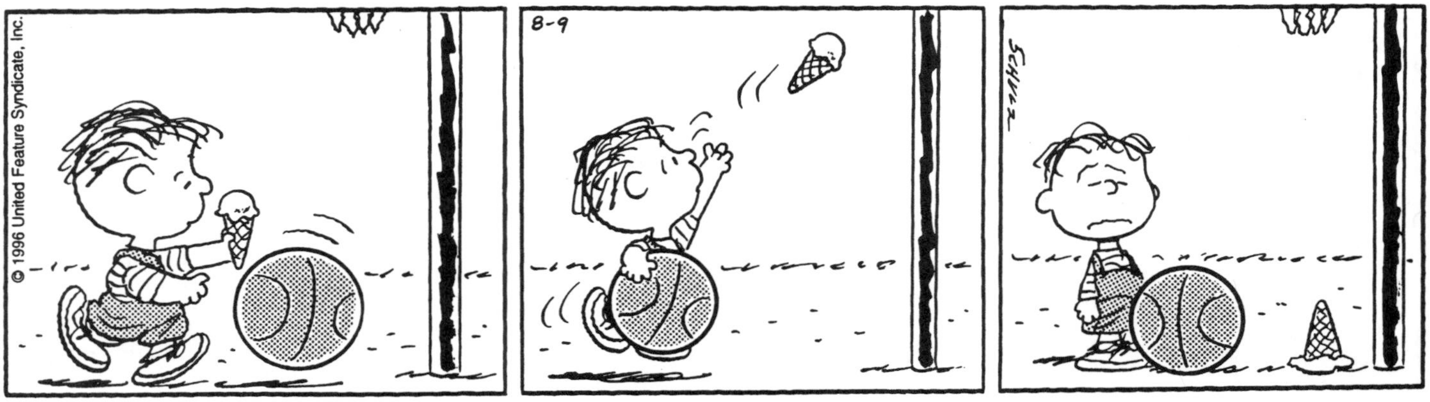
© 1996 United Feature Syndicate, Inc.
8-9
SCHULZ

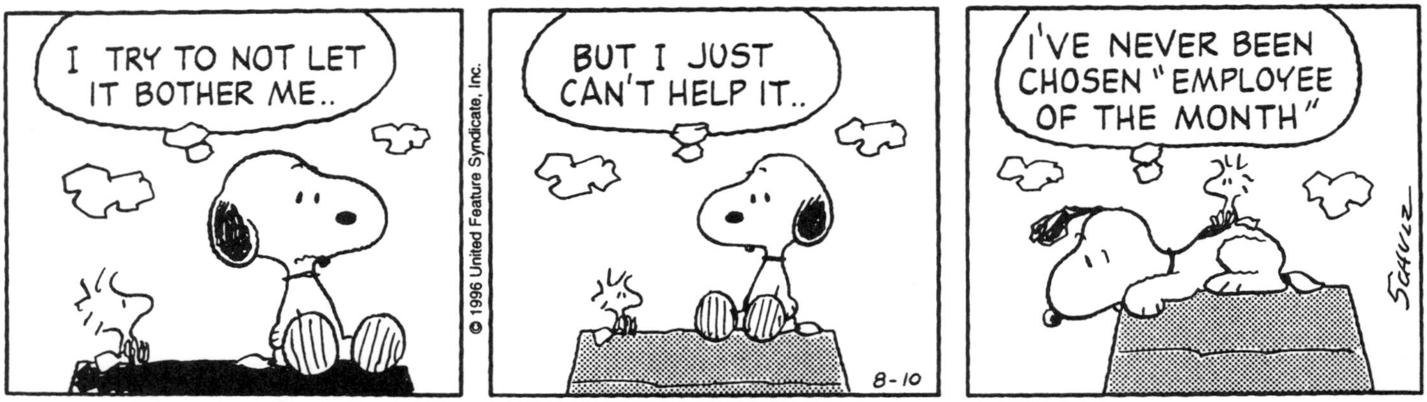
I TRY TO NOT LET IT BOTHER ME..
© 1996 United Feature Syndicate, Inc.
BUT I JUST CAN'T HELP IT..
8-10
I'VE NEVER BEEN CHOSEN "EMPLOYEE OF THE MONTH"
SCHULZ

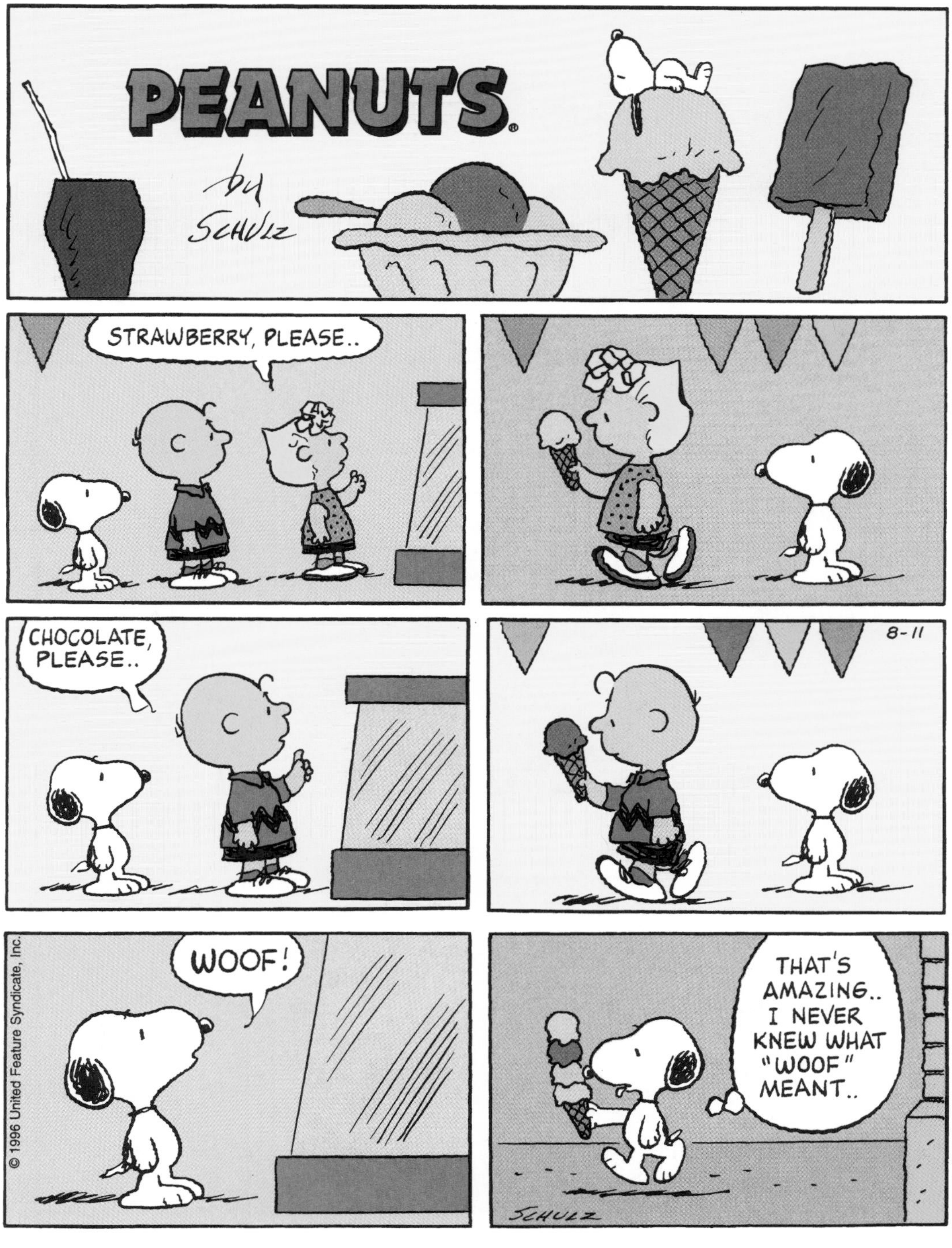
PEANUTS
by SCHULZ
STRAWBERRY, PLEASE..
CHOCOLATE, PLEASE..
8-11
WOOF!
© 1996 United Feature Syndicate, Inc.
THAT'S AMAZING.. I NEVER KNEW WHAT "WOOF" MEANT..
SCHULZ

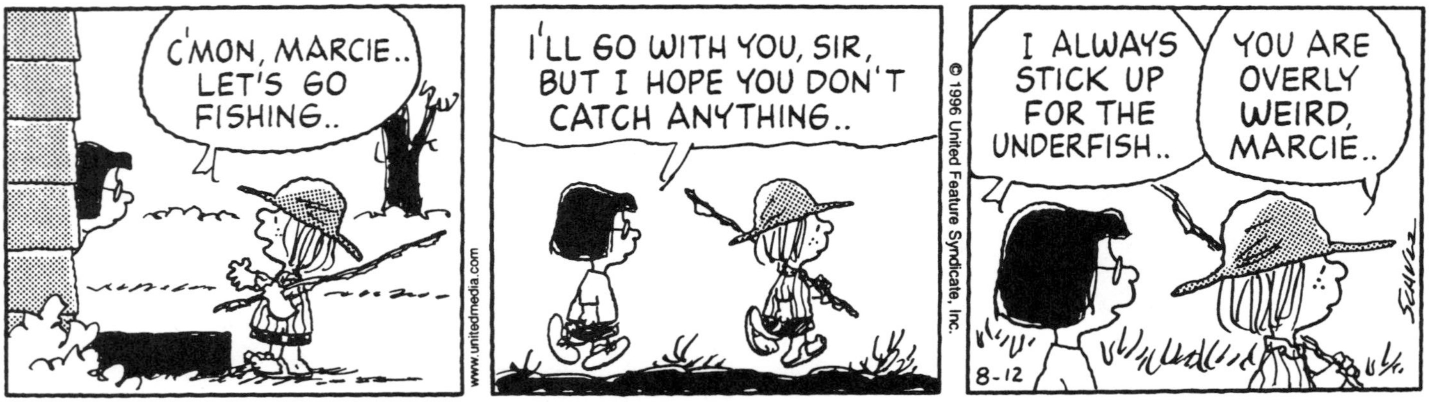
C'MON, MARCIE.. LET'S GO FISHING..
I'LL GO WITH YOU, SIR, BUT I HOPE YOU DON'T CATCH ANYTHING..
I ALWAYS STICK UP FOR THE UNDERFISH..
YOU ARE OVERLY WEIRD, MARCIE..
8-12
SCHULZ

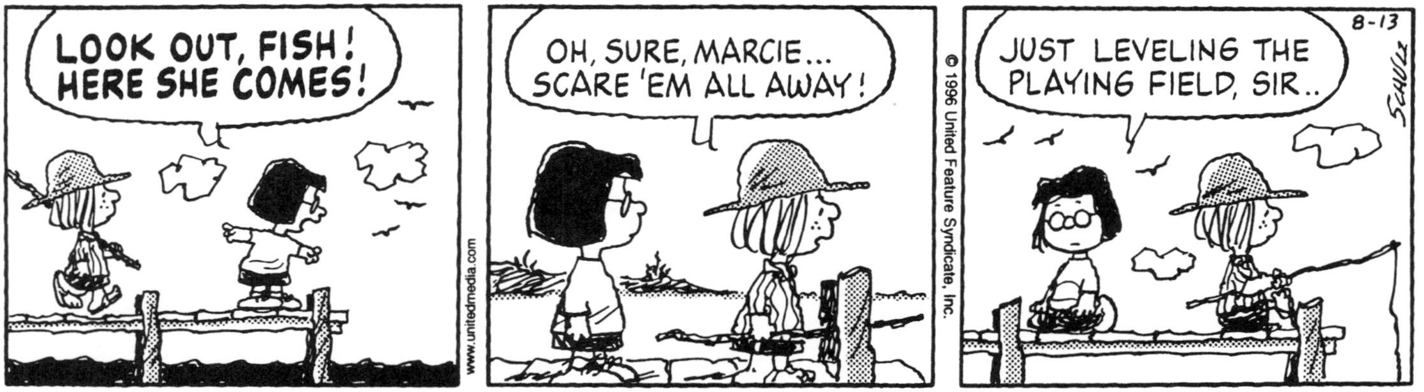
LOOK OUT, FISH! HERE SHE COMES!
OH, SURE, MARCIE... SCARE 'EM ALL AWAY!
JUST LEVELING THE PLAYING FIELD, SIR..
8-13
SCHULZ

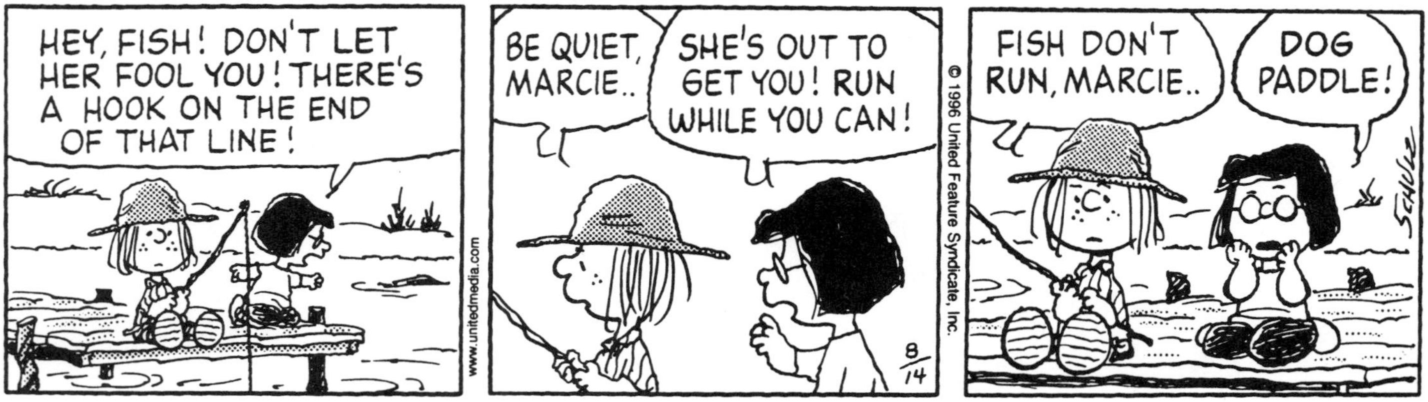
HEY, FISH! DON'T LET HER FOOL YOU! THERE'S A HOOK ON THE END OF THAT LINE!
BE QUIET, MARCIE..
SHE'S OUT TO GET YOU! RUN WHILE YOU CAN!
8/14
FISH DON'T RUN, MARCIE..
DOG PADDLE!
SCHULZ

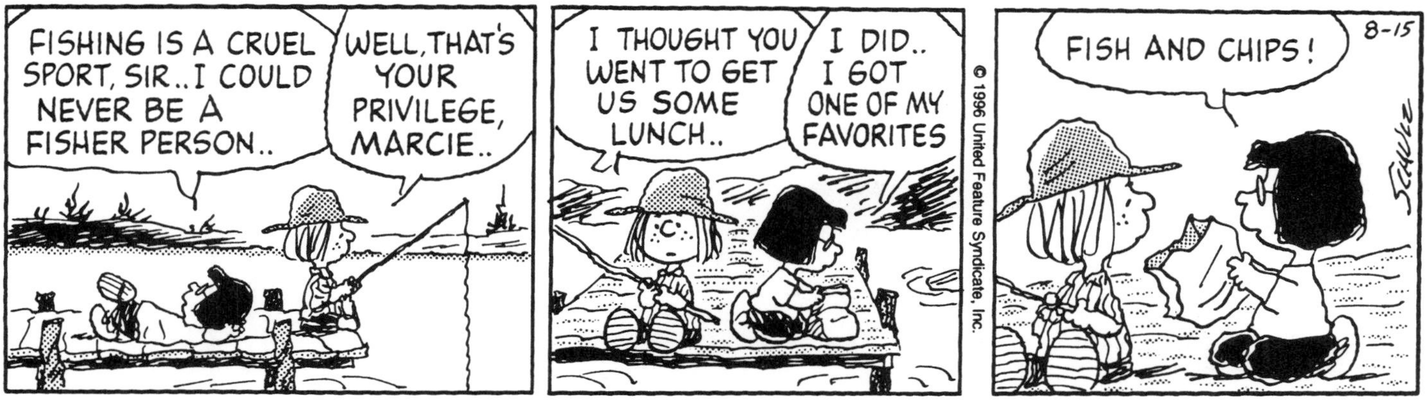
FISHING IS A CRUEL SPORT, SIR.. I COULD NEVER BE A FISHER PERSON..
WELL, THAT'S YOUR PRIVILEGE, MARCIE..
I THOUGHT YOU WENT TO GET US SOME LUNCH..
I DID.. I GOT ONE OF MY FAVORITES
© 1996 United Feature Syndicate, Inc.
FISH AND CHIPS!
8-15
SCHULZ

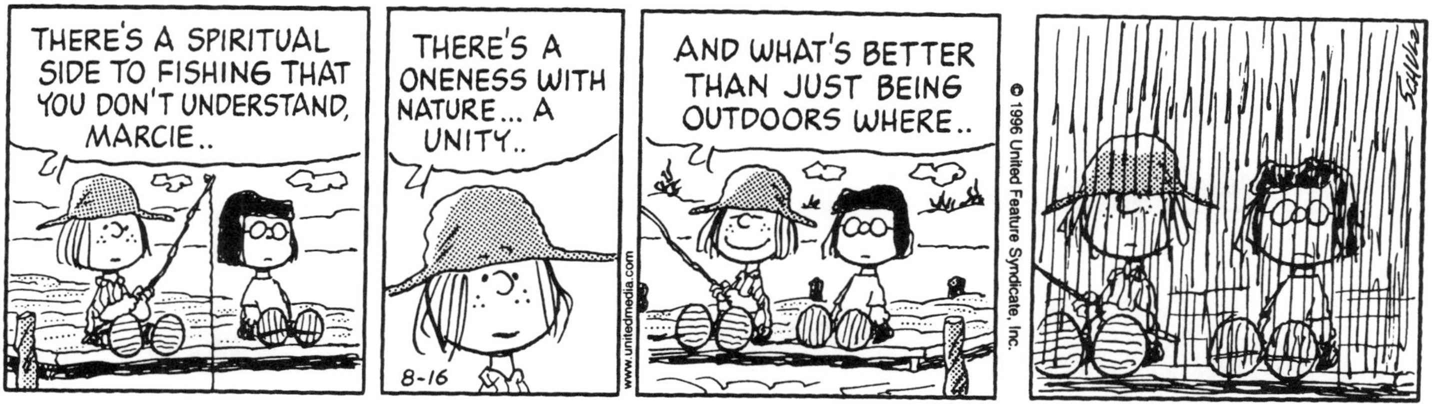
THERE'S A SPIRITUAL SIDE TO FISHING THAT YOU DON'T UNDERSTAND, MARCIE..
THERE'S A ONENESS WITH NATURE... A UNITY..
8-16
www.unitedmedia.com
AND WHAT'S BETTER THAN JUST BEING OUTDOORS WHERE..
© 1996 United Feature Syndicate, Inc.
SCHULZ

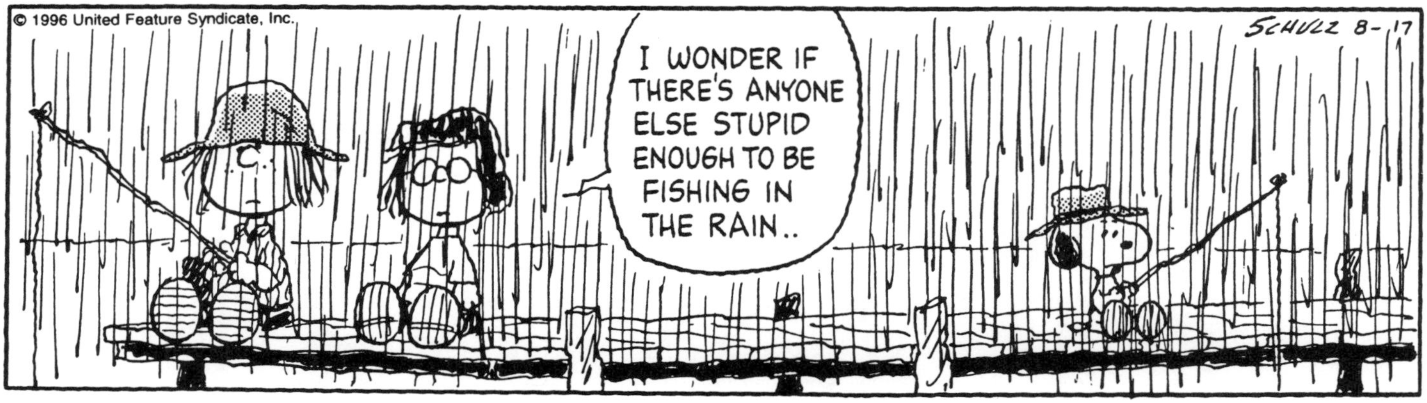
© 1996 United Feature Syndicate, Inc.
SCHULZ 8-17
I WONDER IF THERE'S ANYONE ELSE STUPID ENOUGH TO BE FISHING IN THE RAIN..

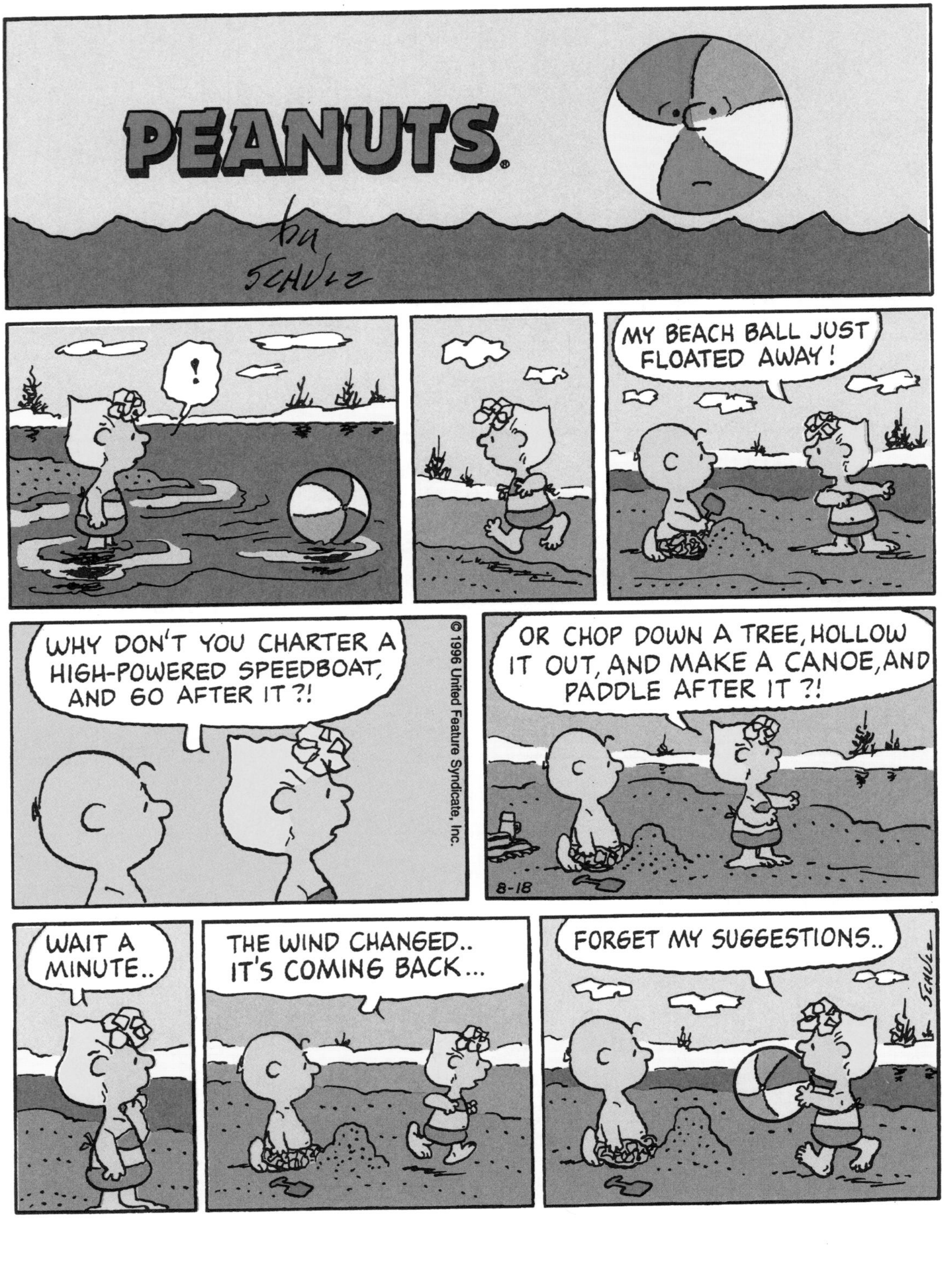
PEANUTS®
by SCHULZ
!
MY BEACH BALL JUST FLOATED AWAY!
WHY DON'T YOU CHARTER A HIGH-POWERED SPEEDBOAT, AND GO AFTER IT?!
© 1996 United Feature Syndicate, Inc.
OR CHOP DOWN A TREE, HOLLOW IT OUT, AND MAKE A CANOE, AND PADDLE AFTER IT?!
8-18
WAIT A MINUTE..
THE WIND CHANGED.. IT'S COMING BACK...
FORGET MY SUGGESTIONS..
SCHULZ

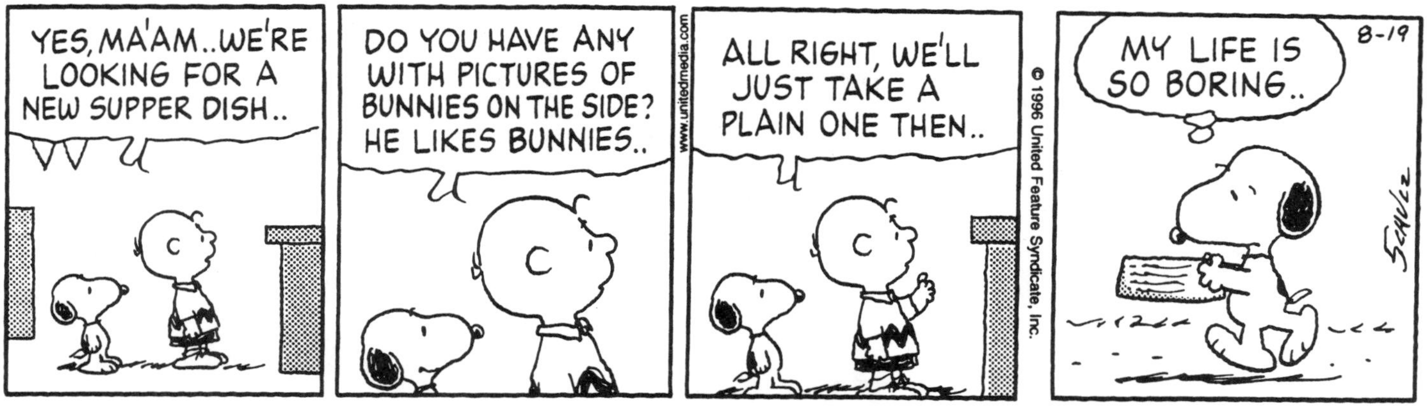
YES, MA'AM..WE'RE LOOKING FOR A NEW SUPPER DISH..
DO YOU HAVE ANY WITH PICTURES OF BUNNIES ON THE SIDE? HE LIKES BUNNIES..
ALL RIGHT, WE'LL JUST TAKE A PLAIN ONE THEN..
MY LIFE IS SO BORING..
8-19
SCHULZ
www.unitedmedia.com
© 1996 United Feature Syndicate, Inc.

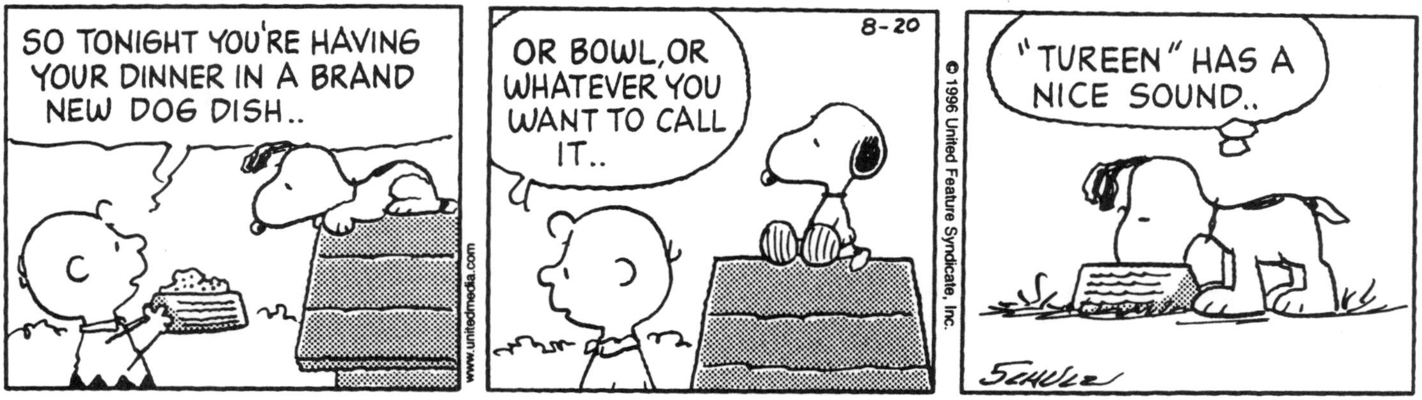
SO TONIGHT YOU'RE HAVING YOUR DINNER IN A BRAND NEW DOG DISH..
OR BOWL, OR WHATEVER YOU WANT TO CALL IT..
"TUREEN" HAS A NICE SOUND..
8-20
SCHULZ
www.unitedmedia.com
© 1996 United Feature Syndicate, Inc.

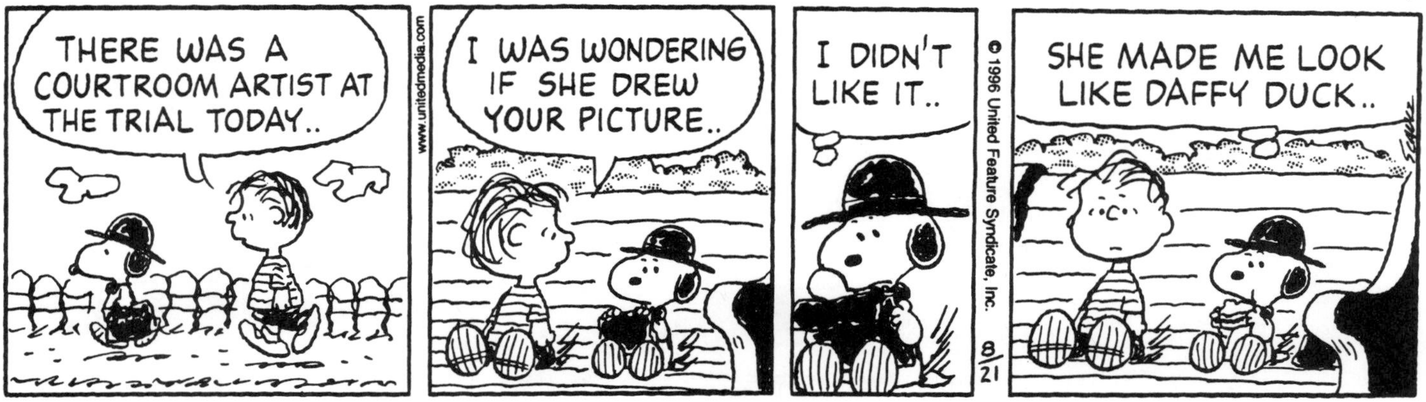
THERE WAS A COURTROOM ARTIST AT THE TRIAL TODAY..
I WAS WONDERING IF SHE DREW YOUR PICTURE..
I DIDN'T LIKE IT..
SHE MADE ME LOOK LIKE DAFFY DUCK..
8/21
SCHULZ
www.unitedmedia.com
© 1996 United Feature Syndicate, Inc.

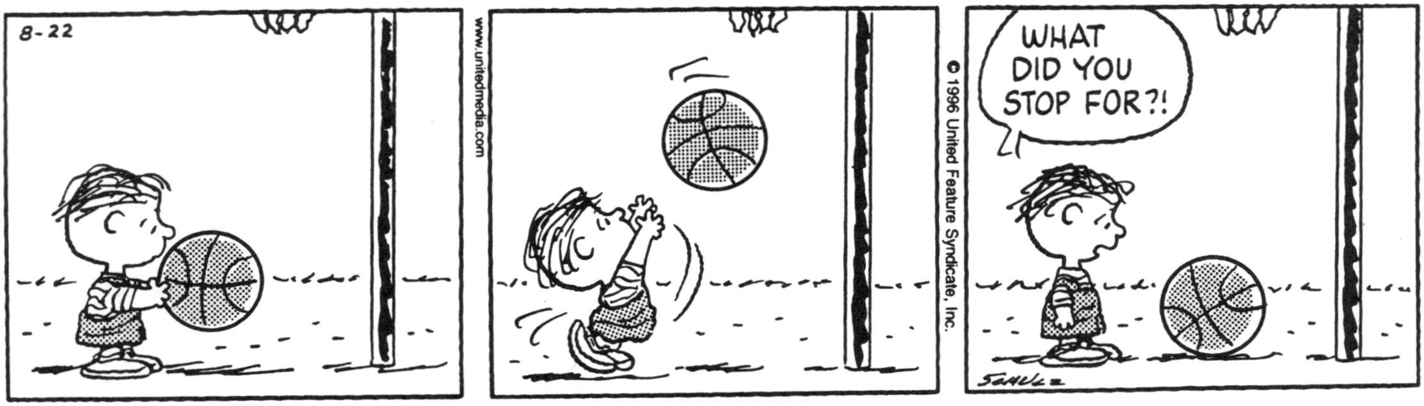
8-22
www.unitedmedia.com
© 1996 United Feature Syndicate, Inc.
WHAT DID YOU STOP FOR?!
SCHULZ

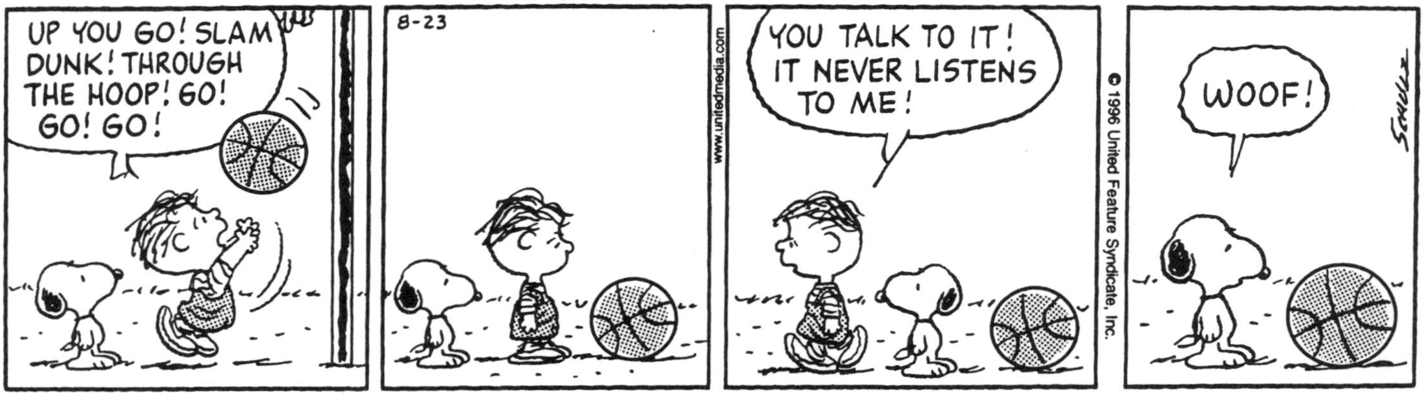
UP YOU GO! SLAM DUNK! THROUGH THE HOOP! GO! GO! GO!
8-23
www.unitedmedia.com
YOU TALK TO IT! IT NEVER LISTENS TO ME!
© 1996 United Feature Syndicate, Inc.
WOOF!
SCHULZ

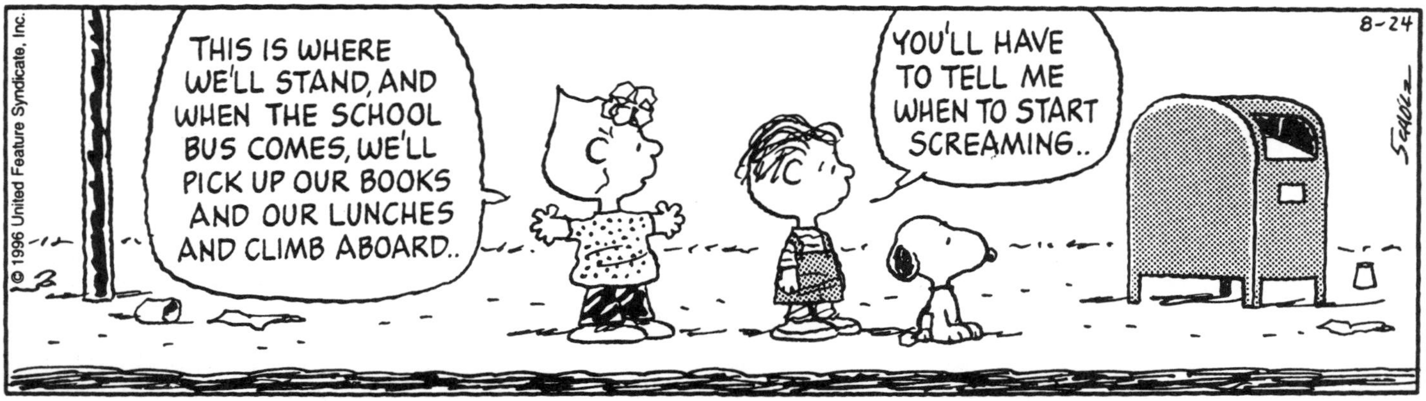
© 1996 United Feature Syndicate, Inc.
THIS IS WHERE WE'LL STAND, AND WHEN THE SCHOOL BUS COMES, WE'LL PICK UP OUR BOOKS AND OUR LUNCHES AND CLIMB ABOARD..
YOU'LL HAVE TO TELL ME WHEN TO START SCREAMING..
8-24
SCHULZ

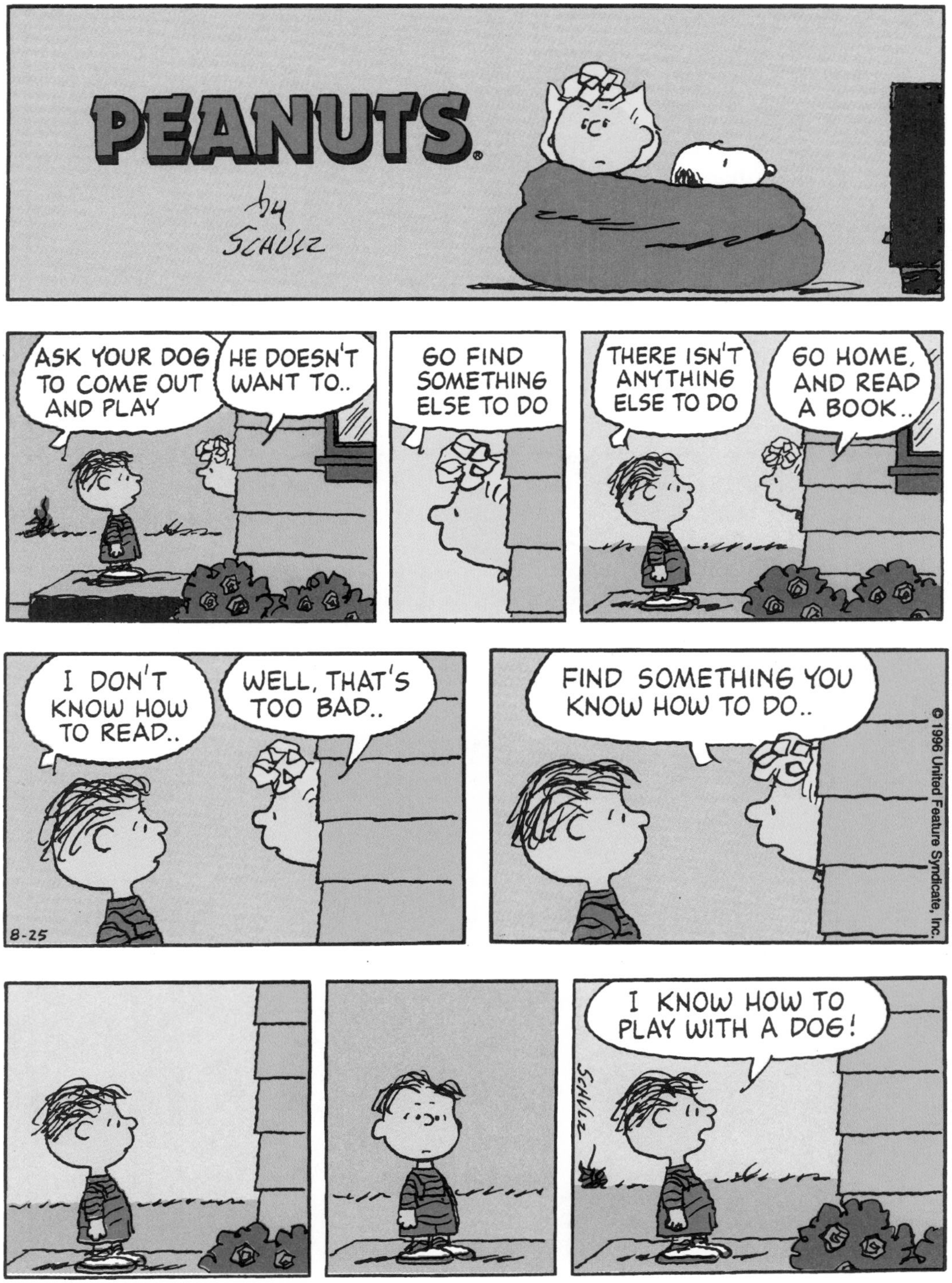
PEANUTS
by SCHULZ
ASK YOUR DOG TO COME OUT AND PLAY
HE DOESN'T WANT TO..
GO FIND SOMETHING ELSE TO DO
THERE ISN'T ANYTHING ELSE TO DO
GO HOME, AND READ A BOOK..
I DON'T KNOW HOW TO READ..
WELL, THAT'S TOO BAD..
8-25
FIND SOMETHING YOU KNOW HOW TO DO..
© 1996 United Feature Syndicate, Inc.
I KNOW HOW TO PLAY WITH A DOG!
SCHULZ

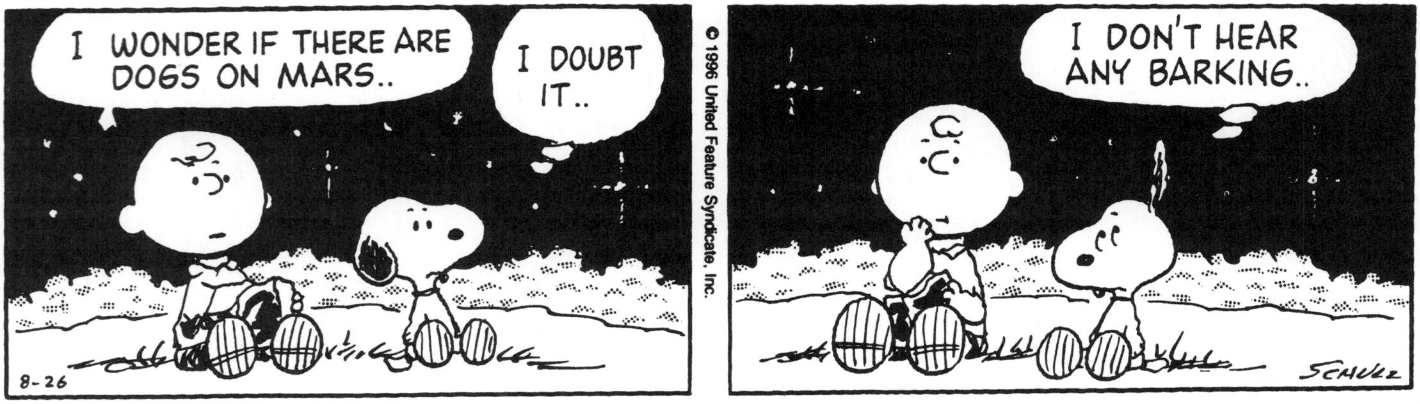
I WONDER IF THERE ARE DOGS ON MARS..
I DOUBT IT..
© 1996 United Feature Syndicate, Inc.
I DON'T HEAR ANY BARKING..
8-26
SCHULZ

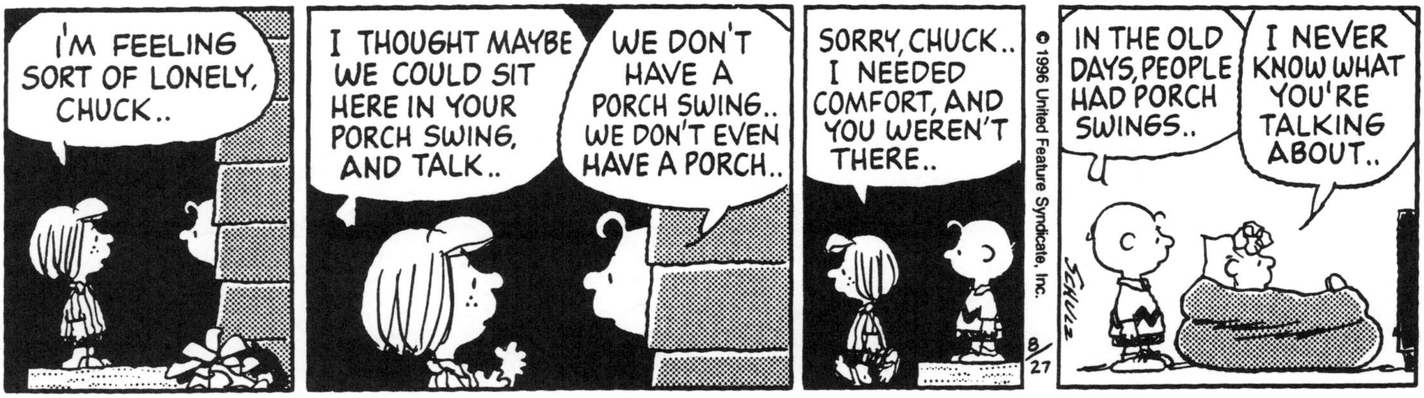
I'M FEELING SORT OF LONELY, CHUCK..
I THOUGHT MAYBE WE COULD SIT HERE IN YOUR PORCH SWING, AND TALK..
WE DON'T HAVE A PORCH SWING.. WE DON'T EVEN HAVE A PORCH..
SORRY, CHUCK.. I NEEDED COMFORT, AND YOU WEREN'T THERE..
© 1996 United Feature Syndicate, Inc.
8/27
SCHULZ
IN THE OLD DAYS, PEOPLE HAD PORCH SWINGS..
I NEVER KNOW WHAT YOU'RE TALKING ABOUT..

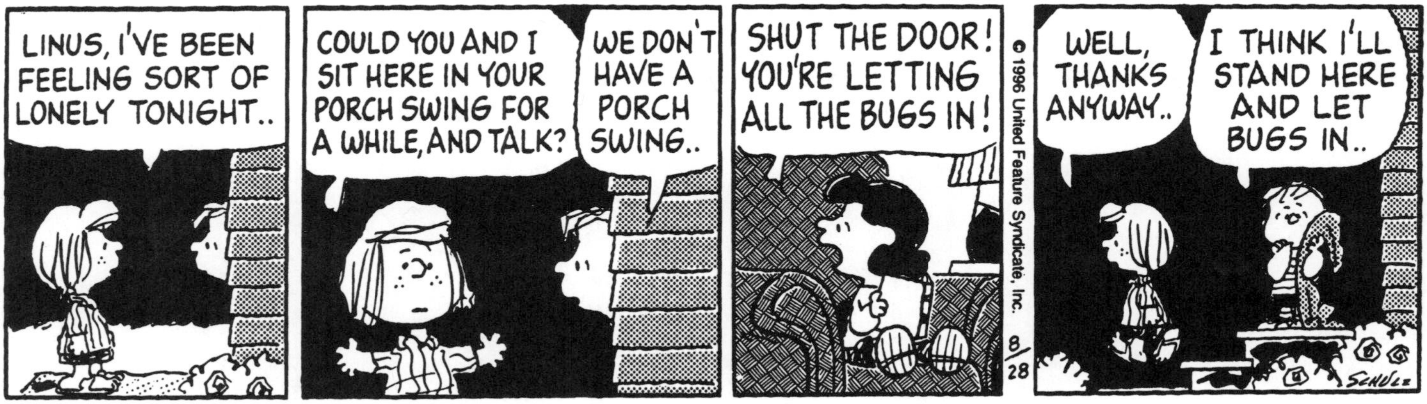
LINUS, I'VE BEEN FEELING SORT OF LONELY TONIGHT..
COULD YOU AND I SIT HERE IN YOUR PORCH SWING FOR A WHILE, AND TALK?
WE DON'T HAVE A PORCH SWING..
SHUT THE DOOR! YOU'RE LETTING ALL THE BUGS IN!
© 1996 United Feature Syndicate, Inc.
8/28
WELL, THANKS ANYWAY..
I THINK I'LL STAND HERE AND LET BUGS IN..
SCHULZ

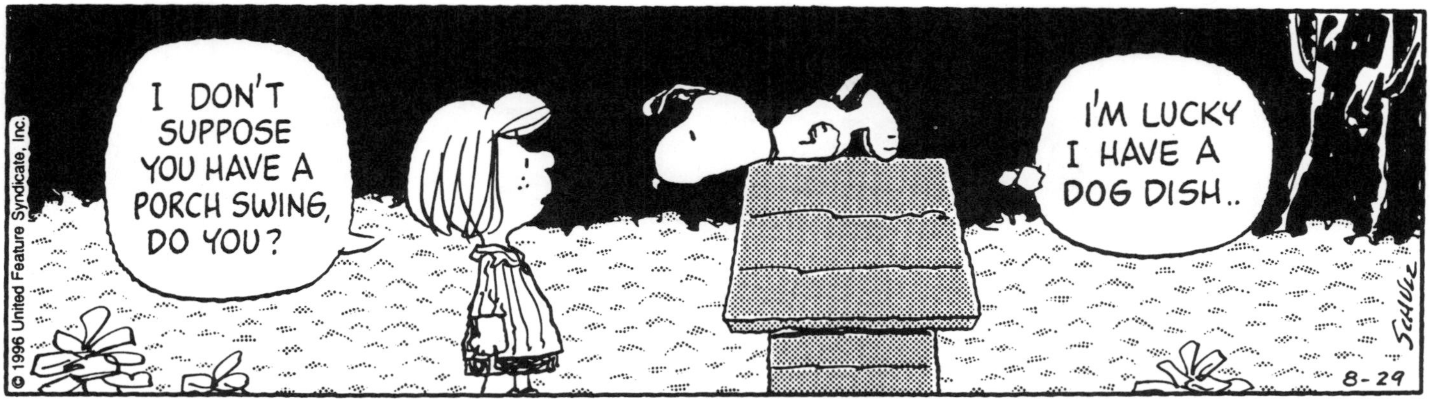
© 1996 United Feature Syndicate, Inc.
I DON'T SUPPOSE YOU HAVE A PORCH SWING, DO YOU?
I'M LUCKY I HAVE A DOG DISH..
SCHULZ
8-29

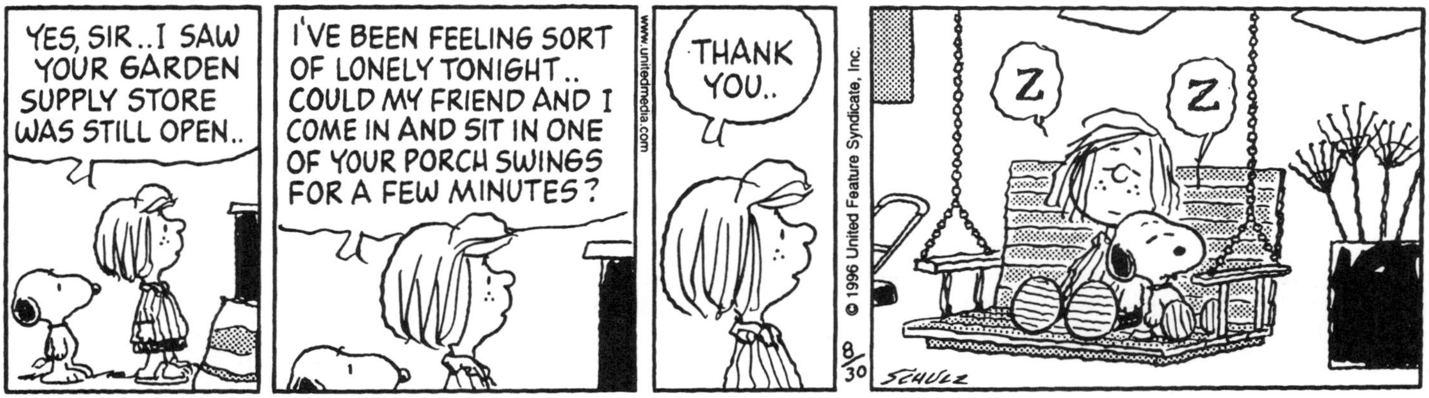
YES, SIR..I SAW YOUR GARDEN SUPPLY STORE WAS STILL OPEN..
I'VE BEEN FEELING SORT OF LONELY TONIGHT.. COULD MY FRIEND AND I COME IN AND SIT IN ONE OF YOUR PORCH SWINGS FOR A FEW MINUTES?
www.unitedmedia.com
THANK YOU..
© 1996 United Feature Syndicate, Inc.
8/30
SCHULZ
Z
Z

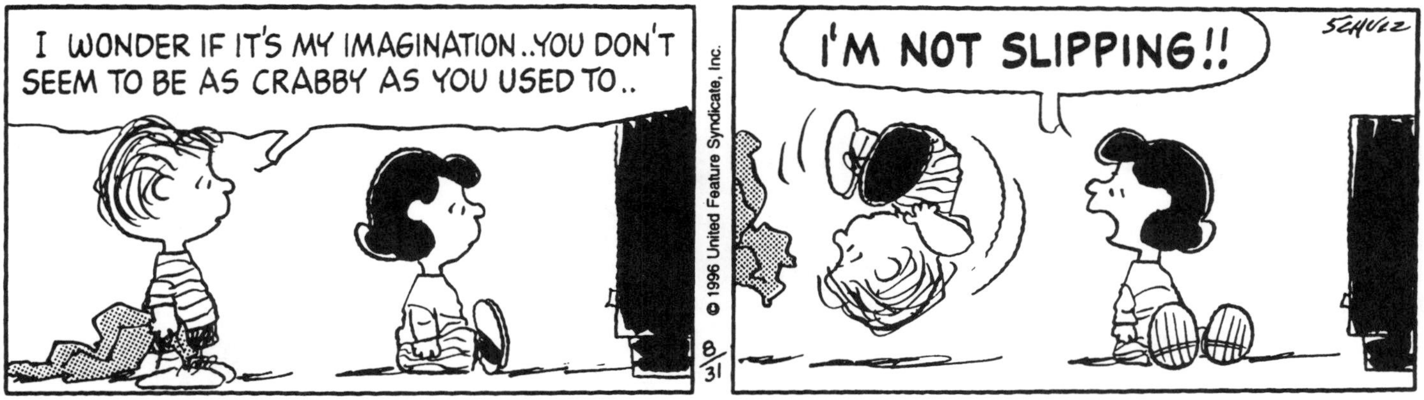
I WONDER IF IT'S MY IMAGINATION..YOU DON'T SEEM TO BE AS CRABBY AS YOU USED TO..
© 1996 United Feature Syndicate, Inc.
8/31
I'M NOT SLIPPING!!
SCHULZ

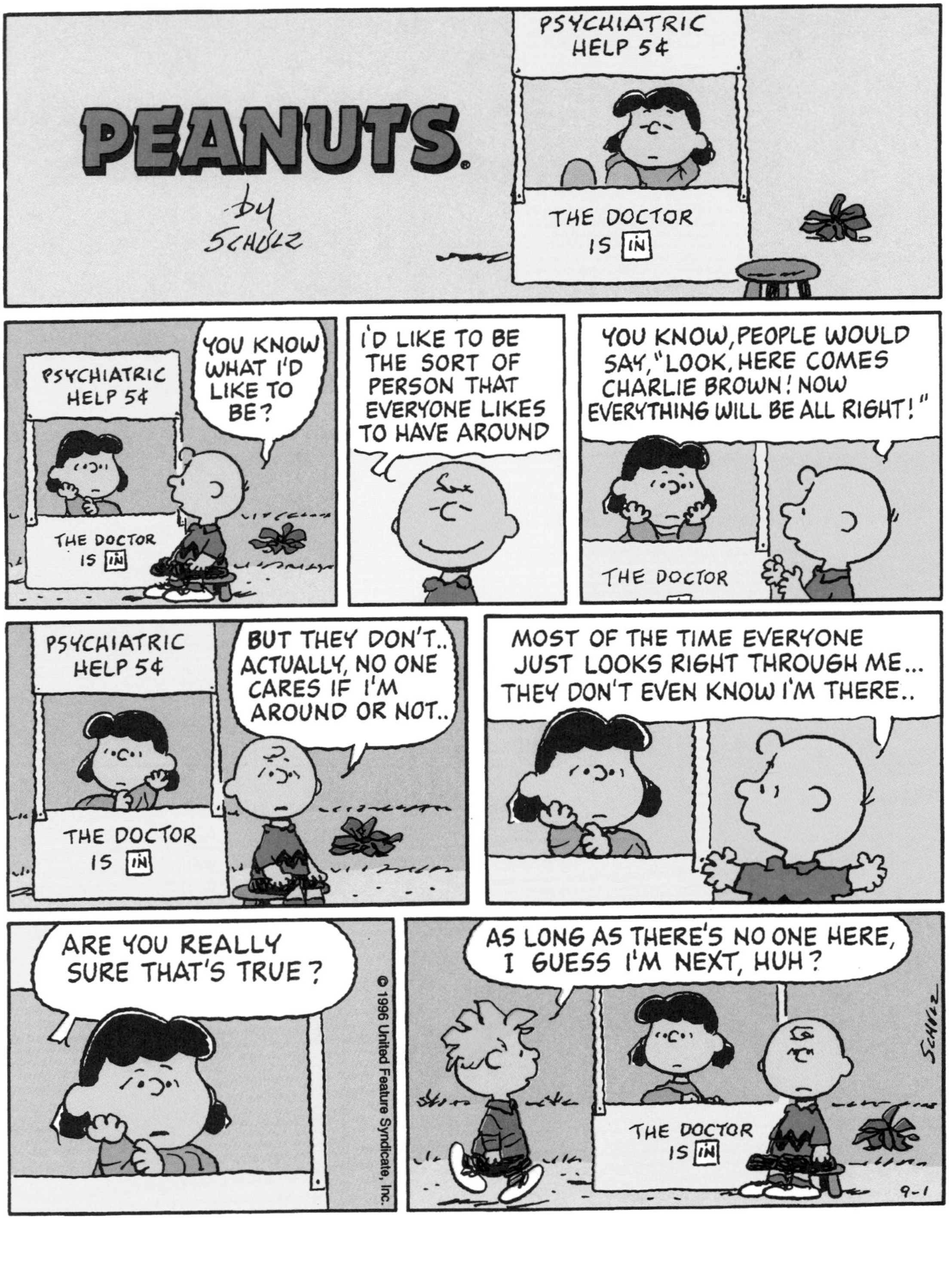
PEANUTS
by SCHULZ
PSYCHIATRIC HELP 5¢
THE DOCTOR IS IN
YOU KNOW WHAT I'D LIKE TO BE?
I'D LIKE TO BE THE SORT OF PERSON THAT EVERYONE LIKES TO HAVE AROUND
YOU KNOW, PEOPLE WOULD SAY, "LOOK, HERE COMES CHARLIE BROWN! NOW EVERYTHING WILL BE ALL RIGHT!"
BUT THEY DON'T.. ACTUALLY, NO ONE CARES IF I'M AROUND OR NOT..
MOST OF THE TIME EVERYONE JUST LOOKS RIGHT THROUGH ME... THEY DON'T EVEN KNOW I'M THERE..
ARE YOU REALLY SURE THAT'S TRUE?
© 1996 United Feature Syndicate, Inc.
AS LONG AS THERE'S NO ONE HERE, I GUESS I'M NEXT, HUH?
SCHULZ
9-1

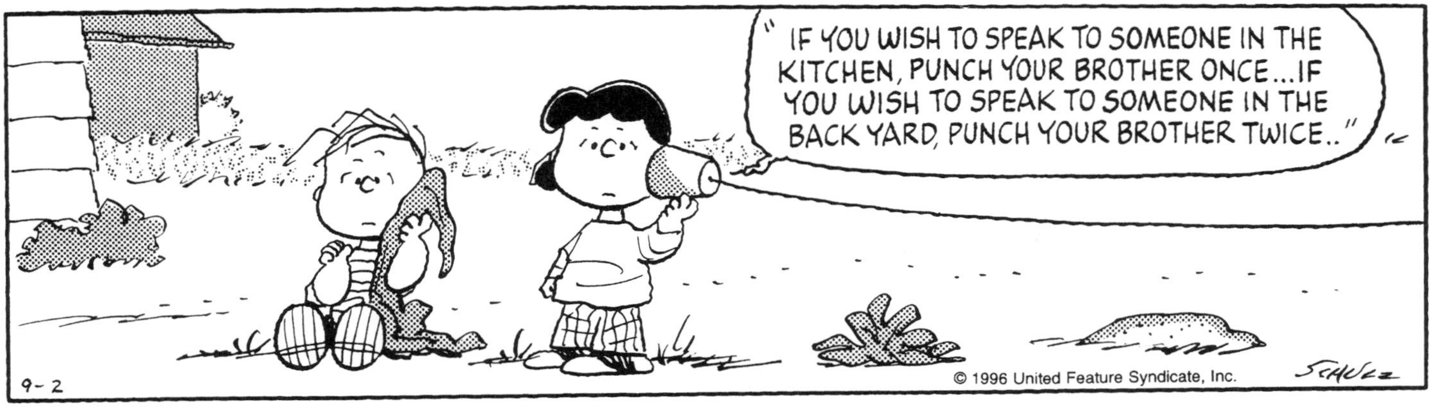
"IF YOU WISH TO SPEAK TO SOMEONE IN THE KITCHEN, PUNCH YOUR BROTHER ONCE...IF YOU WISH TO SPEAK TO SOMEONE IN THE BACK YARD, PUNCH YOUR BROTHER TWICE.."
9-2
© 1996 United Feature Syndicate, Inc.
SCHULZ

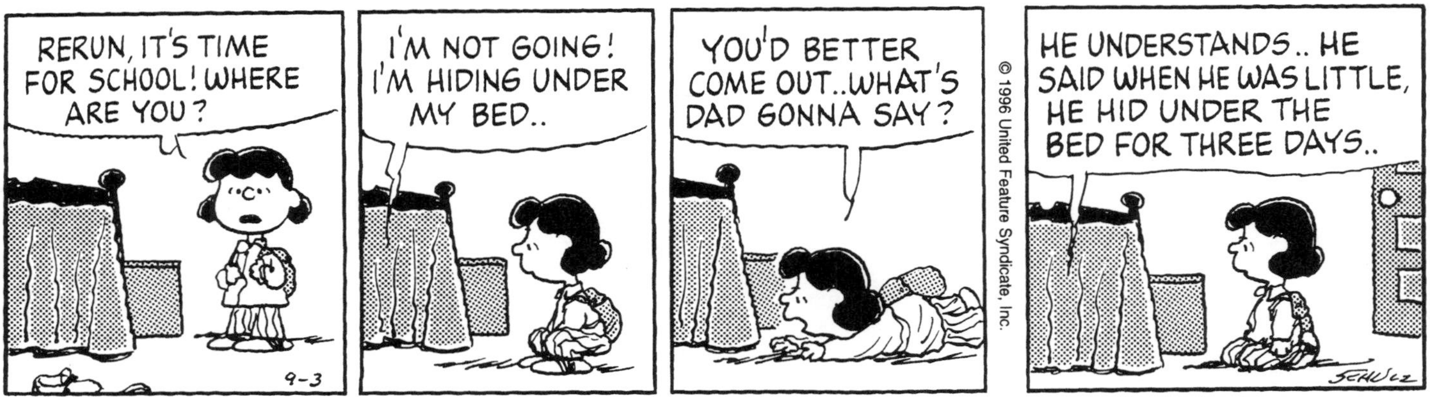
RERUN, IT'S TIME FOR SCHOOL! WHERE ARE YOU?
9-3
I'M NOT GOING! I'M HIDING UNDER MY BED..
YOU'D BETTER COME OUT..WHAT'S DAD GONNA SAY?
© 1996 United Feature Syndicate, Inc.
HE UNDERSTANDS.. HE SAID WHEN HE WAS LITTLE, HE HID UNDER THE BED FOR THREE DAYS..
SCHULZ

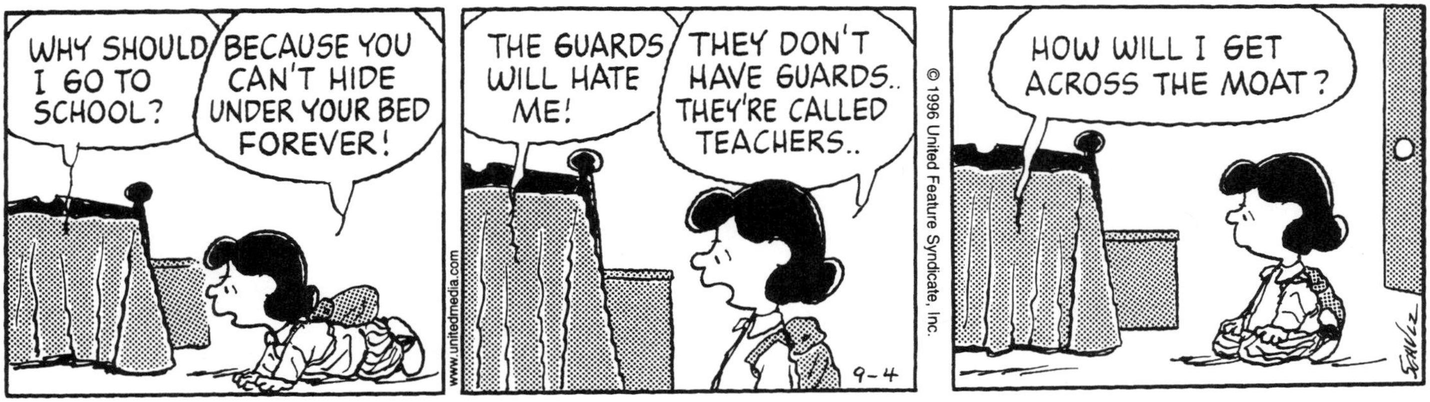
WHY SHOULD I GO TO SCHOOL?
BECAUSE YOU CAN'T HIDE UNDER YOUR BED FOREVER!
www.unitedmedia.com
THE GUARDS WILL HATE ME!
THEY DON'T HAVE GUARDS.. THEY'RE CALLED TEACHERS..
9-4
© 1996 United Feature Syndicate, Inc.
HOW WILL I GET ACROSS THE MOAT?
SCHULZ

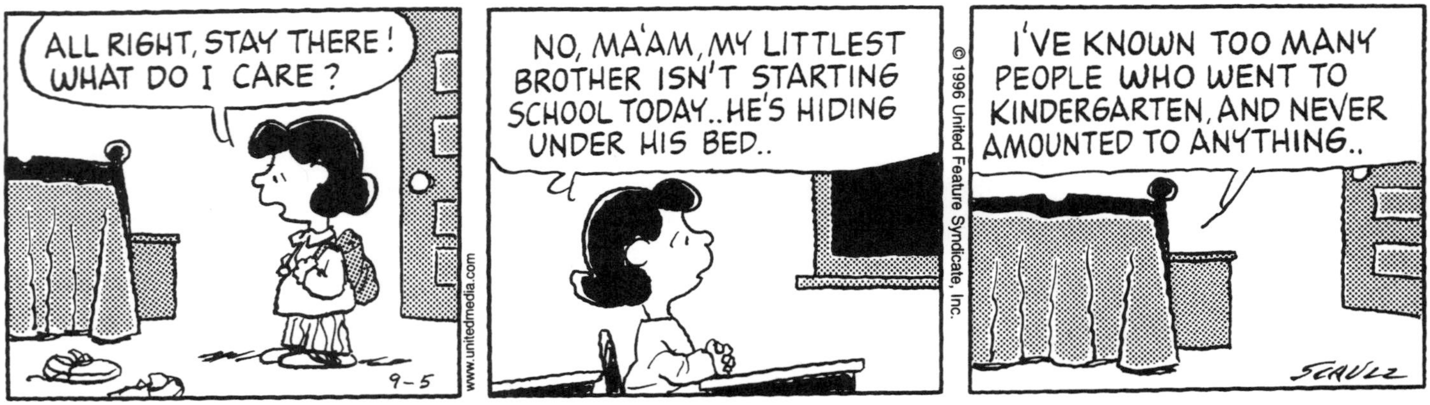
ALL RIGHT, STAY THERE! WHAT DO I CARE?
NO, MA'AM, MY LITTLEST BROTHER ISN'T STARTING SCHOOL TODAY..HE'S HIDING UNDER HIS BED..
I'VE KNOWN TOO MANY PEOPLE WHO WENT TO KINDERGARTEN, AND NEVER AMOUNTED TO ANYTHING..
9-5
www.unitedmedia.com
© 1996 United Feature Syndicate, Inc.
SCHULZ

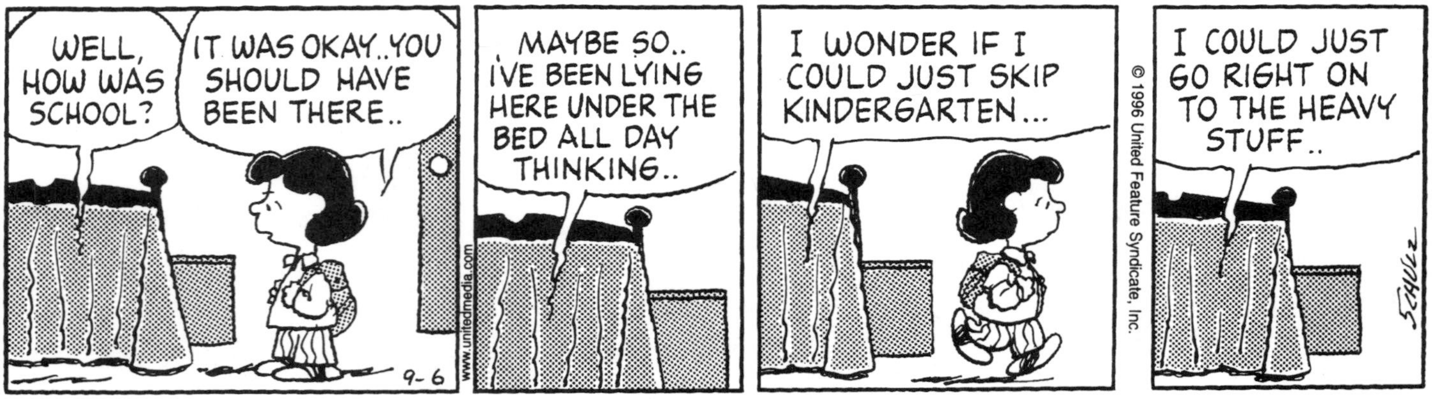
WELL, HOW WAS SCHOOL?
IT WAS OKAY..YOU SHOULD HAVE BEEN THERE..
MAYBE SO.. I'VE BEEN LYING HERE UNDER THE BED ALL DAY THINKING..
I WONDER IF I COULD JUST SKIP KINDERGARTEN...
I COULD JUST GO RIGHT ON TO THE HEAVY STUFF..
9-6
www.unitedmedia.com
© 1996 United Feature Syndicate, Inc.
SCHULZ

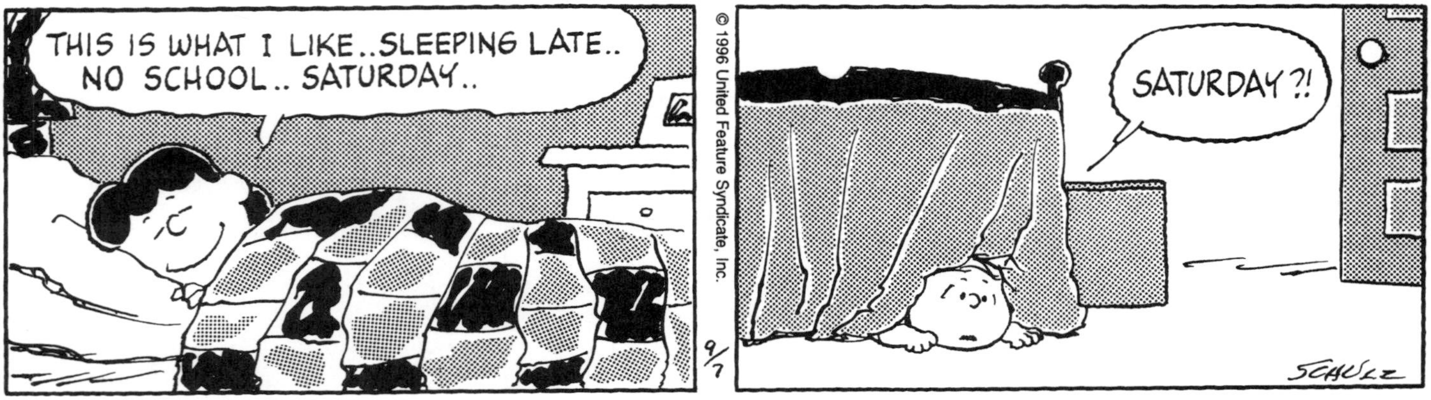
THIS IS WHAT I LIKE..SLEEPING LATE.. NO SCHOOL.. SATURDAY..
SATURDAY?!
9/7
© 1996 United Feature Syndicate, Inc.
SCHULZ

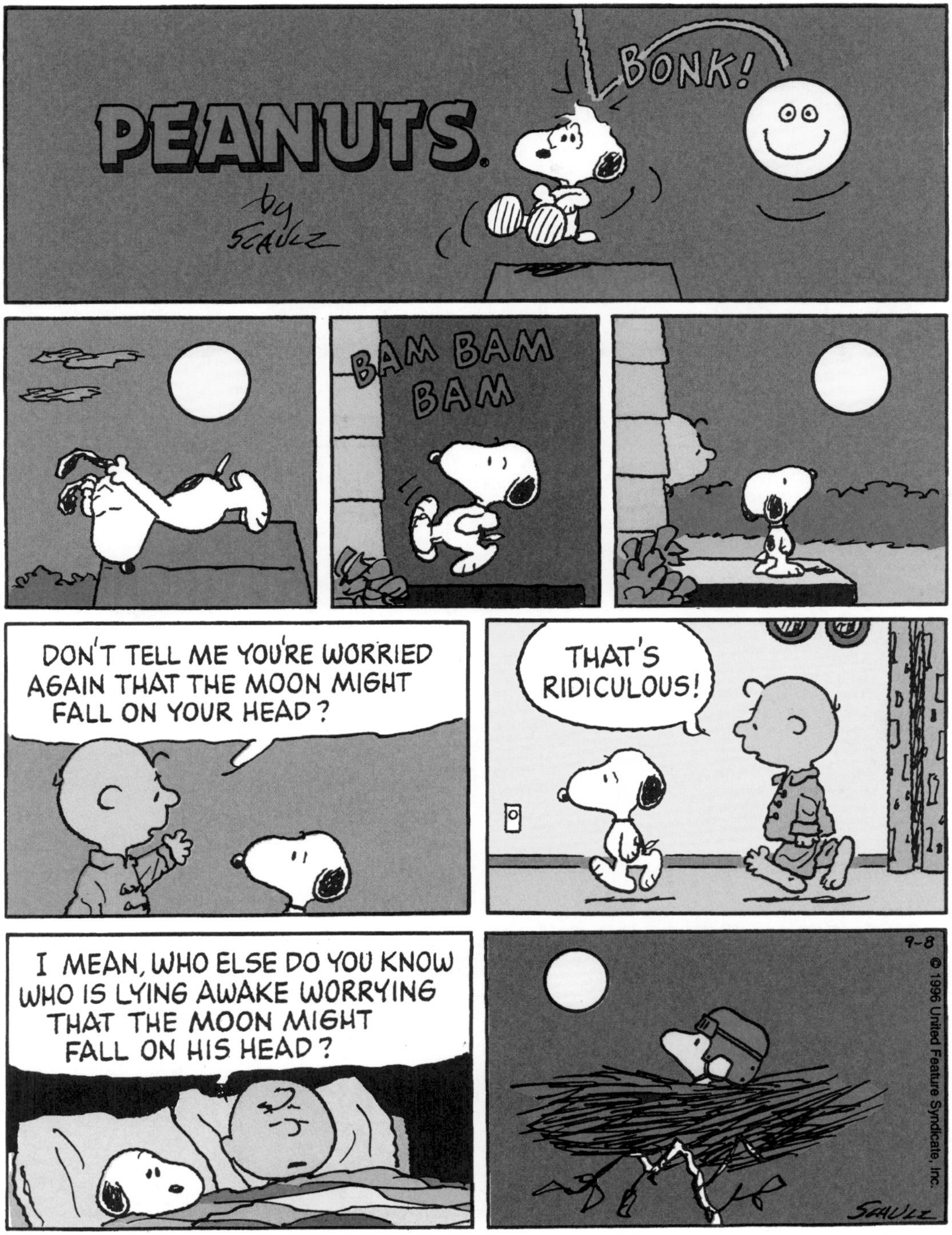
PEANUTS
by SCHULZ
BONK!
BAM BAM BAM
DON'T TELL ME YOU'RE WORRIED AGAIN THAT THE MOON MIGHT FALL ON YOUR HEAD?
THAT'S RIDICULOUS!
I MEAN, WHO ELSE DO YOU KNOW WHO IS LYING AWAKE WORRYING THAT THE MOON MIGHT FALL ON HIS HEAD?
9-8
© 1996 United Feature Syndicate, Inc.
SCHULZ

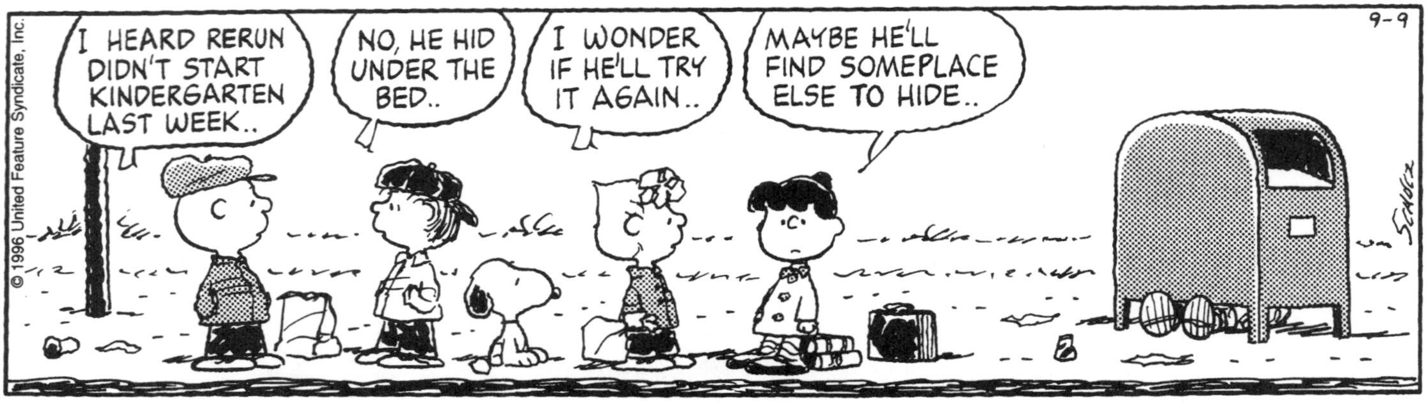
I HEARD RERUN DIDN'T START KINDERGARTEN LAST WEEK..
NO, HE HID UNDER THE BED..
I WONDER IF HE'LL TRY IT AGAIN..
MAYBE HE'LL FIND SOMEPLACE ELSE TO HIDE..
9-9

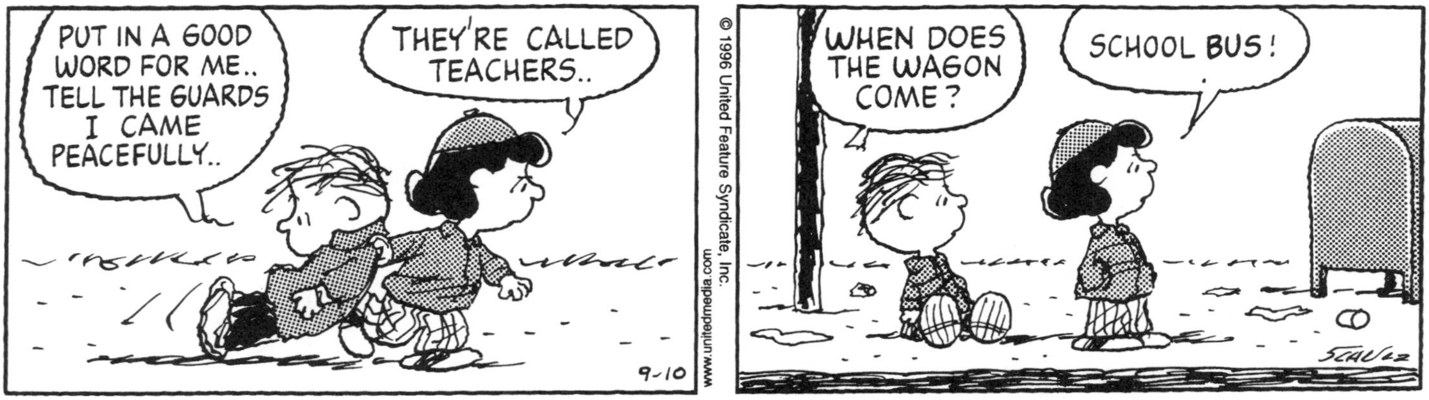
PUT IN A GOOD WORD FOR ME.. TELL THE GUARDS I CAME PEACEFULLY..
THEY'RE CALLED TEACHERS..
9-10
WHEN DOES THE WAGON COME?
SCHOOL BUS!

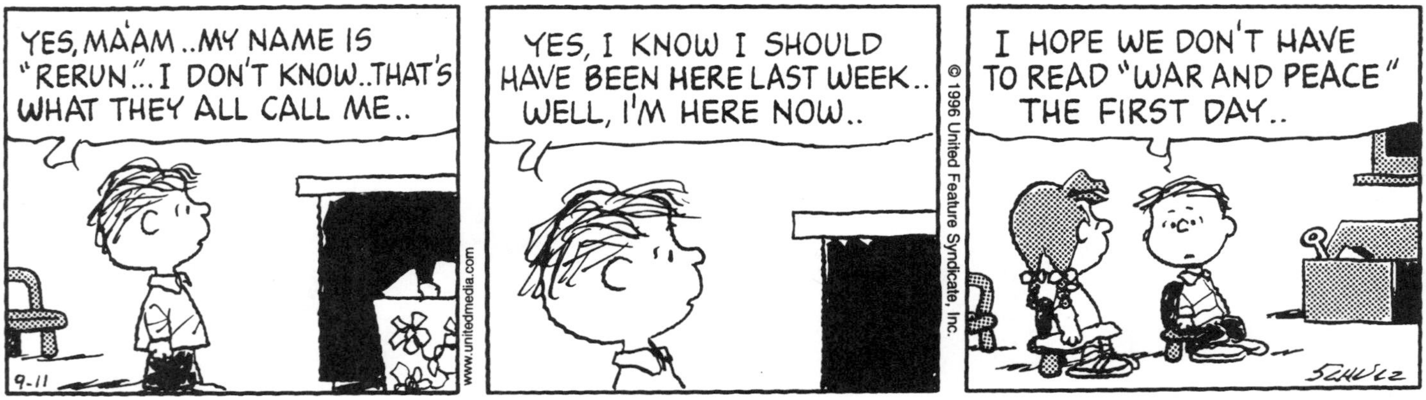
YES, MA'AM..MY NAME IS "RERUN"..I DON'T KNOW..THAT'S WHAT THEY ALL CALL ME..
9-11
YES, I KNOW I SHOULD HAVE BEEN HERE LAST WEEK.. WELL, I'M HERE NOW..
I HOPE WE DON'T HAVE TO READ "WAR AND PEACE" THE FIRST DAY..

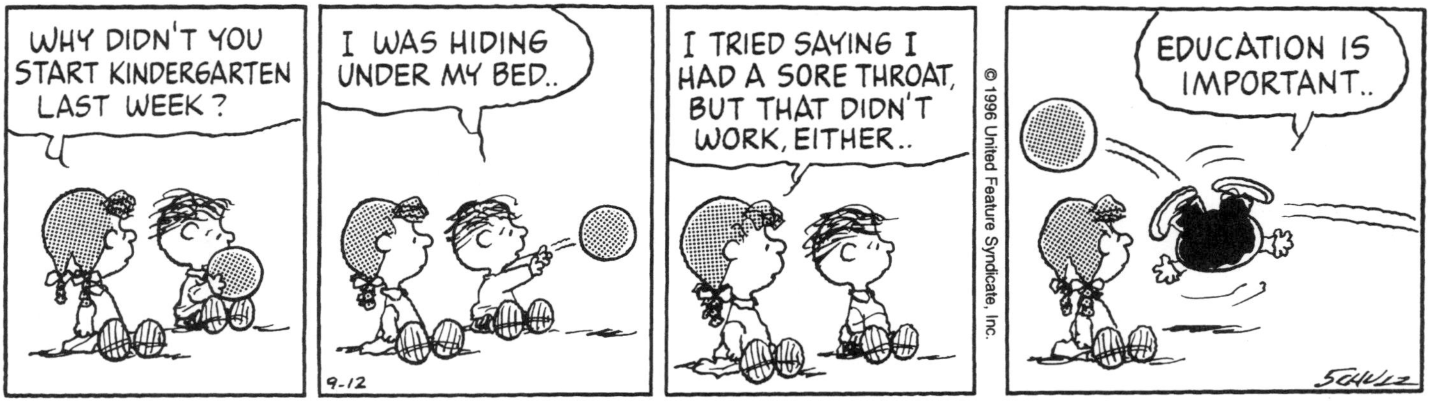
WHY DIDN'T YOU START KINDERGARTEN LAST WEEK?
I WAS HIDING UNDER MY BED..
9-12
I TRIED SAYING I HAD A SORE THROAT, BUT THAT DIDN'T WORK, EITHER..
© 1996 United Feature Syndicate, Inc.
EDUCATION IS IMPORTANT..
SCHULZ

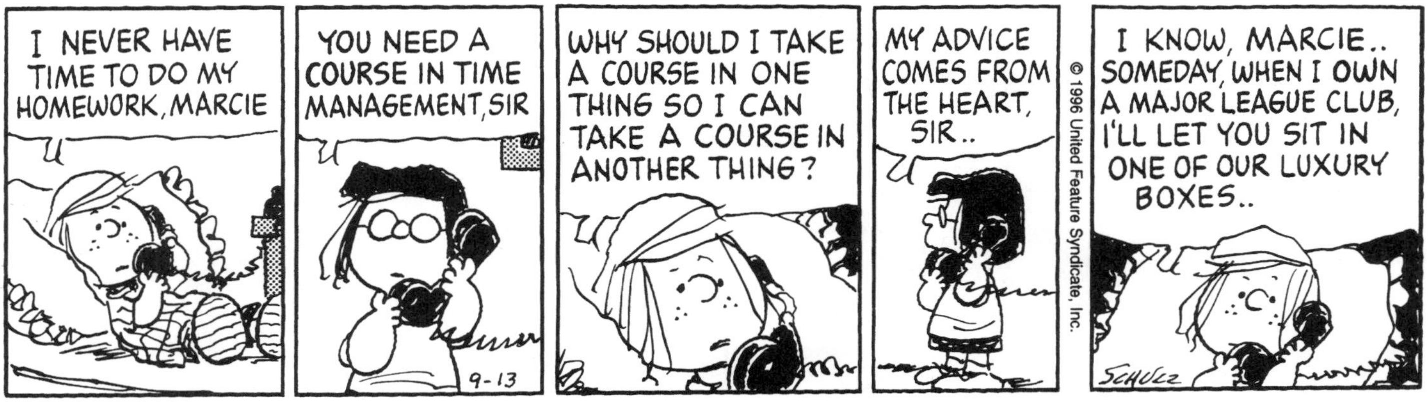
I NEVER HAVE TIME TO DO MY HOMEWORK, MARCIE
YOU NEED A COURSE IN TIME MANAGEMENT, SIR
9-13
WHY SHOULD I TAKE A COURSE IN ONE THING SO I CAN TAKE A COURSE IN ANOTHER THING?
MY ADVICE COMES FROM THE HEART, SIR..
© 1996 United Feature Syndicate, Inc.
I KNOW, MARCIE.. SOMEDAY, WHEN I OWN A MAJOR LEAGUE CLUB, I'LL LET YOU SIT IN ONE OF OUR LUXURY BOXES..
SCHULZ

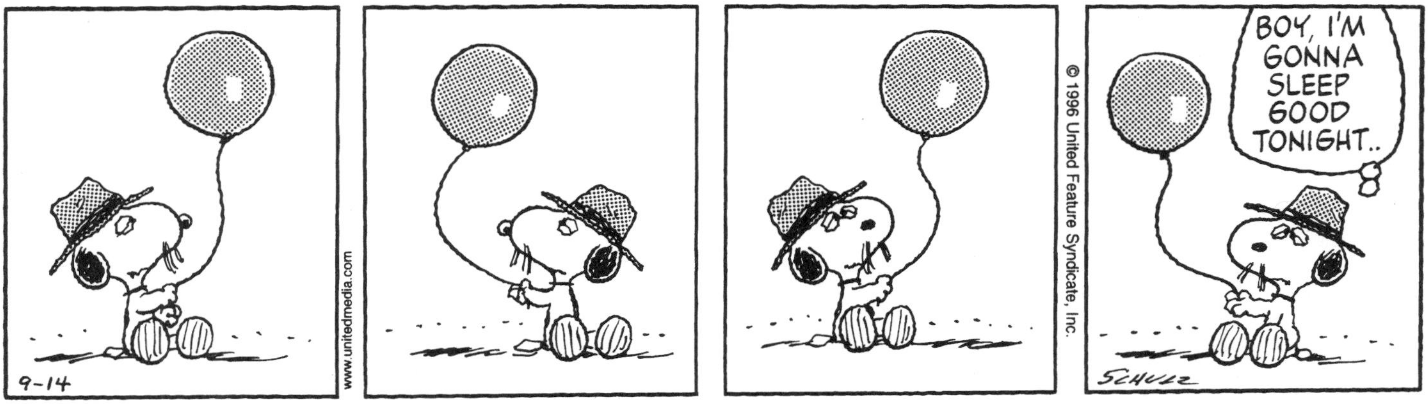
9-14
www.unitedmedia.com
© 1996 United Feature Syndicate, Inc.
BOY, I'M GONNA SLEEP GOOD TONIGHT..
SCHULZ

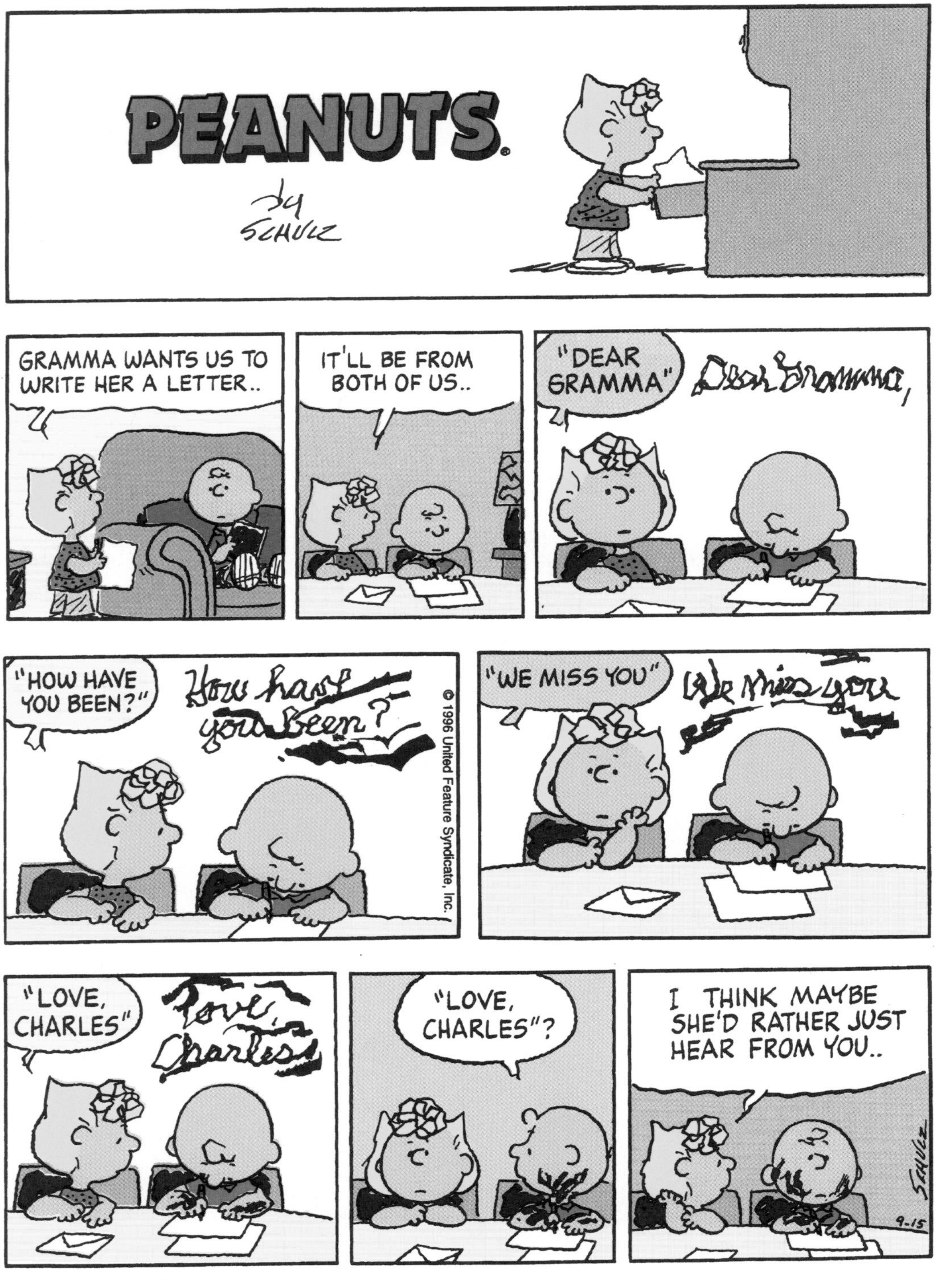
PEANUTS
GRAMMA WANTS US TO WRITE HER A LETTER..
IT'LL BE FROM BOTH OF US..
"DEAR GRAMMA"
"HOW HAVE YOU BEEN?"
© 1996 United Feature Syndicate, Inc.
"WE MISS YOU"
"LOVE, CHARLES"
"LOVE, CHARLES"?
I THINK MAYBE SHE'D RATHER JUST HEAR FROM YOU..

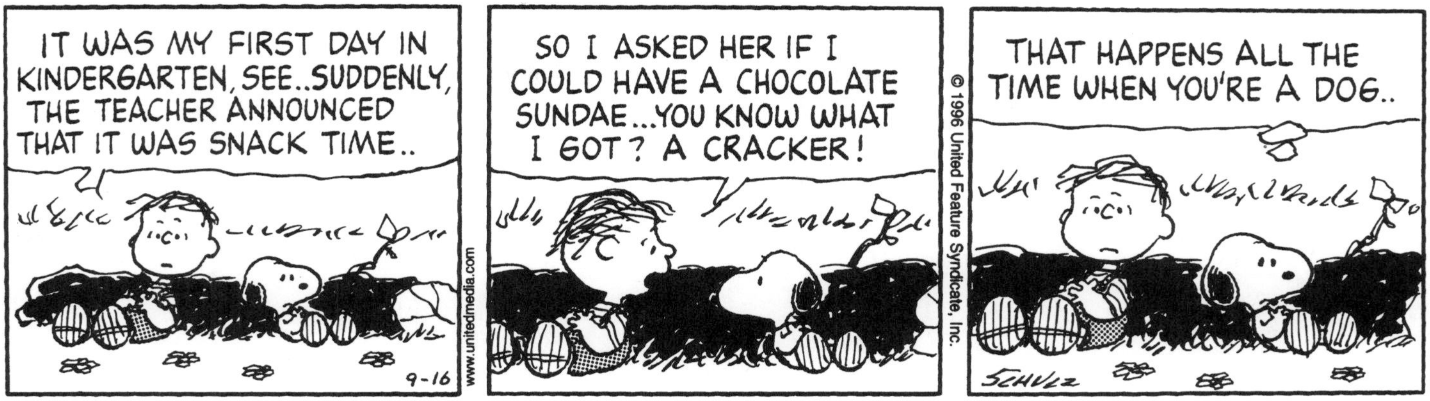
IT WAS MY FIRST DAY IN KINDERGARTEN, SEE..SUDDENLY, THE TEACHER ANNOUNCED THAT IT WAS SNACK TIME..
SO I ASKED HER IF I COULD HAVE A CHOCOLATE SUNDAE...YOU KNOW WHAT I GOT? A CRACKER!
THAT HAPPENS ALL THE TIME WHEN YOU'RE A DOG..
9-16
www.unitedmedia.com
© 1996 United Feature Syndicate, Inc.
SCHULZ

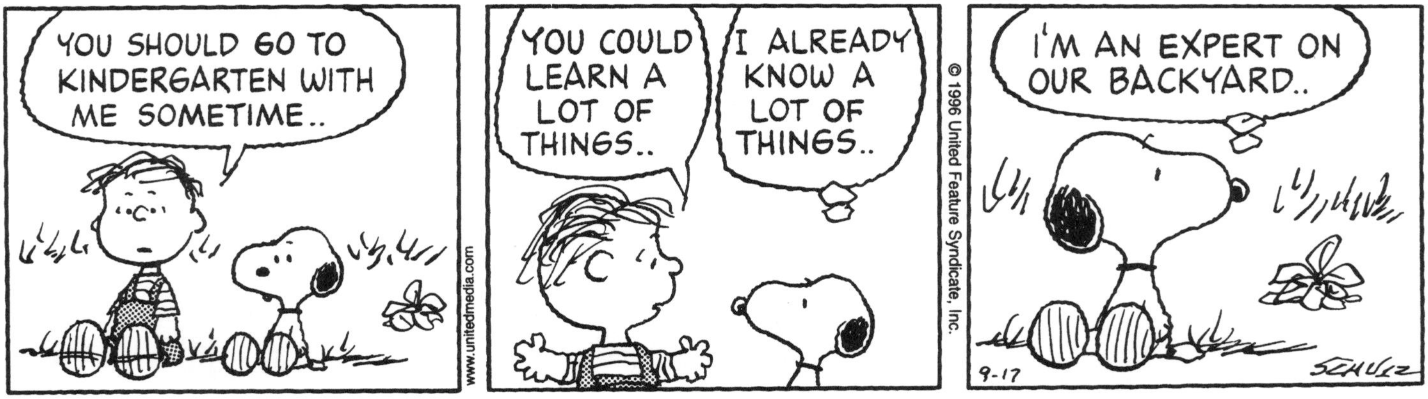
YOU SHOULD GO TO KINDERGARTEN WITH ME SOMETIME..
YOU COULD LEARN A LOT OF THINGS..
I ALREADY KNOW A LOT OF THINGS..
I'M AN EXPERT ON OUR BACKYARD..
www.unitedmedia.com
© 1996 United Feature Syndicate, Inc.
9-17
SCHULZ

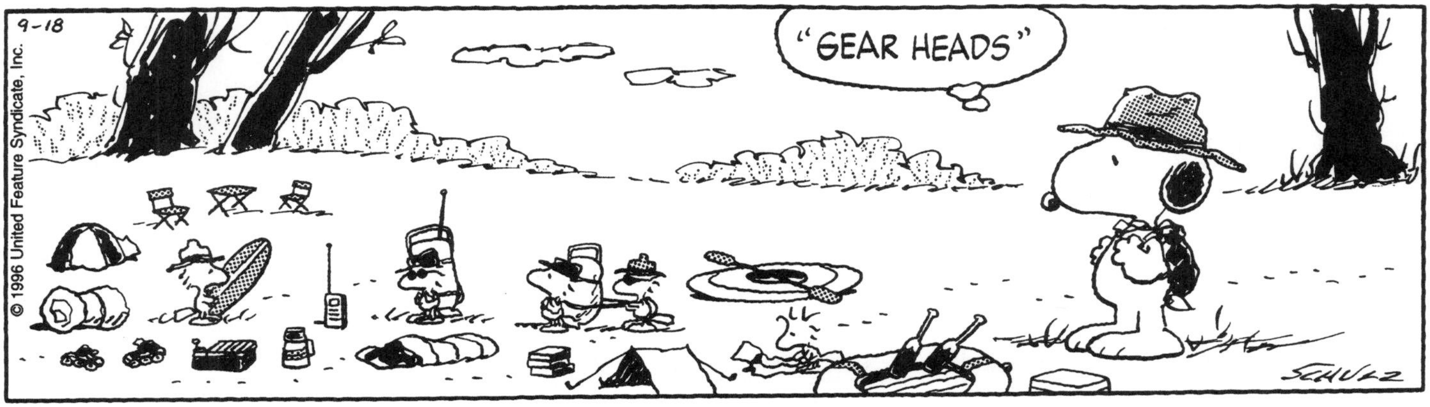
9-18
© 1996 United Feature Syndicate, Inc.
"GEAR HEADS"
SCHULZ

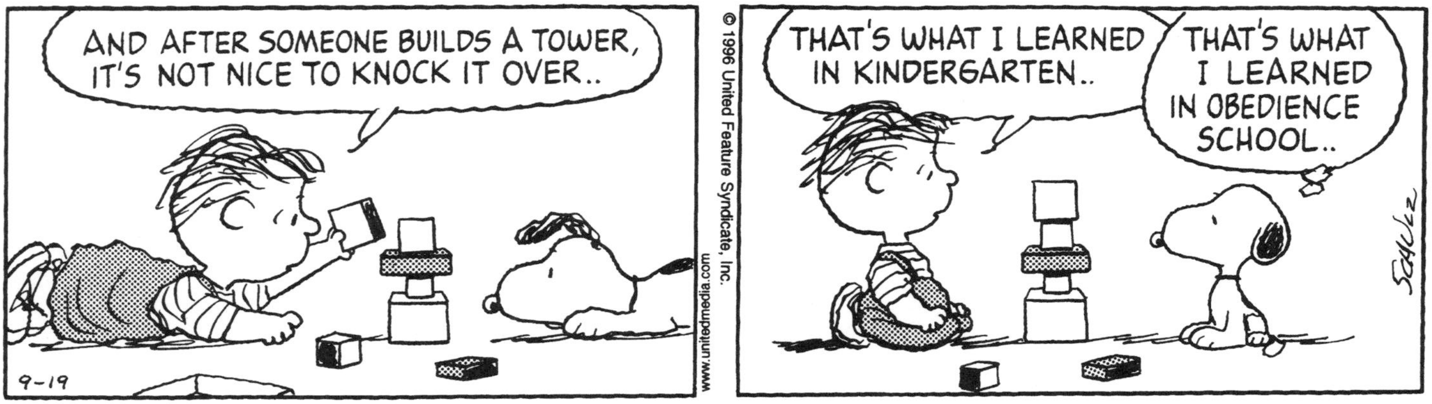
AND AFTER SOMEONE BUILDS A TOWER, IT'S NOT NICE TO KNOCK IT OVER..
9-19
THAT'S WHAT I LEARNED IN KINDERGARTEN..
THAT'S WHAT I LEARNED IN OBEDIENCE SCHOOL..
SCHULZ

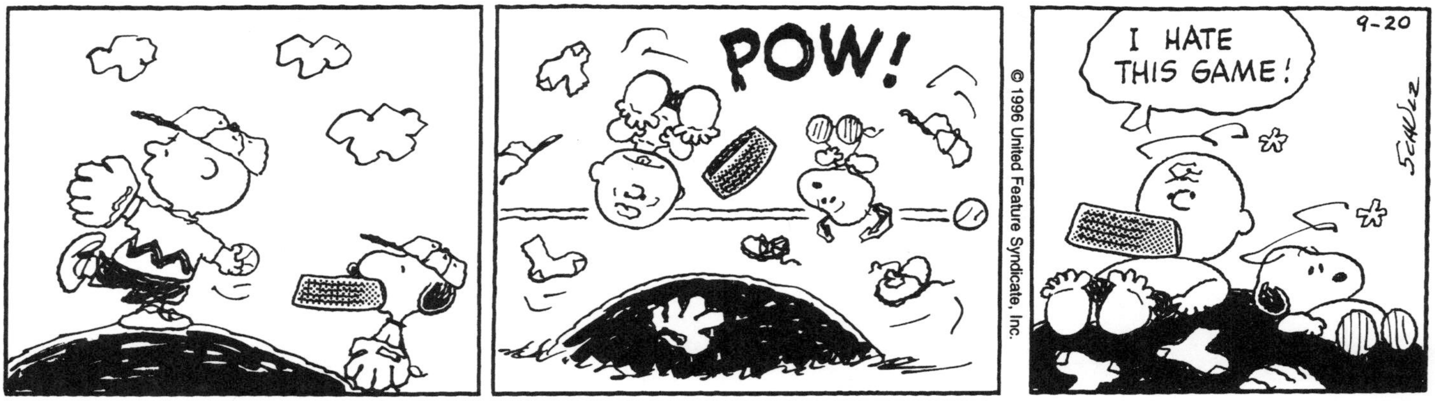
POW!
9-20
I HATE THIS GAME!
SCHULZ

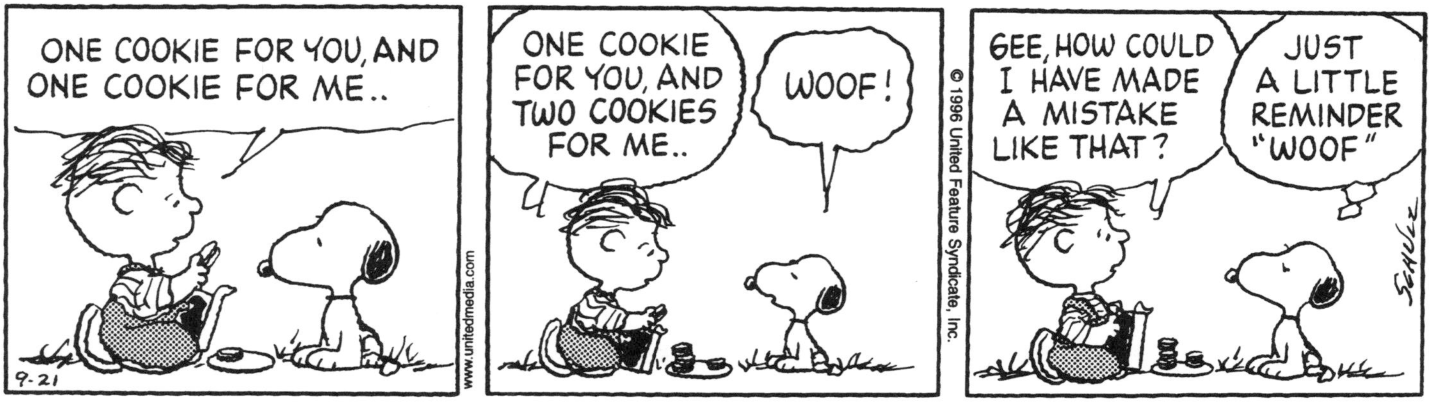
ONE COOKIE FOR YOU, AND ONE COOKIE FOR ME..
9-21
ONE COOKIE FOR YOU, AND TWO COOKIES FOR ME..
WOOF!
GEE, HOW COULD I HAVE MADE A MISTAKE LIKE THAT?
JUST A LITTLE REMINDER "WOOF"
SCHULZ

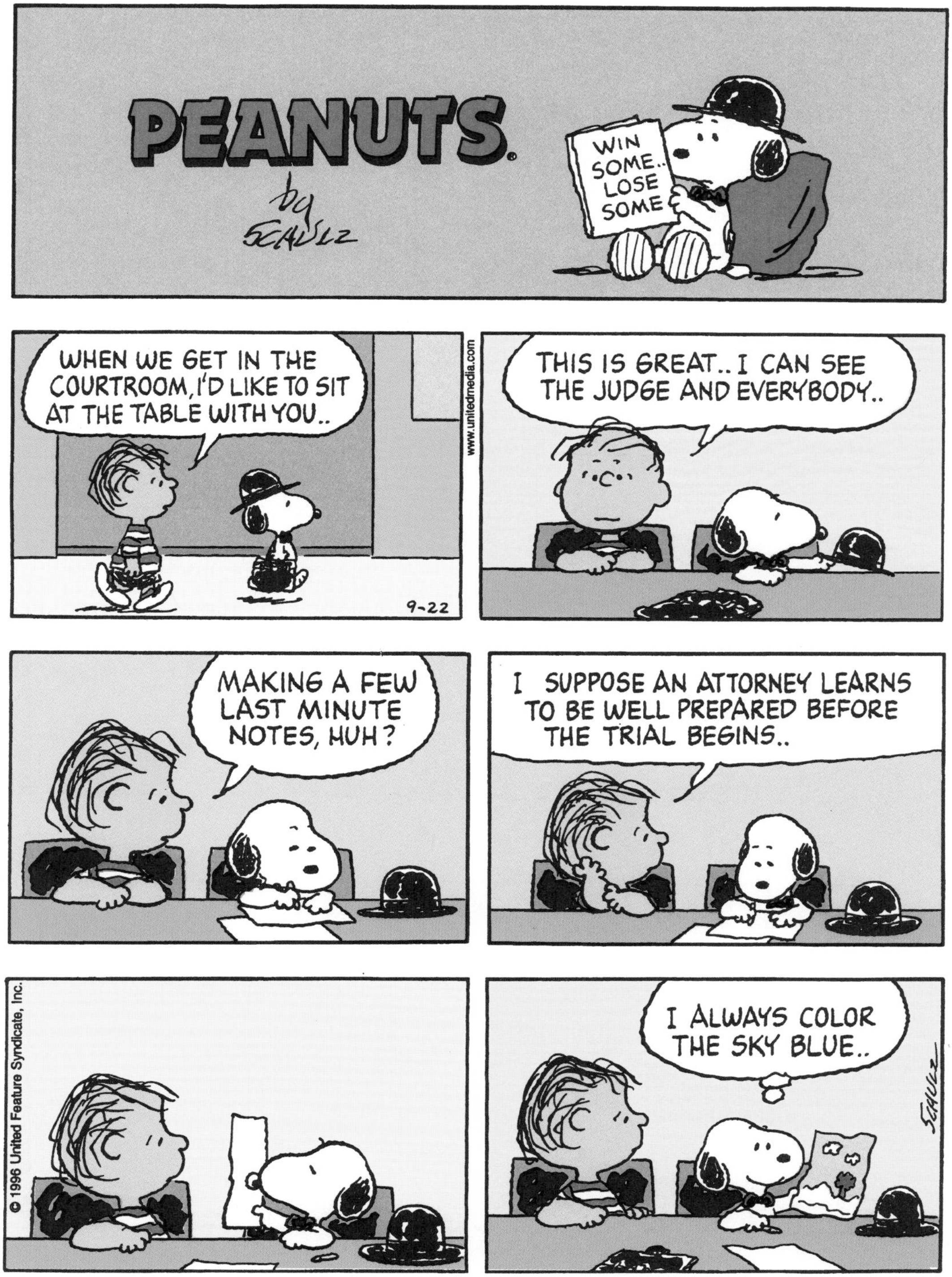
PEANUTS
by SCHULZ
WIN SOME.. LOSE SOME
WHEN WE GET IN THE COURTROOM, I'D LIKE TO SIT AT THE TABLE WITH YOU..
www.unitedmedia.com
9-22
THIS IS GREAT.. I CAN SEE THE JUDGE AND EVERYBODY..
MAKING A FEW LAST MINUTE NOTES, HUH?
I SUPPOSE AN ATTORNEY LEARNS TO BE WELL PREPARED BEFORE THE TRIAL BEGINS..
© 1996 United Feature Syndicate, Inc.
I ALWAYS COLOR THE SKY BLUE..
SCHULZ

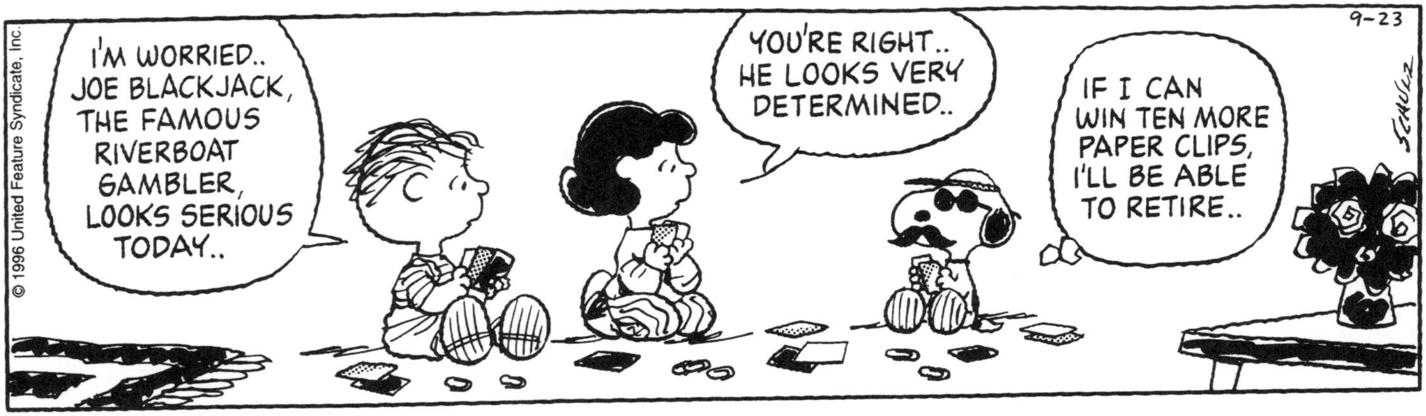
I'M WORRIED.. JOE BLACKJACK, THE FAMOUS RIVERBOAT GAMBLER, LOOKS SERIOUS TODAY..
YOU'RE RIGHT.. HE LOOKS VERY DETERMINED..
IF I CAN WIN TEN MORE PAPER CLIPS, I'LL BE ABLE TO RETIRE..
9-23
SCHULZ
© 1996 United Feature Syndicate, Inc.

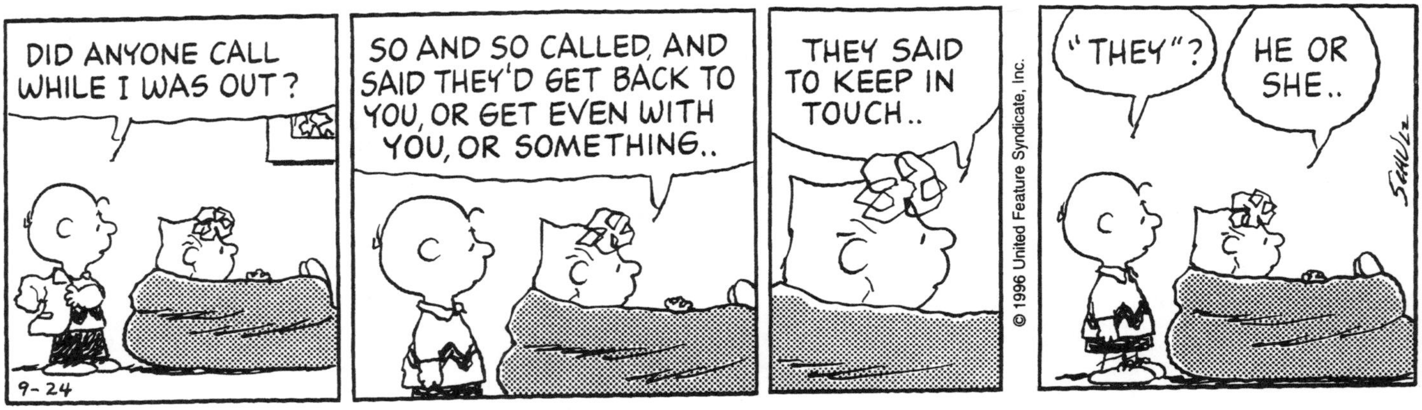
DID ANYONE CALL WHILE I WAS OUT?
SO AND SO CALLED, AND SAID THEY'D GET BACK TO YOU, OR GET EVEN WITH YOU, OR SOMETHING..
THEY SAID TO KEEP IN TOUCH..
"THEY"?
HE OR SHE..
9-24
SCHULZ
© 1996 United Feature Syndicate, Inc.

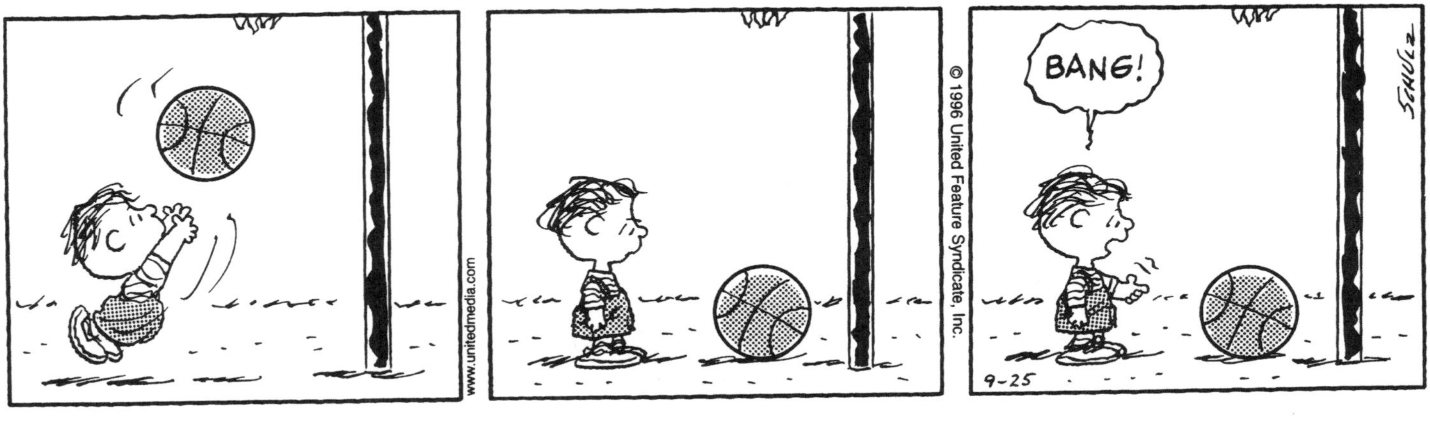
BANG!
9-25
SCHULZ
www.unitedmedia.com
© 1996 United Feature Syndicate, Inc.

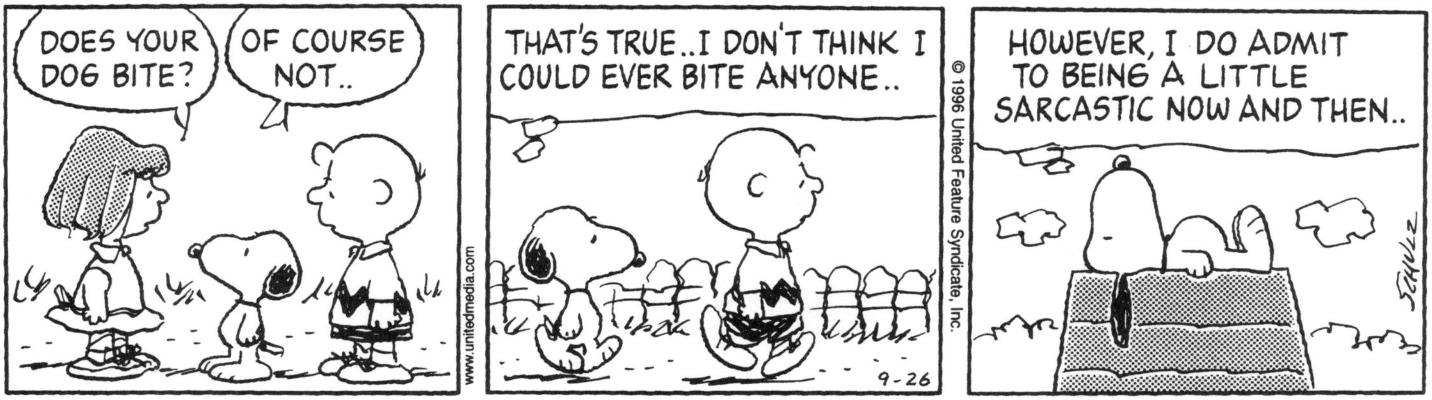
DOES YOUR DOG BITE?
OF COURSE NOT..
THAT'S TRUE..I DON'T THINK I COULD EVER BITE ANYONE..
HOWEVER, I DO ADMIT TO BEING A LITTLE SARCASTIC NOW AND THEN..
9-26
© 1996 United Feature Syndicate, Inc.
www.unitedmedia.com
SCHULZ

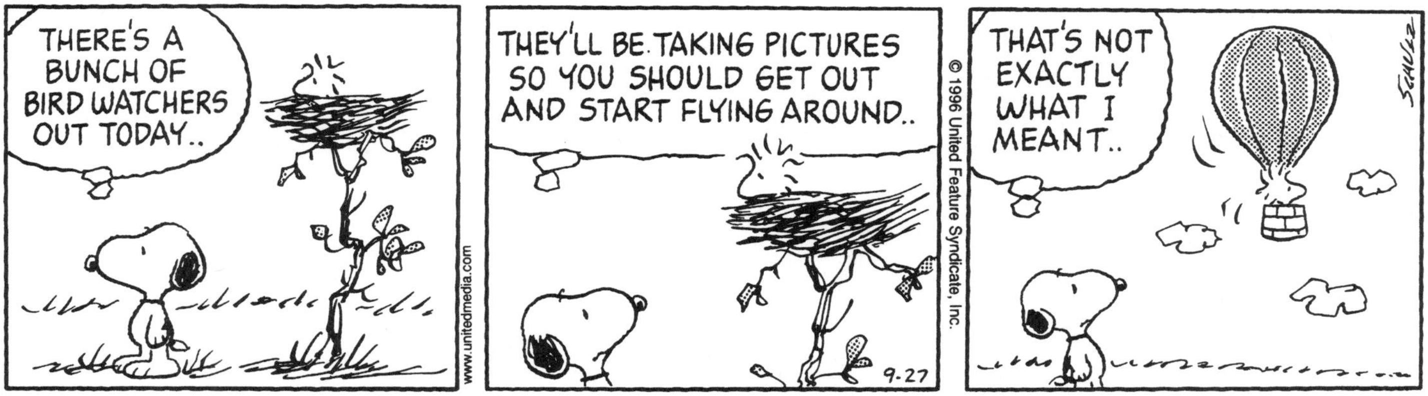
THERE'S A BUNCH OF BIRD WATCHERS OUT TODAY..
THEY'LL BE TAKING PICTURES SO YOU SHOULD GET OUT AND START FLYING AROUND..
THAT'S NOT EXACTLY WHAT I MEANT..
9-27
© 1996 United Feature Syndicate, Inc.
www.unitedmedia.com
SCHULZ

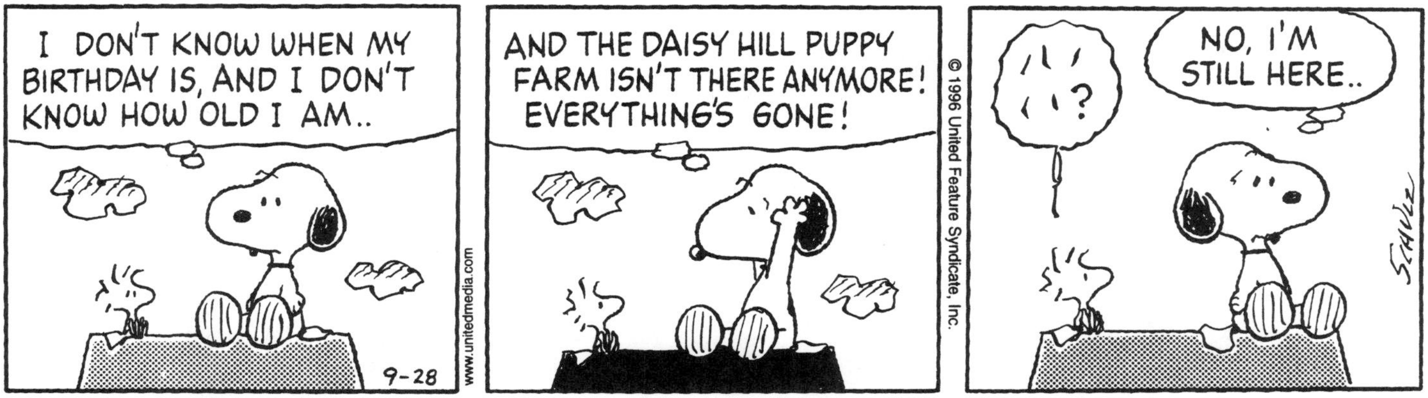
I DON'T KNOW WHEN MY BIRTHDAY IS, AND I DON'T KNOW HOW OLD I AM..
AND THE DAISY HILL PUPPY FARM ISN'T THERE ANYMORE! EVERYTHING'S GONE!
?
NO, I'M STILL HERE..
9-28
© 1996 United Feature Syndicate, Inc.
www.unitedmedia.com
SCHULZ

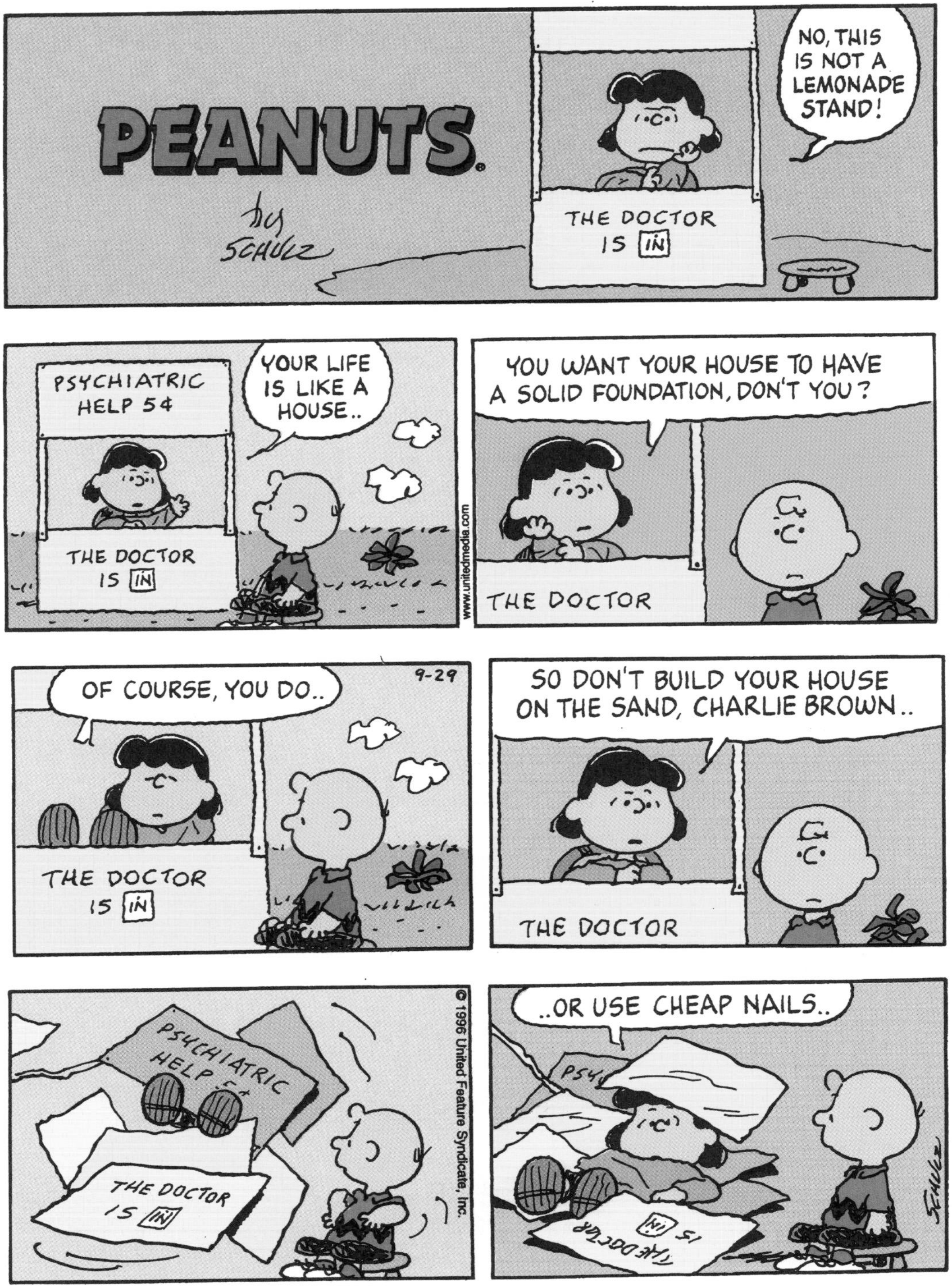
PEANUTS
by SCHULZ
NO, THIS IS NOT A LEMONADE STAND!
THE DOCTOR IS IN
PSYCHIATRIC HELP 5¢
YOUR LIFE IS LIKE A HOUSE..
THE DOCTOR IS IN
www.unitedmedia.com
YOU WANT YOUR HOUSE TO HAVE A SOLID FOUNDATION, DON'T YOU?
THE DOCTOR
9-29
OF COURSE, YOU DO..
THE DOCTOR IS IN
SO DON'T BUILD YOUR HOUSE ON THE SAND, CHARLIE BROWN..
THE DOCTOR
PSYCHIATRIC HELP
THE DOCTOR IS IN
© 1996 United Feature Syndicate, Inc.
..OR USE CHEAP NAILS..
SCHULZ

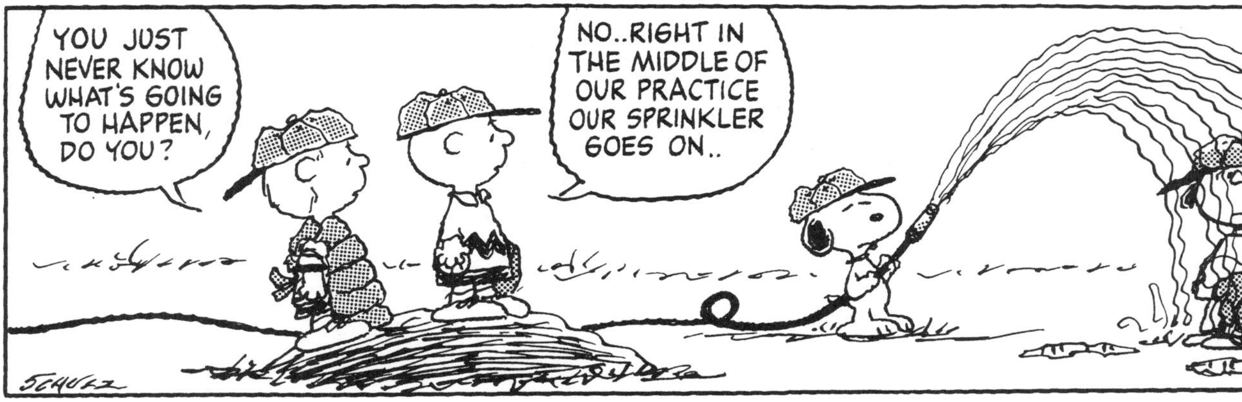
9-30
© 1996 United Feature Syndicate, Inc.
YOU JUST NEVER KNOW WHAT'S GOING TO HAPPEN, DO YOU?
NO..RIGHT IN THE MIDDLE OF OUR PRACTICE OUR SPRINKLER GOES ON..
SCHULZ

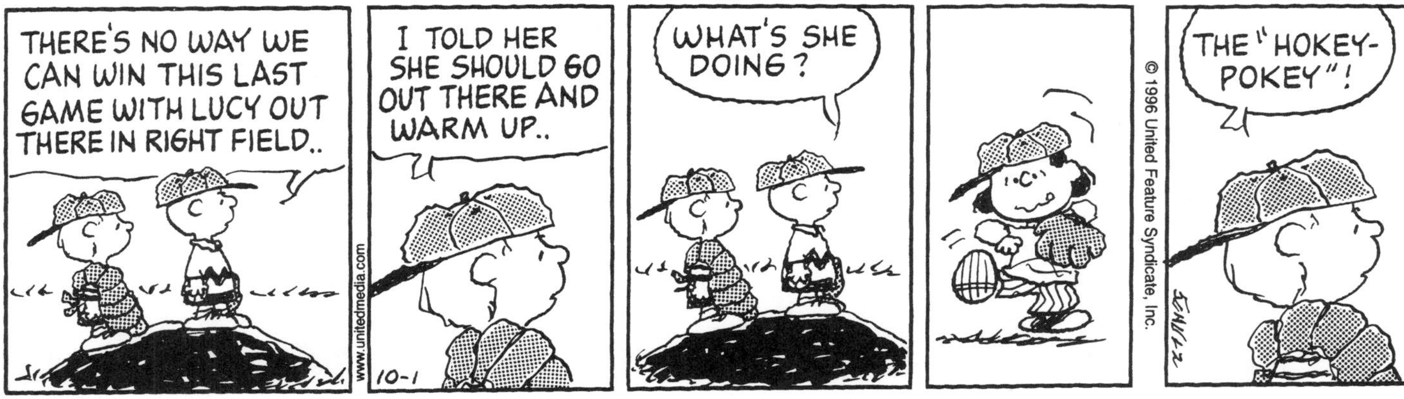
THERE'S NO WAY WE CAN WIN THIS LAST GAME WITH LUCY OUT THERE IN RIGHT FIELD..
www.unitedmedia.com
I TOLD HER SHE SHOULD GO OUT THERE AND WARM UP..
10-1
WHAT'S SHE DOING?
© 1996 United Feature Syndicate, Inc.
THE "HOKEY-POKEY"!
SCHULZ

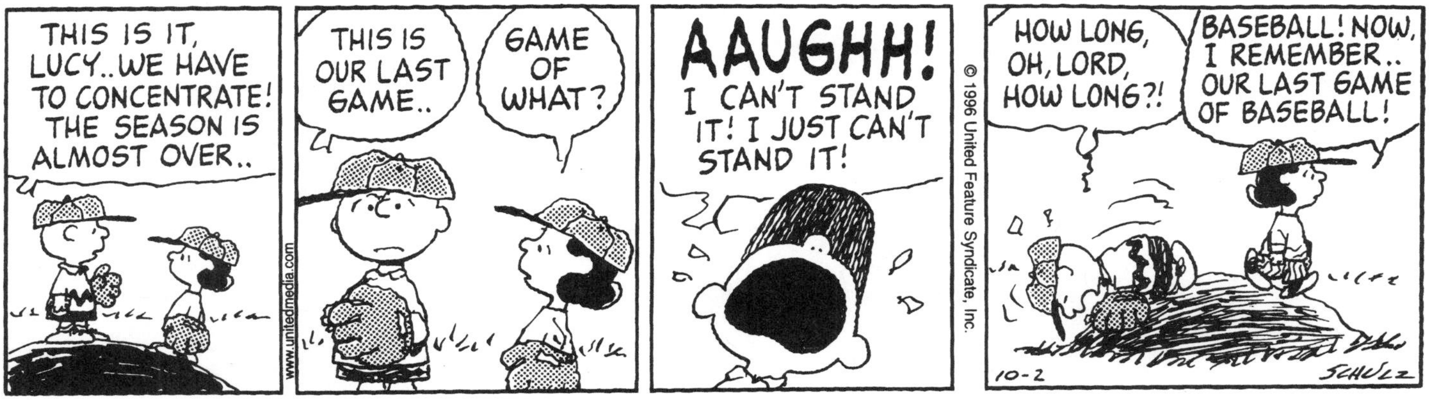
THIS IS IT, LUCY..WE HAVE TO CONCENTRATE! THE SEASON IS ALMOST OVER..
www.unitedmedia.com
THIS IS OUR LAST GAME..
GAME OF WHAT?
AAUGHH!
I CAN'T STAND IT! I JUST CAN'T STAND IT!
© 1996 United Feature Syndicate, Inc.
HOW LONG, OH, LORD, HOW LONG?!
BASEBALL! NOW, I REMEMBER.. OUR LAST GAME OF BASEBALL!
10-2
SCHULZ

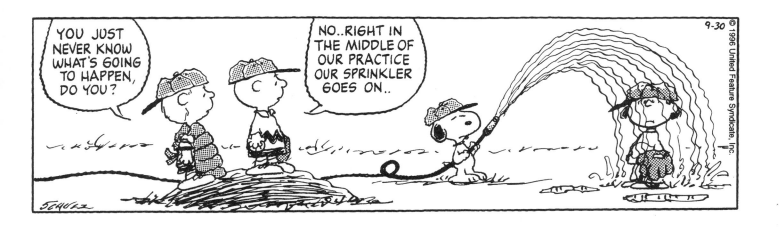

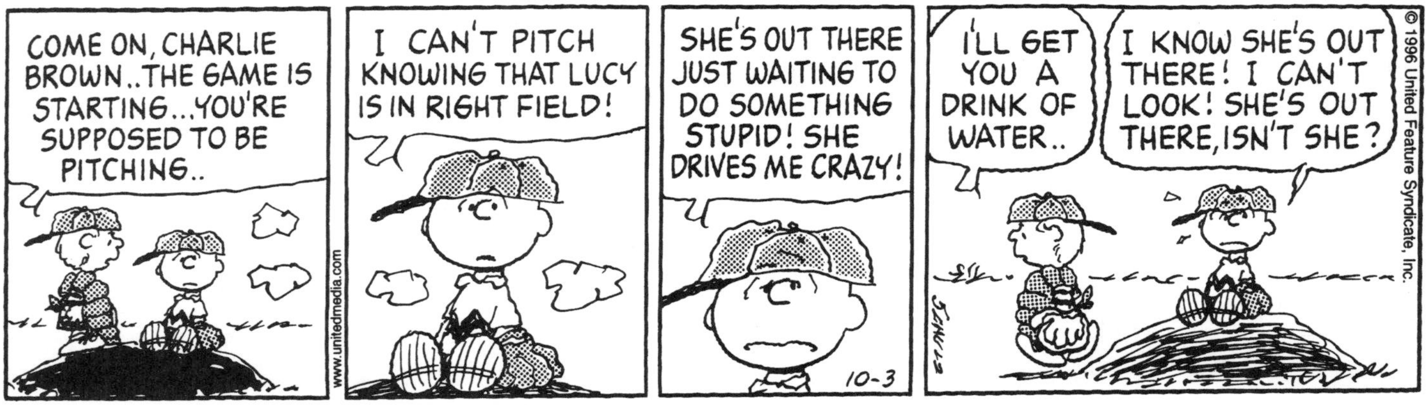
COME ON, CHARLIE BROWN..THE GAME IS STARTING...YOU'RE SUPPOSED TO BE PITCHING..
www.unitedmedia.com
I CAN'T PITCH KNOWING THAT LUCY IS IN RIGHT FIELD!
SHE'S OUT THERE JUST WAITING TO DO SOMETHING STUPID! SHE DRIVES ME CRAZY!
10-3
I'LL GET YOU A DRINK OF WATER..
I KNOW SHE'S OUT THERE! I CAN'T LOOK! SHE'S OUT THERE, ISN'T SHE?
© 1996 United Feature Syndicate, Inc.
SCHULZ

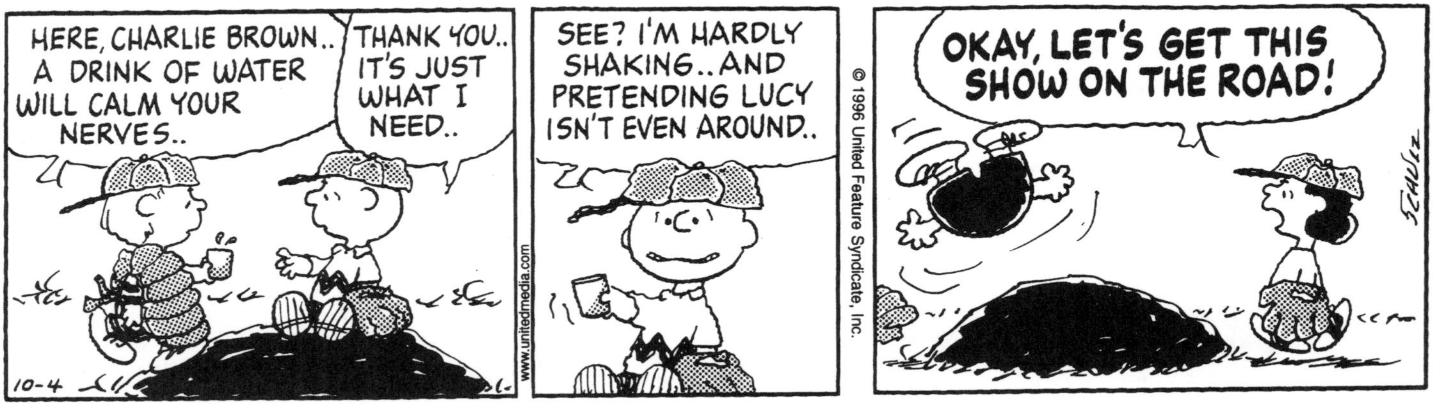
HERE, CHARLIE BROWN.. A DRINK OF WATER WILL CALM YOUR NERVES..
THANK YOU.. IT'S JUST WHAT I NEED..
10-4
www.unitedmedia.com
SEE? I'M HARDLY SHAKING..AND PRETENDING LUCY ISN'T EVEN AROUND..
© 1996 United Feature Syndicate, Inc.
OKAY, LET'S GET THIS SHOW ON THE ROAD!
SCHULZ

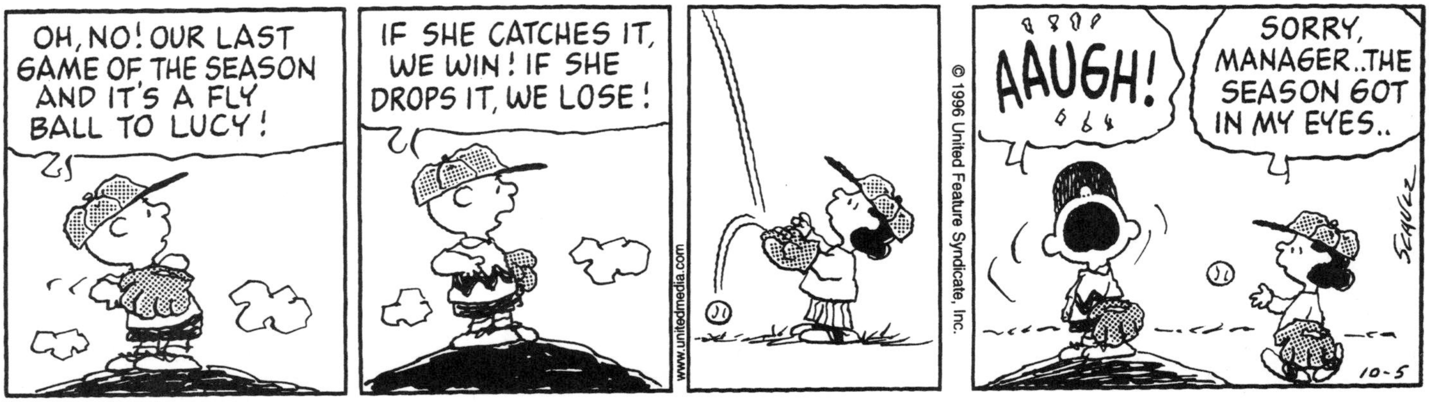
OH, NO! OUR LAST GAME OF THE SEASON AND IT'S A FLY BALL TO LUCY!
IF SHE CATCHES IT, WE WIN! IF SHE DROPS IT, WE LOSE!
www.unitedmedia.com
© 1996 United Feature Syndicate, Inc.
AAUGH!
SORRY, MANAGER..THE SEASON GOT IN MY EYES..
SCHULZ
10-5

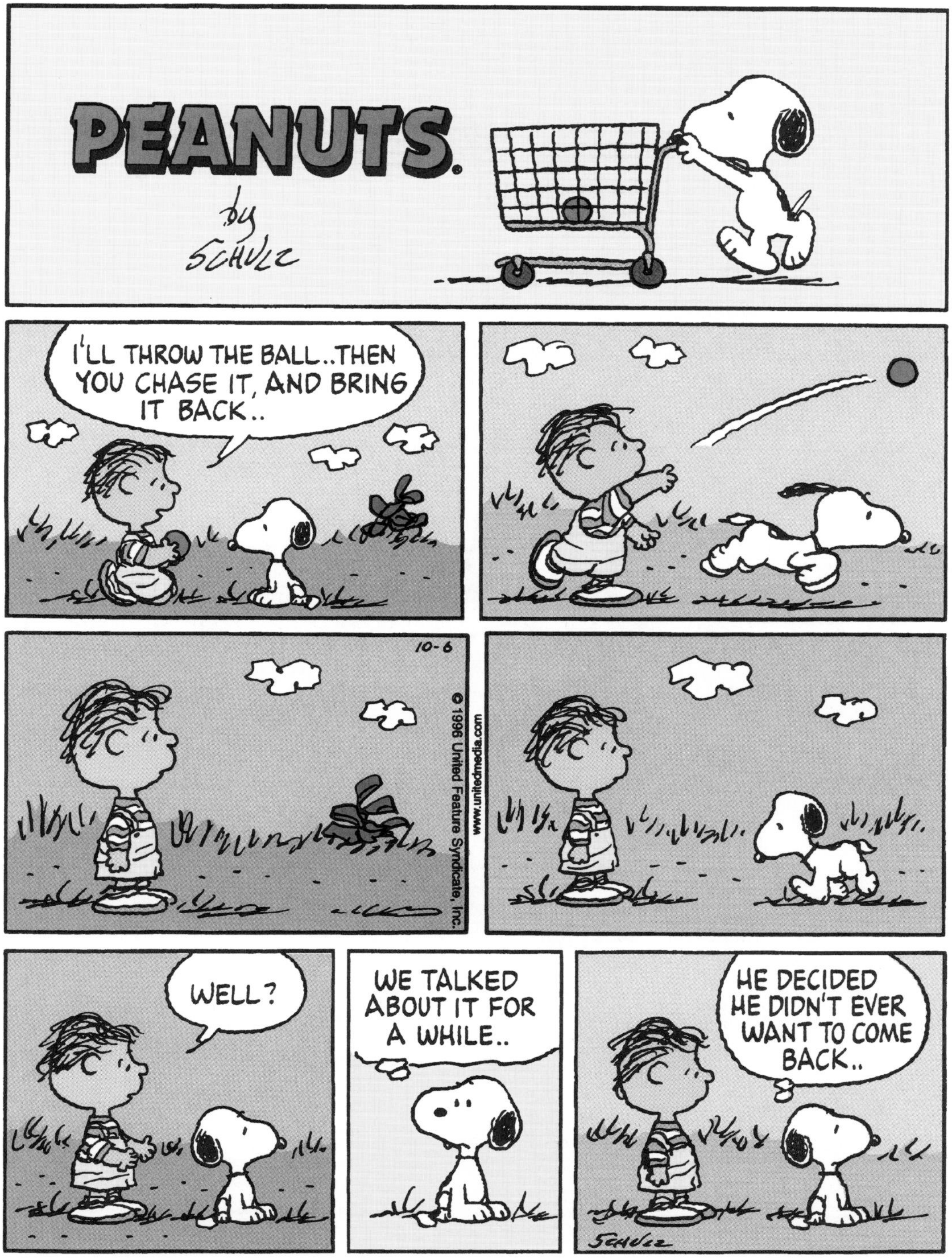
PEANUTS
by SCHULZ
I'LL THROW THE BALL..THEN YOU CHASE IT, AND BRING IT BACK..
10-6
© 1996 United Feature Syndicate, Inc.
www.unitedmedia.com
WELL?
WE TALKED ABOUT IT FOR A WHILE..
HE DECIDED HE DIDN'T EVER WANT TO COME BACK..
SCHULZ

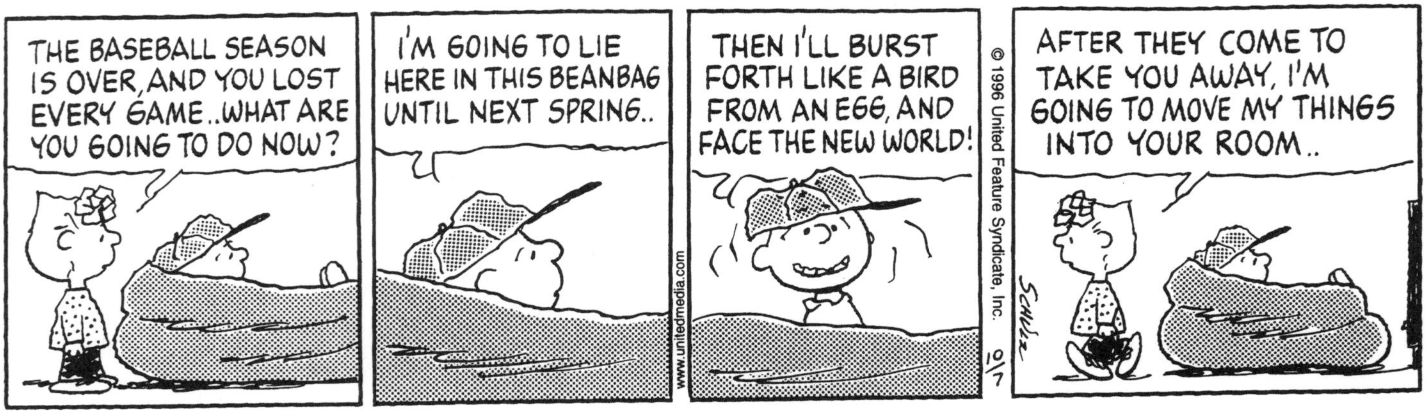
THE BASEBALL SEASON IS OVER, AND YOU LOST EVERY GAME..WHAT ARE YOU GOING TO DO NOW?
I'M GOING TO LIE HERE IN THIS BEANBAG UNTIL NEXT SPRING..
THEN I'LL BURST FORTH LIKE A BIRD FROM AN EGG, AND FACE THE NEW WORLD!
AFTER THEY COME TO TAKE YOU AWAY, I'M GOING TO MOVE MY THINGS INTO YOUR ROOM..
www.unitedmedia.com
© 1996 United Feature Syndicate, Inc.
10/7

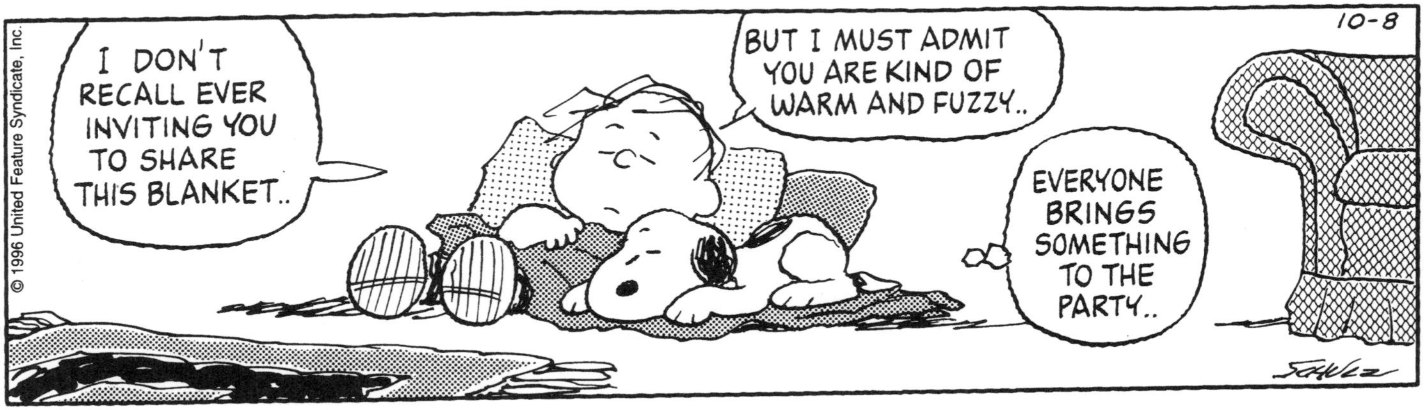
© 1996 United Feature Syndicate, Inc.
10-8
I DON'T RECALL EVER INVITING YOU TO SHARE THIS BLANKET..
BUT I MUST ADMIT YOU ARE KIND OF WARM AND FUZZY..
EVERYONE BRINGS SOMETHING TO THE PARTY..

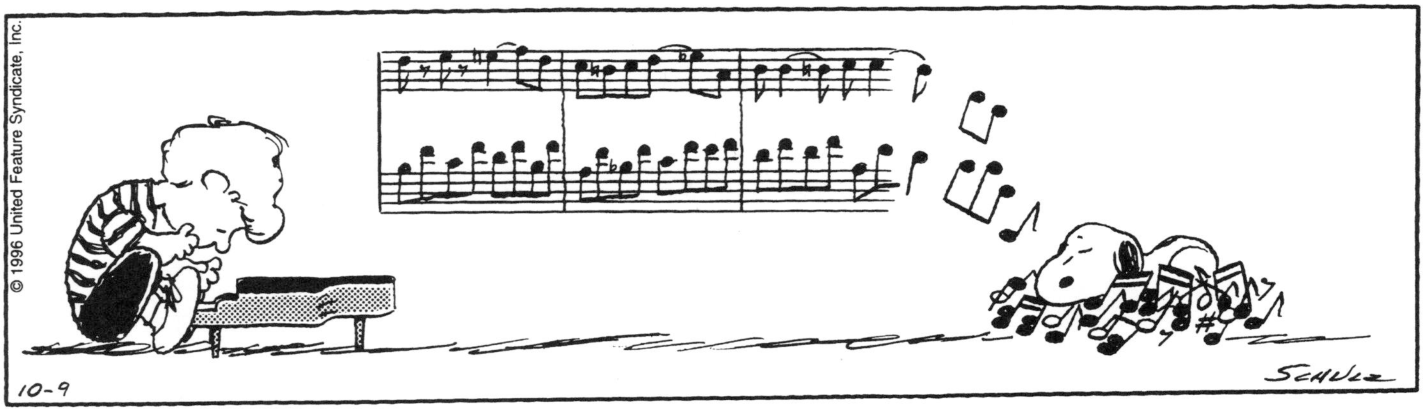
© 1996 United Feature Syndicate, Inc.
10-9

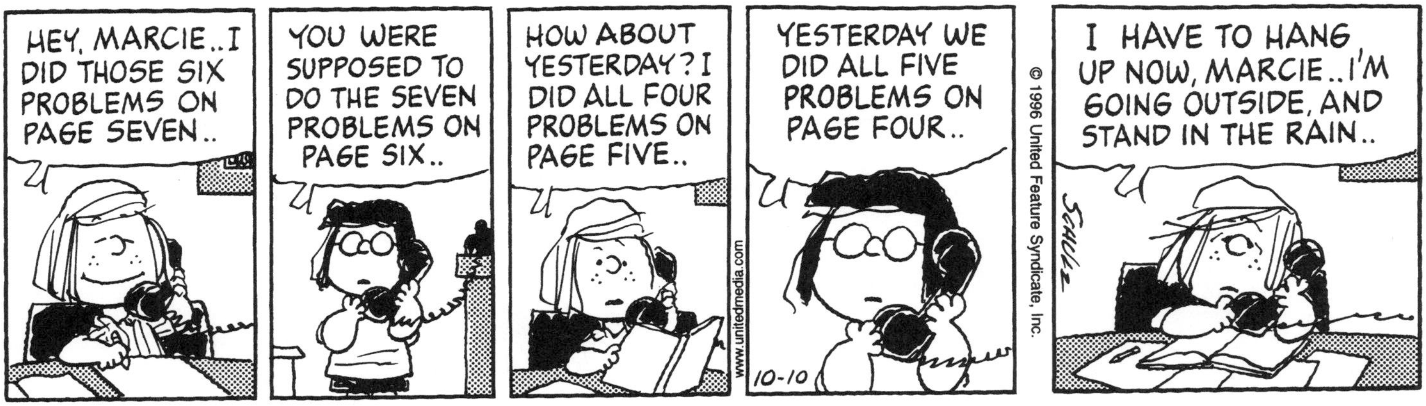
HEY, MARCIE..I DID THOSE SIX PROBLEMS ON PAGE SEVEN..
YOU WERE SUPPOSED TO DO THE SEVEN PROBLEMS ON PAGE SIX..
HOW ABOUT YESTERDAY? I DID ALL FOUR PROBLEMS ON PAGE FIVE..
www.unitedmedia.com
10-10
YESTERDAY WE DID ALL FIVE PROBLEMS ON PAGE FOUR..
© 1996 United Feature Syndicate, Inc.
I HAVE TO HANG UP NOW, MARCIE..I'M GOING OUTSIDE, AND STAND IN THE RAIN..
SCHULZ

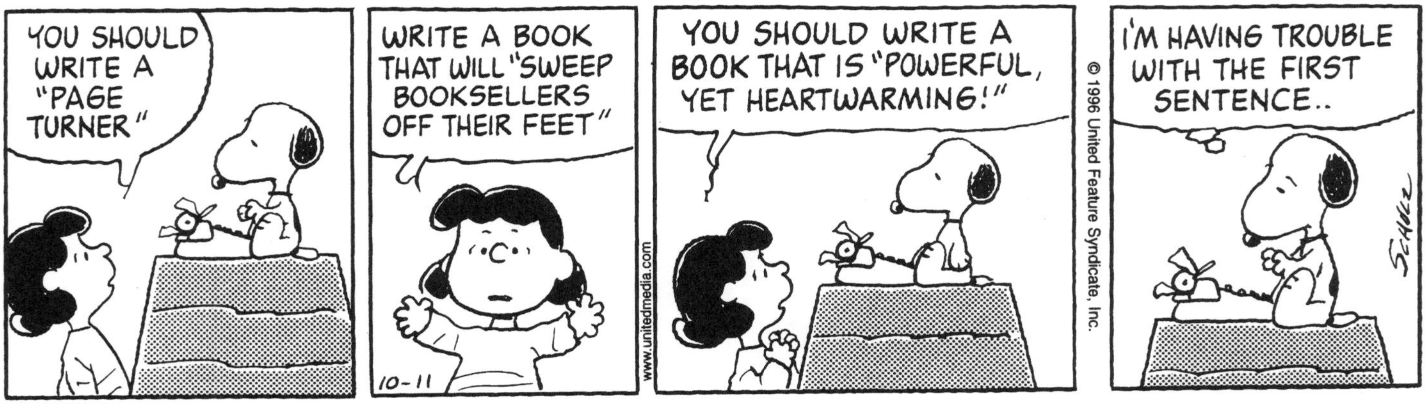
YOU SHOULD WRITE A "PAGE TURNER"
WRITE A BOOK THAT WILL "SWEEP BOOKSELLERS OFF THEIR FEET"
10-11
www.unitedmedia.com
YOU SHOULD WRITE A BOOK THAT IS "POWERFUL, YET HEARTWARMING!"
© 1996 United Feature Syndicate, Inc.
I'M HAVING TROUBLE WITH THE FIRST SENTENCE..
SCHULZ

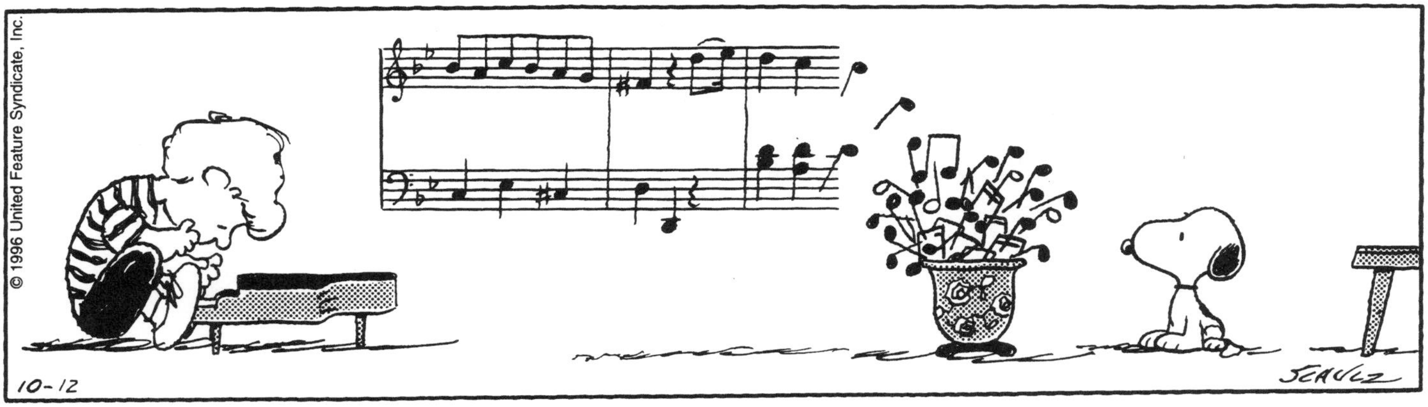
© 1996 United Feature Syndicate, Inc.
10-12
SCHULZ

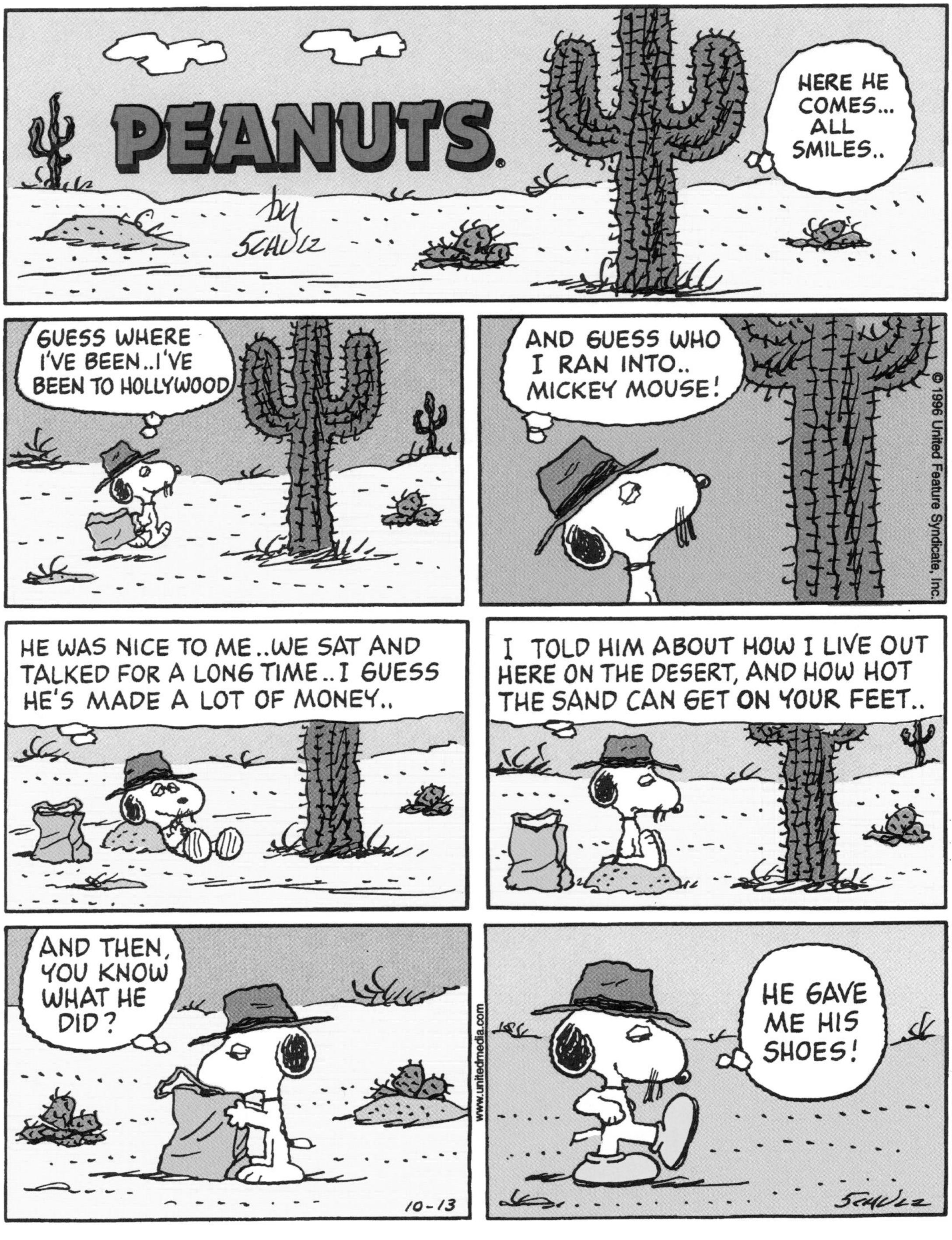
PEANUTS
by SCHULZ
HERE HE COMES... ALL SMILES..
GUESS WHERE I'VE BEEN..I'VE BEEN TO HOLLYWOOD
AND GUESS WHO I RAN INTO.. MICKEY MOUSE!
© 1996 United Feature Syndicate, Inc.
HE WAS NICE TO ME..WE SAT AND TALKED FOR A LONG TIME..I GUESS HE'S MADE A LOT OF MONEY..
I TOLD HIM ABOUT HOW I LIVE OUT HERE ON THE DESERT, AND HOW HOT THE SAND CAN GET ON YOUR FEET..
AND THEN, YOU KNOW WHAT HE DID?
www.unitedmedia.com
10-13
HE GAVE ME HIS SHOES!
SCHULZ

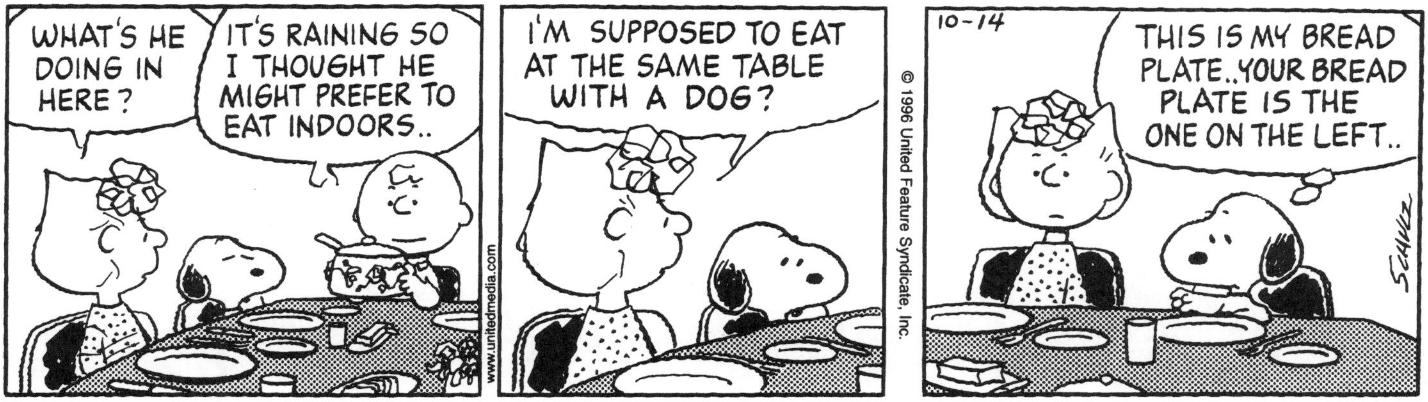
WHAT'S HE DOING IN HERE?
IT'S RAINING SO I THOUGHT HE MIGHT PREFER TO EAT INDOORS..
I'M SUPPOSED TO EAT AT THE SAME TABLE WITH A DOG?
10-14
THIS IS MY BREAD PLATE..YOUR BREAD PLATE IS THE ONE ON THE LEFT..
© 1996 United Feature Syndicate, Inc.
www.unitedmedia.com
SCHULZ

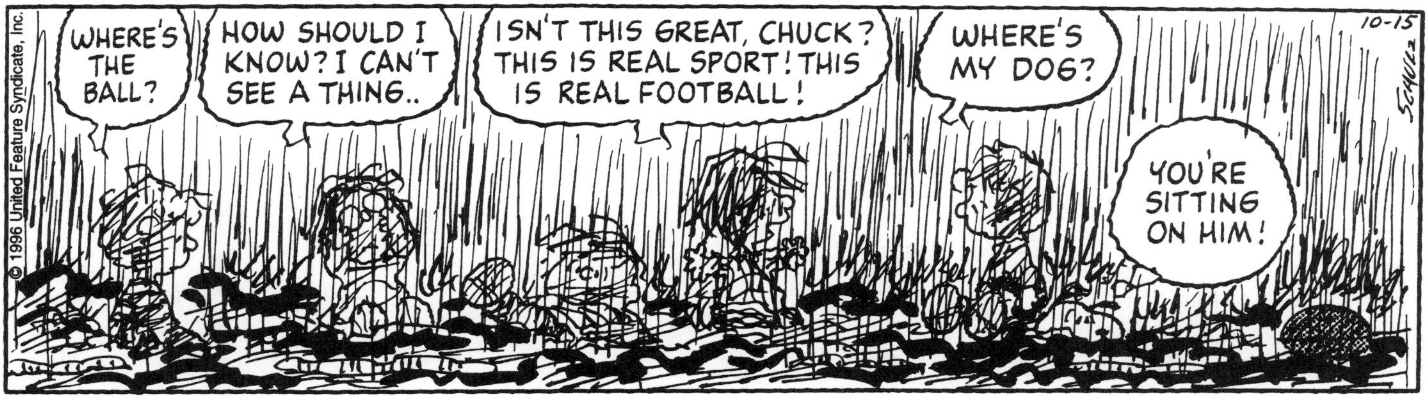
WHERE'S THE BALL?
HOW SHOULD I KNOW? I CAN'T SEE A THING..
ISN'T THIS GREAT, CHUCK? THIS IS REAL SPORT! THIS IS REAL FOOTBALL!
WHERE'S MY DOG?
YOU'RE SITTING ON HIM!
10-15
© 1996 United Feature Syndicate, Inc.
SCHULZ

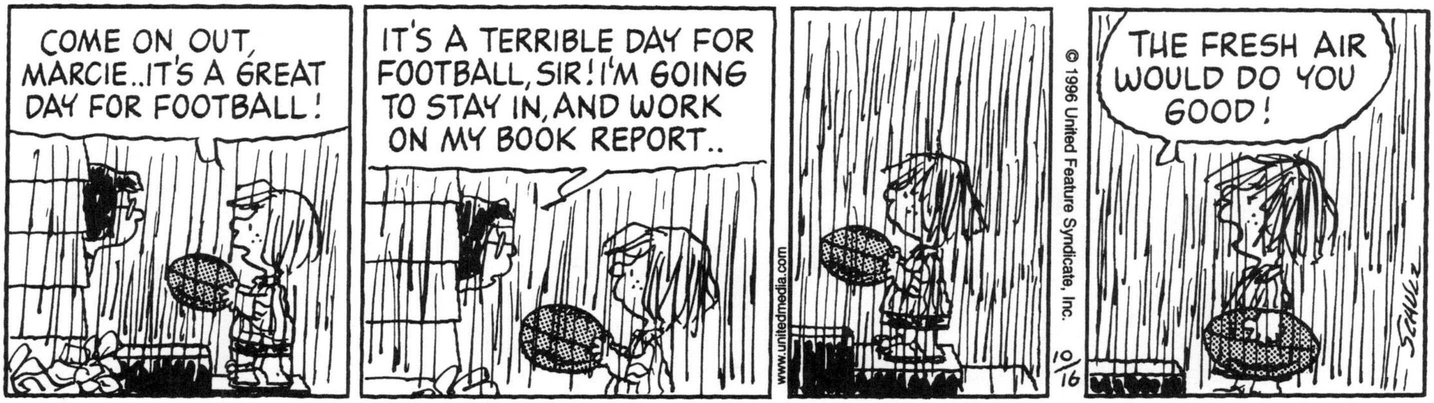
COME ON OUT, MARCIE..IT'S A GREAT DAY FOR FOOTBALL!
IT'S A TERRIBLE DAY FOR FOOTBALL, SIR! I'M GOING TO STAY IN, AND WORK ON MY BOOK REPORT..
THE FRESH AIR WOULD DO YOU GOOD!
10/16
© 1996 United Feature Syndicate, Inc.
www.unitedmedia.com
SCHULZ

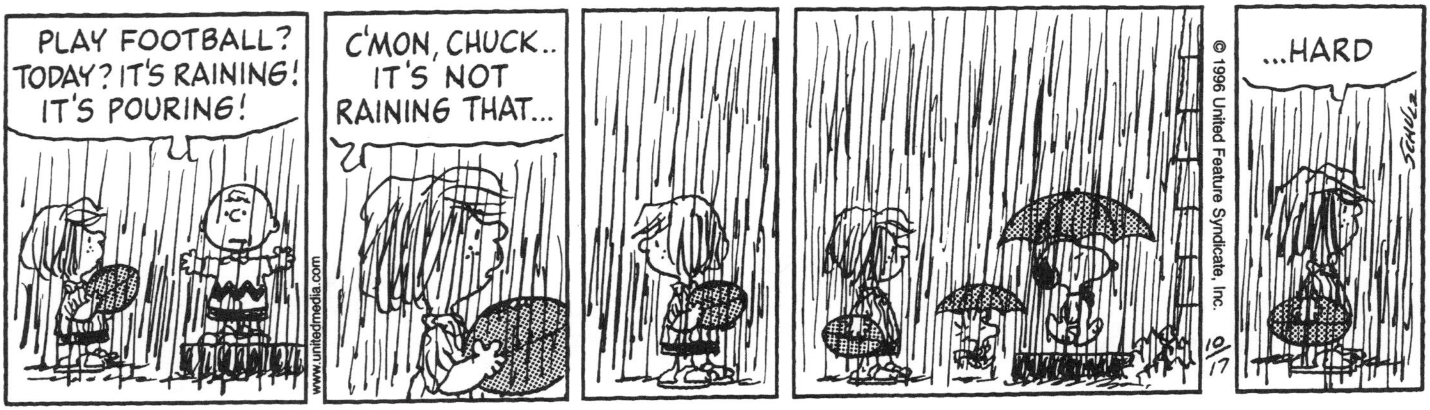
PLAY FOOTBALL? TODAY? IT'S RAINING! IT'S POURING!
C'MON, CHUCK.. IT'S NOT RAINING THAT...
...HARD

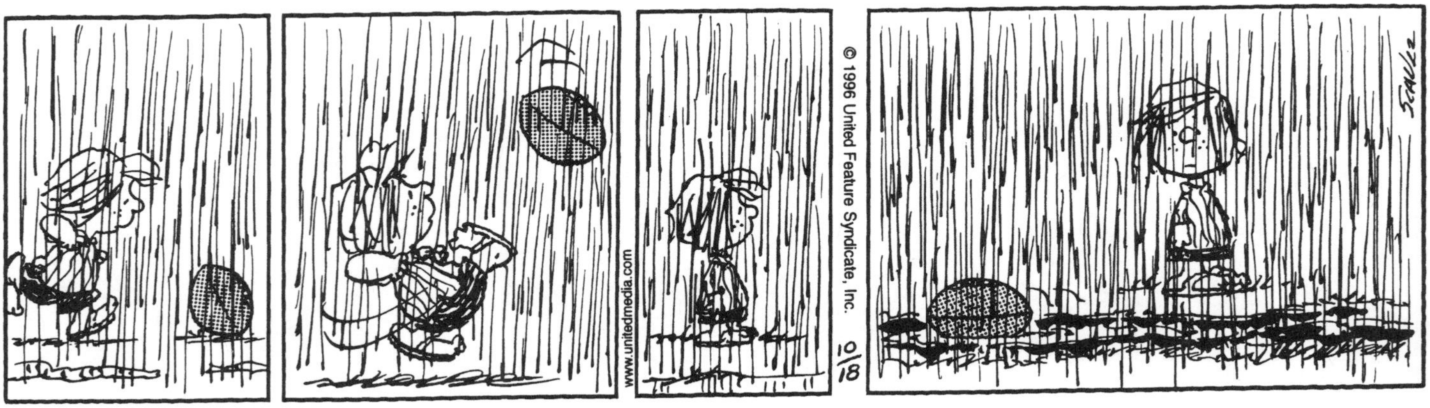

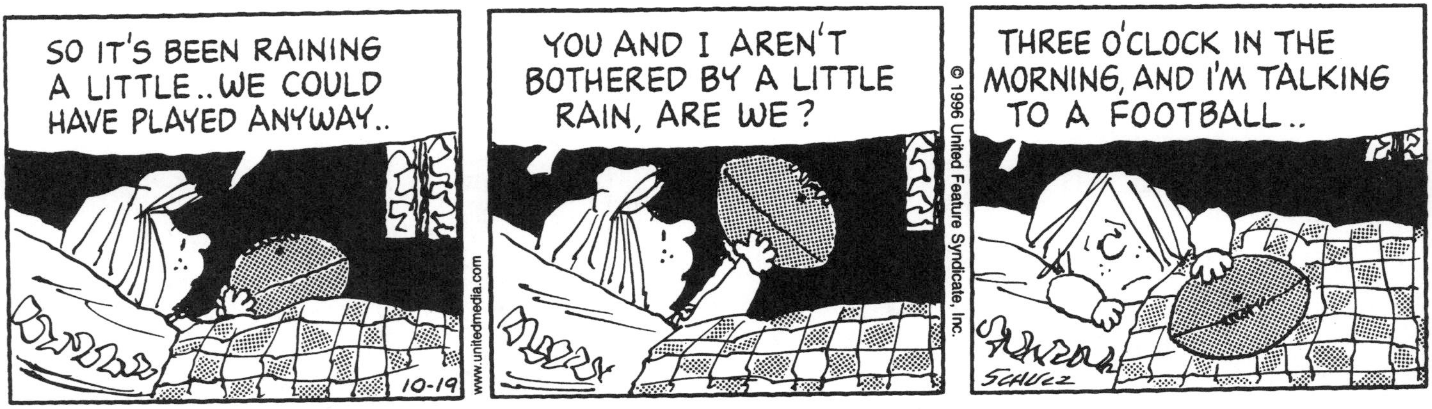
SO IT'S BEEN RAINING A LITTLE..WE COULD HAVE PLAYED ANYWAY..
YOU AND I AREN'T BOTHERED BY A LITTLE RAIN, ARE WE?
THREE O'CLOCK IN THE MORNING, AND I'M TALKING TO A FOOTBALL..

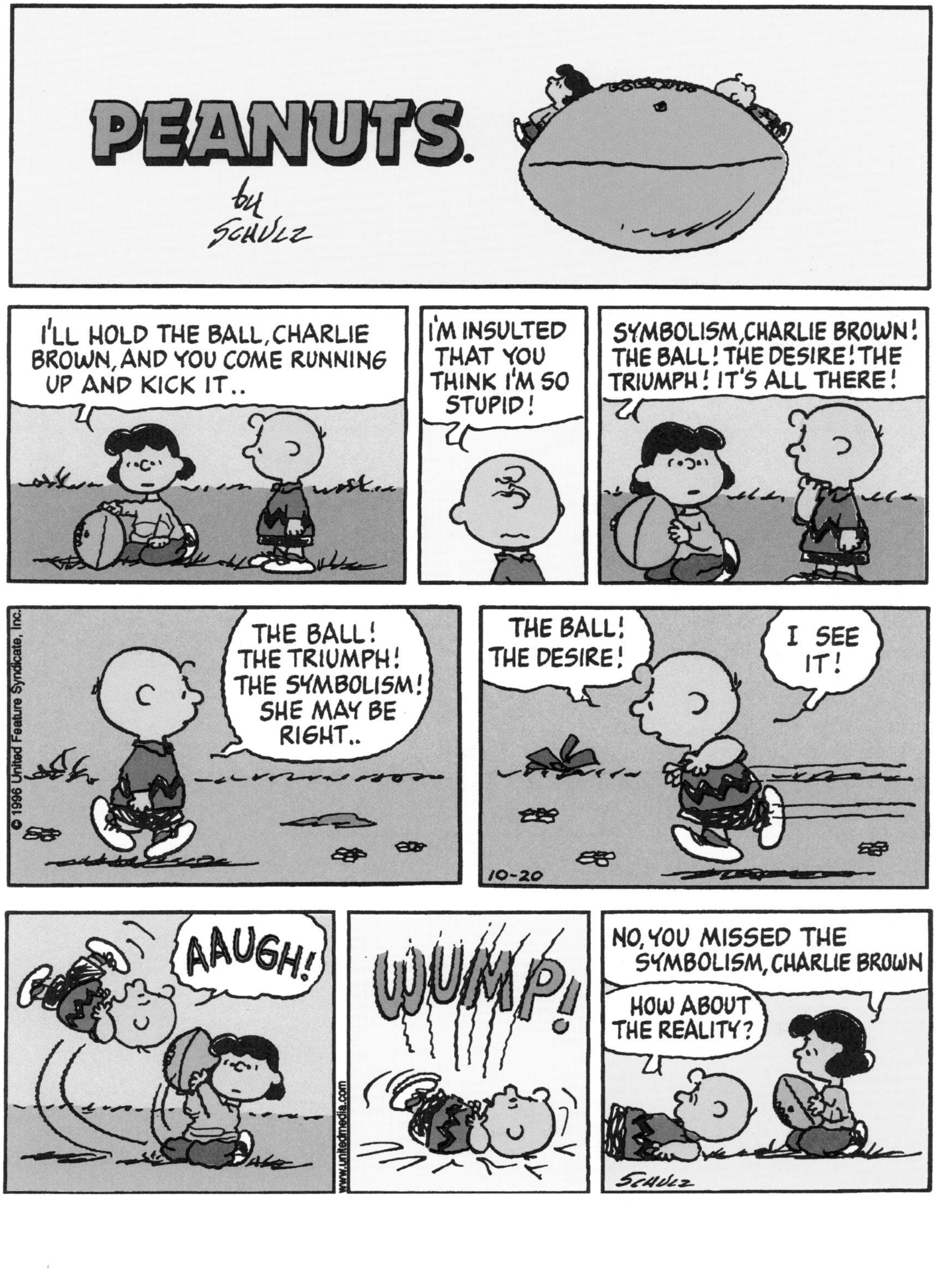
PEANUTS.
by SCHULZ
I'LL HOLD THE BALL, CHARLIE BROWN, AND YOU COME RUNNING UP AND KICK IT..
I'M INSULTED THAT YOU THINK I'M SO STUPID!
SYMBOLISM, CHARLIE BROWN! THE BALL! THE DESIRE! THE TRIUMPH! IT'S ALL THERE!
© 1996 United Feature Syndicate, Inc.
THE BALL! THE TRIUMPH! THE SYMBOLISM! SHE MAY BE RIGHT..
THE BALL! THE DESIRE!
I SEE IT!
10-20
AAUGH!
www.unitedmedia.com
WUMP!
NO, YOU MISSED THE SYMBOLISM, CHARLIE BROWN
HOW ABOUT THE REALITY?
SCHULZ

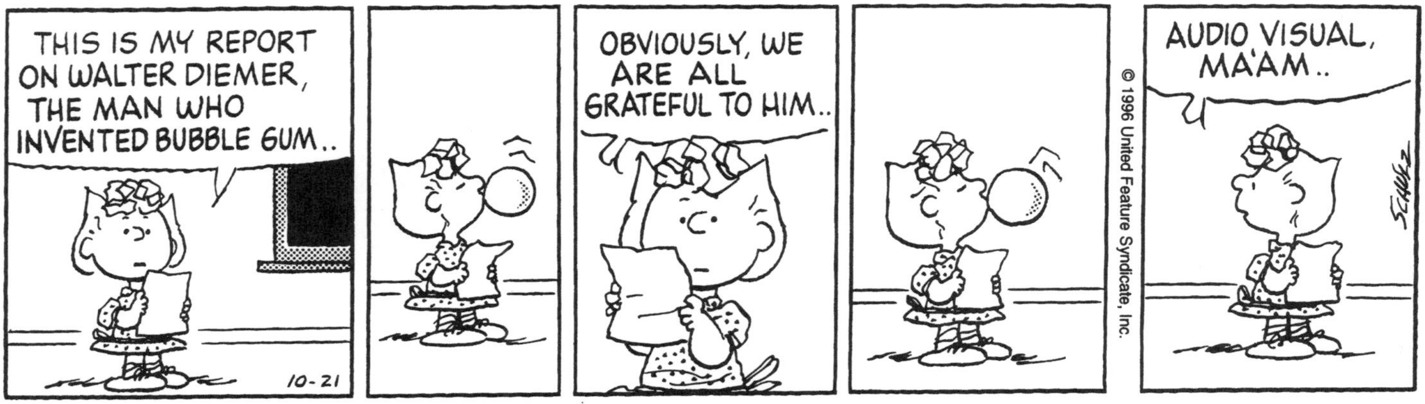
THIS IS MY REPORT ON WALTER DIEMER, THE MAN WHO INVENTED BUBBLE GUM..
OBVIOUSLY, WE ARE ALL GRATEFUL TO HIM..
AUDIO VISUAL, MA'AM..
10-21
© 1996 United Feature Syndicate, Inc.
SCHULZ

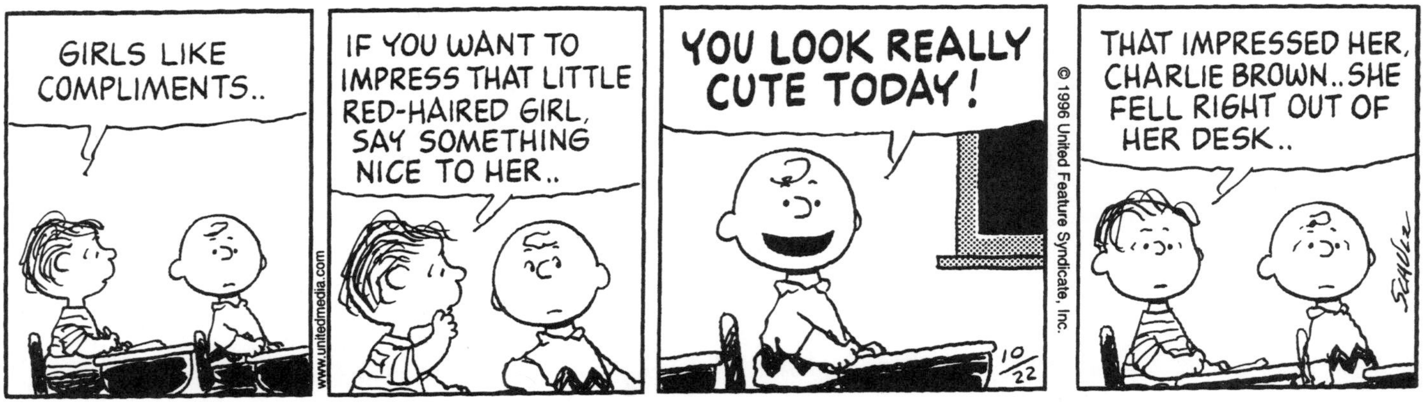
GIRLS LIKE COMPLIMENTS..
IF YOU WANT TO IMPRESS THAT LITTLE RED-HAIRED GIRL, SAY SOMETHING NICE TO HER..
YOU LOOK REALLY CUTE TODAY!
THAT IMPRESSED HER, CHARLIE BROWN..SHE FELL RIGHT OUT OF HER DESK..
www.unitedmedia.com
10/22
© 1996 United Feature Syndicate, Inc.
SCHULZ

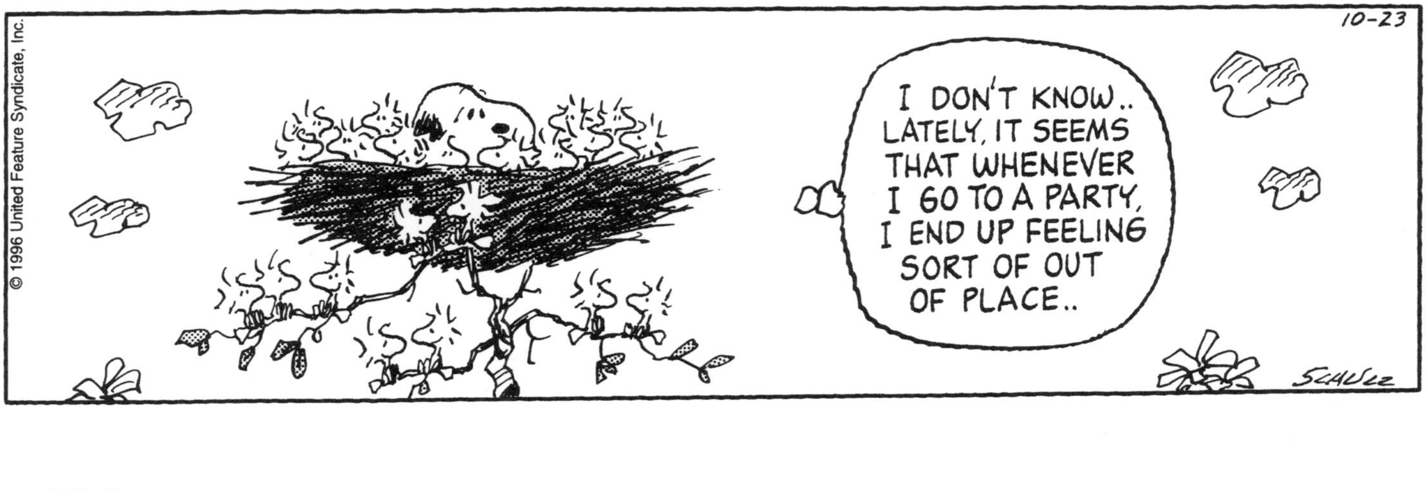
10-23
© 1996 United Feature Syndicate, Inc.
I DON'T KNOW.. LATELY, IT SEEMS THAT WHENEVER I GO TO A PARTY, I END UP FEELING SORT OF OUT OF PLACE..
SCHULZ

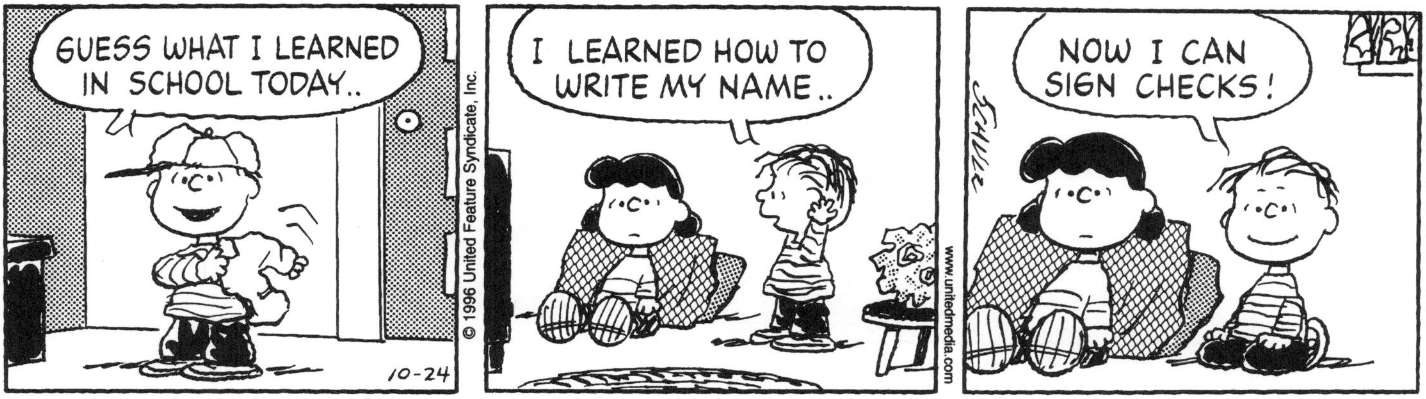
GUESS WHAT I LEARNED IN SCHOOL TODAY..
10-24
© 1996 United Feature Syndicate, Inc.
I LEARNED HOW TO WRITE MY NAME..
www.unitedmedia.com
NOW I CAN SIGN CHECKS!
SCHULZ

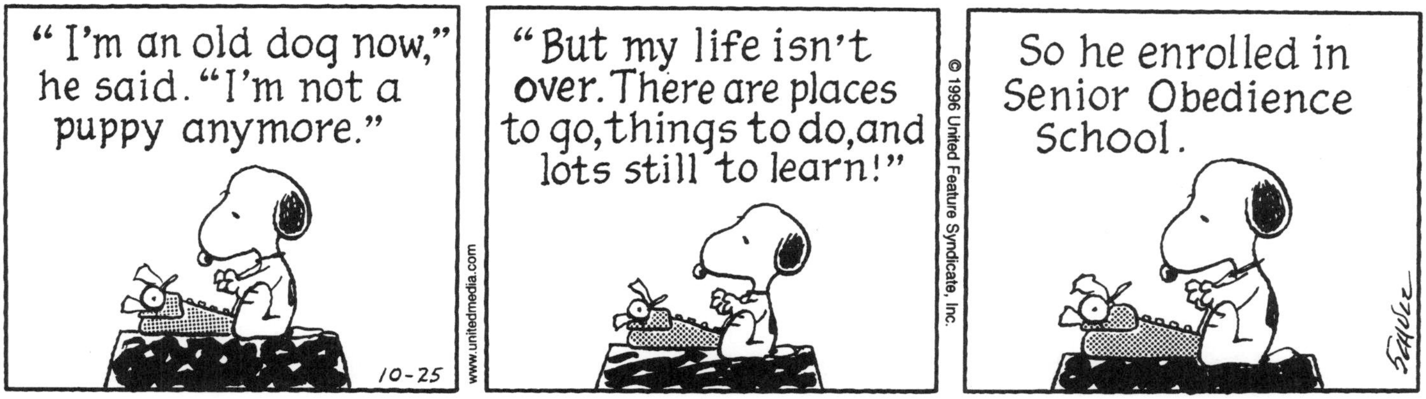
"I'm an old dog now," he said. "I'm not a puppy anymore."
10-25
www.unitedmedia.com
"But my life isn't over. There are places to go, things to do, and lots still to learn!"
© 1996 United Feature Syndicate, Inc.
So he enrolled in Senior Obedience School.
SCHULZ

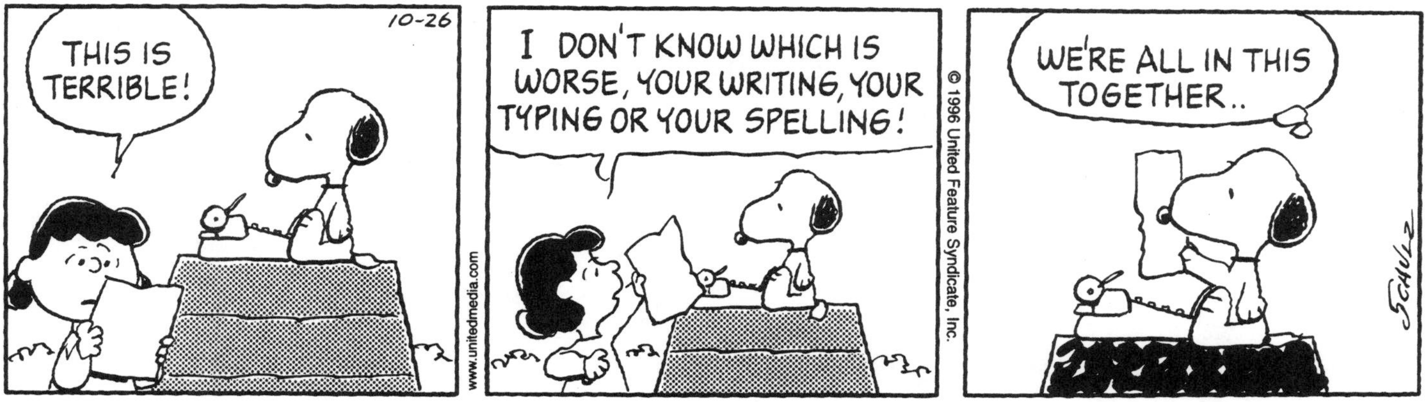
10-26
THIS IS TERRIBLE!
www.unitedmedia.com
I DON'T KNOW WHICH IS WORSE, YOUR WRITING, YOUR TYPING OR YOUR SPELLING!
© 1996 United Feature Syndicate, Inc.
WE'RE ALL IN THIS TOGETHER..
SCHULZ

PEANUTS by SCHULZ

GOOD MORNING, YOUNG LADY..

AS YOU KNOW, HALLOWEEN IS COMING SO WE'RE HERE TO TELL YOU ABOUT THE GREAT PUMPKIN..

THE GREAT WHO?

PUMPKIN! ON HALLOWEEN NIGHT THE GREAT PUMPKIN RISES OUT OF THE PUMPKIN PATCH..

THEN HE FLIES THROUGH THE AIR, AND BRINGS TOYS TO ALL THE CHILDREN IN THE WORLD!

ARE YOU FOR REAL? IS THAT A DOG?

www.unitedmedia.com

I'LL TELL YOU WHAT.. YOU WAIT RIGHT THERE.. I'M GOING TO GO IN AND DIAL 911, AND TELL THEM TO COME AND TAKE YOU AWAY!

ANY SUGGESTIONS?

© 1996 United Feature Syndicate, Inc.

DOGS ALWAYS KNOW WHAT TO DO..

10-27

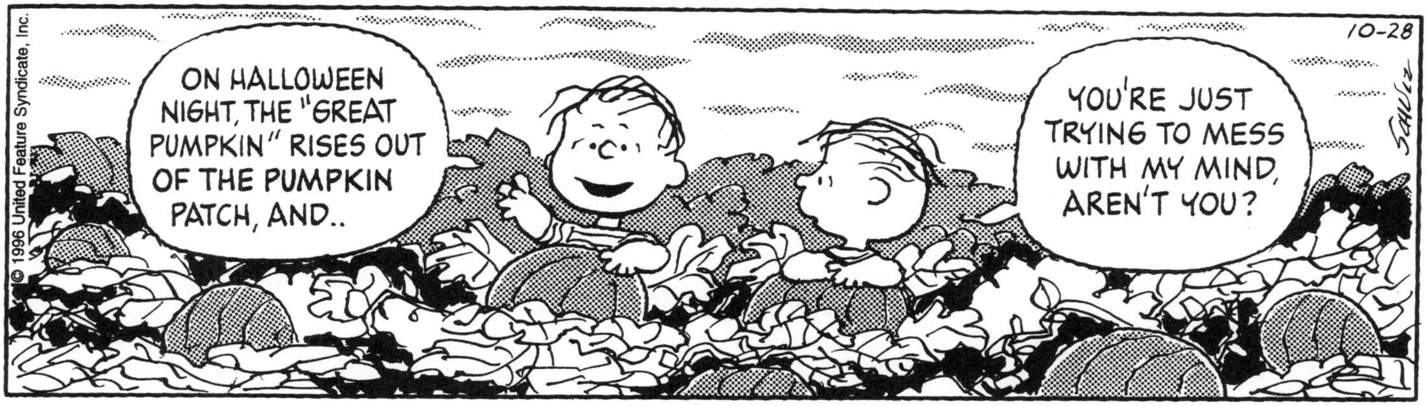
© 1996 United Feature Syndicate, Inc.
10-28
ON HALLOWEEN NIGHT, THE "GREAT PUMPKIN" RISES OUT OF THE PUMPKIN PATCH, AND..
YOU'RE JUST TRYING TO MESS WITH MY MIND, AREN'T YOU?
SCHULZ

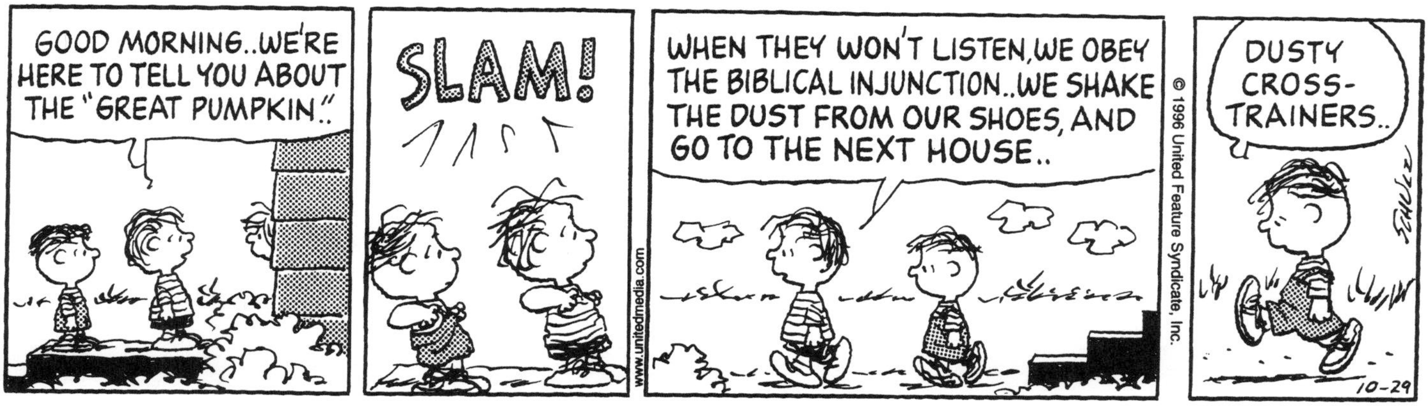
GOOD MORNING..WE'RE HERE TO TELL YOU ABOUT THE "GREAT PUMPKIN"..
SLAM!
www.unitedmedia.com
WHEN THEY WON'T LISTEN, WE OBEY THE BIBLICAL INJUNCTION..WE SHAKE THE DUST FROM OUR SHOES, AND GO TO THE NEXT HOUSE..
© 1996 United Feature Syndicate, Inc.
DUSTY CROSS-TRAINERS..
SCHULZ
10-29

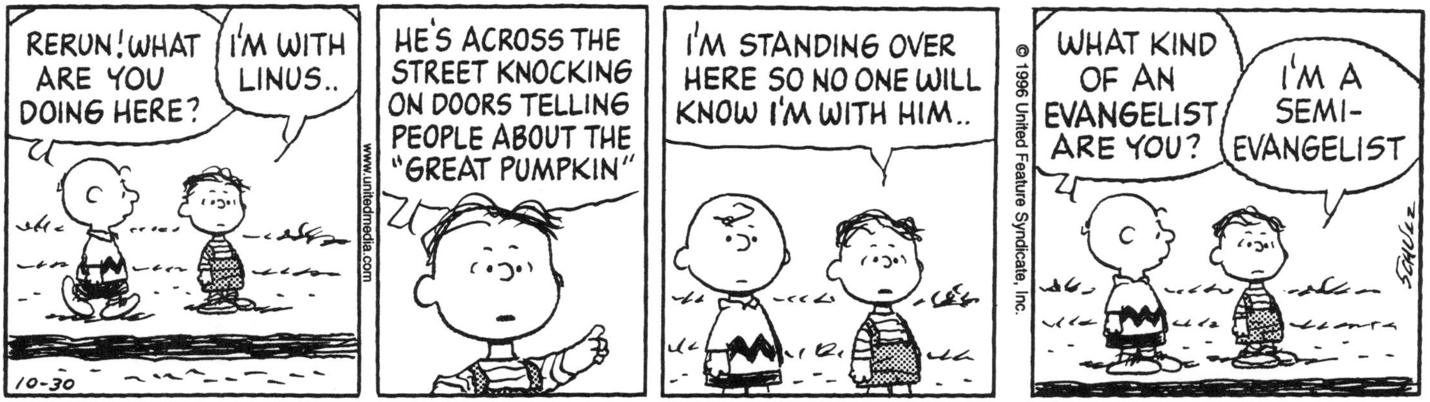
RERUN! WHAT ARE YOU DOING HERE?
I'M WITH LINUS..
10-30
www.unitedmedia.com
HE'S ACROSS THE STREET KNOCKING ON DOORS TELLING PEOPLE ABOUT THE "GREAT PUMPKIN"
I'M STANDING OVER HERE SO NO ONE WILL KNOW I'M WITH HIM..
© 1996 United Feature Syndicate, Inc.
WHAT KIND OF AN EVANGELIST ARE YOU?
I'M A SEMI-EVANGELIST
SCHULZ

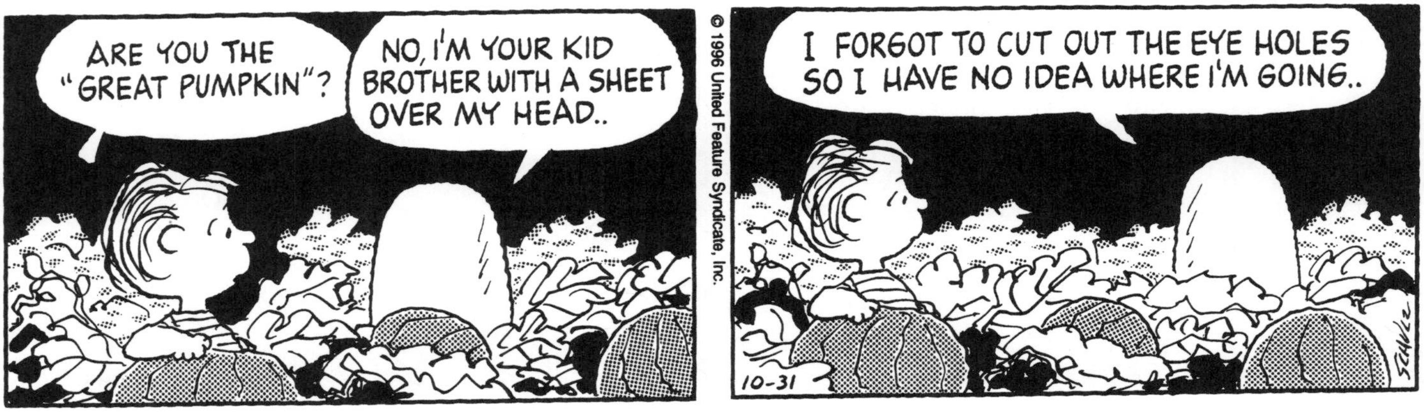
ARE YOU THE "GREAT PUMPKIN"?
NO, I'M YOUR KID BROTHER WITH A SHEET OVER MY HEAD..
© 1996 United Feature Syndicate, Inc.
I FORGOT TO CUT OUT THE EYE HOLES SO I HAVE NO IDEA WHERE I'M GOING..
10-31
SCHULZ

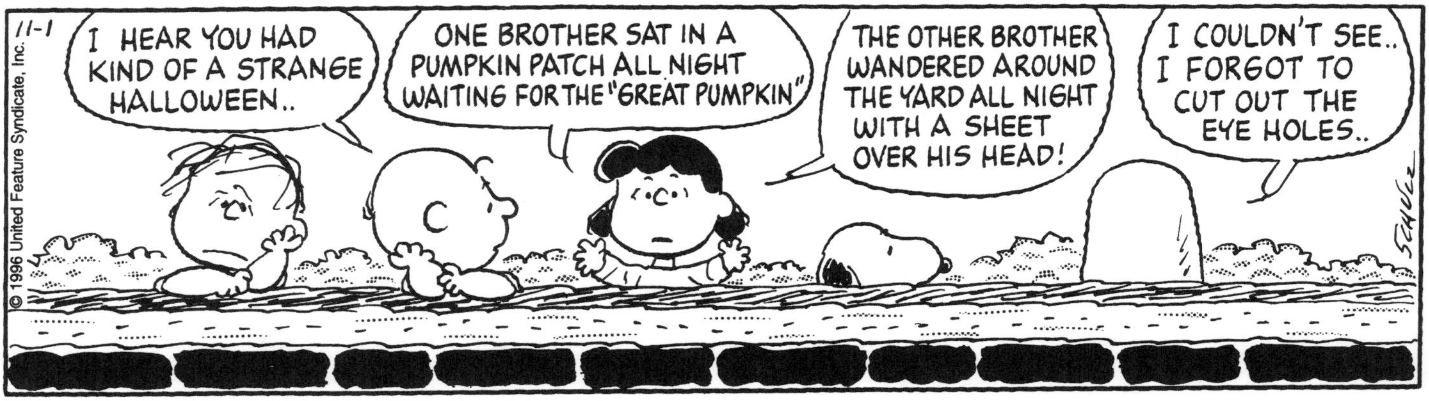
11-1
© 1996 United Feature Syndicate, Inc.
I HEAR YOU HAD KIND OF A STRANGE HALLOWEEN..
ONE BROTHER SAT IN A PUMPKIN PATCH ALL NIGHT WAITING FOR THE "GREAT PUMPKIN"
THE OTHER BROTHER WANDERED AROUND THE YARD ALL NIGHT WITH A SHEET OVER HIS HEAD!
I COULDN'T SEE.. I FORGOT TO CUT OUT THE EYE HOLES..
SCHULZ

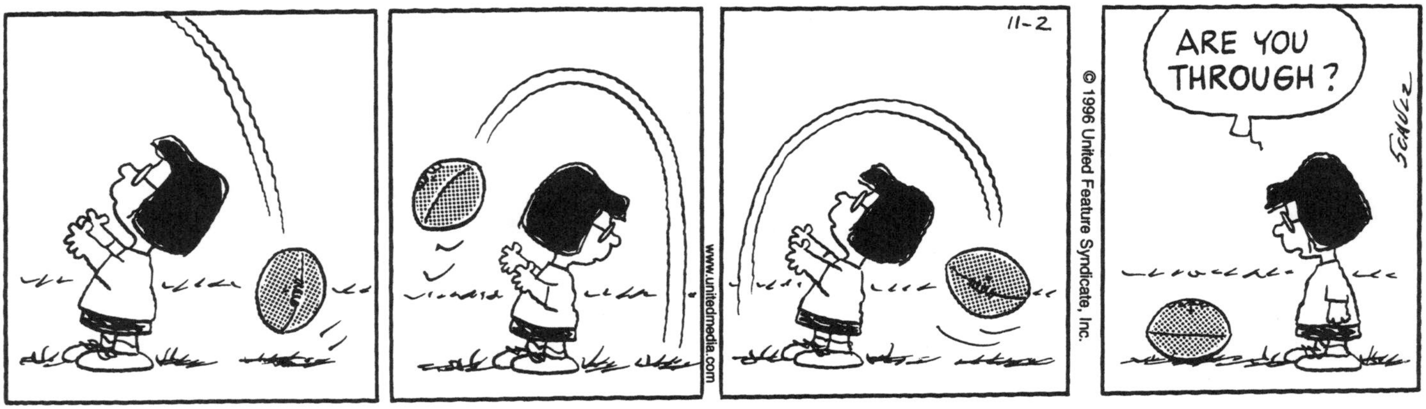
www.unitedmedia.com
11-2
© 1996 United Feature Syndicate, Inc.
ARE YOU THROUGH?
SCHULZ

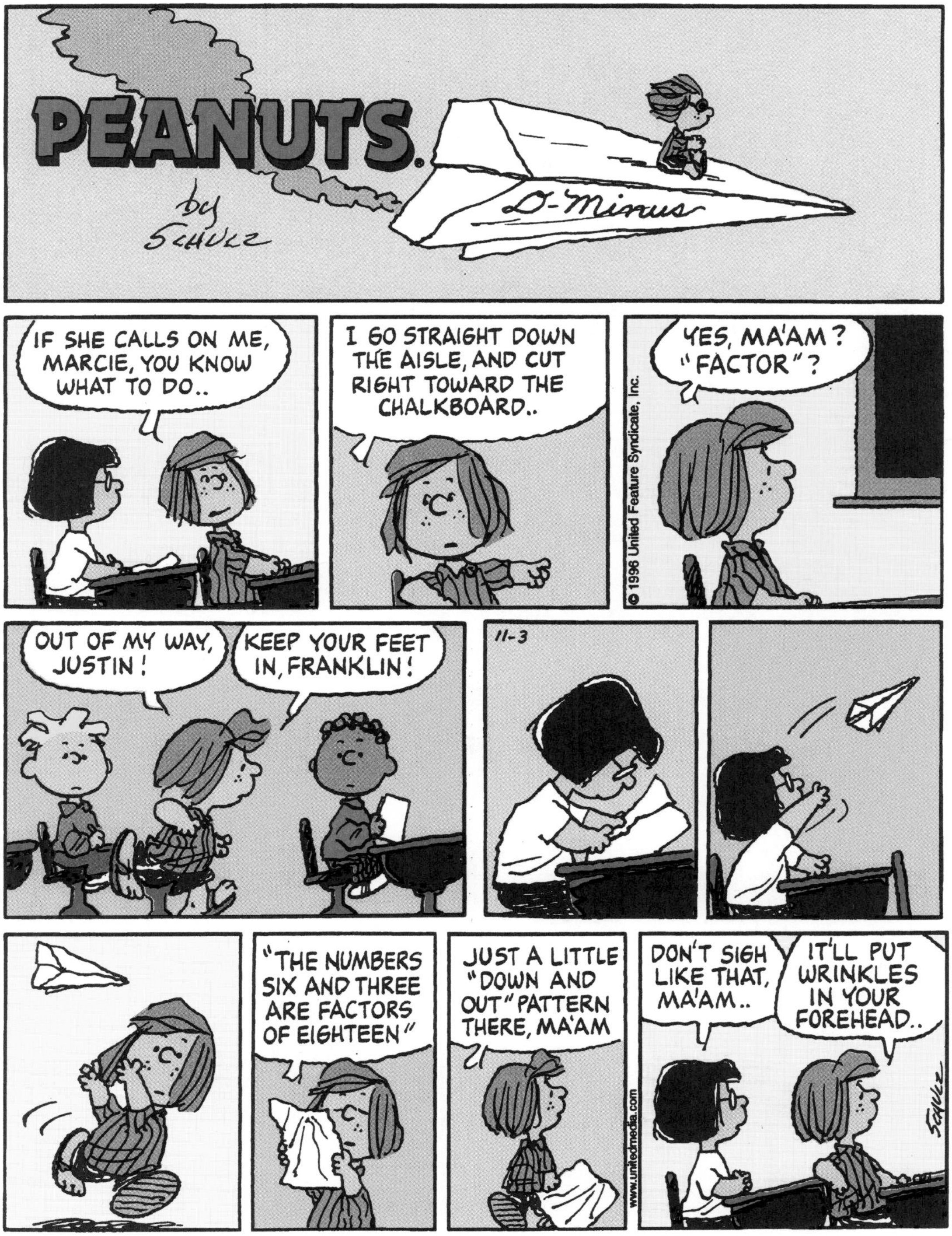
PEANUTS
by SCHULZ
D-Minus
IF SHE CALLS ON ME, MARCIE, YOU KNOW WHAT TO DO..
I GO STRAIGHT DOWN THE AISLE, AND CUT RIGHT TOWARD THE CHALKBOARD..
© 1996 United Feature Syndicate, Inc.
YES, MA'AM? "FACTOR"?
OUT OF MY WAY, JUSTIN!
KEEP YOUR FEET IN, FRANKLIN!
11-3
"THE NUMBERS SIX AND THREE ARE FACTORS OF EIGHTEEN"
JUST A LITTLE "DOWN AND OUT" PATTERN THERE, MA'AM
www.unitedmedia.com
DON'T SIGH LIKE THAT, MA'AM..
IT'LL PUT WRINKLES IN YOUR FOREHEAD..
SCHULZ

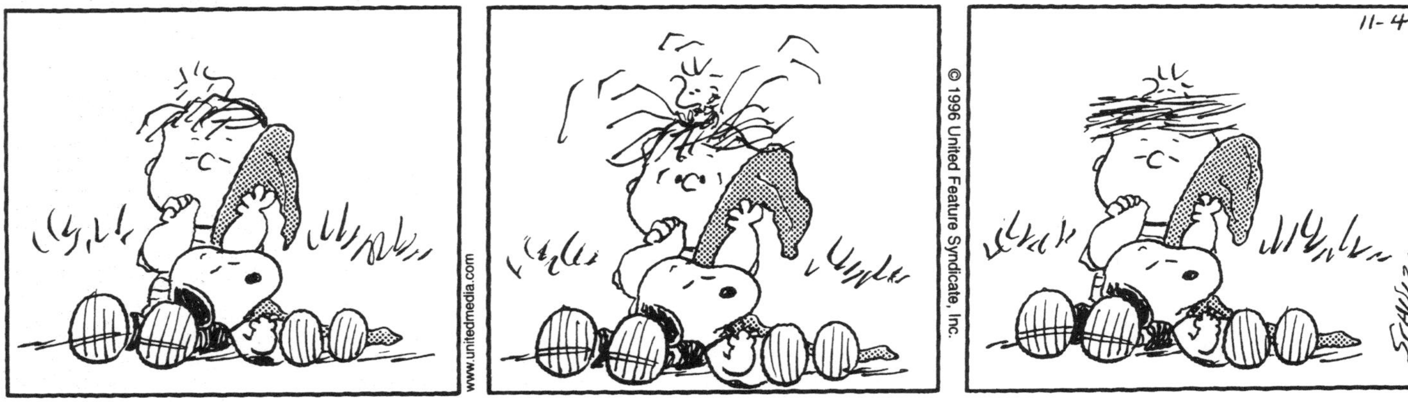
11-4
© 1996 United Feature Syndicate, Inc.
www.unitedmedia.com
SCHULZ

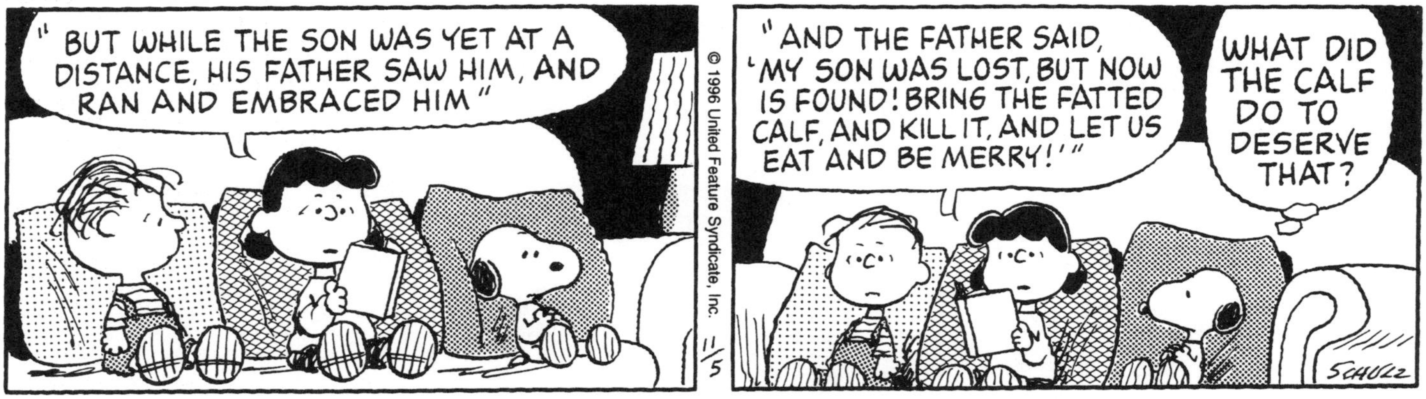
" BUT WHILE THE SON WAS YET AT A DISTANCE, HIS FATHER SAW HIM, AND RAN AND EMBRACED HIM "
"AND THE FATHER SAID, 'MY SON WAS LOST, BUT NOW IS FOUND! BRING THE FATTED CALF, AND KILL IT, AND LET US EAT AND BE MERRY!' "
WHAT DID THE CALF DO TO DESERVE THAT?
© 1996 United Feature Syndicate, Inc.
11/5
SCHULZ

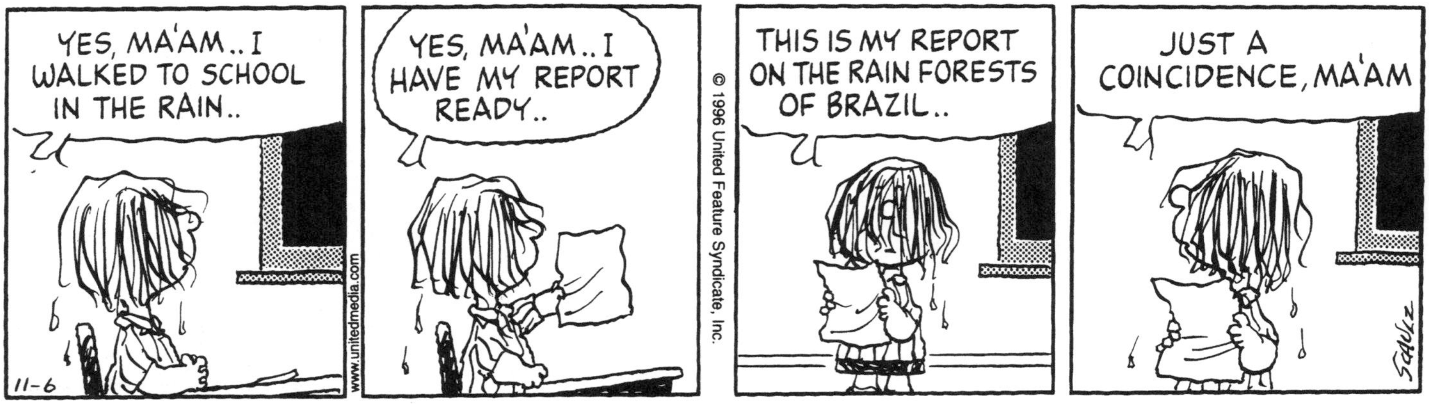
YES, MA'AM.. I WALKED TO SCHOOL IN THE RAIN..
YES, MA'AM.. I HAVE MY REPORT READY..
THIS IS MY REPORT ON THE RAIN FORESTS OF BRAZIL..
JUST A COINCIDENCE, MA'AM
11-6
www.unitedmedia.com
© 1996 United Feature Syndicate, Inc.
SCHULZ

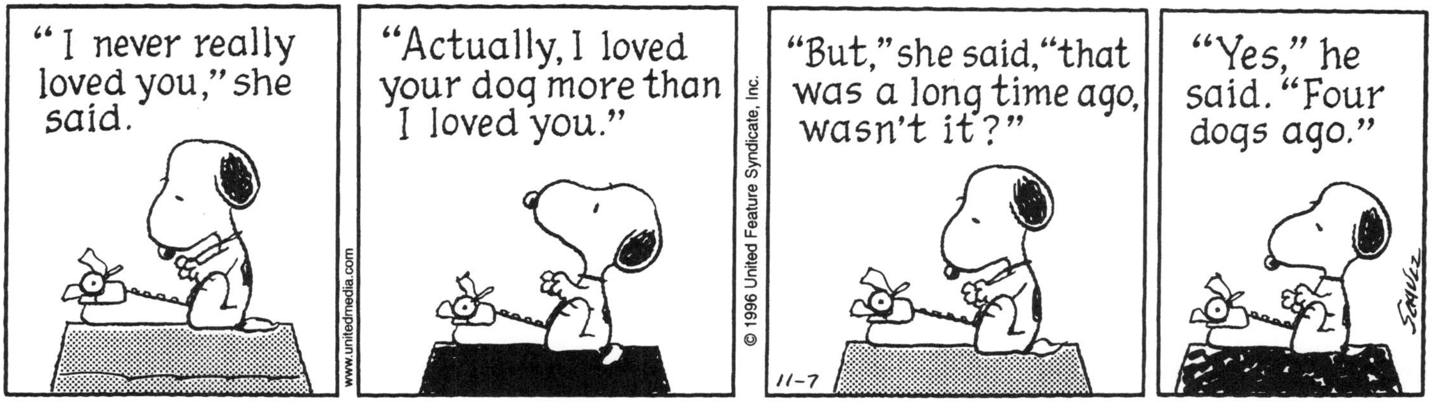
"I never really loved you," she said.
"Actually, I loved your dog more than I loved you."
"But," she said, "that was a long time ago, wasn't it?"
"Yes," he said. "Four dogs ago."
11-7
www.unitedmedia.com
© 1996 United Feature Syndicate, Inc.
SCHULZ

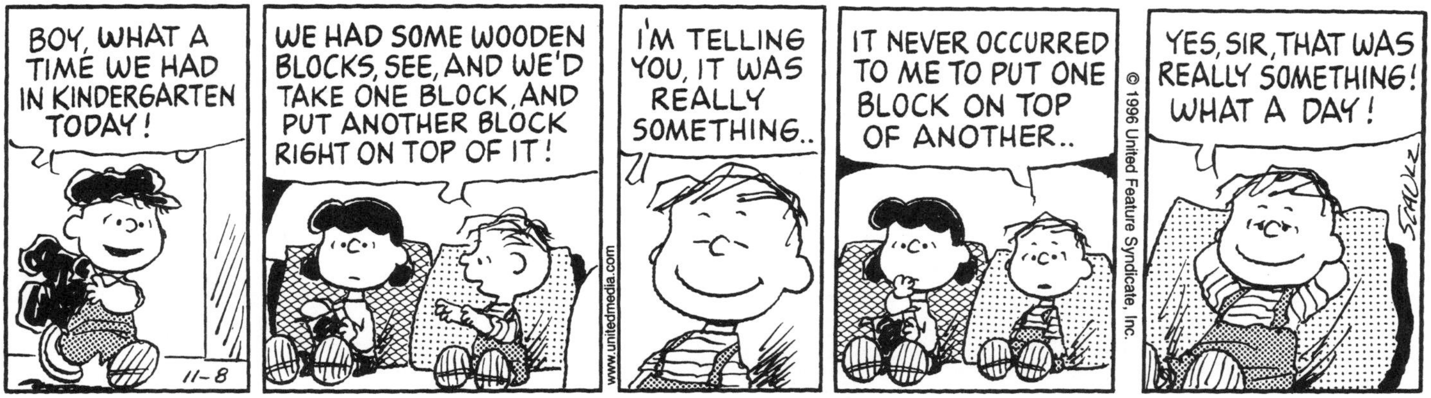
BOY, WHAT A TIME WE HAD IN KINDERGARTEN TODAY!
WE HAD SOME WOODEN BLOCKS, SEE, AND WE'D TAKE ONE BLOCK, AND PUT ANOTHER BLOCK RIGHT ON TOP OF IT!
I'M TELLING YOU, IT WAS REALLY SOMETHING..
IT NEVER OCCURRED TO ME TO PUT ONE BLOCK ON TOP OF ANOTHER..
YES, SIR, THAT WAS REALLY SOMETHING! WHAT A DAY!
11-8
www.unitedmedia.com
© 1996 United Feature Syndicate, Inc.
SCHULZ

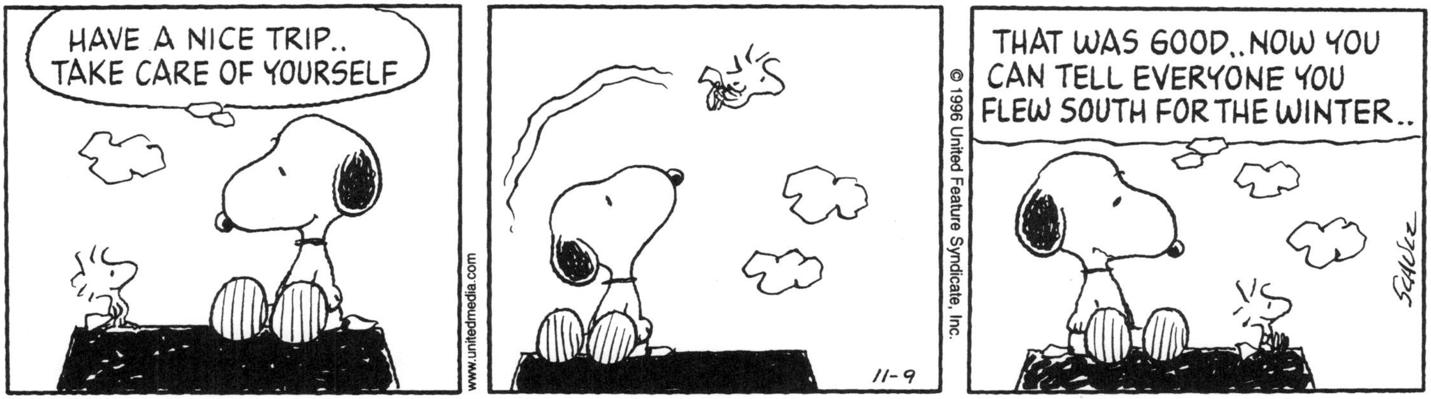
HAVE A NICE TRIP.. TAKE CARE OF YOURSELF
THAT WAS GOOD..NOW YOU CAN TELL EVERYONE YOU FLEW SOUTH FOR THE WINTER..
11-9
www.unitedmedia.com
© 1996 United Feature Syndicate, Inc.
SCHULZ

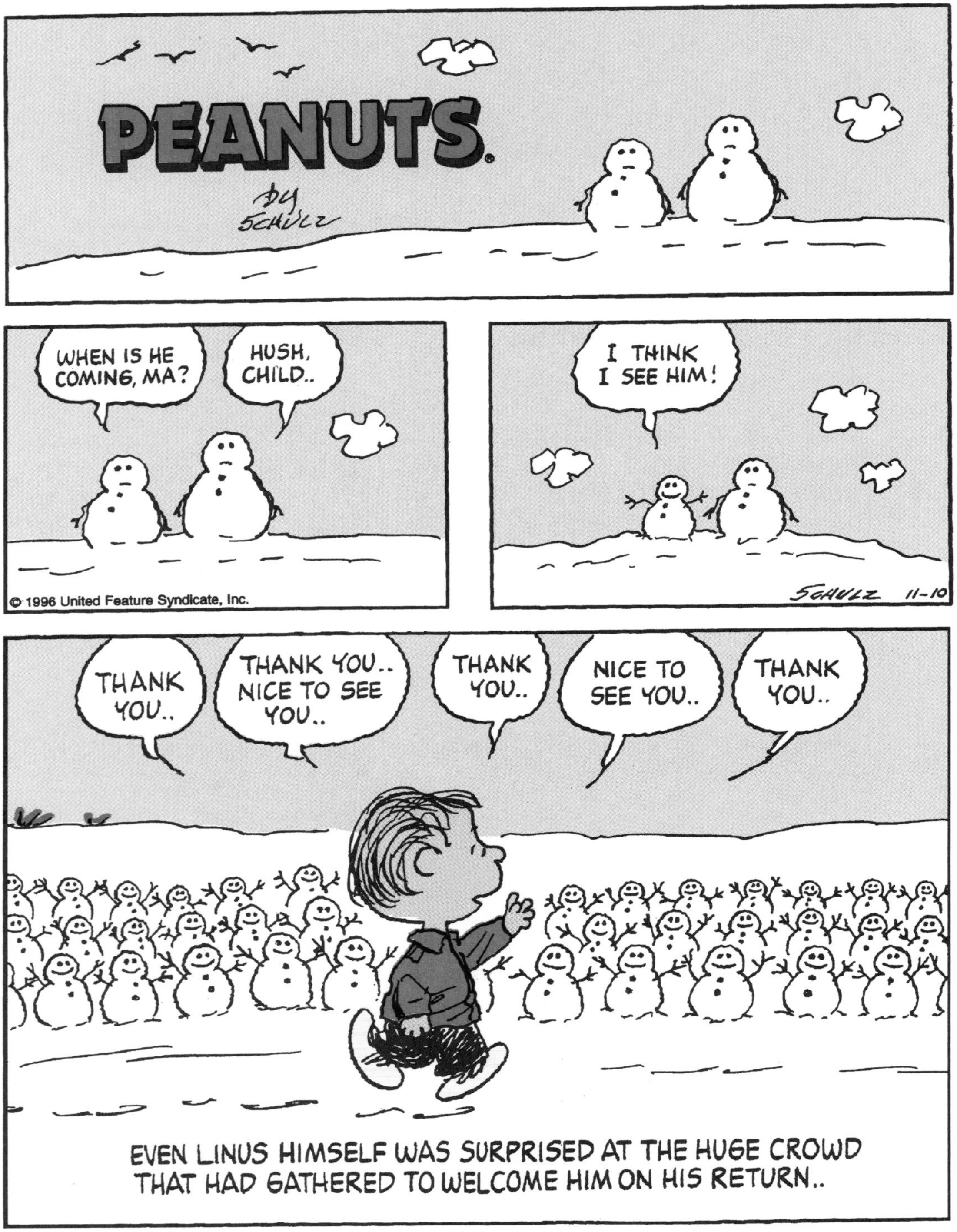
PEANUTS
by SCHULZ
WHEN IS HE COMING, MA?
HUSH, CHILD..
© 1996 United Feature Syndicate, Inc.
I THINK I SEE HIM!
SCHULZ 11-10
THANK YOU..
THANK YOU.. NICE TO SEE YOU..
THANK YOU..
NICE TO SEE YOU..
THANK YOU..
EVEN LINUS HIMSELF WAS SURPRISED AT THE HUGE CROWD THAT HAD GATHERED TO WELCOME HIM ON HIS RETURN..

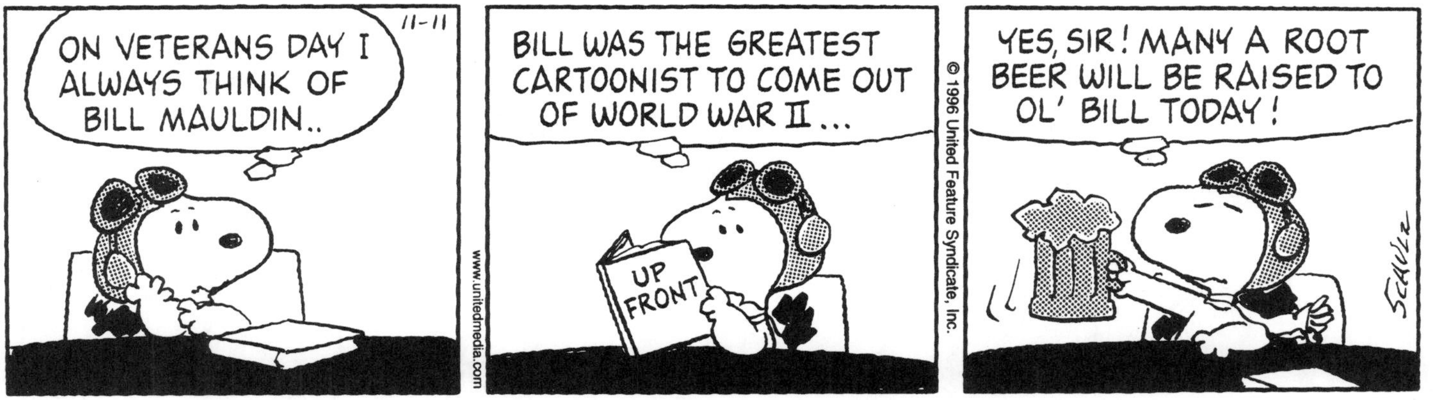
11-11
ON VETERANS DAY I ALWAYS THINK OF BILL MAULDIN..
www.unitedmedia.com
BILL WAS THE GREATEST CARTOONIST TO COME OUT OF WORLD WAR II ...
UP FRONT
© 1996 United Feature Syndicate, Inc.
YES, SIR! MANY A ROOT BEER WILL BE RAISED TO OL' BILL TODAY!
SCHULZ

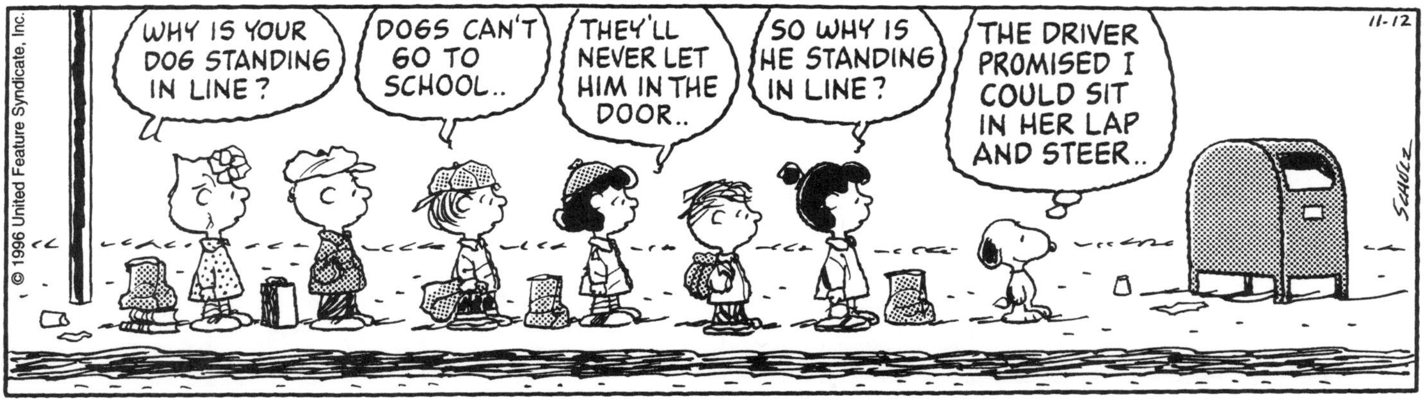
© 1996 United Feature Syndicate, Inc.
11-12
WHY IS YOUR DOG STANDING IN LINE?
DOGS CAN'T GO TO SCHOOL..
THEY'LL NEVER LET HIM IN THE DOOR..
SO WHY IS HE STANDING IN LINE?
THE DRIVER PROMISED I COULD SIT IN HER LAP AND STEER..
SCHULZ

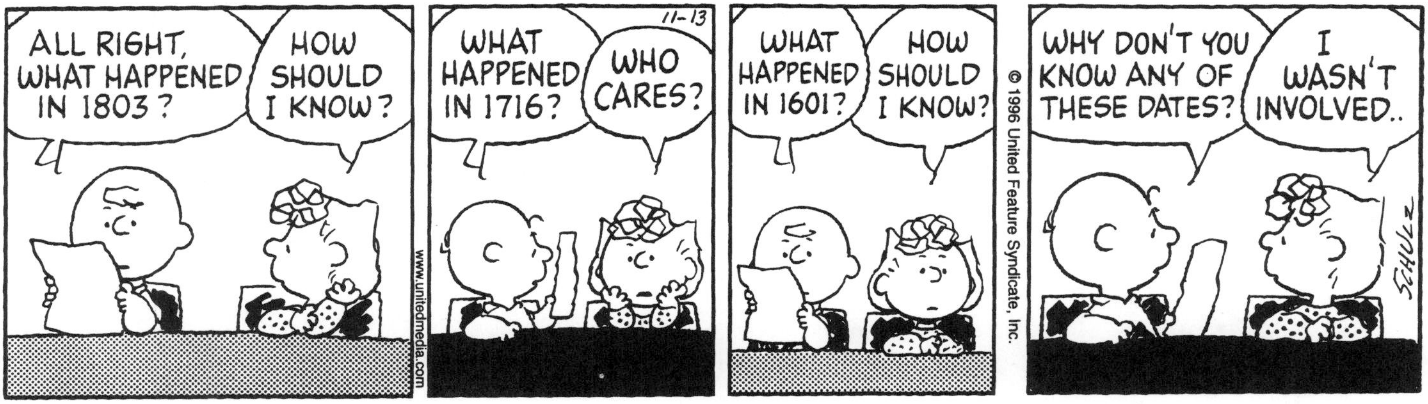
ALL RIGHT, WHAT HAPPENED IN 1803?
HOW SHOULD I KNOW?
www.unitedmedia.com
11-13
WHAT HAPPENED IN 1716?
WHO CARES?
WHAT HAPPENED IN 1601?
HOW SHOULD I KNOW?
© 1996 United Feature Syndicate, Inc.
WHY DON'T YOU KNOW ANY OF THESE DATES?
I WASN'T INVOLVED..
SCHULZ

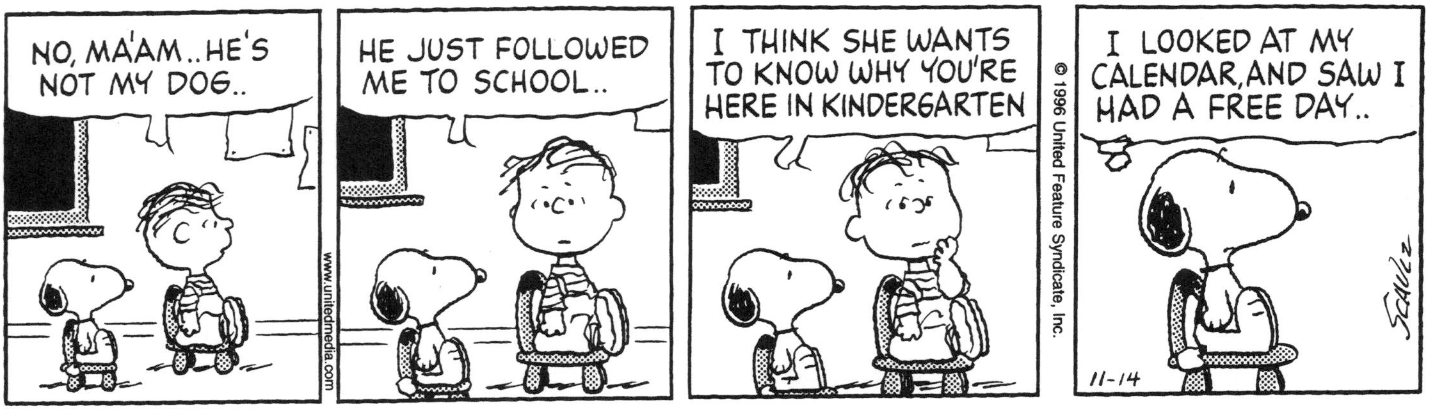
NO, MA'AM..HE'S NOT MY DOG..
HE JUST FOLLOWED ME TO SCHOOL..
I THINK SHE WANTS TO KNOW WHY YOU'RE HERE IN KINDERGARTEN
I LOOKED AT MY CALENDAR, AND SAW I HAD A FREE DAY..
www.unitedmedia.com
© 1996 United Feature Syndicate, Inc.
11-14

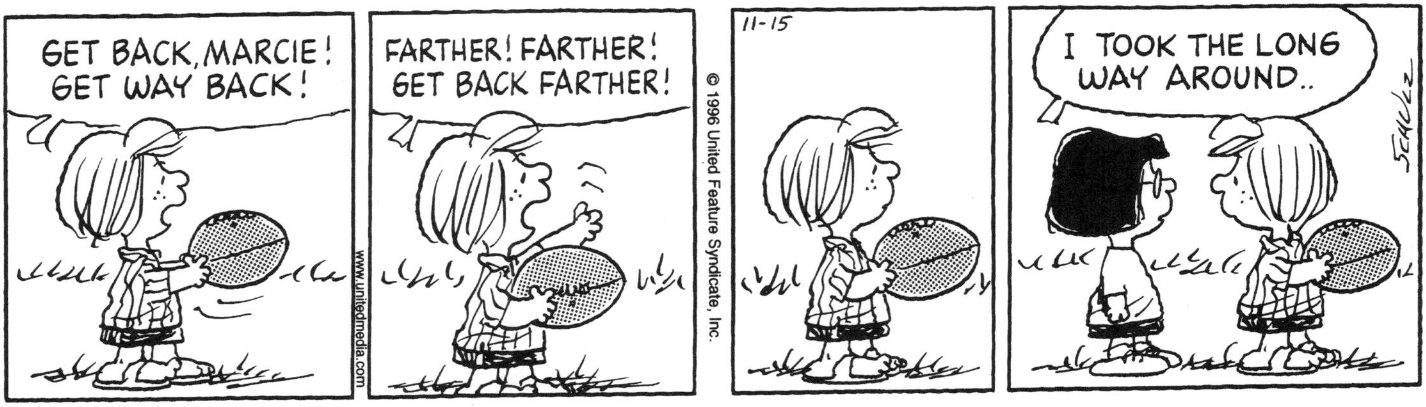
GET BACK, MARCIE! GET WAY BACK!
FARTHER! FARTHER! GET BACK FARTHER!
I TOOK THE LONG WAY AROUND..
www.unitedmedia.com
© 1996 United Feature Syndicate, Inc.
11-15

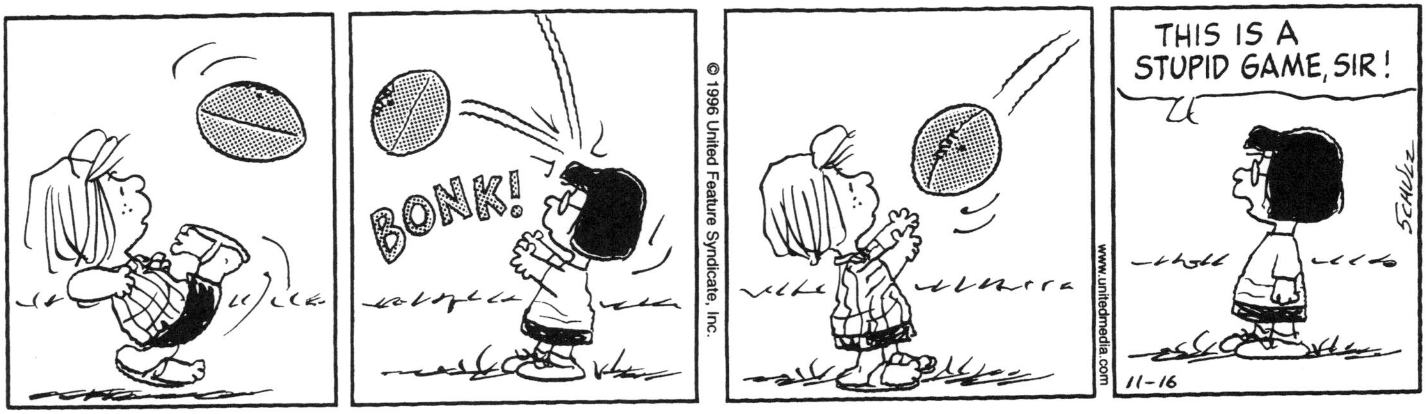
BONK!
THIS IS A STUPID GAME, SIR!
© 1996 United Feature Syndicate, Inc.
www.unitedmedia.com
11-16

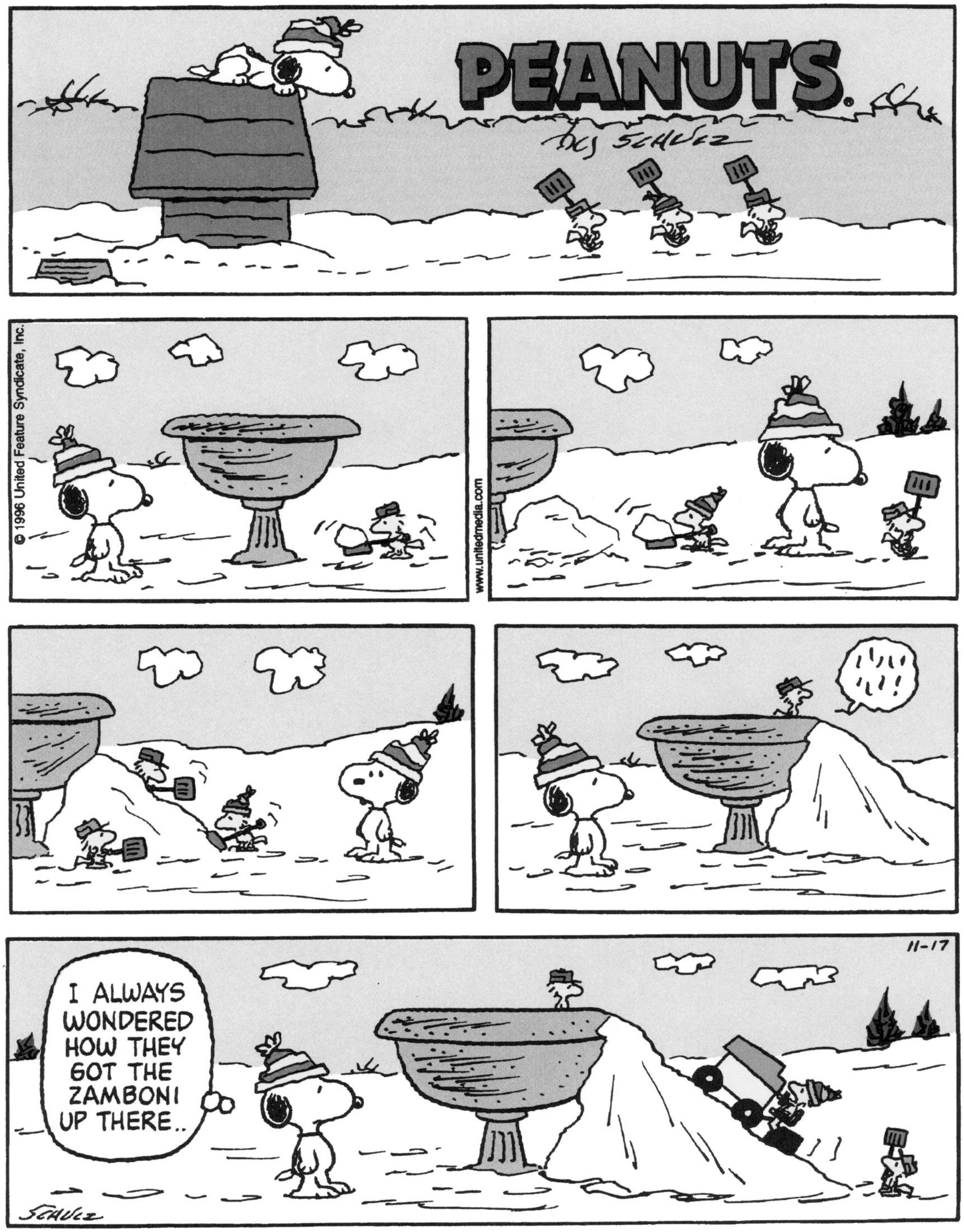
PEANUTS
© 1996 United Feature Syndicate, Inc.
www.unitedmedia.com
11-17
I ALWAYS WONDERED HOW THEY GOT THE ZAMBONI UP THERE..

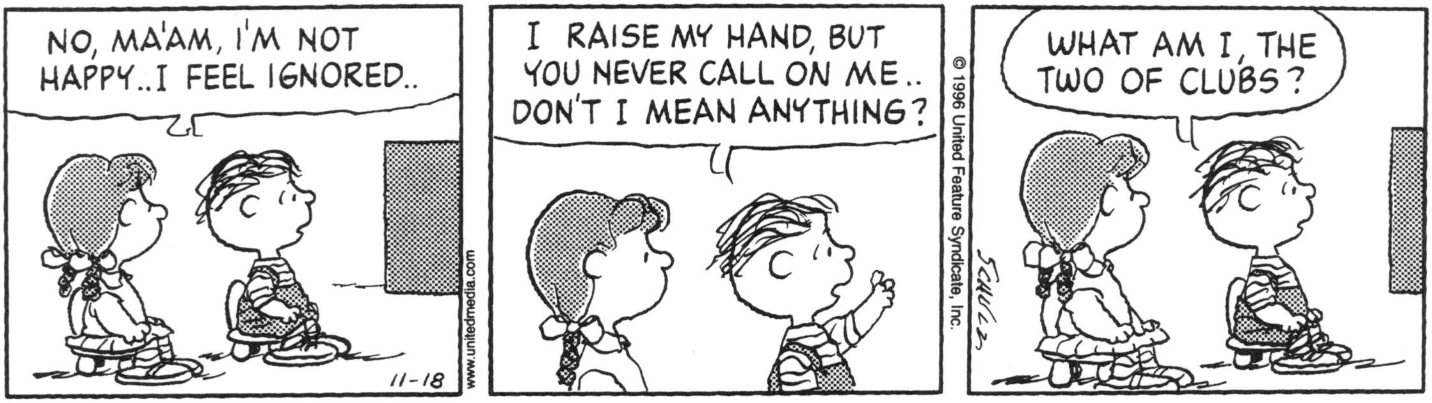
NO, MA'AM, I'M NOT HAPPY..I FEEL IGNORED..
11-18
www.unitedmedia.com
I RAISE MY HAND, BUT YOU NEVER CALL ON ME.. DON'T I MEAN ANYTHING?
© 1996 United Feature Syndicate, Inc.
WHAT AM I, THE TWO OF CLUBS?
SCHULZ

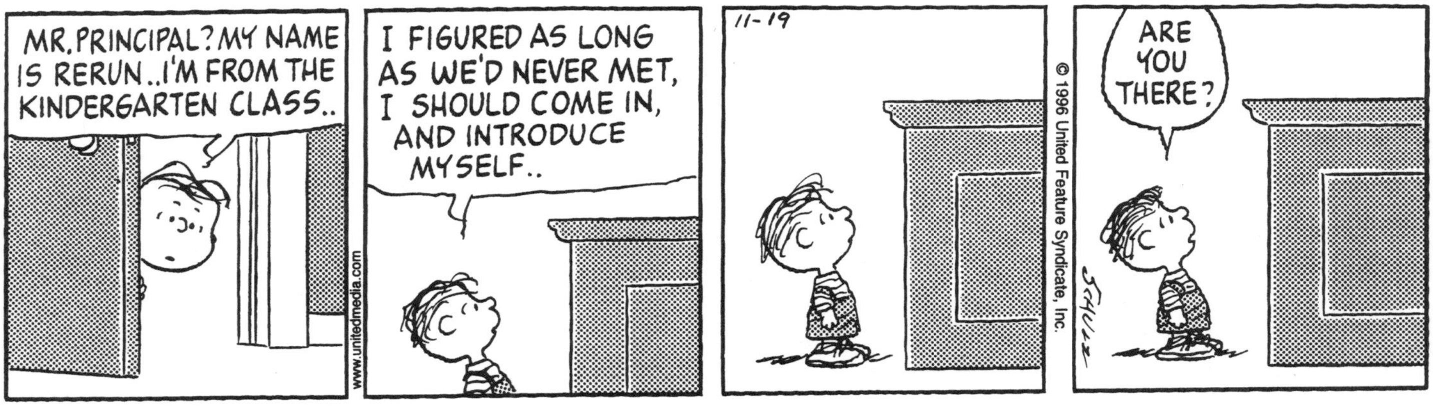
MR. PRINCIPAL? MY NAME IS RERUN..I'M FROM THE KINDERGARTEN CLASS..
www.unitedmedia.com
I FIGURED AS LONG AS WE'D NEVER MET, I SHOULD COME IN, AND INTRODUCE MYSELF..
11-19
© 1996 United Feature Syndicate, Inc.
ARE YOU THERE?
SCHULZ

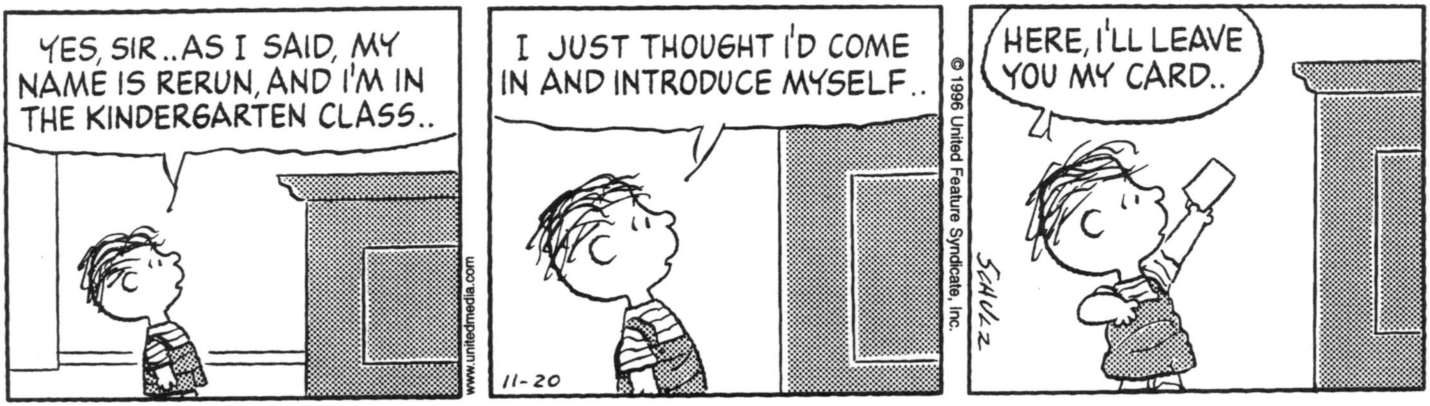
YES, SIR..AS I SAID, MY NAME IS RERUN, AND I'M IN THE KINDERGARTEN CLASS..
www.unitedmedia.com
I JUST THOUGHT I'D COME IN AND INTRODUCE MYSELF..
11-20
© 1996 United Feature Syndicate, Inc.
HERE, I'LL LEAVE YOU MY CARD..
SCHULZ

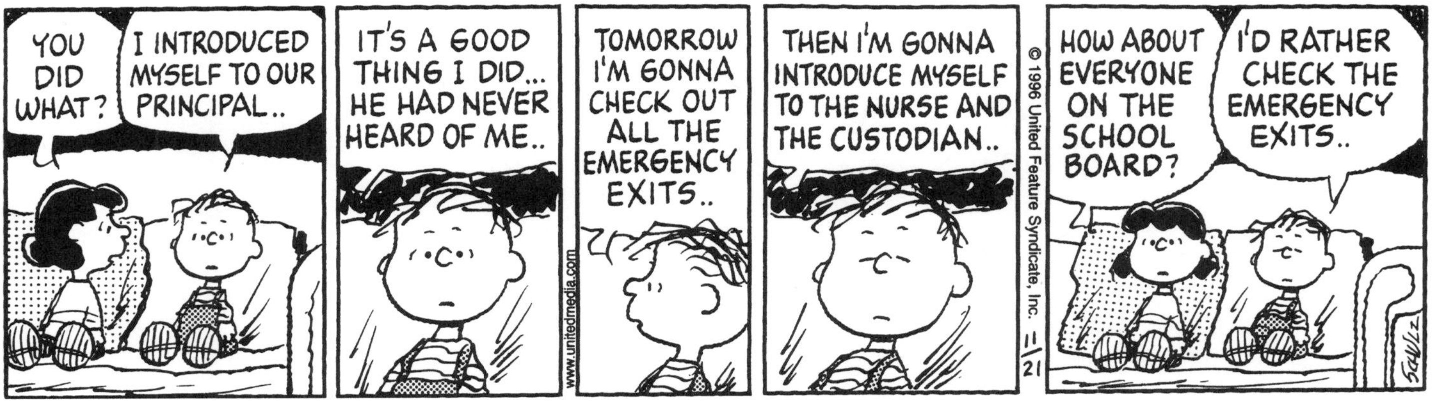
YOU DID WHAT?
I INTRODUCED MYSELF TO OUR PRINCIPAL..
IT'S A GOOD THING I DID... HE HAD NEVER HEARD OF ME..
TOMORROW I'M GONNA CHECK OUT ALL THE EMERGENCY EXITS..
THEN I'M GONNA INTRODUCE MYSELF TO THE NURSE AND THE CUSTODIAN..
HOW ABOUT EVERYONE ON THE SCHOOL BOARD?
I'D RATHER CHECK THE EMERGENCY EXITS..
www.unitedmedia.com
© 1996 United Feature Syndicate, Inc.
11/21
SCHULZ

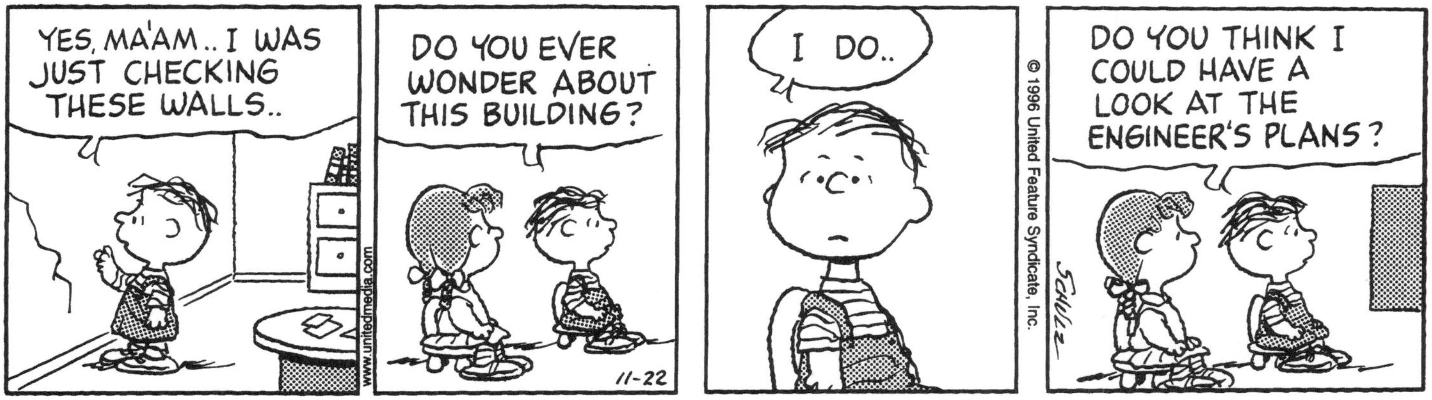
YES, MA'AM.. I WAS JUST CHECKING THESE WALLS..
DO YOU EVER WONDER ABOUT THIS BUILDING?
I DO..
DO YOU THINK I COULD HAVE A LOOK AT THE ENGINEER'S PLANS?
www.unitedmedia.com
11-22
© 1996 United Feature Syndicate, Inc.
SCHULZ

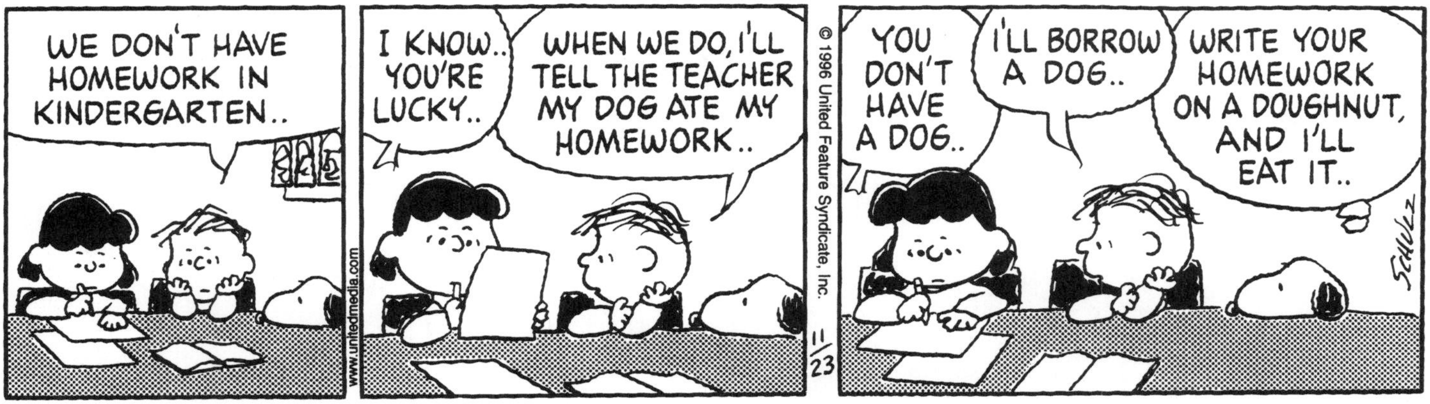
WE DON'T HAVE HOMEWORK IN KINDERGARTEN..
I KNOW.. YOU'RE LUCKY..
WHEN WE DO, I'LL TELL THE TEACHER MY DOG ATE MY HOMEWORK..
YOU DON'T HAVE A DOG..
I'LL BORROW A DOG..
WRITE YOUR HOMEWORK ON A DOUGHNUT, AND I'LL EAT IT..
www.unitedmedia.com
© 1996 United Feature Syndicate, Inc.
11/23
SCHULZ

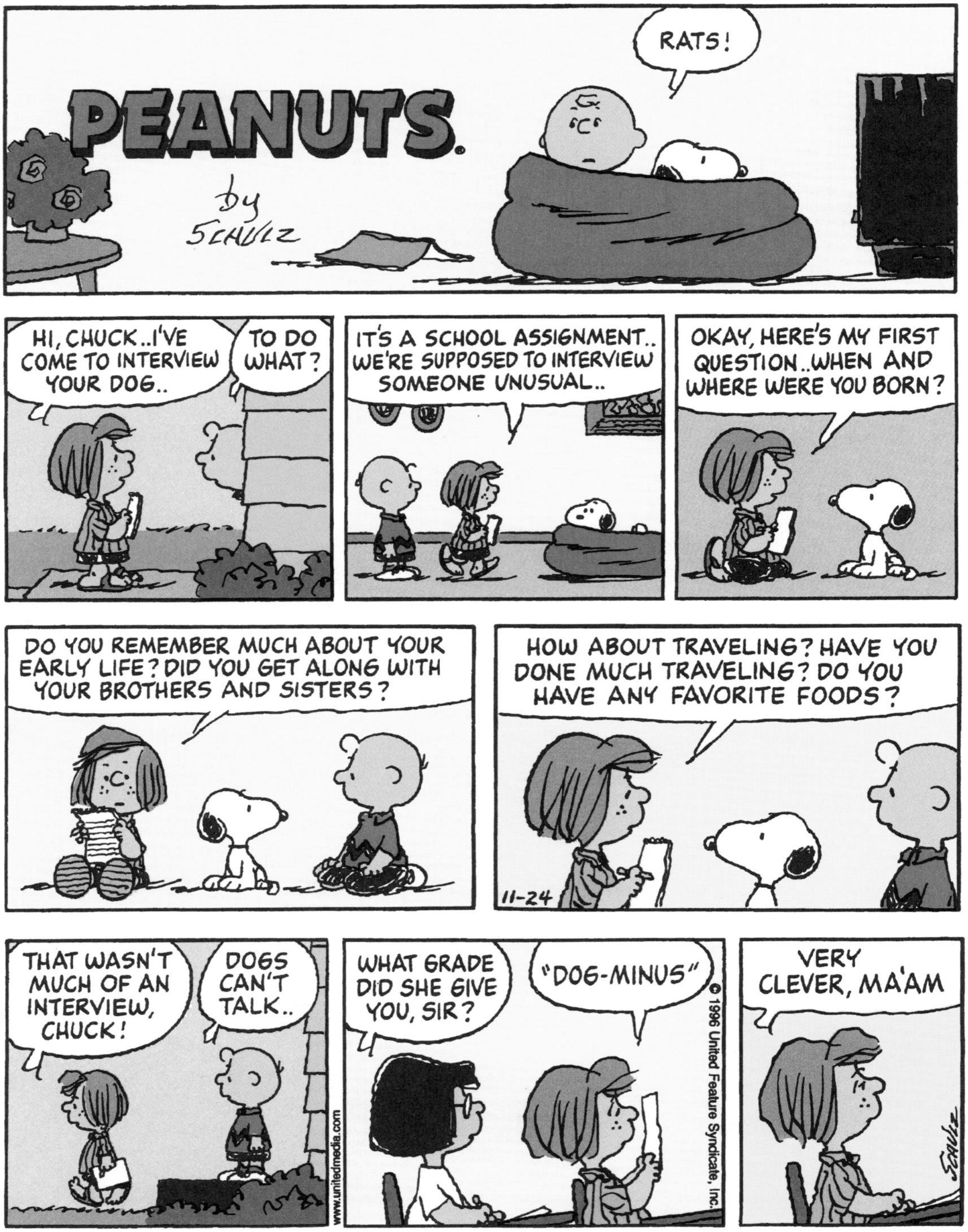
PEANUTS
by SCHULZ
RATS!
HI, CHUCK..I'VE COME TO INTERVIEW YOUR DOG..
TO DO WHAT?
IT'S A SCHOOL ASSIGNMENT.. WE'RE SUPPOSED TO INTERVIEW SOMEONE UNUSUAL..
OKAY, HERE'S MY FIRST QUESTION..WHEN AND WHERE WERE YOU BORN?
DO YOU REMEMBER MUCH ABOUT YOUR EARLY LIFE? DID YOU GET ALONG WITH YOUR BROTHERS AND SISTERS?
HOW ABOUT TRAVELING? HAVE YOU DONE MUCH TRAVELING? DO YOU HAVE ANY FAVORITE FOODS?
11-24
THAT WASN'T MUCH OF AN INTERVIEW, CHUCK!
DOGS CAN'T TALK..
www.unitedmedia.com
WHAT GRADE DID SHE GIVE YOU, SIR?
"DOG-MINUS"
© 1996 United Feature Syndicate, Inc.
VERY CLEVER, MA'AM
SCHULZ

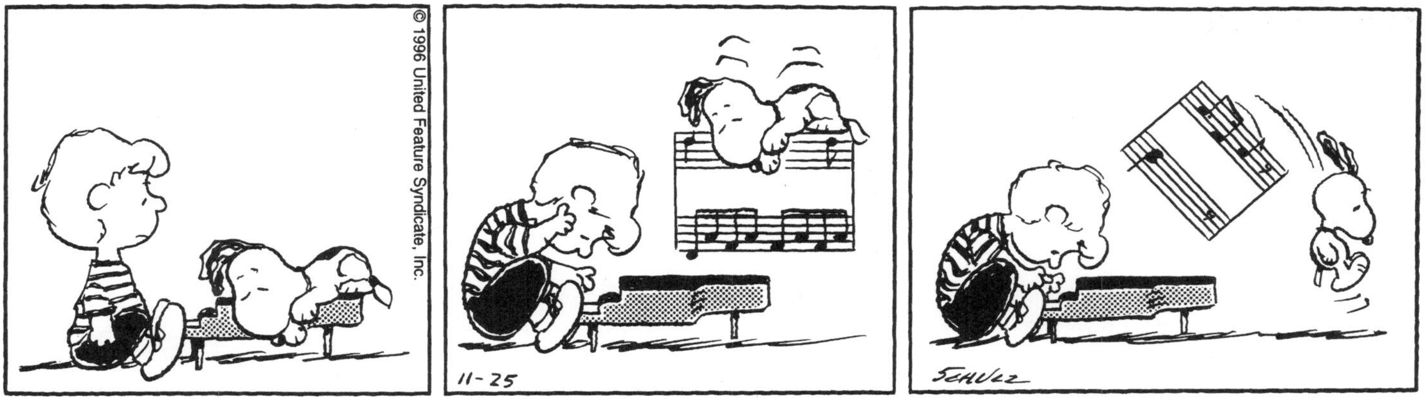
© 1996 United Feature Syndicate, Inc.
11-25
SCHULZ

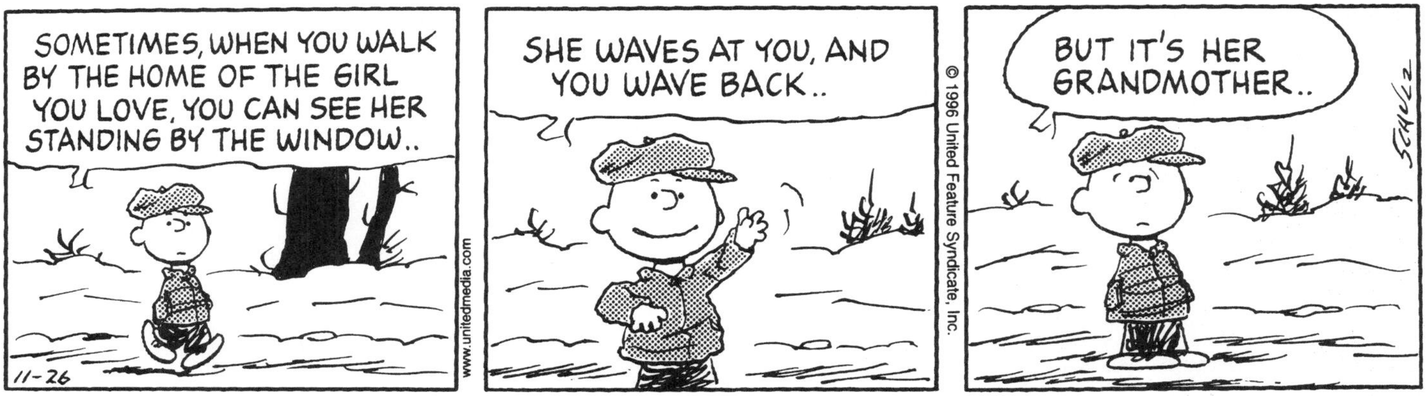
SOMETIMES, WHEN YOU WALK BY THE HOME OF THE GIRL YOU LOVE, YOU CAN SEE HER STANDING BY THE WINDOW..
11-26
www.unitedmedia.com
SHE WAVES AT YOU, AND YOU WAVE BACK..
© 1996 United Feature Syndicate, Inc.
BUT IT'S HER GRANDMOTHER..
SCHULZ

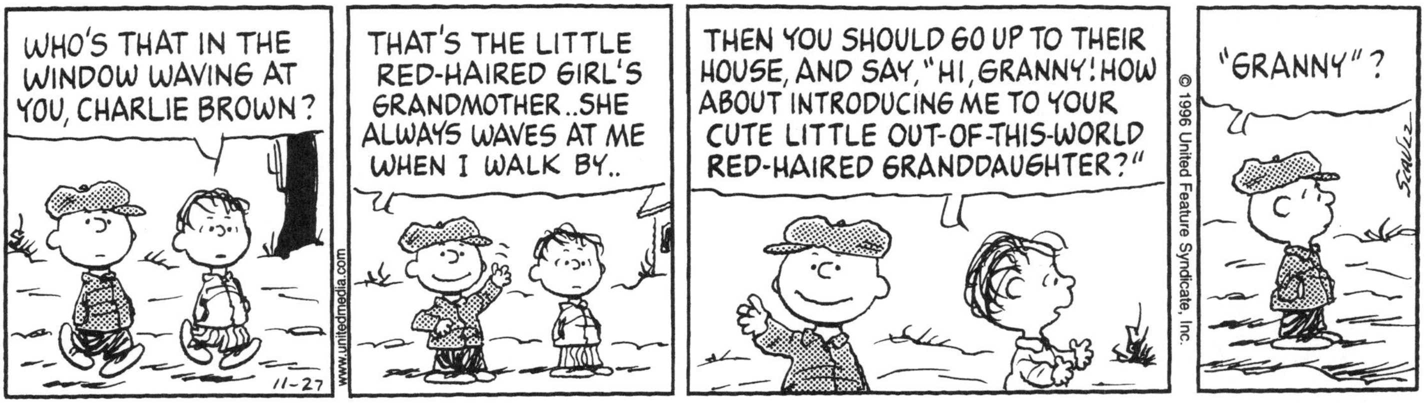
WHO'S THAT IN THE WINDOW WAVING AT YOU, CHARLIE BROWN?
11-27
www.unitedmedia.com
THAT'S THE LITTLE RED-HAIRED GIRL'S GRANDMOTHER..SHE ALWAYS WAVES AT ME WHEN I WALK BY..
THEN YOU SHOULD GO UP TO THEIR HOUSE, AND SAY, "HI, GRANNY! HOW ABOUT INTRODUCING ME TO YOUR CUTE LITTLE OUT-OF-THIS-WORLD RED-HAIRED GRANDDAUGHTER?"
© 1996 United Feature Syndicate, Inc.
"GRANNY"?
SCHULZ

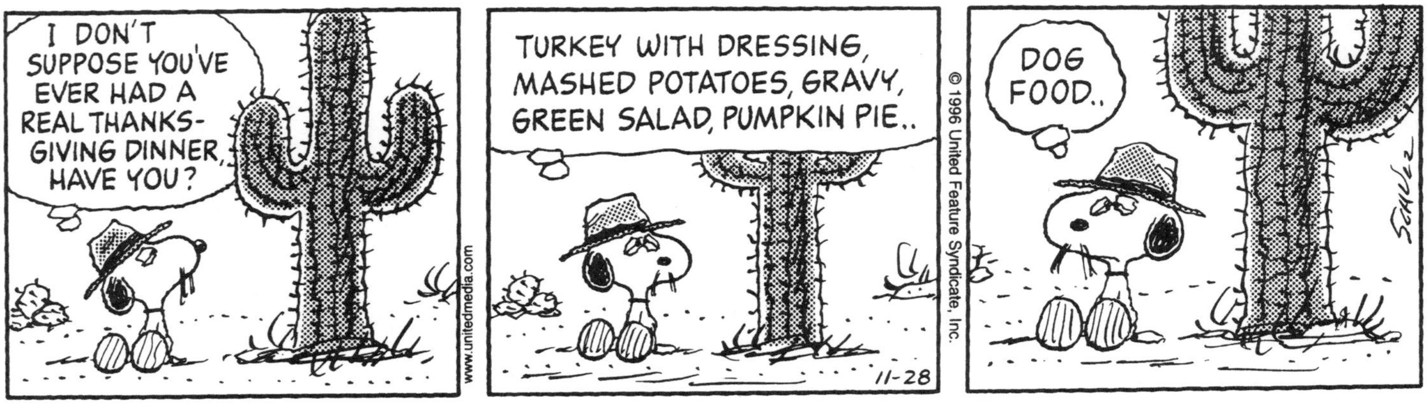
I DON'T SUPPOSE YOU'VE EVER HAD A REAL THANKSGIVING DINNER, HAVE YOU?
TURKEY WITH DRESSING, MASHED POTATOES, GRAVY, GREEN SALAD, PUMPKIN PIE..
DOG FOOD..
www.unitedmedia.com
© 1996 United Feature Syndicate, Inc.
11-28
SCHULZ

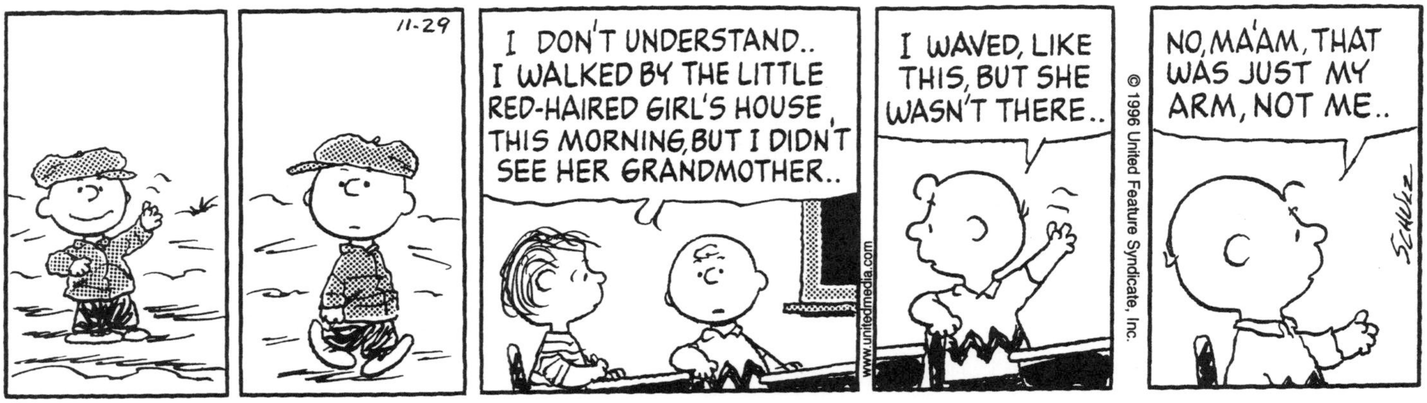
11-29
I DON'T UNDERSTAND.. I WALKED BY THE LITTLE RED-HAIRED GIRL'S HOUSE THIS MORNING, BUT I DIDN'T SEE HER GRANDMOTHER..
I WAVED, LIKE THIS, BUT SHE WASN'T THERE..
NO, MA'AM, THAT WAS JUST MY ARM, NOT ME..
www.unitedmedia.com
© 1996 United Feature Syndicate, Inc.
SCHULZ

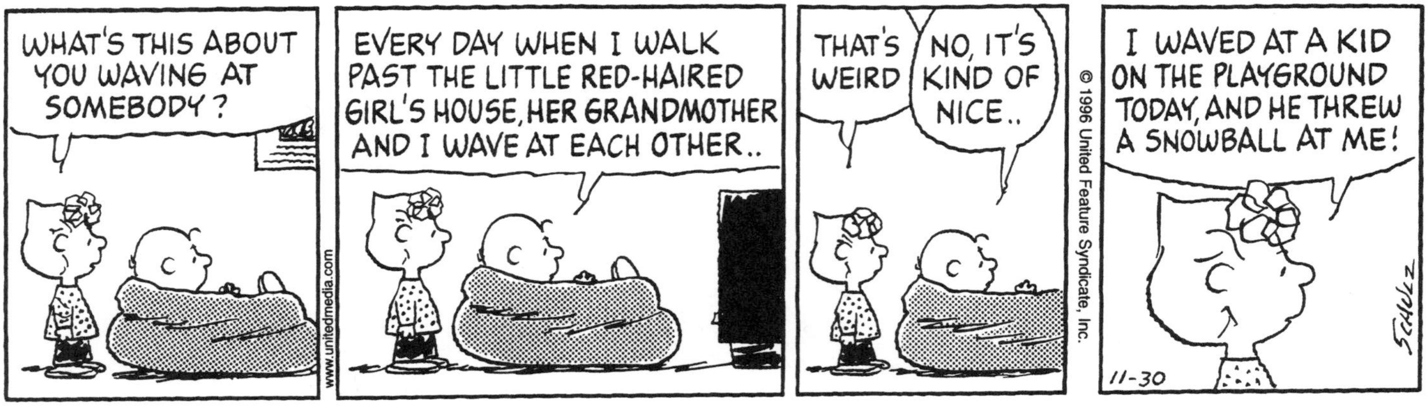
WHAT'S THIS ABOUT YOU WAVING AT SOMEBODY?
EVERY DAY WHEN I WALK PAST THE LITTLE RED-HAIRED GIRL'S HOUSE, HER GRANDMOTHER AND I WAVE AT EACH OTHER..
THAT'S WEIRD
NO, IT'S KIND OF NICE..
I WAVED AT A KID ON THE PLAYGROUND TODAY, AND HE THREW A SNOWBALL AT ME!
www.unitedmedia.com
© 1996 United Feature Syndicate, Inc.
SCHULZ
11-30

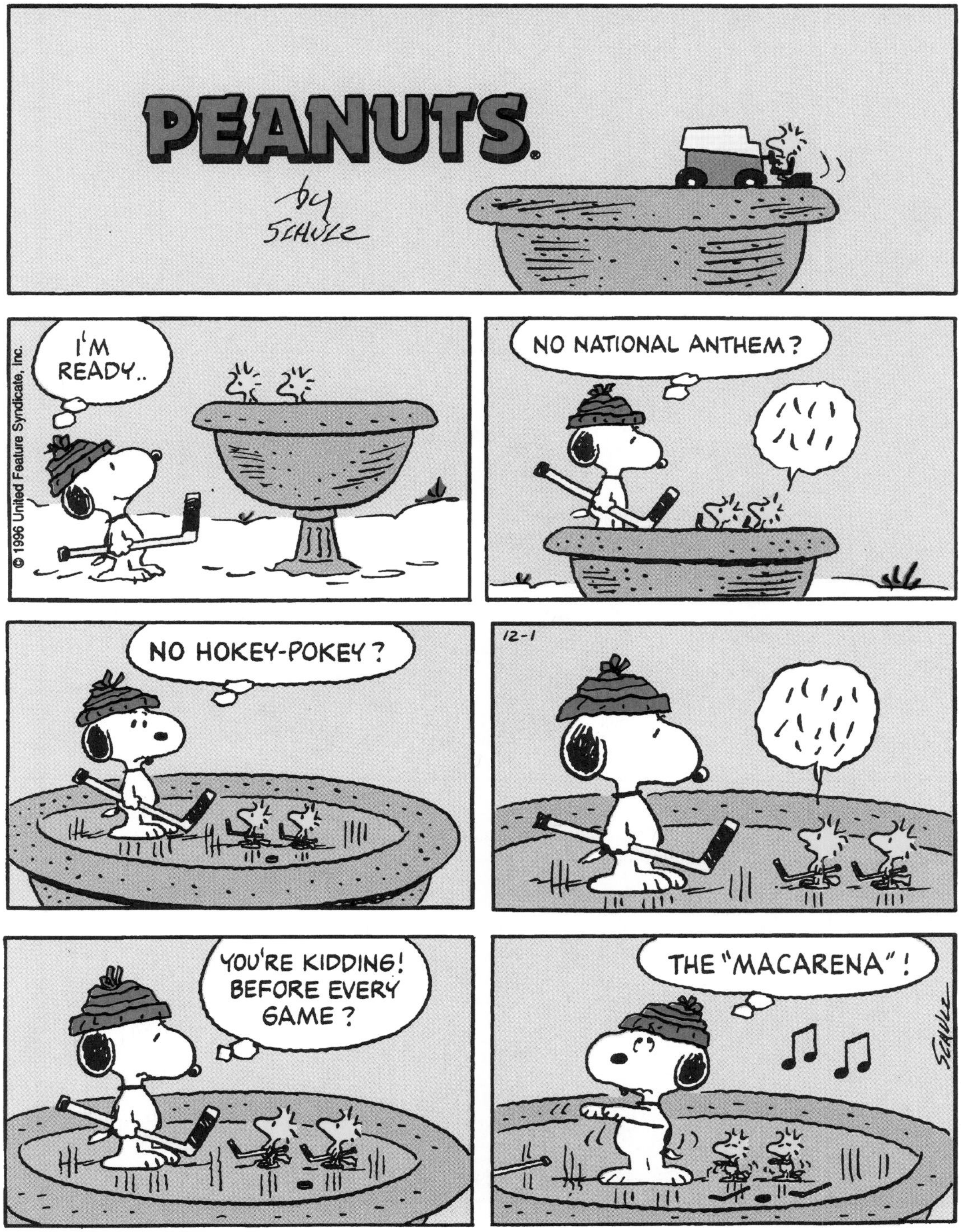
PEANUTS
by SCHULZ
© 1996 United Feature Syndicate, Inc.
I'M READY..
NO NATIONAL ANTHEM?
NO HOKEY-POKEY?
12-1
YOU'RE KIDDING! BEFORE EVERY GAME?
THE "MACARENA"!
SCHULZ

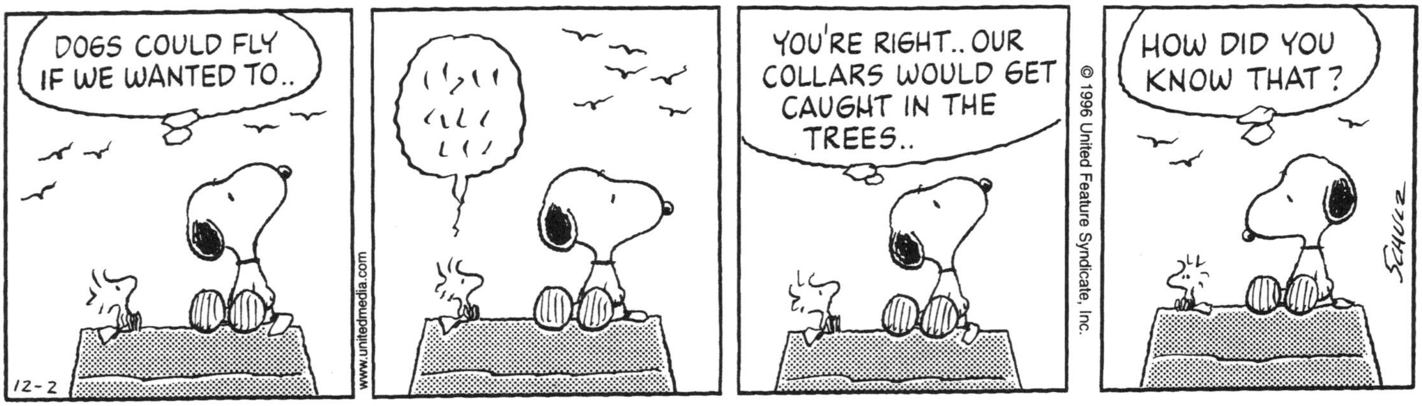
DOGS COULD FLY IF WE WANTED TO..
YOU'RE RIGHT.. OUR COLLARS WOULD GET CAUGHT IN THE TREES..
HOW DID YOU KNOW THAT?
12-2
www.unitedmedia.com
© 1996 United Feature Syndicate, Inc.
SCHULZ

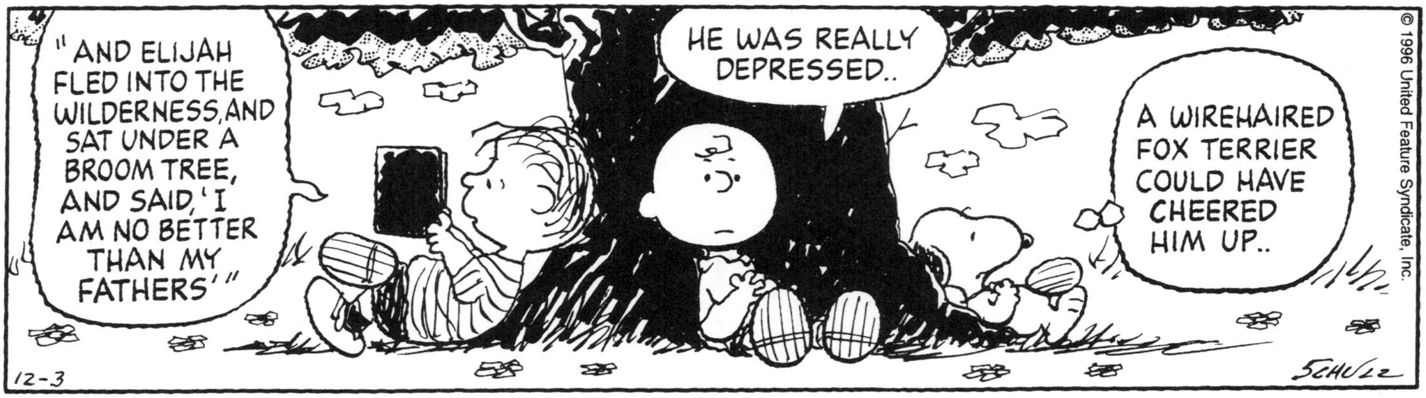
"AND ELIJAH FLED INTO THE WILDERNESS, AND SAT UNDER A BROOM TREE, AND SAID, 'I AM NO BETTER THAN MY FATHERS' "
HE WAS REALLY DEPRESSED..
A WIREHAIRED FOX TERRIER COULD HAVE CHEERED HIM UP..
12-3
© 1996 United Feature Syndicate, Inc.
SCHULZ

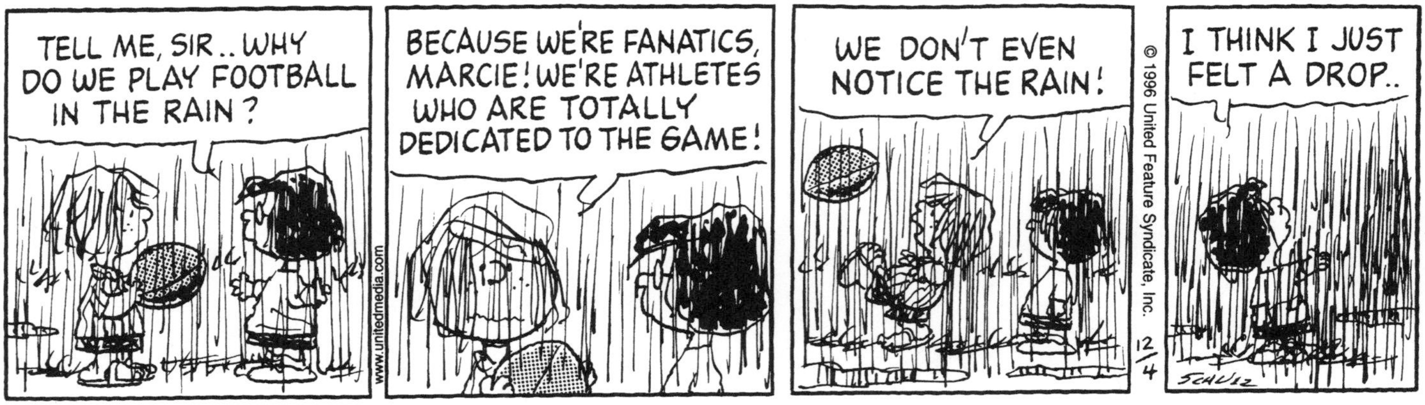
TELL ME, SIR.. WHY DO WE PLAY FOOTBALL IN THE RAIN?
BECAUSE WE'RE FANATICS, MARCIE! WE'RE ATHLETES WHO ARE TOTALLY DEDICATED TO THE GAME!
WE DON'T EVEN NOTICE THE RAIN!
I THINK I JUST FELT A DROP..
www.unitedmedia.com
© 1996 United Feature Syndicate, Inc.
12/4
SCHULZ

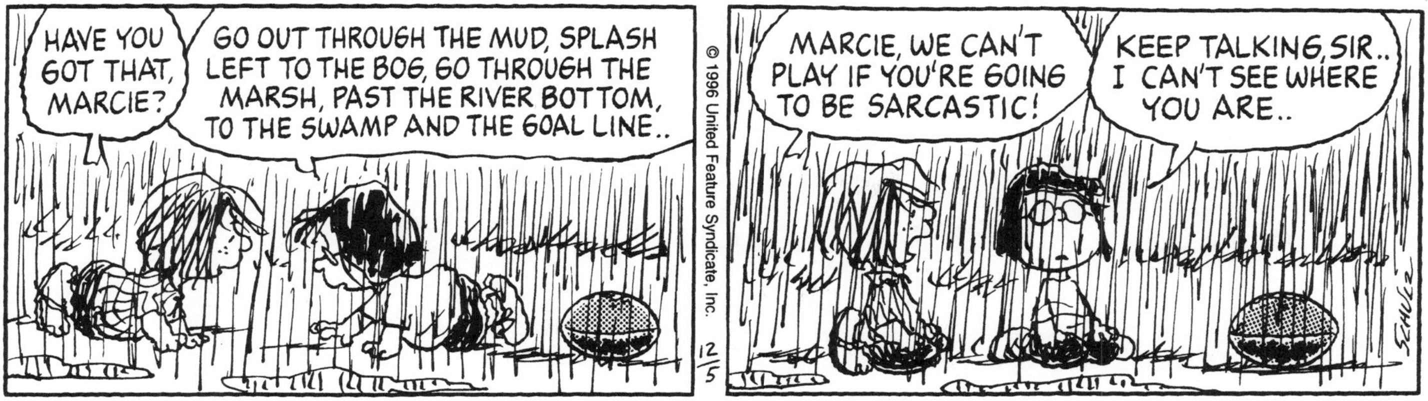
HAVE YOU GOT THAT, MARCIE?
GO OUT THROUGH THE MUD, SPLASH LEFT TO THE BOG, GO THROUGH THE MARSH, PAST THE RIVER BOTTOM, TO THE SWAMP AND THE GOAL LINE..
© 1996 United Feature Syndicate, Inc.
12/5
MARCIE, WE CAN'T PLAY IF YOU'RE GOING TO BE SARCASTIC!
KEEP TALKING, SIR.. I CAN'T SEE WHERE YOU ARE..
SCHULZ

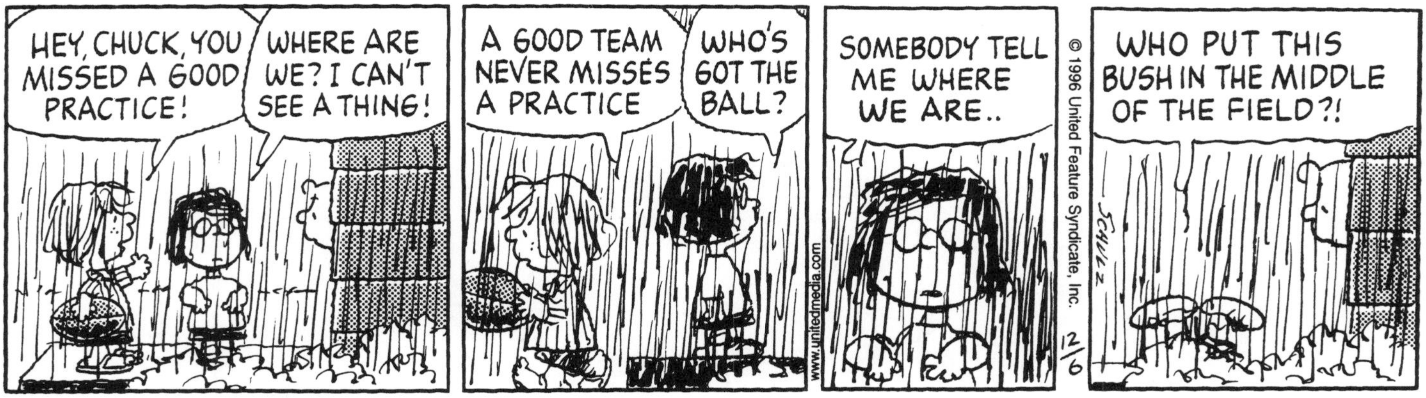
HEY, CHUCK, YOU MISSED A GOOD PRACTICE!
WHERE ARE WE? I CAN'T SEE A THING!
A GOOD TEAM NEVER MISSES A PRACTICE
WHO'S GOT THE BALL?
www.unitedmedia.com
SOMEBODY TELL ME WHERE WE ARE..
SCHULZ
© 1996 United Feature Syndicate, Inc.
12/6
WHO PUT THIS BUSH IN THE MIDDLE OF THE FIELD?!

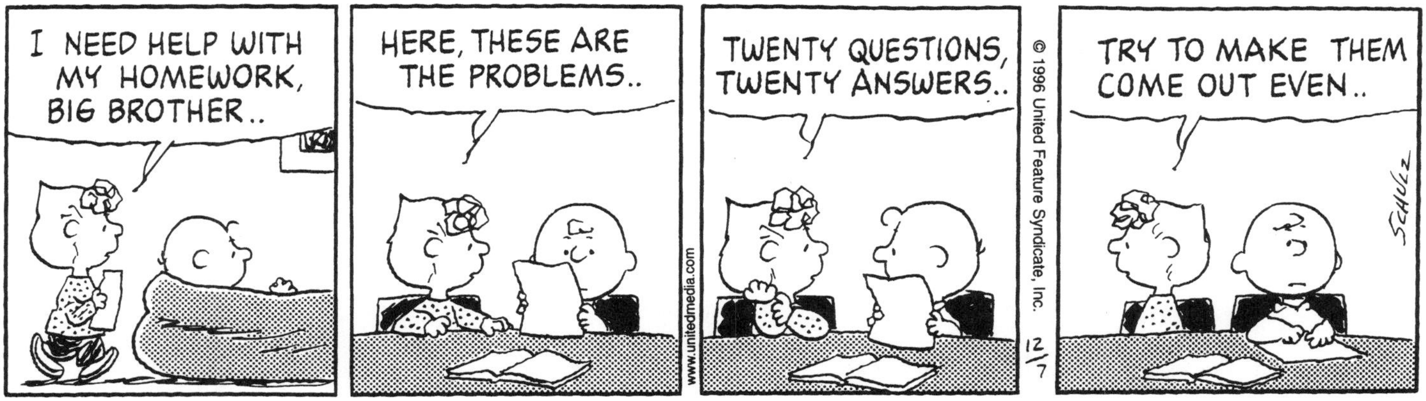
I NEED HELP WITH MY HOMEWORK, BIG BROTHER..
HERE, THESE ARE THE PROBLEMS..
www.unitedmedia.com
TWENTY QUESTIONS, TWENTY ANSWERS..
© 1996 United Feature Syndicate, Inc.
12/7
TRY TO MAKE THEM COME OUT EVEN..
SCHULZ

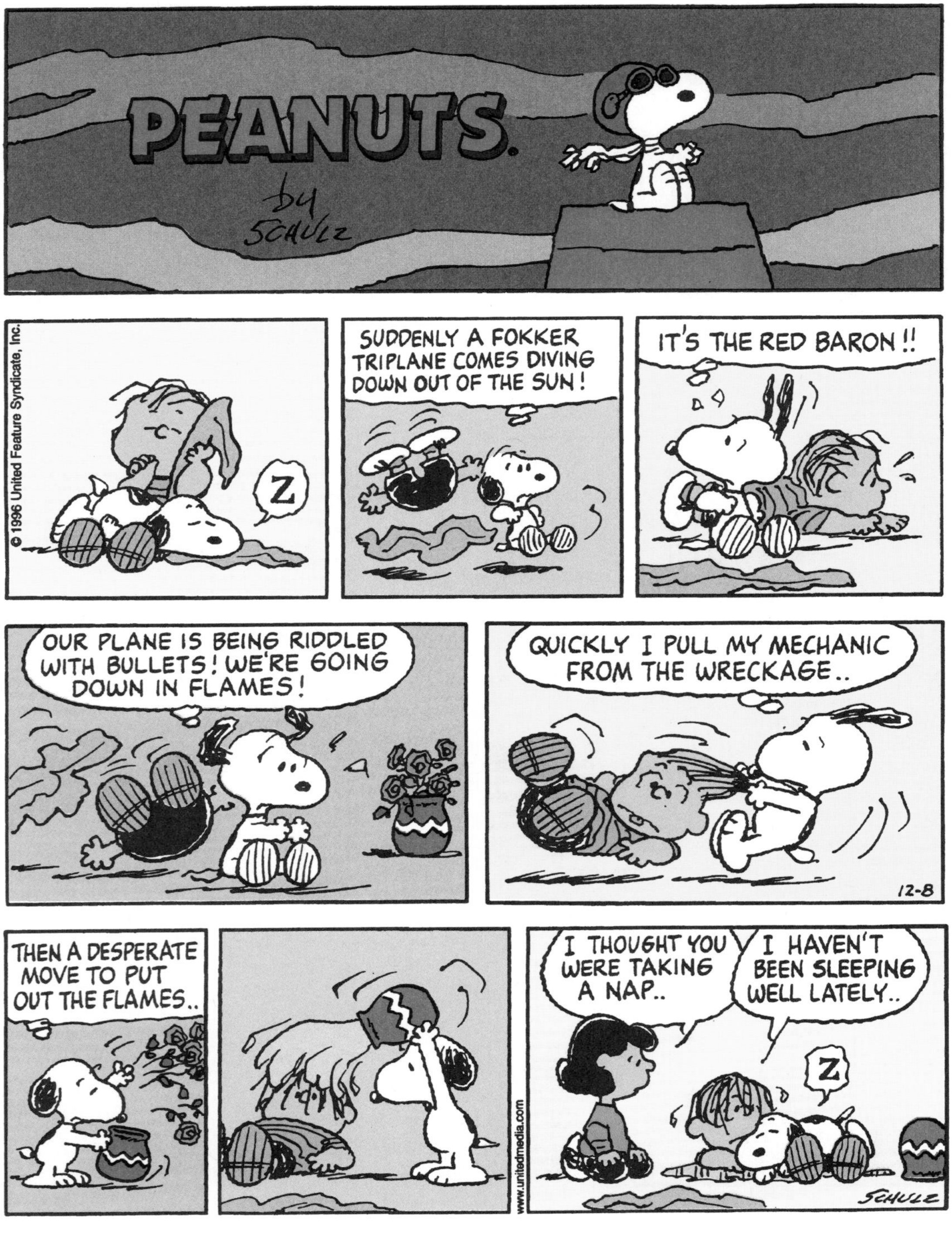
PEANUTS.
by SCHULZ
© 1996 United Feature Syndicate, Inc.
Z
SUDDENLY A FOKKER TRIPLANE COMES DIVING DOWN OUT OF THE SUN!
IT'S THE RED BARON!!
OUR PLANE IS BEING RIDDLED WITH BULLETS! WE'RE GOING DOWN IN FLAMES!
QUICKLY I PULL MY MECHANIC FROM THE WRECKAGE..
12-8
THEN A DESPERATE MOVE TO PUT OUT THE FLAMES..
www.unitedmedia.com
I THOUGHT YOU WERE TAKING A NAP..
I HAVEN'T BEEN SLEEPING WELL LATELY..
Z
SCHULZ

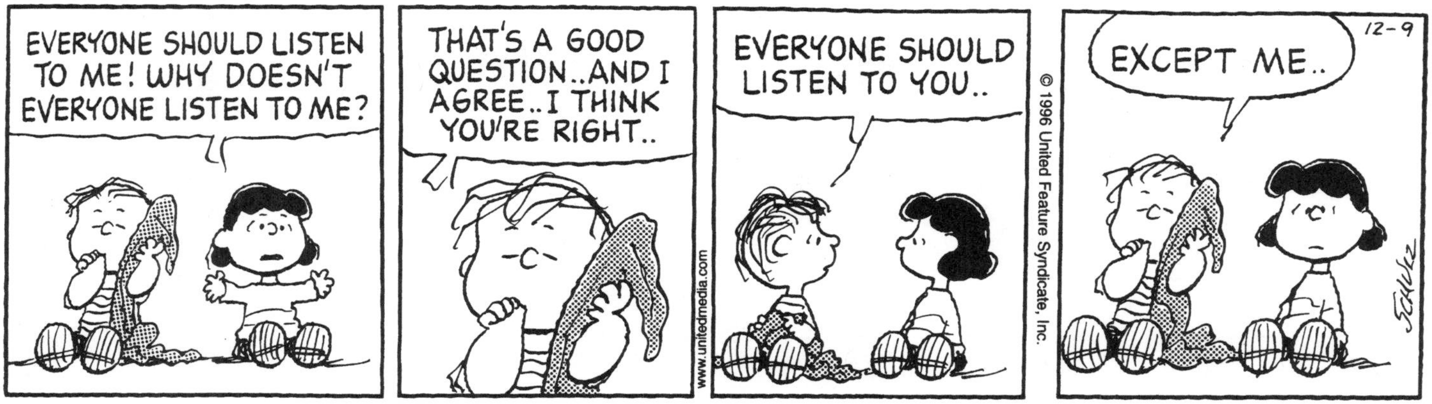
EVERYONE SHOULD LISTEN TO ME! WHY DOESN'T EVERYONE LISTEN TO ME?
THAT'S A GOOD QUESTION..AND I AGREE..I THINK YOU'RE RIGHT..
www.unitedmedia.com
EVERYONE SHOULD LISTEN TO YOU..
© 1996 United Feature Syndicate, Inc.
12-9
EXCEPT ME..
SCHULZ

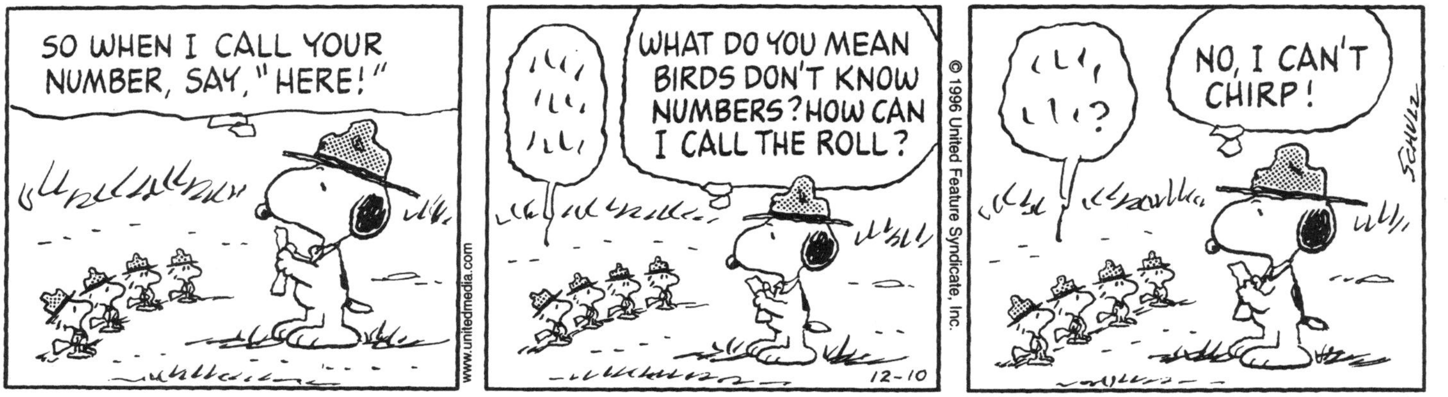
SO WHEN I CALL YOUR NUMBER, SAY, "HERE!"
www.unitedmedia.com
WHAT DO YOU MEAN BIRDS DON'T KNOW NUMBERS? HOW CAN I CALL THE ROLL?
12-10
© 1996 United Feature Syndicate, Inc.
NO, I CAN'T CHIRP!
SCHULZ

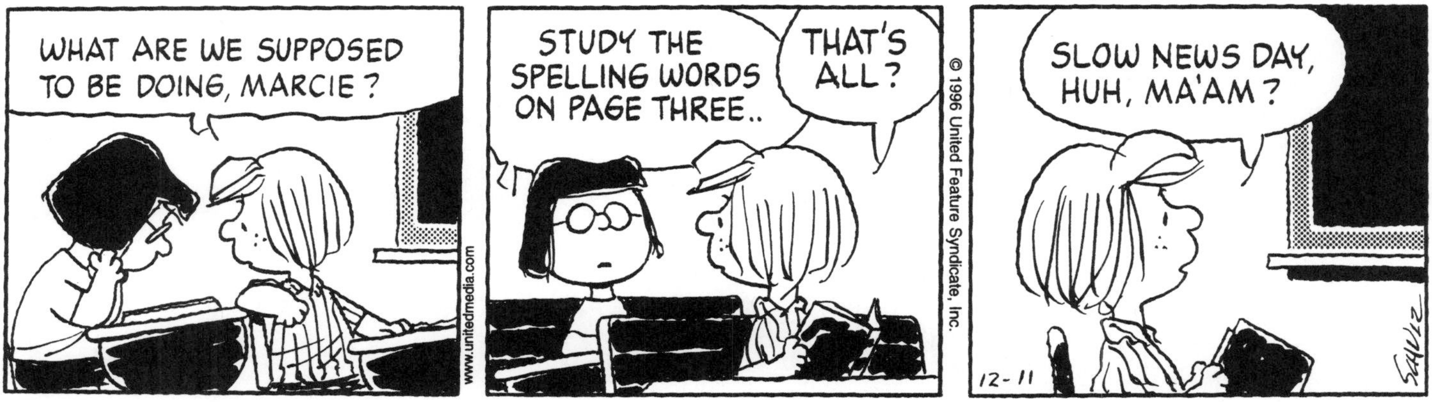
WHAT ARE WE SUPPOSED TO BE DOING, MARCIE?
www.unitedmedia.com
STUDY THE SPELLING WORDS ON PAGE THREE..
THAT'S ALL?
© 1996 United Feature Syndicate, Inc.
SLOW NEWS DAY, HUH, MA'AM?
12-11
SCHULZ

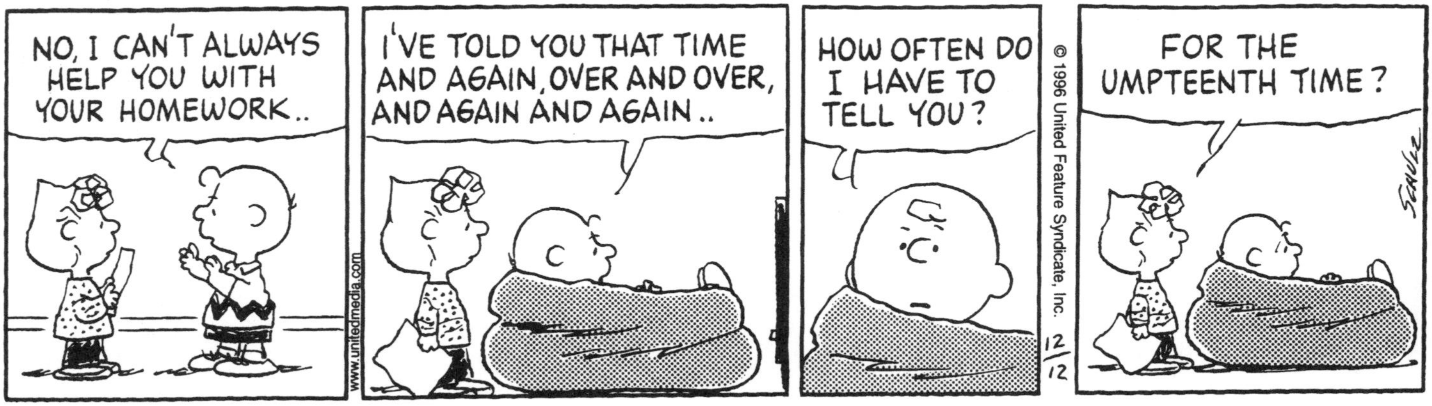
NO, I CAN'T ALWAYS HELP YOU WITH YOUR HOMEWORK..
I'VE TOLD YOU THAT TIME AND AGAIN, OVER AND OVER, AND AGAIN AND AGAIN..
HOW OFTEN DO I HAVE TO TELL YOU?
FOR THE UMPTEENTH TIME?
© 1996 United Feature Syndicate, Inc.
www.unitedmedia.com
12/12
SCHULZ

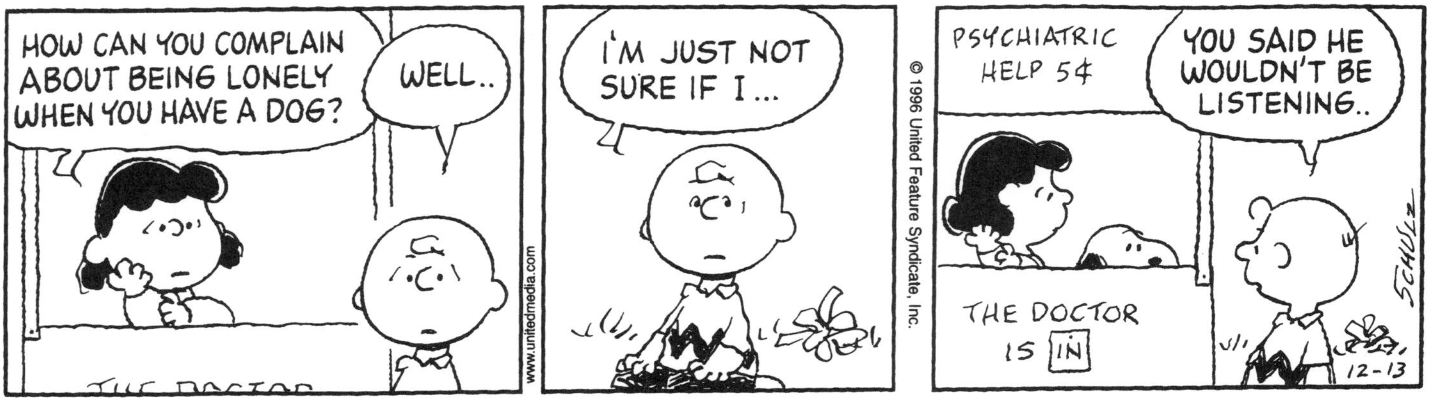
HOW CAN YOU COMPLAIN ABOUT BEING LONELY WHEN YOU HAVE A DOG?
WELL..
I'M JUST NOT SURE IF I...
PSYCHIATRIC HELP 5¢
YOU SAID HE WOULDN'T BE LISTENING..
THE DOCTOR IS IN
© 1996 United Feature Syndicate, Inc.
www.unitedmedia.com
12-13
SCHULZ

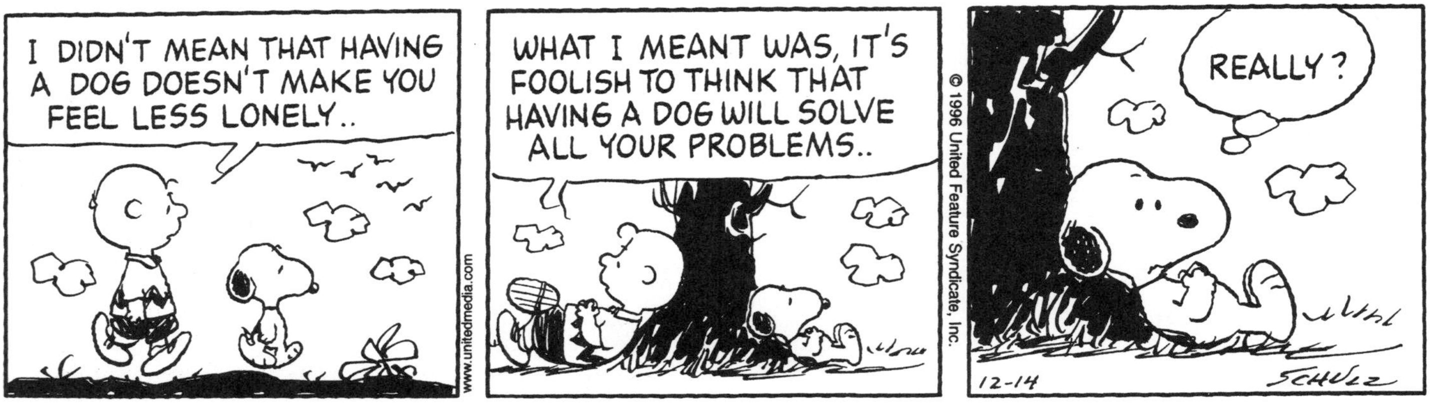
I DIDN'T MEAN THAT HAVING A DOG DOESN'T MAKE YOU FEEL LESS LONELY..
WHAT I MEANT WAS, IT'S FOOLISH TO THINK THAT HAVING A DOG WILL SOLVE ALL YOUR PROBLEMS..
REALLY?
© 1996 United Feature Syndicate, Inc.
www.unitedmedia.com
12-14
SCHULZ

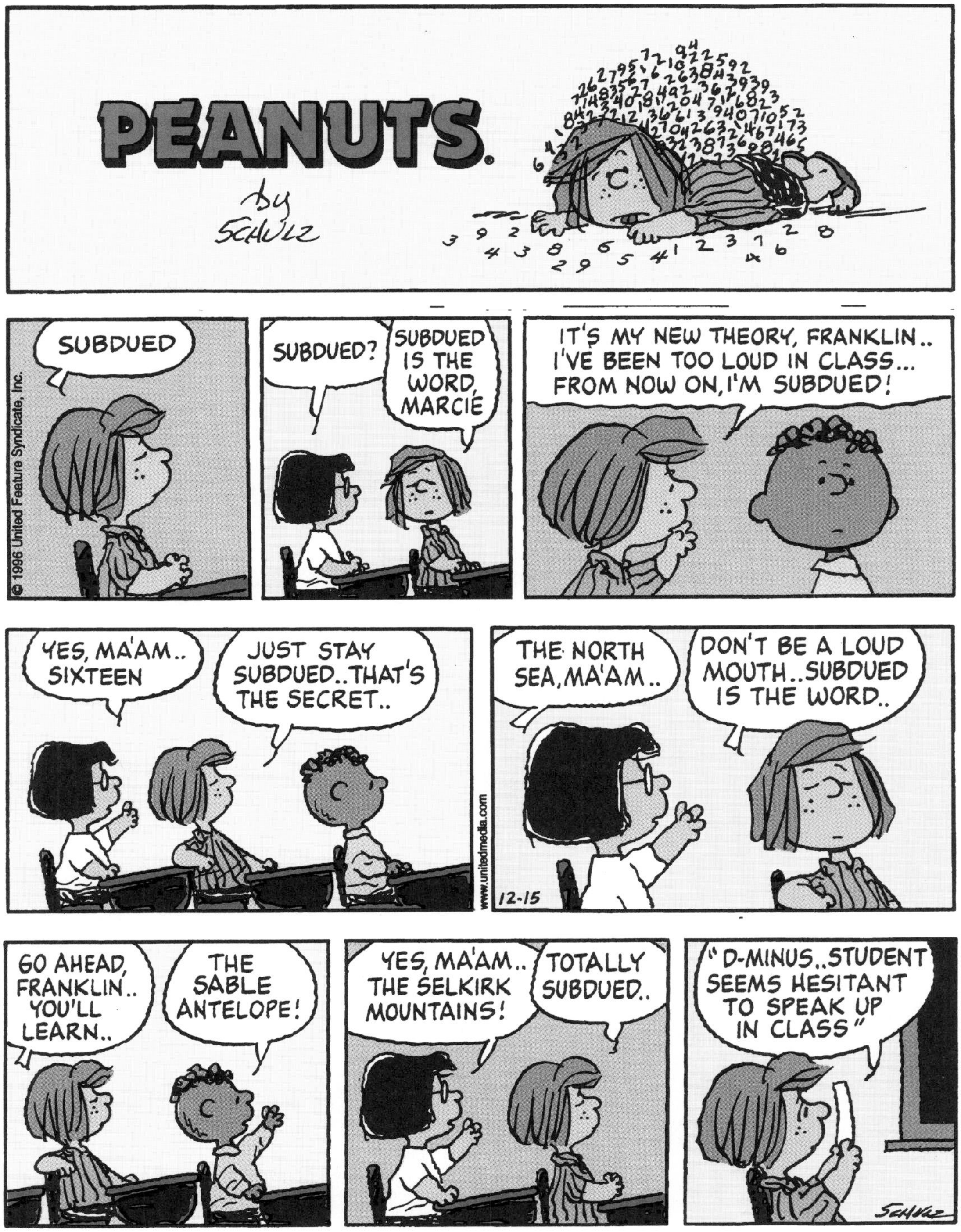
PEANUTS
by SCHULZ
© 1996 United Feature Syndicate, Inc.
SUBDUED
SUBDUED?
SUBDUED IS THE WORD, MARCIE
IT'S MY NEW THEORY, FRANKLIN.. I'VE BEEN TOO LOUD IN CLASS... FROM NOW ON, I'M SUBDUED!
YES, MA'AM.. SIXTEEN
JUST STAY SUBDUED..THAT'S THE SECRET..
www.unitedmedia.com
12-15
THE NORTH SEA, MA'AM..
DON'T BE A LOUD MOUTH..SUBDUED IS THE WORD..
GO AHEAD, FRANKLIN.. YOU'LL LEARN..
THE SABLE ANTELOPE!
YES, MA'AM.. THE SELKIRK MOUNTAINS!
TOTALLY SUBDUED..
"D-MINUS..STUDENT SEEMS HESITANT TO SPEAK UP IN CLASS"
SCHULZ

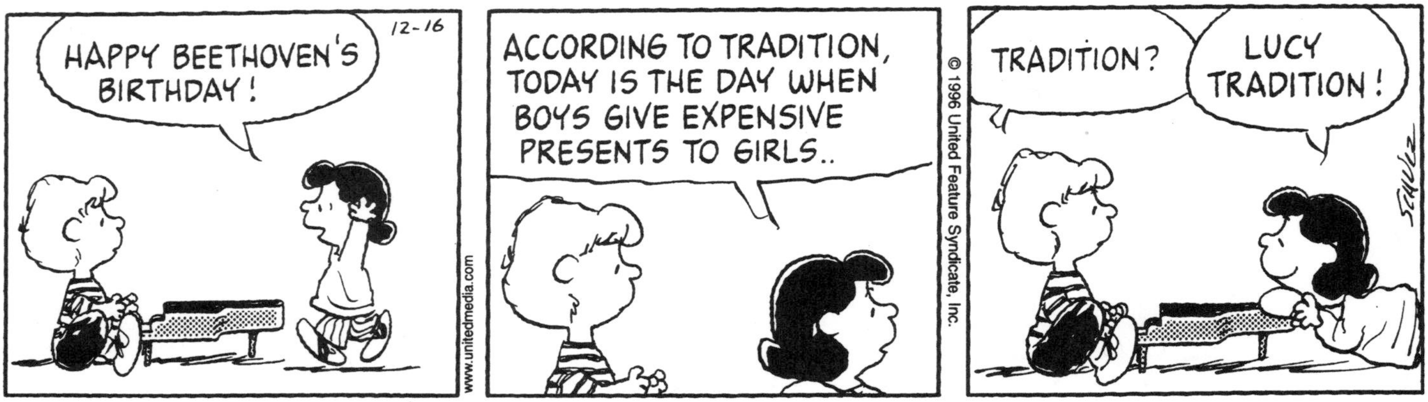
12-16
HAPPY BEETHOVEN'S BIRTHDAY!
ACCORDING TO TRADITION, TODAY IS THE DAY WHEN BOYS GIVE EXPENSIVE PRESENTS TO GIRLS..
TRADITION?
LUCY TRADITION!
SCHULZ
© 1996 United Feature Syndicate, Inc.
www.unitedmedia.com

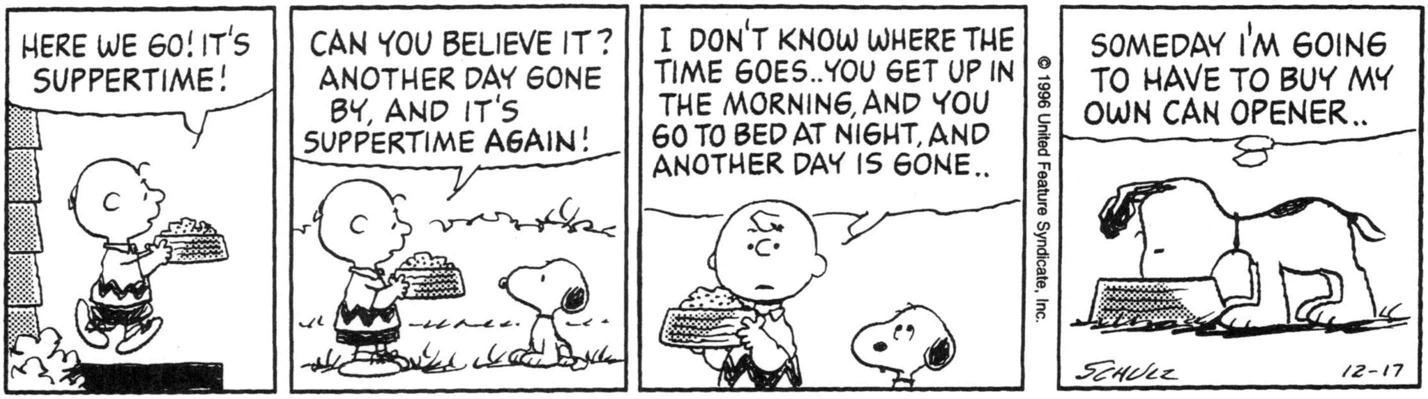
HERE WE GO! IT'S SUPPERTIME!
CAN YOU BELIEVE IT? ANOTHER DAY GONE BY, AND IT'S SUPPERTIME AGAIN!
I DON'T KNOW WHERE THE TIME GOES..YOU GET UP IN THE MORNING, AND YOU GO TO BED AT NIGHT, AND ANOTHER DAY IS GONE..
SOMEDAY I'M GOING TO HAVE TO BUY MY OWN CAN OPENER..
SCHULZ
12-17
© 1996 United Feature Syndicate, Inc.

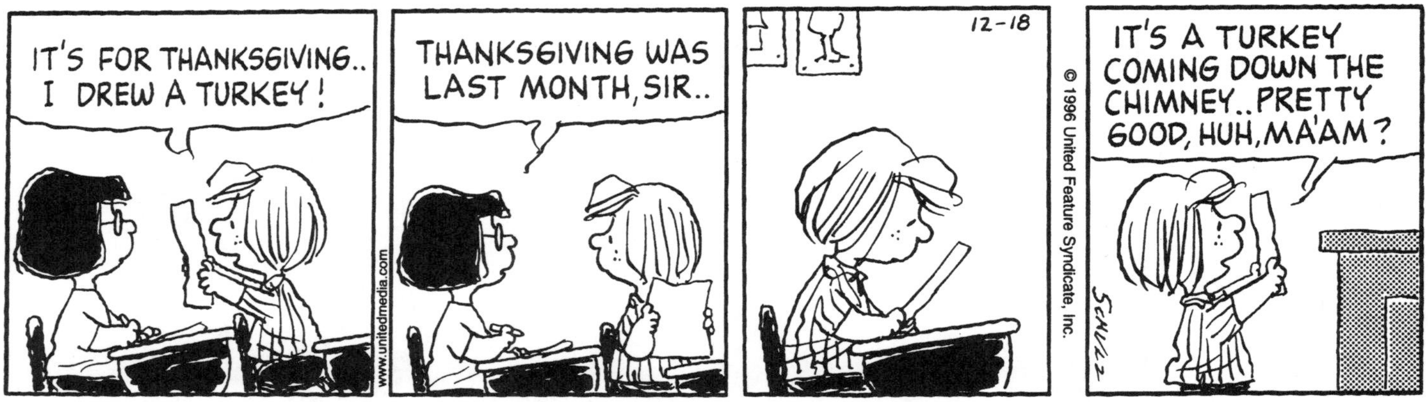
IT'S FOR THANKSGIVING.. I DREW A TURKEY!
THANKSGIVING WAS LAST MONTH, SIR..
12-18
IT'S A TURKEY COMING DOWN THE CHIMNEY..PRETTY GOOD, HUH, MA'AM?
SCHULZ
© 1996 United Feature Syndicate, Inc.
www.unitedmedia.com

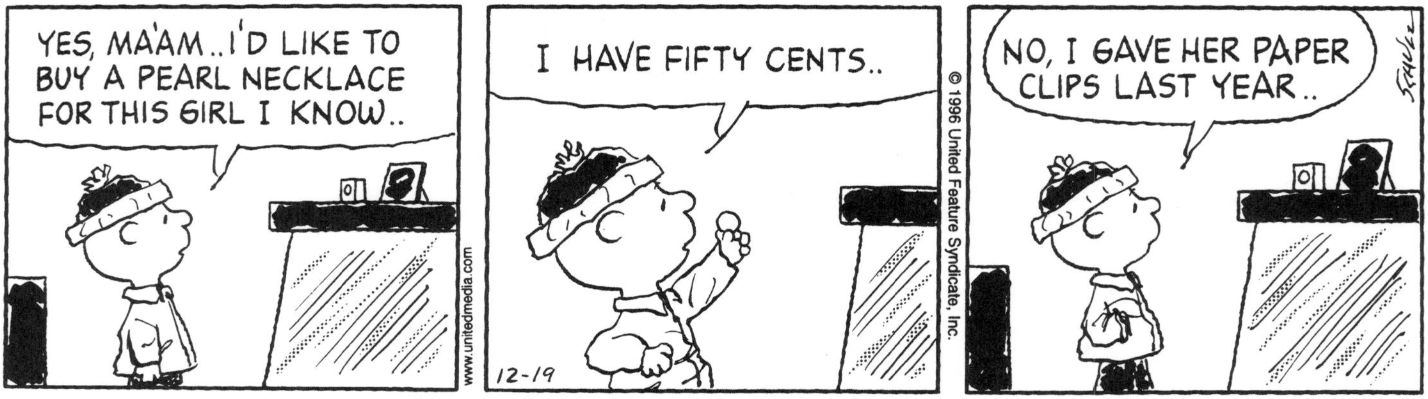
YES, MA'AM..I'D LIKE TO BUY A PEARL NECKLACE FOR THIS GIRL I KNOW..
I HAVE FIFTY CENTS..
NO, I GAVE HER PAPER CLIPS LAST YEAR..
www.unitedmedia.com
12-19
© 1996 United Feature Syndicate, Inc.
SCHULZ

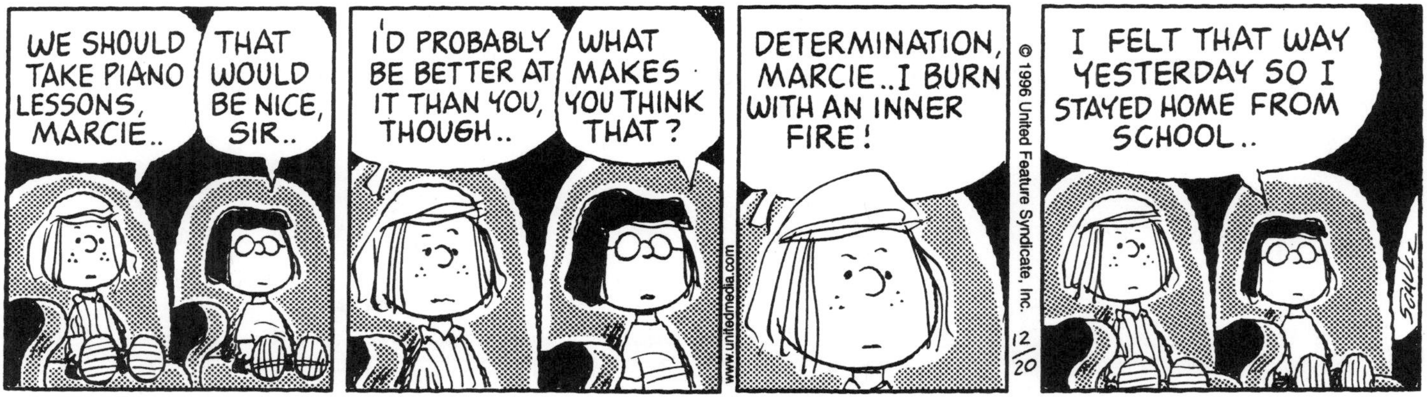
WE SHOULD TAKE PIANO LESSONS, MARCIE..
THAT WOULD BE NICE, SIR..
I'D PROBABLY BE BETTER AT IT THAN YOU, THOUGH..
WHAT MAKES YOU THINK THAT?
www.unitedmedia.com
DETERMINATION, MARCIE..I BURN WITH AN INNER FIRE!
© 1996 United Feature Syndicate, Inc.
12/20
I FELT THAT WAY YESTERDAY SO I STAYED HOME FROM SCHOOL..
SCHULZ

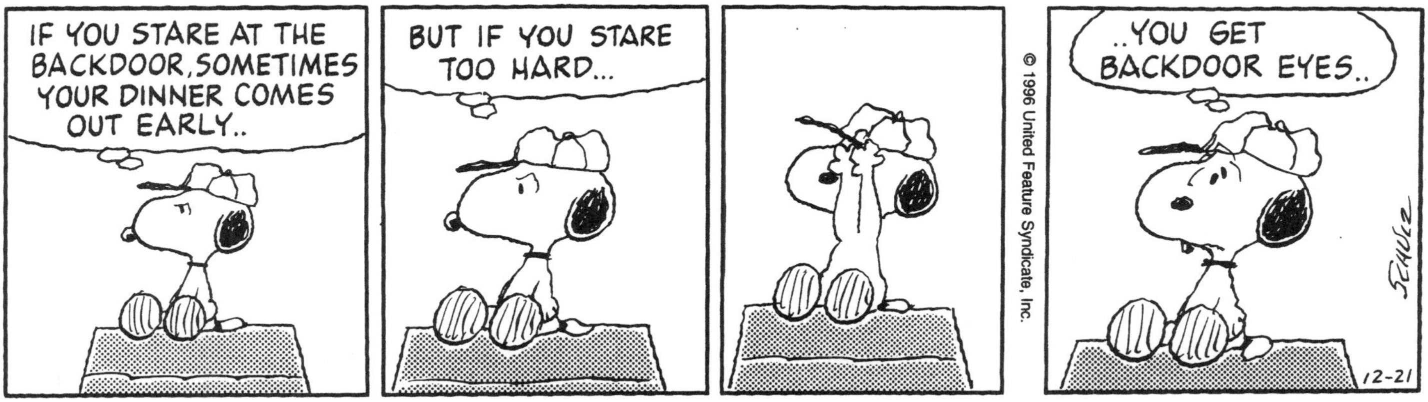
IF YOU STARE AT THE BACKDOOR, SOMETIMES YOUR DINNER COMES OUT EARLY..
BUT IF YOU STARE TOO HARD...
© 1996 United Feature Syndicate, Inc.
..YOU GET BACKDOOR EYES..
SCHULZ
12-21

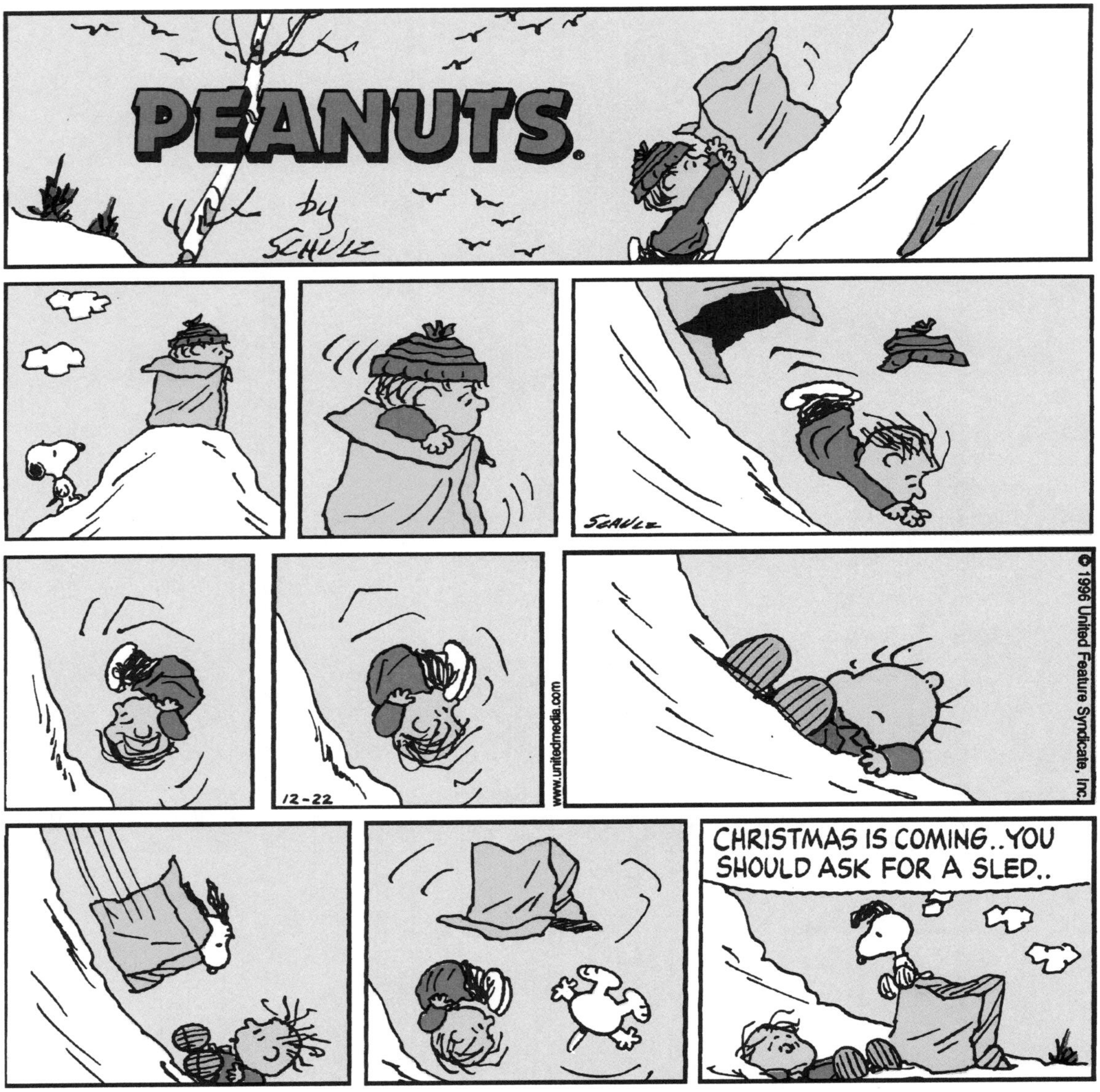
PEANUTS
by SCHULZ
SCHULZ
12-22
www.unitedmedia.com
© 1996 United Feature Syndicate, Inc.
CHRISTMAS IS COMING..YOU SHOULD ASK FOR A SLED..

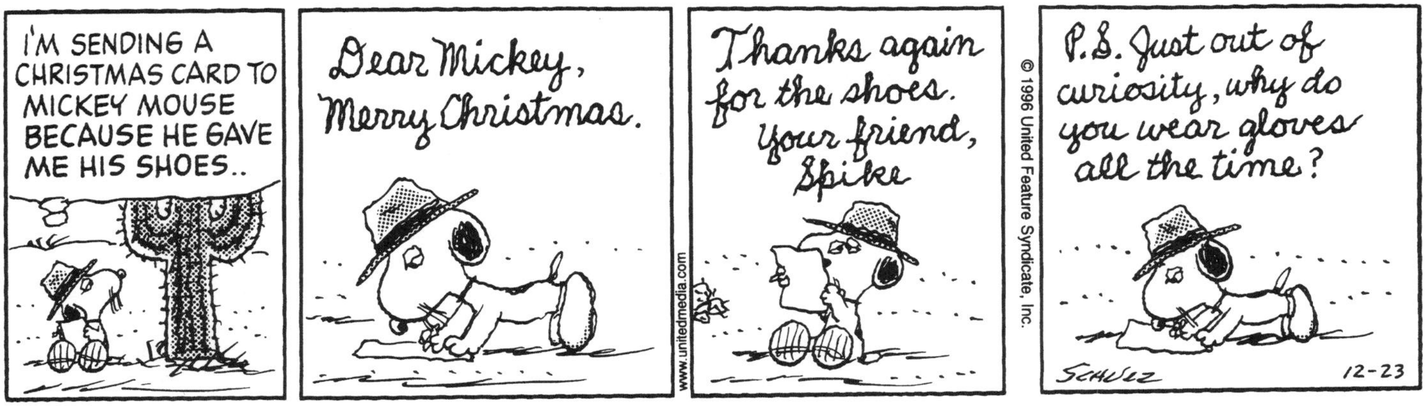
I'M SENDING A CHRISTMAS CARD TO MICKEY MOUSE BECAUSE HE GAVE ME HIS SHOES..
Dear Mickey, Merry Christmas.
Thanks again for the shoes. Your friend, Spike
P.S. Just out of curiosity, why do you wear gloves all the time?
www.unitedmedia.com
© 1996 United Feature Syndicate, Inc.
SCHULZ
12-23

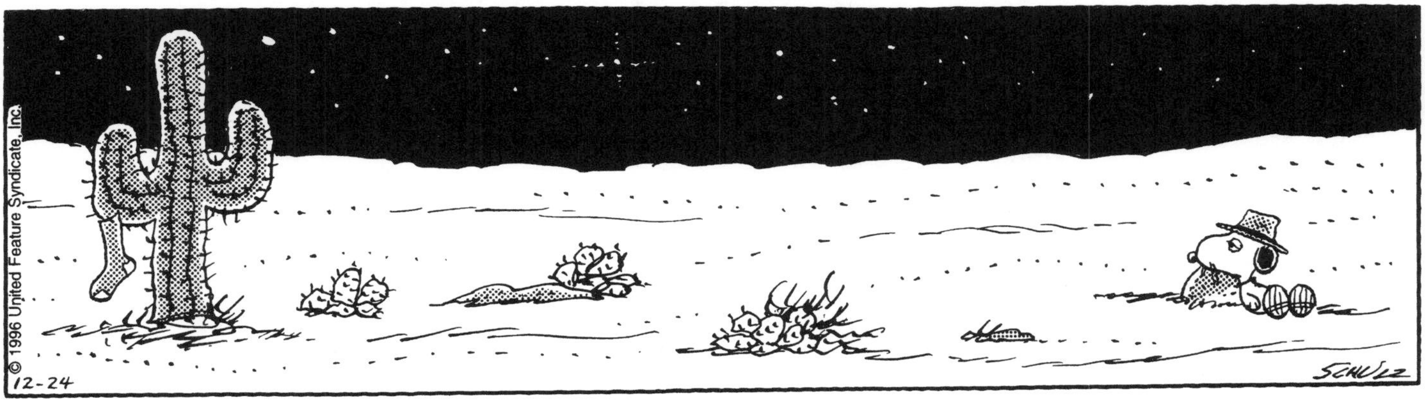
© 1996 United Feature Syndicate, Inc.
12-24
SCHULZ

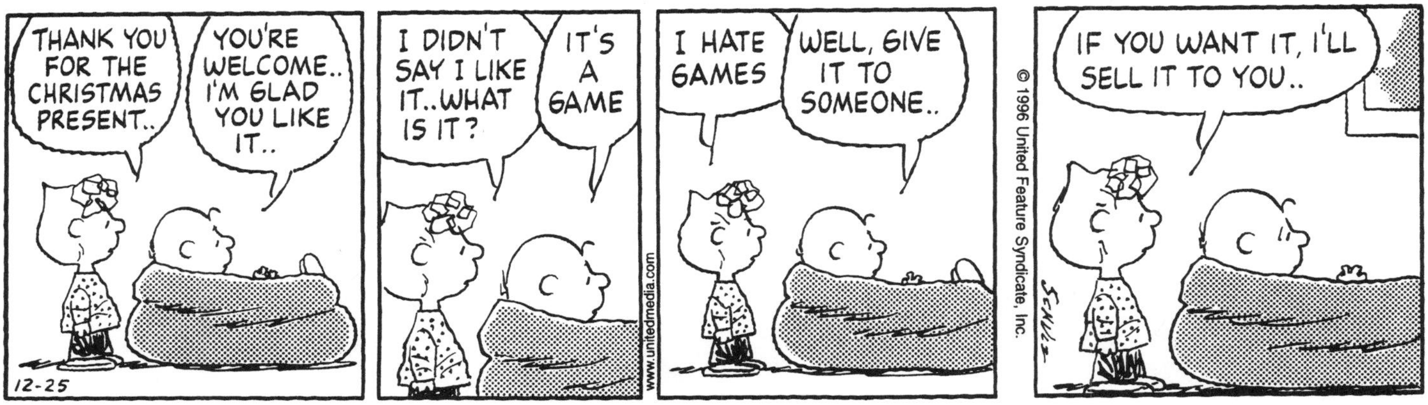
THANK YOU FOR THE CHRISTMAS PRESENT..
YOU'RE WELCOME.. I'M GLAD YOU LIKE IT..
I DIDN'T SAY I LIKE IT..WHAT IS IT?
IT'S A GAME
I HATE GAMES
WELL, GIVE IT TO SOMEONE..
IF YOU WANT IT, I'LL SELL IT TO YOU..
12-25
www.unitedmedia.com
© 1996 United Feature Syndicate, Inc.
SCHULZ

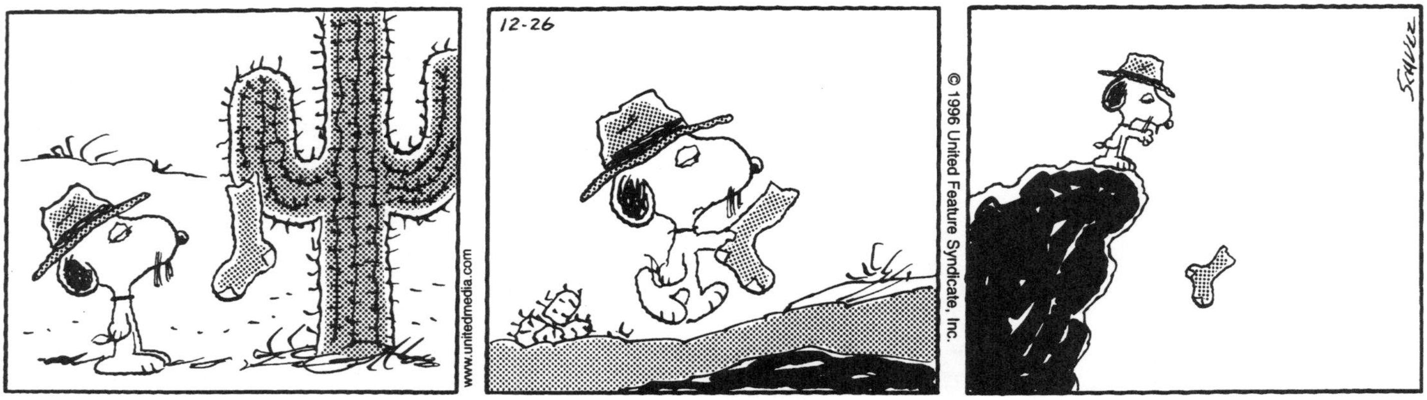
12-26
© 1996 United Feature Syndicate, Inc.
www.unitedmedia.com
SCHULZ

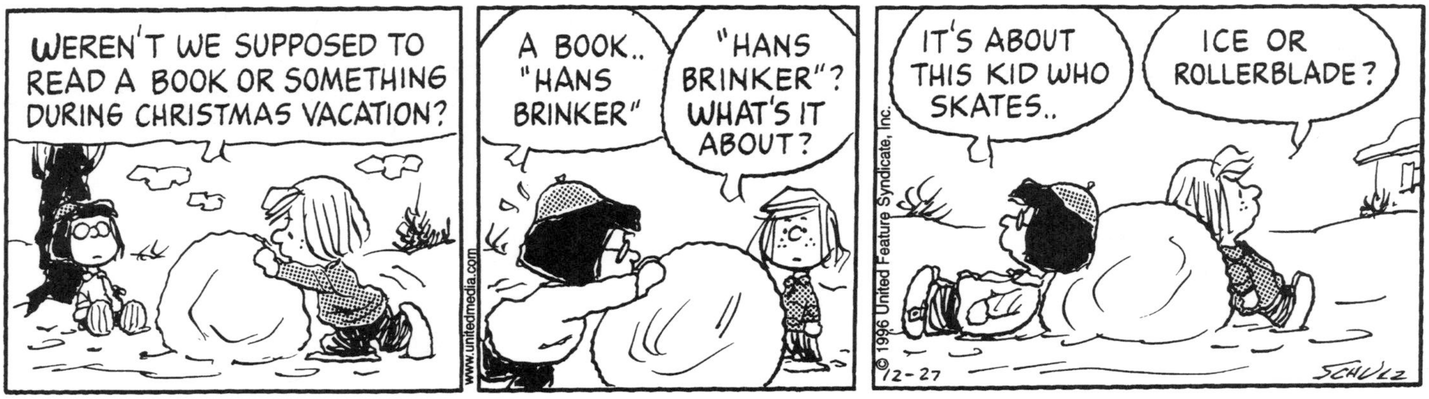
WEREN'T WE SUPPOSED TO READ A BOOK OR SOMETHING DURING CHRISTMAS VACATION?
A BOOK.. "HANS BRINKER"
"HANS BRINKER"? WHAT'S IT ABOUT?
IT'S ABOUT THIS KID WHO SKATES..
ICE OR ROLLERBLADE?
12-27
© 1996 United Feature Syndicate, Inc.
www.unitedmedia.com
SCHULZ

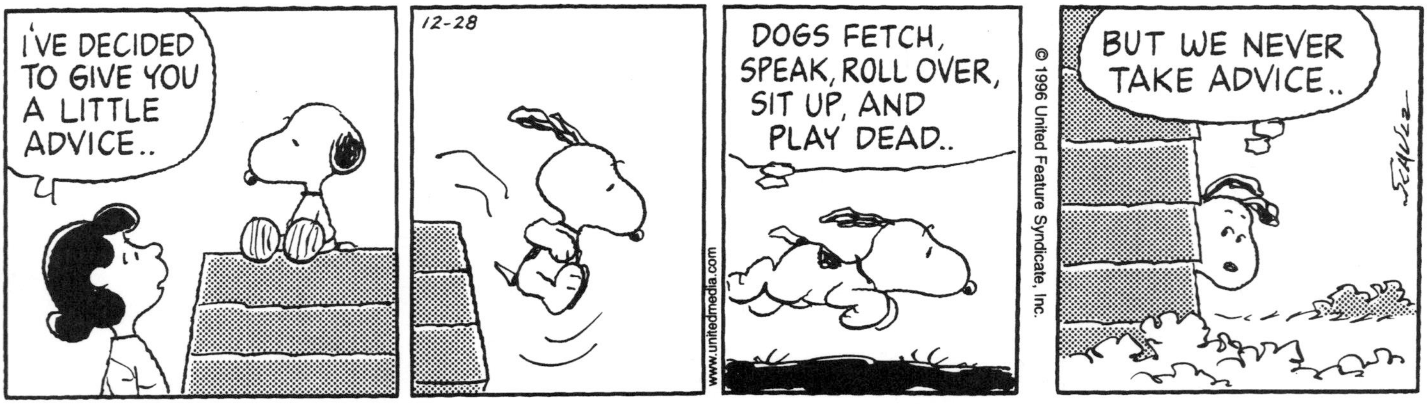
I'VE DECIDED TO GIVE YOU A LITTLE ADVICE..
12-28
DOGS FETCH, SPEAK, ROLL OVER, SIT UP, AND PLAY DEAD..
BUT WE NEVER TAKE ADVICE..
© 1996 United Feature Syndicate, Inc.
www.unitedmedia.com
SCHULZ

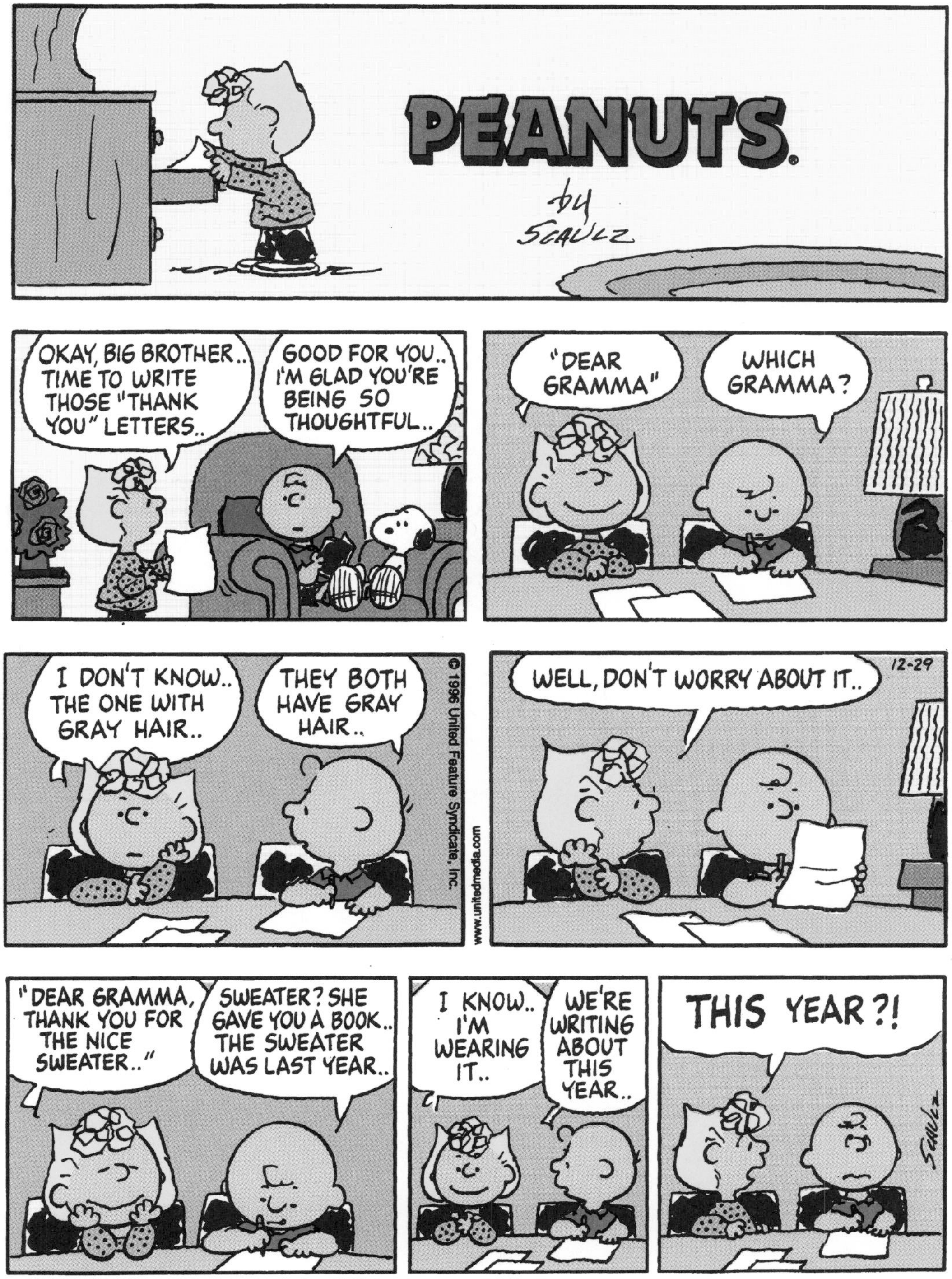
PEANUTS.
by SCHULZ
OKAY, BIG BROTHER.. TIME TO WRITE THOSE "THANK YOU" LETTERS..
GOOD FOR YOU.. I'M GLAD YOU'RE BEING SO THOUGHTFUL..
"DEAR GRAMMA"
WHICH GRAMMA?
I DON'T KNOW.. THE ONE WITH GRAY HAIR..
THEY BOTH HAVE GRAY HAIR..
© 1996 United Feature Syndicate, Inc.
www.unitedmedia.com
12-29
WELL, DON'T WORRY ABOUT IT..
"DEAR GRAMMA, THANK YOU FOR THE NICE SWEATER.."
SWEATER? SHE GAVE YOU A BOOK.. THE SWEATER WAS LAST YEAR..
I KNOW.. I'M WEARING IT..
WE'RE WRITING ABOUT THIS YEAR..
THIS YEAR?!
SCHULZ

YES, SIR.. IS THIS WHERE YOU'RE SELLING ATHLETE'S AUTOGRAPHS?
I'D LIKE A BASEBALL WITH JOE SHLABOTNIK'S AUTOGRAPH.. WHO IS HE? HE'S MY HERO!
www.unitedmedia.com
IS HE HERE? WELL, JUST ASK HIM TO SIGN A BALL, AND I'LL PAY FOR IT..
© 1996 United Feature Syndicate, Inc.
I USED TO HAVE A LASSIE DOG DISH, BUT SHE NEVER SIGNED IT..
SCHULZ
12-30

IS THIS JOE SHLABOTNIK'S AUTOGRAPH? WOW!
www.unitedmedia.com
WHERE IS HE? MAY I SEE HIM, AND THANK HIM?
WELL, TELL HIM I APPRECIATE THE AUTOGRAPH..
..EVEN THOUGH IT TOOK ALL THE MONEY I'VE GOT..
12-31
© 1996 United Feature Syndicate, Inc.
WOW! I'LL BE THE ENVY OF EVERY JOE SHLABOTNIK FAN IN THE WORLD!
ALL ONE OF YOU!
SCHULZ

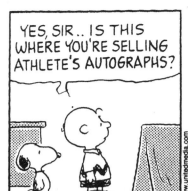

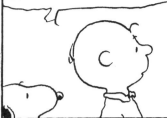

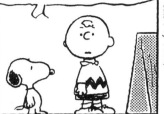

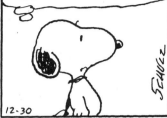

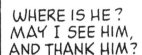

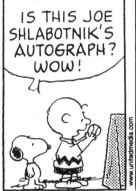

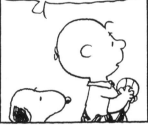

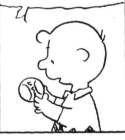

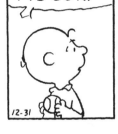

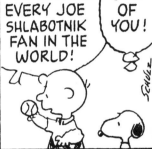